It Tells My Story

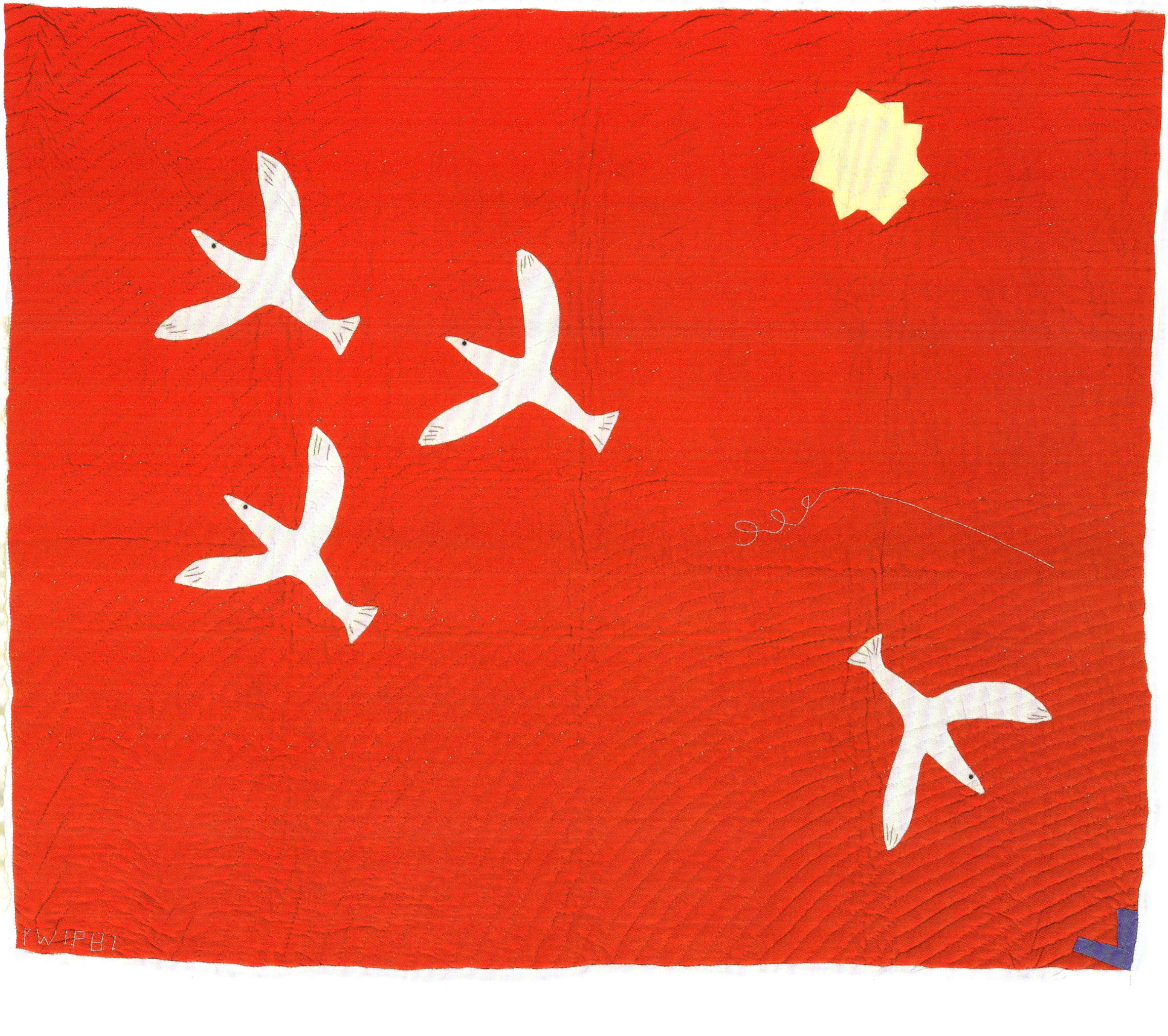

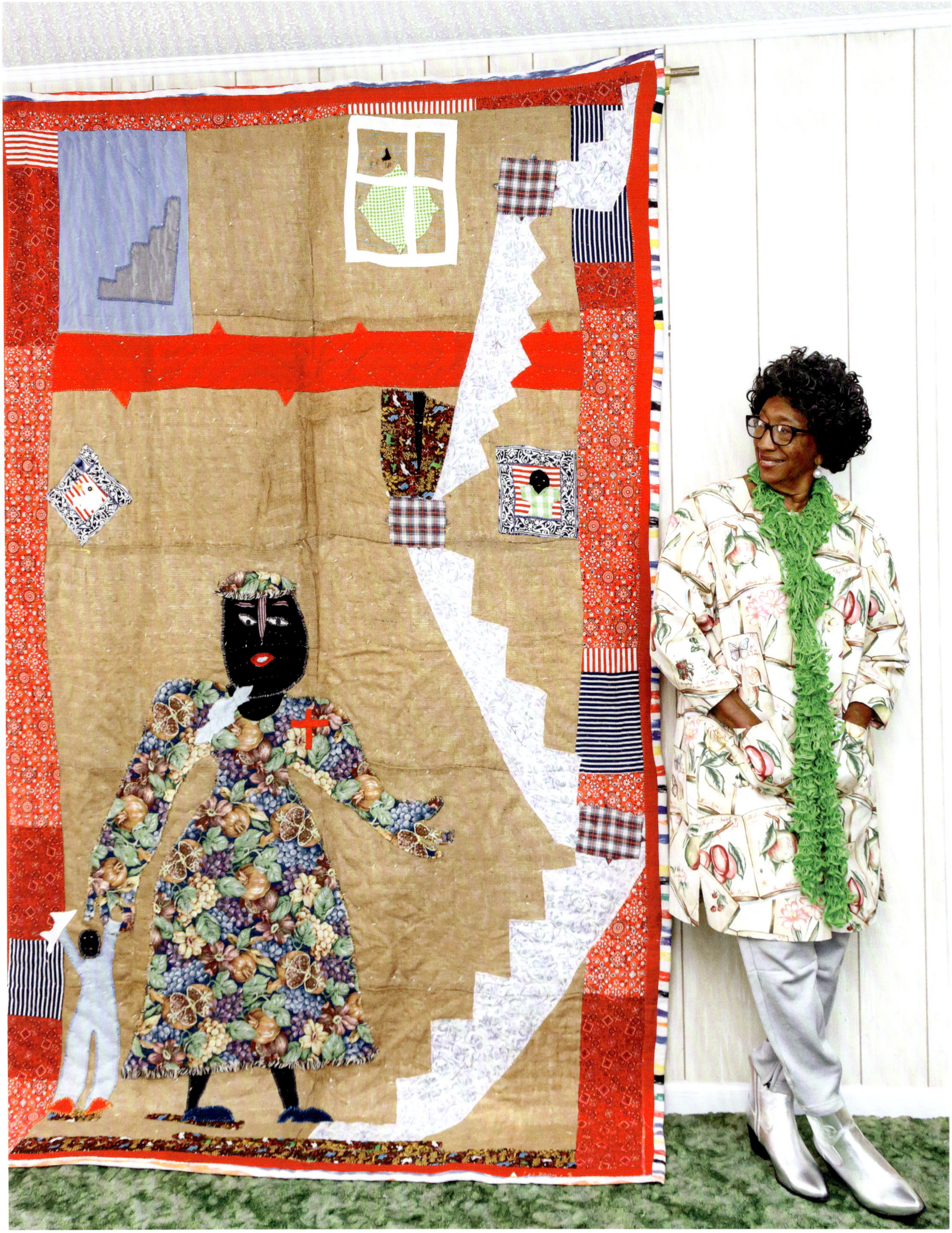

It Tells My Story

The Yvonne Wells Collection at the International Quilt Museum

Featuring Wells's Brilliant Series *The Seven Deadly Sins*

Edited by Teresa Duryea Wong

Foreword by Carolyn Ducey

Contributions by Kyra E. Hicks,

Sharbreon Plummer, and Yvonne Wells

Photography by Dave Walker

Quilt photography by Jamie Swartz

University of Nebraska Press
Lincoln

Frontispiece a: *Going Home* (1987).
Frontispiece b: Yvonne Wells next to her quilt titled *Mother to Son* (2004–5). Photo by Dave Walker.

Manufactured in China

The University of Nebraska Press is part of a land-grant institution with campuses and programs on the past, present, and future homelands of the Pawnee, Ponca, Otoe-Missouria, Omaha, Dakota, Lakota, Kaw, Cheyenne, and Arapaho Peoples, as well as those of the relocated Ho-Chunk, Sac and Fox, and Iowa Peoples.

∞

Support for this publication was provided by the International Quilt Museum, University of Nebraska–Lincoln, and the Joan Laughlin, PhD, Endowment Fund at the International Quilt Museum.

Designed by Teresa Duryea Wong. Typeset in Franklin Gothic Book and Arial.

For customers in the EU with safety/GPSR concerns, contact:
gpsr@mare-nostrum.co.uk
Mare Nostrum Group BV
Doelen 72
4831 GR Breda
The Netherlands

Library of Congress Cataloging-in-Publication Data
Names: International Quilt Museum author | Wong, Teresa Duryea editor | Ducey, Carolyn writer of foreword | Hicks, Kyra E. contributor | Plummer, Sharbreon S. contributor | Wells, Yvonne contributor
Title: It tells my story: the Yvonne Wells collection at the International Quilt Museum / edited by Teresa Duryea Wong; foreword by Carolyn Ducey; contributions by Kyra E. Hicks, Sharbreon Plummer, and Yvonne Wells; photography by Dave Walker; quilt photography by Jamie Swartz.
Description: Lincoln: University of Nebraska Press, [2026] | Includes bibliographical references.
Identifiers: LCCN 2025054733
ISBN 9781496247902 hardback
Subjects: LCSH: Wells, Yvonne—Catalogs | International Quilt Museum—Catalogs | Art quilts—Nebraska—Lincoln—Catalogs | BISAC: BIOGRAPHY & AUTOBIOGRAPHY / Personal Memoirs | ART / Women Artists | LCGFT: Catalogs
Classification: LCC NK9102.L53 I85 2026

"Anything I can stick a
needle in and it
can tell my story,
I got it."

—Yvonne Wells

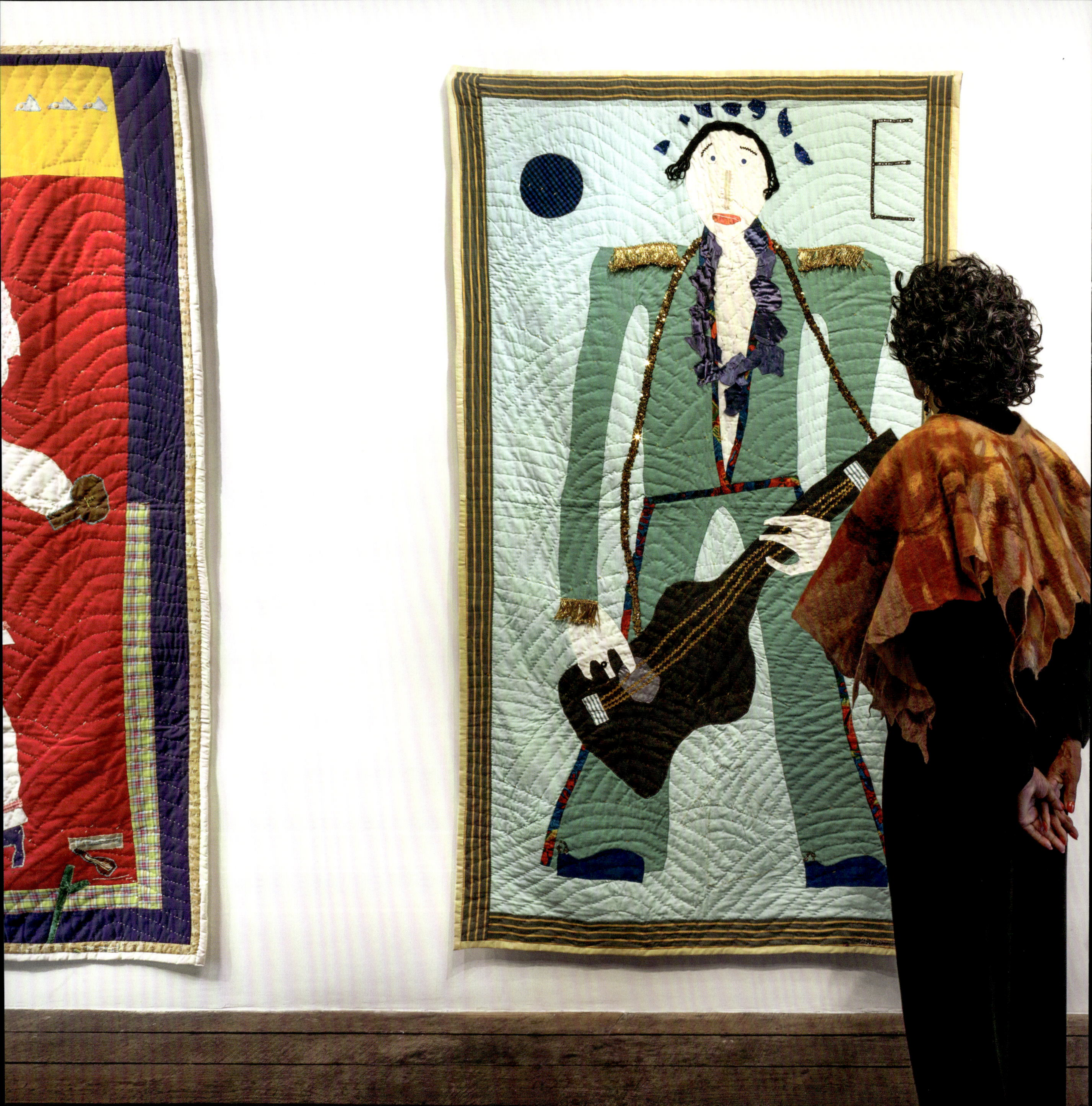
E

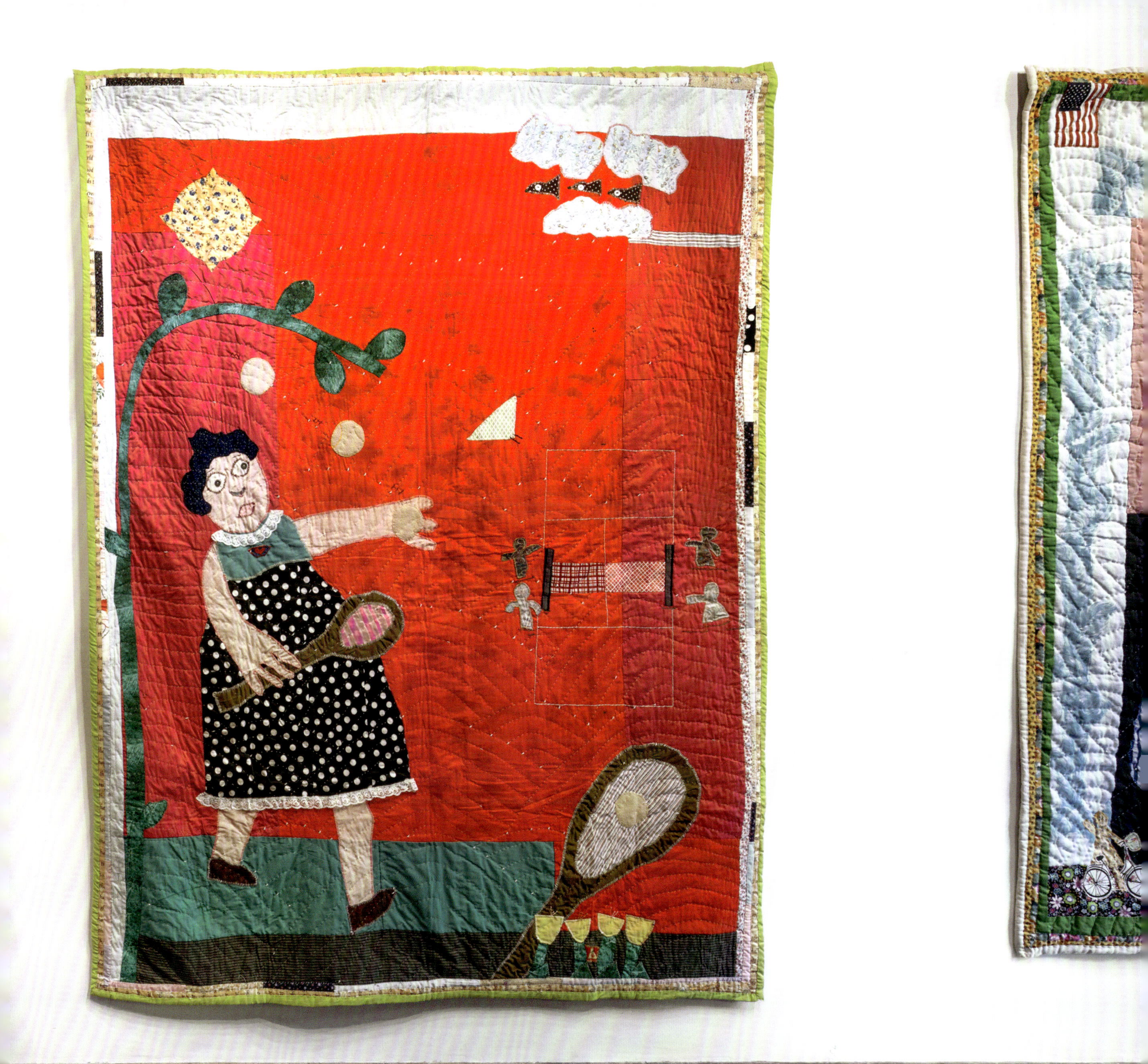

Yvonne Wells: Play the Hand That's Dealt You, Fort Gansevoort, New York, June 8–August 12, 2023.

Following page: *Log Cabin*, c. 1980s.

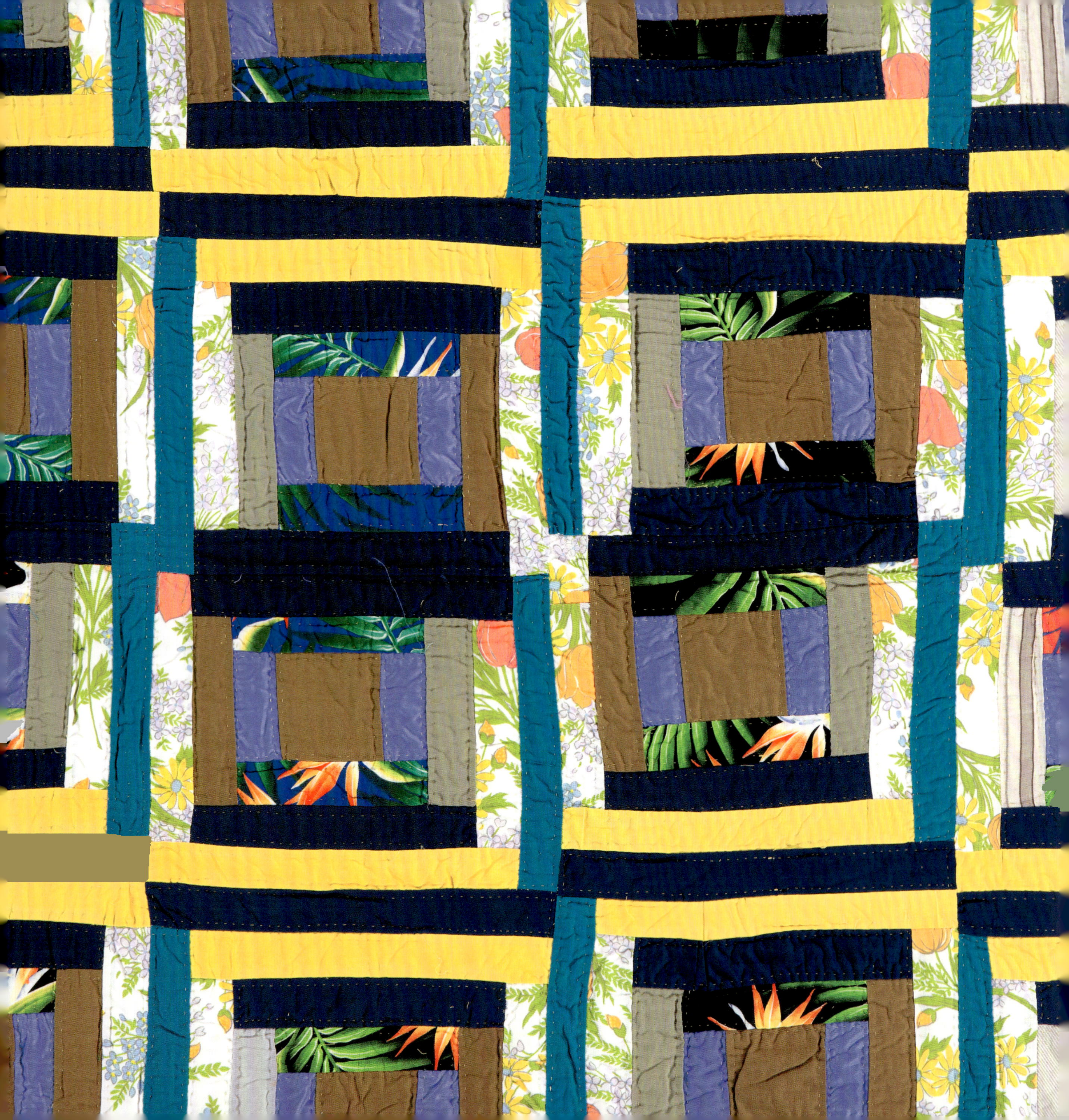

CONTENTS

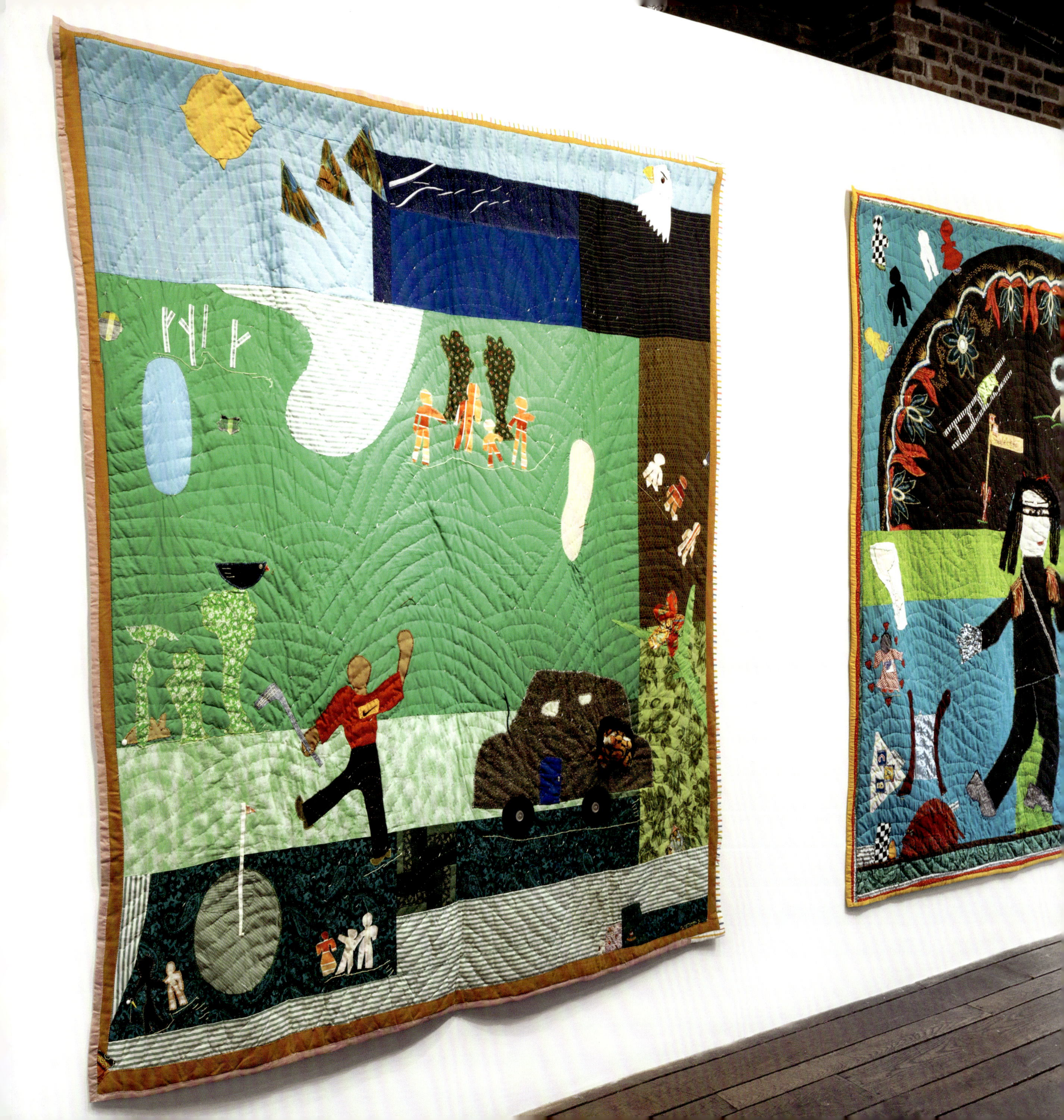

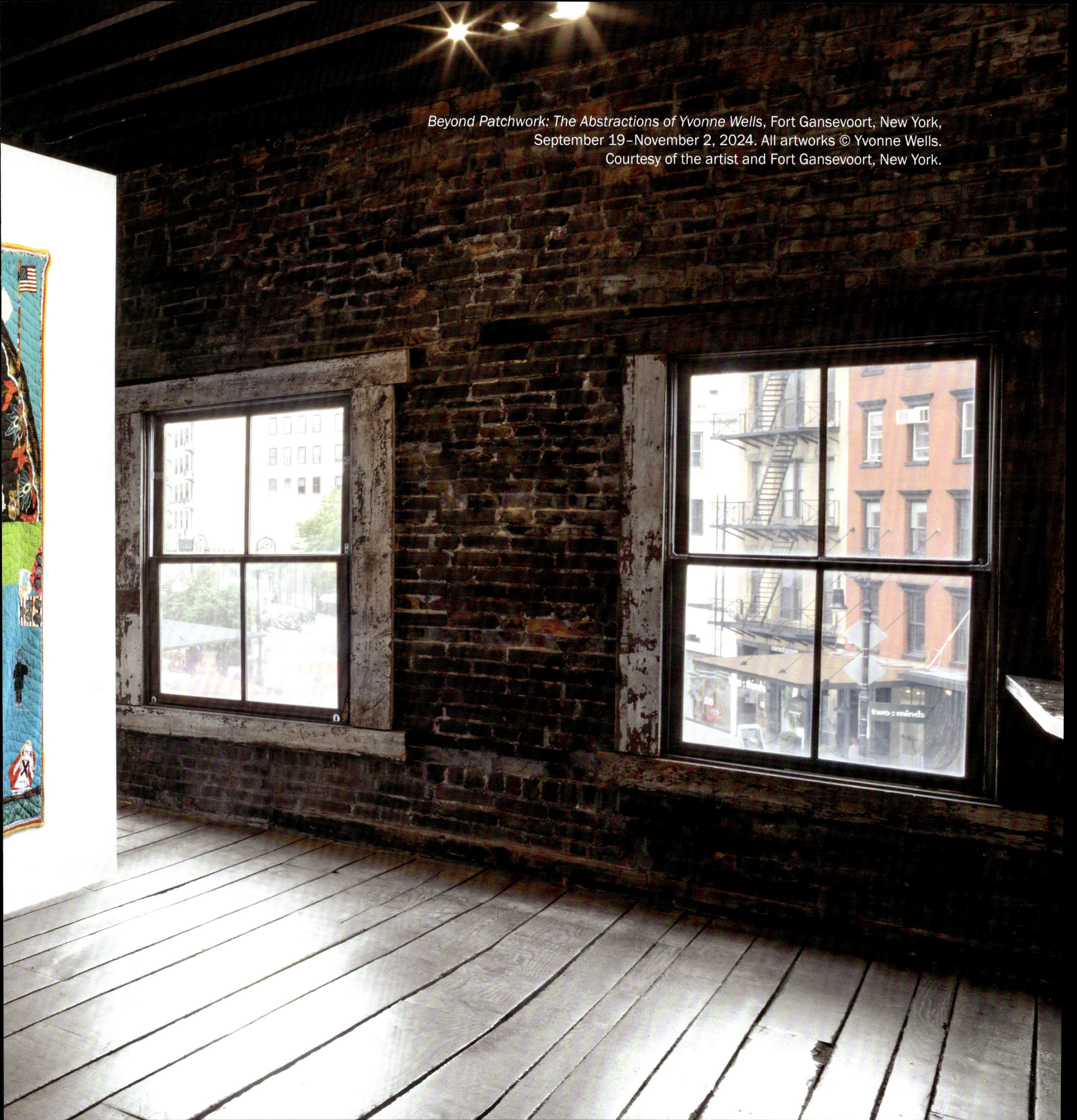

Beyond Patchwork: The Abstractions of Yvonne Wells, Fort Gansevoort, New York, September 19–November 2, 2024. All artworks © Yvonne Wells. Courtesy of the artist and Fort Gansevoort, New York.

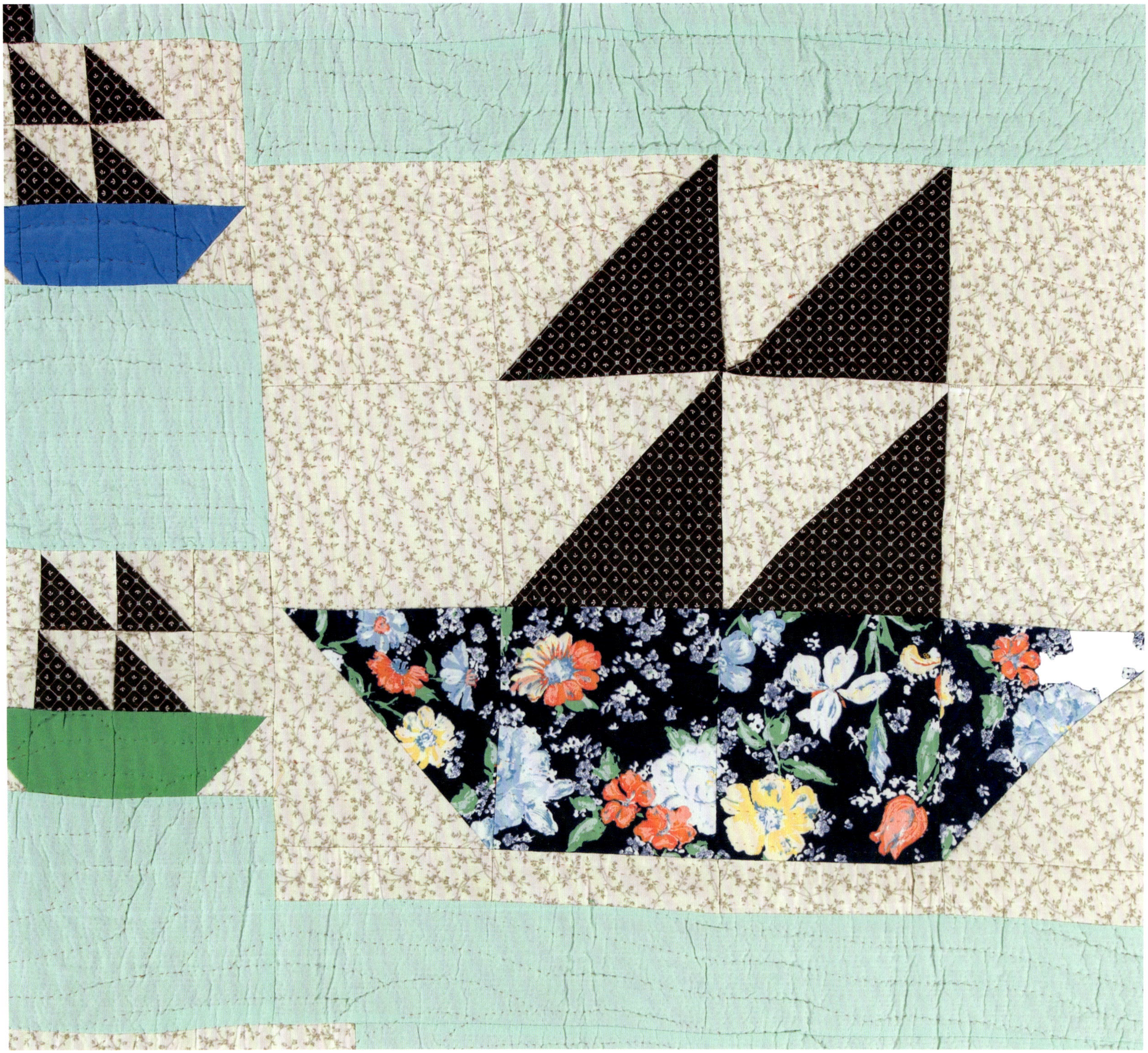

FOREWORD

Discovering Yvonne Wells

Carolyn Ducey

My first interaction with the Robert and Helen Cargo Collection of African American quilts came in 2000, during the process of unpacking and accessioning 156 quilts when they arrived at the International Quilt Museum (then known as the International Quilt Study Center), University of Nebraska–Lincoln. I was blown away.

Even among the explosion of color, line, and pattern from thirty-two quiltmakers included in the Cargo Collection, Yvonne Wells's quilts stood out. They were completely unique. Her appliquéd designs of figures engaged in a variety of activities, with unusual details such as the repetitive use of triangles floating across the body of the quilt or sewn in the borders, spoke volumes to me. In some cases, the design was startingly simple. For example, *First Dark*, with the sun setting as the moon appears, is seemingly simple on the surface, but her choices show a confident and bold artist.

When the Cargo Collection was first established in 2000, those 156 African American quilts became the largest documented museum collection to focus on the work of twentieth-century Black quiltmakers. Though limited to the Alabama area, the collection was vital to the representation of the work of African American makers, which had previously been either ignored or underrepresented in the canon of quilt history.

Left: *The Mother Ship* (c. 1984), detail.
Following page: *Noah's Ark* (1988), detail. Page 15: *Seven Deadly Sins: Envy* (2006), detail.

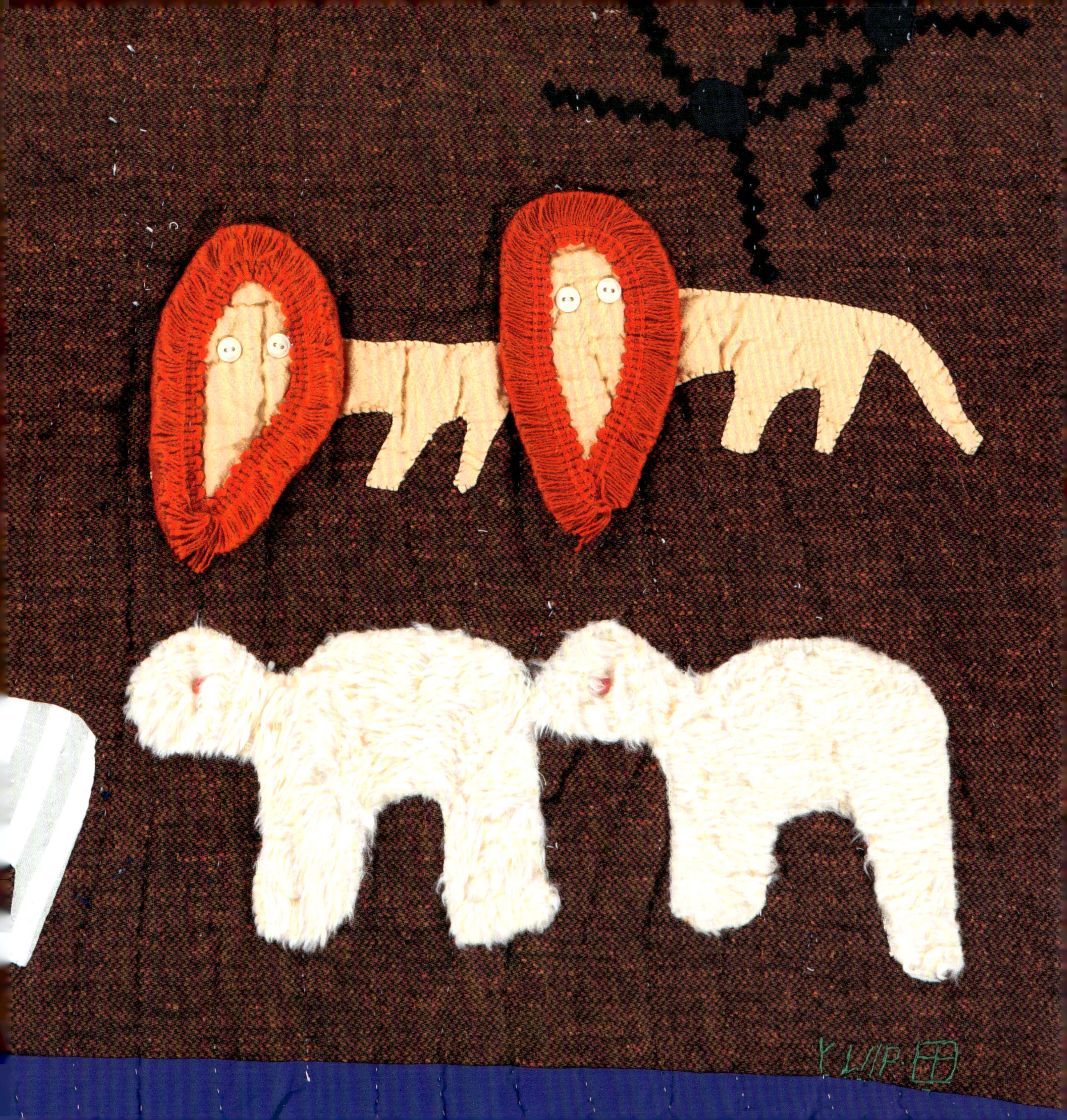

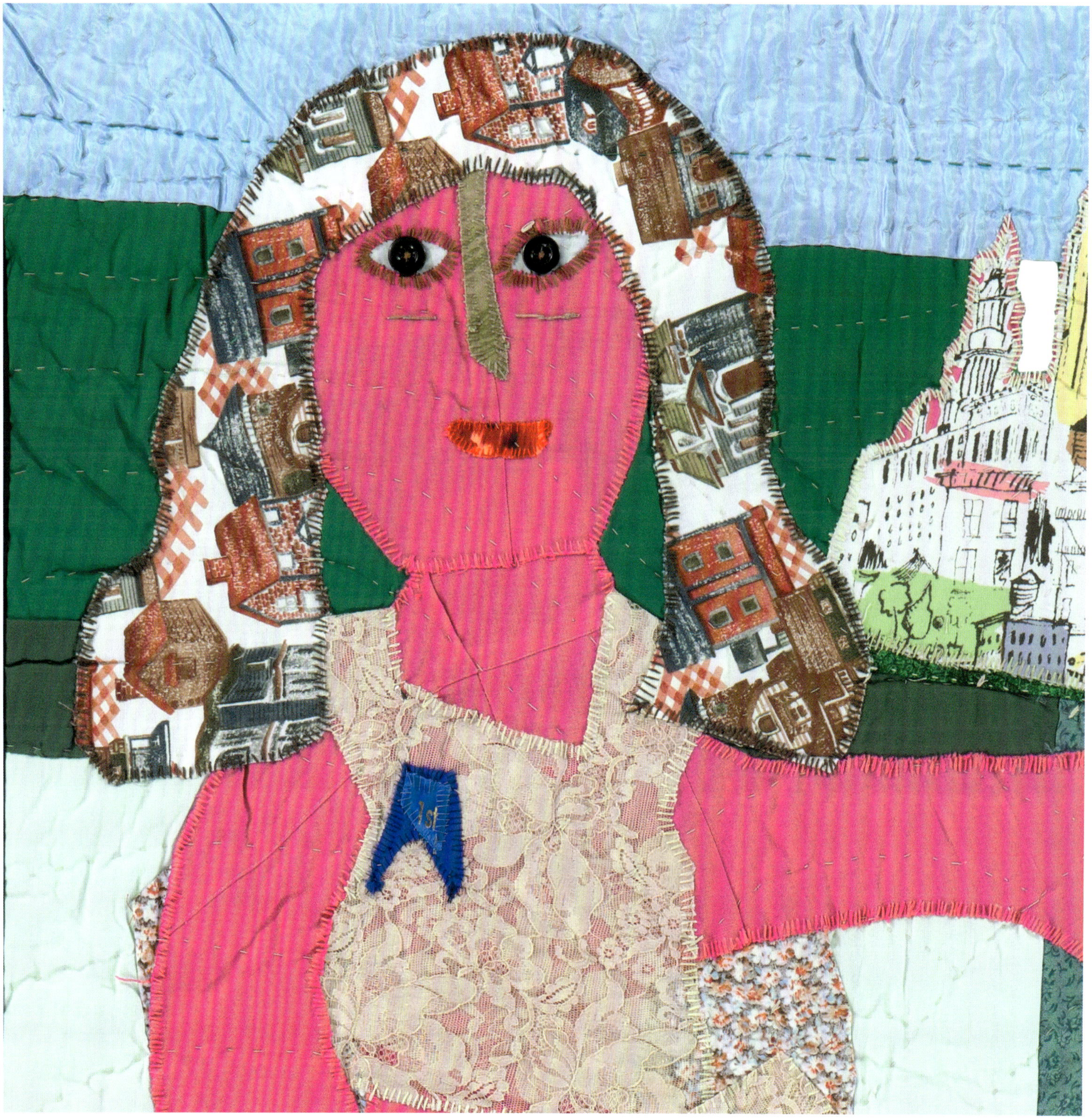
1st

African American quiltmaking gained greater recognition in the 1980s and '90s, due in large part to the work of scholars and collectors Carolyn Mazloomi, Cuesta Benberry, and Roland Freeman. Mazloomi founded the Women of Color Quilter's Network in 1981 to educate, preserve, exhibit, promote, and document quilts made by African Americans. She has also authored numerous books and articles and curated dozens of exhibitions featuring Black quilters. Benberry published a seminal book titled *Always There: The African-American Presence in American Quilts* (University of Pennsylvania Press, 1992), which tells the history of the lengthy and prolific work of Black quiltmakers. Freeman traveled across the entire country documenting the work of quilters and published another seminal book titled *A Communion of the Spirits: African-American Quilters, Preservers, and Their Stories* (Rutledge Hill Press, 1996). These three leaders worked to dispel inaccurate perceptions of what constituted African American quilts and raise awareness of their highly original and diverse styles of art.

Dr. Patricia "Pat" Crews, the inaugural director of the International Quilt Museum (IQM), along with scholar Jonathan Holstein (who wrote a foreword to Cuesta Benberry's book) and members of the IQM's International Advisory Board, prioritized the acquisition of the Robert and Helen Cargo Collection.

Crews commented on the significance of the gift in the press release announcing the addition of the collection: "This exceptional collection superbly illustrates the ongoing role that African American quilt makers play in the larger tradition of American quilt history."

Dr. Robert Cargo taught French literature in the Department of Romance Languages and Classics at the University of Alabama, and Helen McCain Cargo also taught French and was a quilter herself. Helen died in 2008 at age seventy-five, Robert in 2012 at age seventy-nine. The Cargos also operated a folk art gallery in downtown Tuscaloosa for several decades. Robert was a champion of self-taught artists and quiltmakers from his home state, and he had collected Alabama quilts for years, inspired by his own family's quilts. When he noticed African American quilts hanging on clotheslines in the area around Birmingham, he became enthralled by their vitality.

Cargo literally knocked on a lot of doors, and he eventually became a welcome visitor to the homes of numerous quiltmakers, where he actively encouraged the artists to display and sell their quilts. The homes he visited included those of Nora Ezell, Mary Maxtion, Lureca Outland, and Yvonne Wells. He purchased many quilts himself, most of which he then offered for sale at Cargo Folk Art Gallery.

The Cargos' dedication to the documentation of the makers reflected the same efforts that IQM was pursuing to establish collections with known provenance. This information is rare with most antique quilts but has always been a priority of the IQM collection under both Pat Crews's leadership and that of the current executive director, Leslie Campbell-Levy.

During the process of bringing the Cargo Collection to the IQM, Robert and Ardis James (who had donated their own collection of one thousand quilts to the University of Nebraska in 1997) and Pat Crews first visited Tuscaloosa in 2000. Shortly thereafter, a larger group of staff and supporters made a second visit. Crews, IQM curator of exhibitions Marin Hanson, IQM board members Diann Sorenson and Sara Dillow, and University of Nebraska Foundation representative Rachelle Humiston traveled to Tuscaloosa to select and pack quilts to become a part of the IQM permanent collection.

"After seeing the amazing quilts by Yvonne Wells on our trip to Tuscaloosa, we had the opportunity to meet and spend time with her," Marin Hanson explained. "Yvonne was warm, engaging, and generous with stories of her early quiltmaking as well as the inspiration for her story quilts. We knew then that we wanted to represent her as fully as possible in the quilt museum's collection."

The Robert and Helen Cargo Collection of African American quilts was donated in part by the Cargos and supported by funding from Robert and Ardis James. More than thirty-two artists are included in the collection, representing locales all over Alabama, including urban areas such as Birmingham, rural areas like Greene County, and the now-famous community of Gee's Bend.

The quilts mostly date from the fourth quarter of the twentieth century but also include several significant pre-1950 works. Most were purchased directly from the makers.

Over the course of the weeks it took to unpack and accession those quilts, I came to know the artists' work, including Maggie Smith's *Britchy Quilt*, composed of worn denim jeans that brought to mind individuals' lives of hard work; Nora Ezell's *Everybody Quilt*, featuring an assortment of quilt patterns from eight-pointed stars to spinning Dresden plates with jagged edges; a series of flag quilts by Mary Maxtion, who even incorporated camouflage fabrics in a Desert Storm quilt; and Dennis Jones's *Broken Dishes*, composed of thousands of triangles. The freedom in the construction was especially inspiring for me as a maker myself, who could not follow the mainstream "rules" I had been taught in my quilt classes. Through the Cargo quilts, I quickly learned seams did not need to be straight with perfect corners. Lines did not need to march carefully across the surface. The Cargo quilts showed me, through their dynamic and bold designs, that the rules needed to be thrown out.

Of course, I was especially drawn to the twenty-seven highly original quilts made by Yvonne Wells. The way she portrays the lightening sky of the *Crucifixion* quilt, progressing across the top of the quilt, floored me. Then, I saw *Yesterday: Civil Rights in the South.* There is something about *Civil Rights* that reached a deep level of emotion for me and still resonates with me twenty-five years later. The imagery is harsh—scenes from the Civil Rights Movement that Wells lived through are portrayed within the individual vignettes: A lynched man swings from a tree, while another is attacked by a dog whose leash is held by a white man.

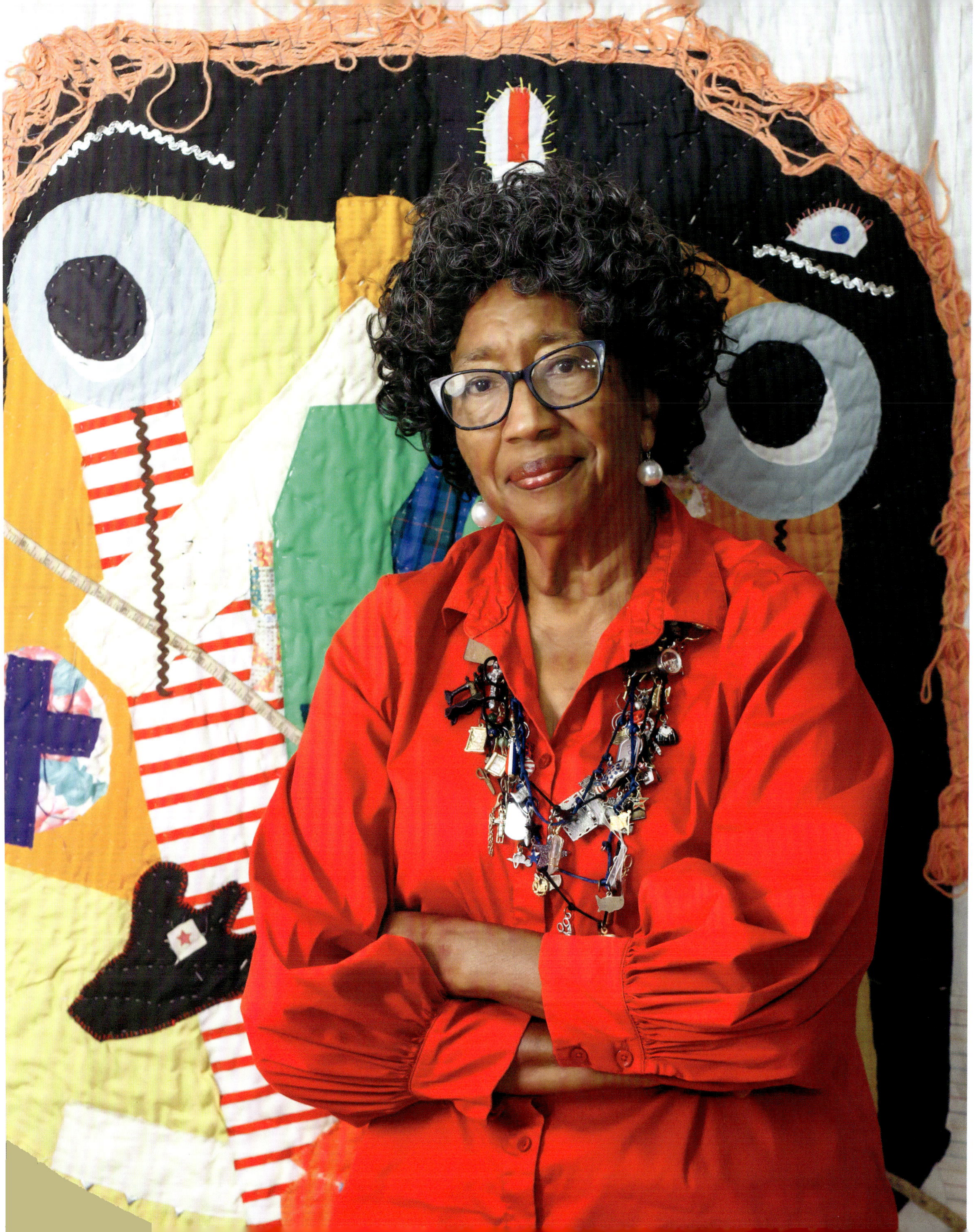

Four crosses mark the 1963 bombing deaths of fourteen-year-olds Addie Mae Collins, Denise McNair, and Carole Robertson and eleven-year-old Cynthia Wesley at the 16th Street Baptist Church in Birmingham. Wells described her need to create *Civil Rights*: "So many activities, so many events were going on at that time. . . . The quilts gave me an outlet to say some of the things that I had seen or how I felt . . . so that it would be part of history."

When I first began to study these quilts a quarter century ago, they quickly took the naivety I had felt about quilts—the warmth and comfort, the history, and the beauty of quilts—to a new realm for me. How could something soft, made simply of cloth, so vividly portray such hateful violence? The juxtaposition of the hard and soft, of the comfort and the reality, exemplified the limits of my own knowledge of quilts and what they could be. Wells's ability to portray her personal reality, as well as the reality of racism in the United States, showed me the true value of expressing these injustices through art.

I first met Wells at the opening of an exhibition of the Cargo Collection at the Sheldon Museum of Art in 2001. She was the featured artist for that exhibition, and I loved hearing her talk about making quilts in her living room as she sat on the floor and stitched. She explained the meaning of the rich details in each quilt. Some were lighthearted and fun, and others were testaments to her deep faith and her life experiences. She had a lovely energy and patience for question after question. Wells's lively sense of humor prevailed, but she also shared the deep emotions she experienced and expressed in her quilts.

Wells returned to Nebraska in 2011 when the IQM held a solo exhibition of her work titled *Yvonne Wells: Quilted Messages*. For that exhibition, we borrowed her seminal piece *Being in Total Control of Herself (BITCH)*, a powerful quilt that expressed her reaction after seeing the Statue of Liberty during a 1990 trip to New York City. Here is her description of how she felt: "When I got off the plane . . . I saw that lady . . . with her hands outstretched holding the keys, it looked like, to everything. She was in control of everything. She had this Black person in her hand, squeezing it, with a piece of tape over her mouth so that this person would be unable to speak. Under her feet stood the Indians, who were crying, 'This is my country! This is my country!' And she steps on them as well, because she was in control."

Once again, Wells's unflinching honesty hit me hard.

Wells gave a special program during that visit to the IQM in 2011. She allowed us to add a pop-up exhibition of a new series she had just completed, in addition to those we showed in our gallery. The new series was the *Seven Deadly Sins*. Wells described each quilt, explaining the details she created to represent each

Yvonne Wells. Photo by Dave Walker.

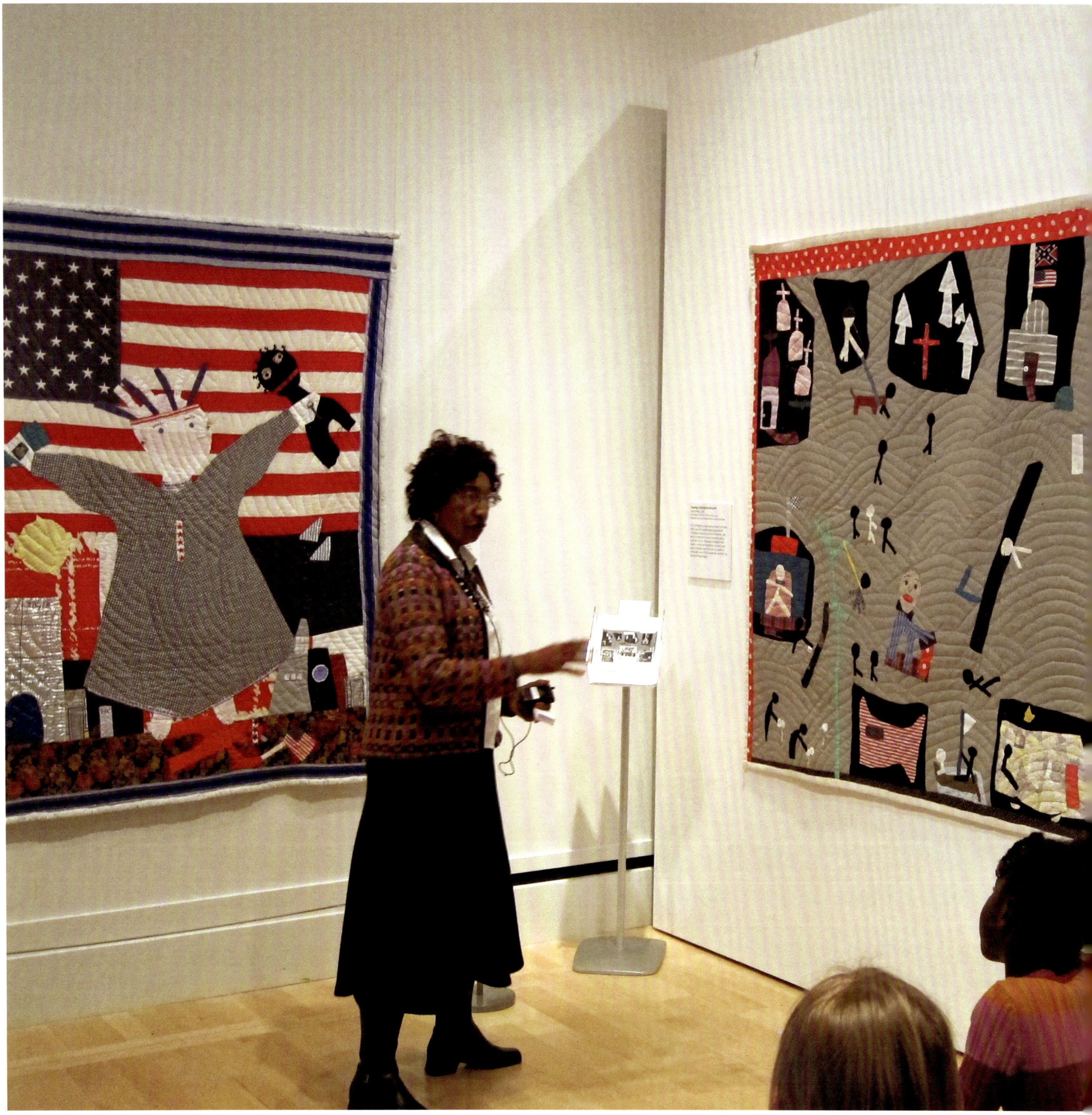

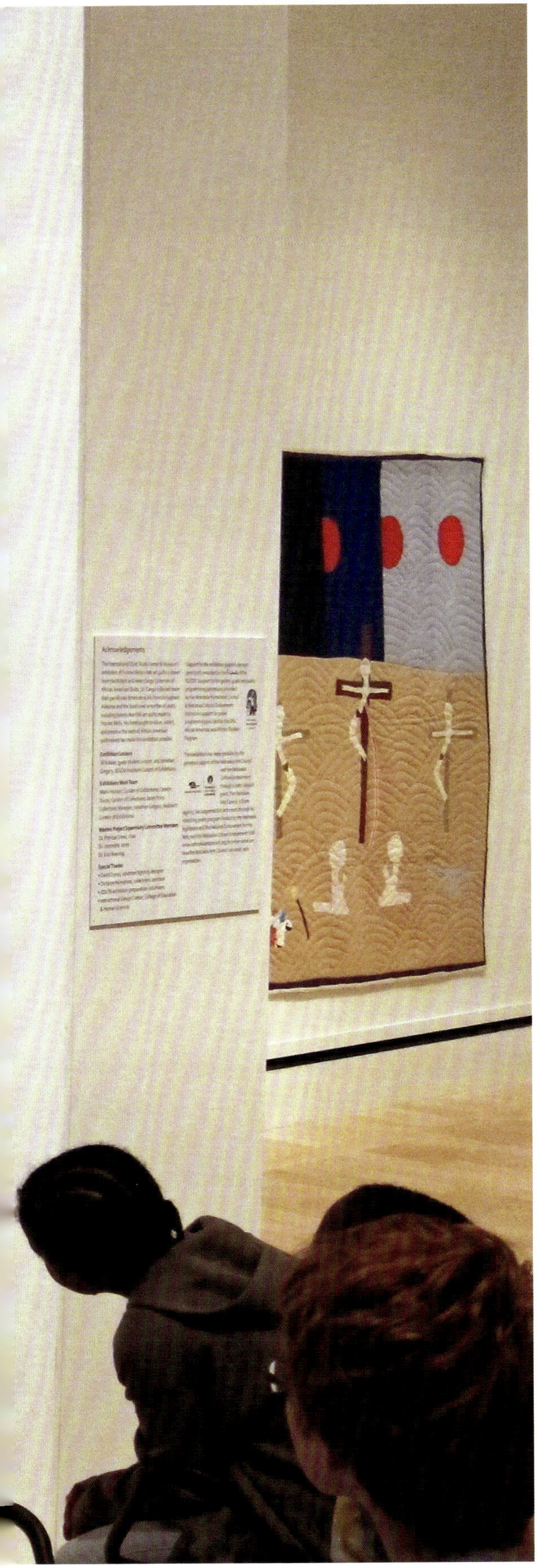

“When I got off the plane . . . I saw that lady . . . with her hands outstretched holding the keys, it looked like, to everything. She was in control of everything. She had this Black person in her hand, squeezing it, with a piece of tape over her mouth so that this person would be unable to speak. Under her feet stood the Indians, who were crying, ‘This is my country! This is my country!’ And she steps on them as well, because she was in control.”

—Yvonne Wells
Speaking about her quilt
Being in Total Control of Herself (BITCH), 2011

Left: Yvonne Wells presenting a talk during her 2011 solo exhibition at the IQM.

sin—lust, gluttony, greed, sloth, anger, envy, and pride. The work reflected all the elements of her inspiration—humor, life experiences, and deep religious faith—and resonated deeply with those at the talk, including me.

Now, so many years later, I am very proud to know that those pieces are a part of the IQM collection. The *Seven Deadly Sins* series, as well as three additional pieces, became a part of the IQM collection in 2023 due in large part to the generosity and passion of Teresa Duryea Wong. She is a member of the IQM's International Advisory Board and a frequent visitor to the IQM. As a quilt historian, Duryea Wong has also featured quilts from the collection in a number of her books. While researching inside the IQM archives in 2015, she encountered Yvonne Wells's quilts and, like me, fell in love with them. Duryea Wong was inspired and decided that the IQM's collection of Wells's work would be next in her line of quilt books. We concocted a plan to add additional pieces to the collection.

Teresa Duryea Wong and I visited Wells's Tuscaloosa home in 2022, where, like the IQM team that visited Robert Cargo twenty-two years earlier, we were treated to a private showing of stacks of quilts in her home. Wells shared fascinating details about many of her quilts, but when she showed us the *Seven Deadly Sins* quilts, our eyes met, and Duryea Wong and I knew we simply had to have them for the IQM.

The *Seven Deadly Sins* series, along with three additional pieces, went through consideration by the IQM's Acquisition Committee. These quilts, acquired with generous support from the Jimmy and Teresa Duryea Wong Foundation and the Robert and Ardis James Foundation, established the Yvonne Wells Collection. We owe these donors a great deal of gratitude. It simply would not have been possible without their support!

Today, besides the IQM, Yvonne Wells's quilts are included in several major museum collections. Her life and career are documented in the book by Stacy Morgan and Wells titled *The Story Quilts of Yvonne Wells* (University of Alabama Press, 2024).

Wells has also, in a sense, returned to New York City, where she is now represented by the gallery Fort Gansevoort. More than a quarter of a century after her 1990 visit, she continues to speak for those silenced by social injustices as a celebrated artist who is honored and collected by people around the world.

As she often states, "What my head sees, my heart feels, my hand creates." Wells has created an unforgettable group of quilts at the IQM that will live on not only as a testament to her creative drive but also as a representation of work that places African American quilts at the heart of the history of quilts in American culture.

ΔΔΔ

Yvonne Wells in front of *Three Wise Men* (2017).
Photo by Dave Walker.

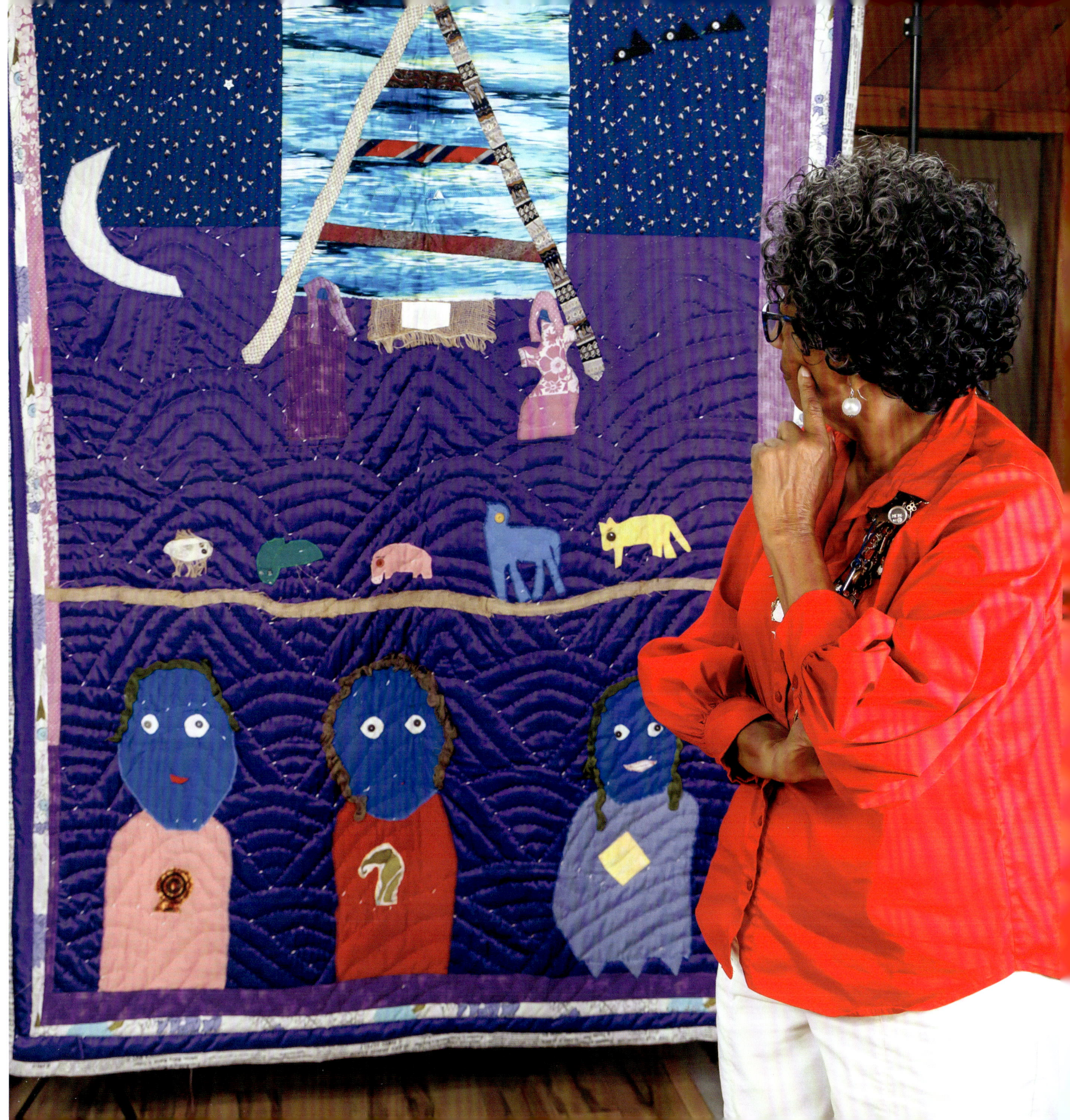

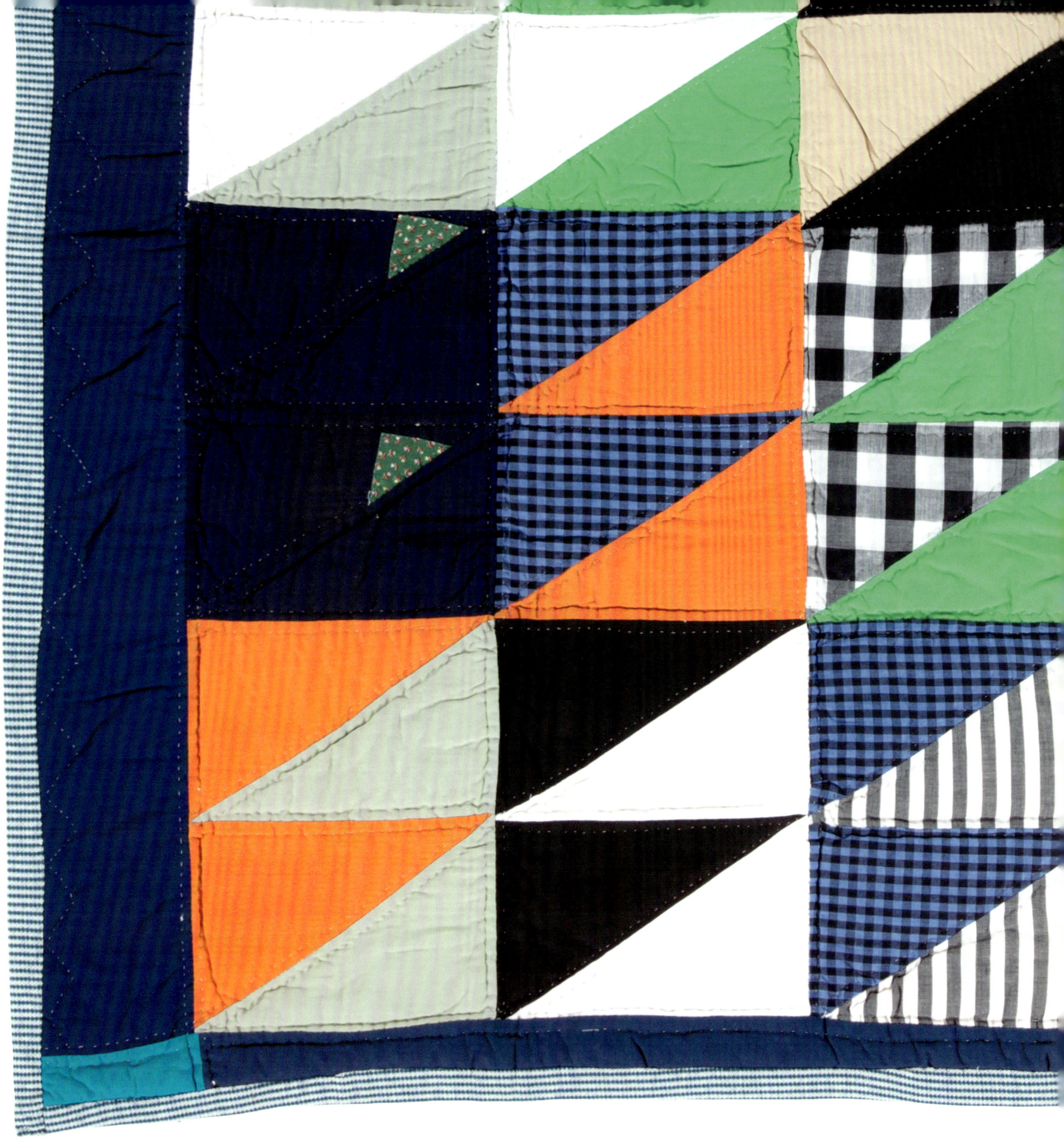

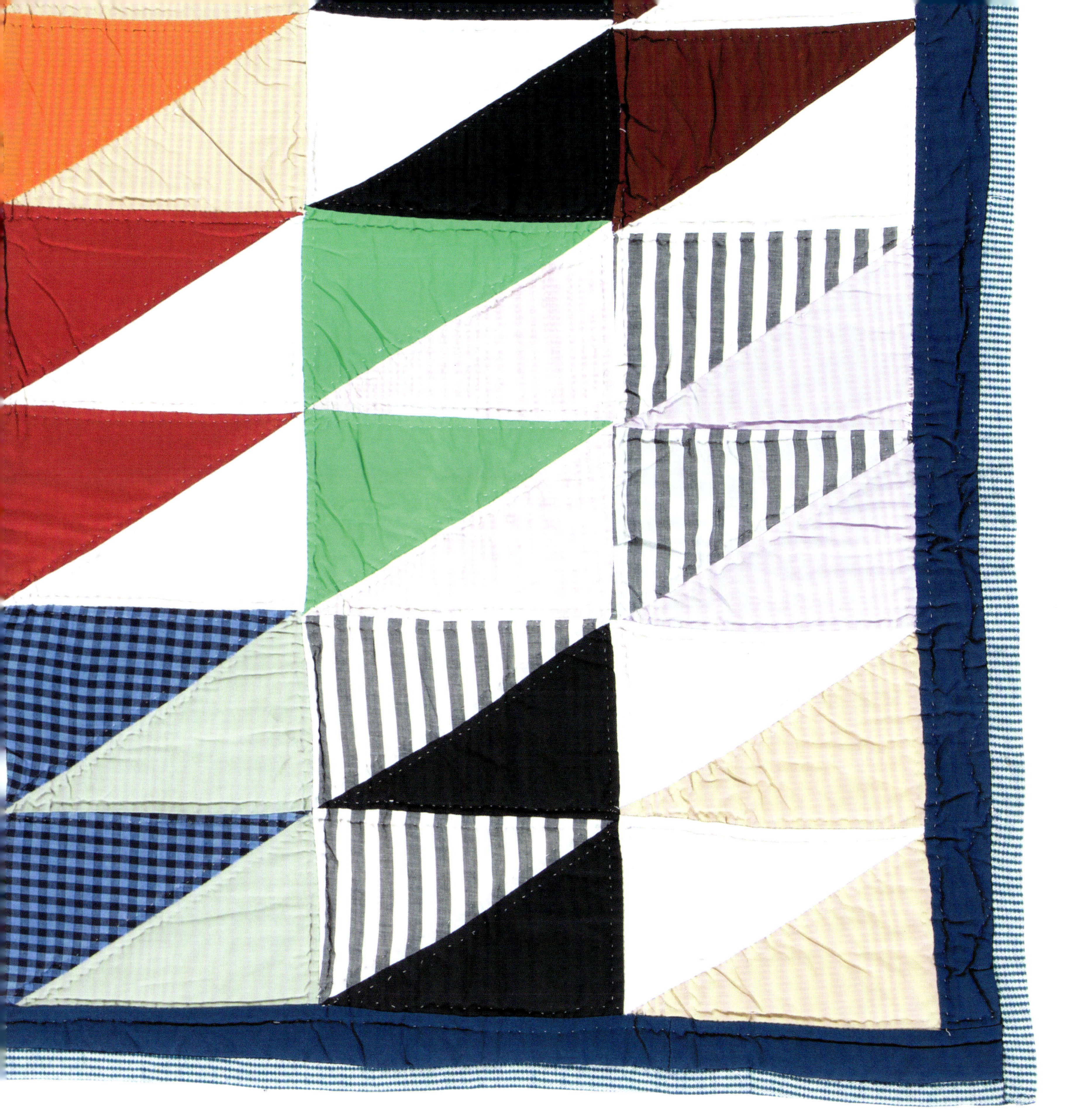

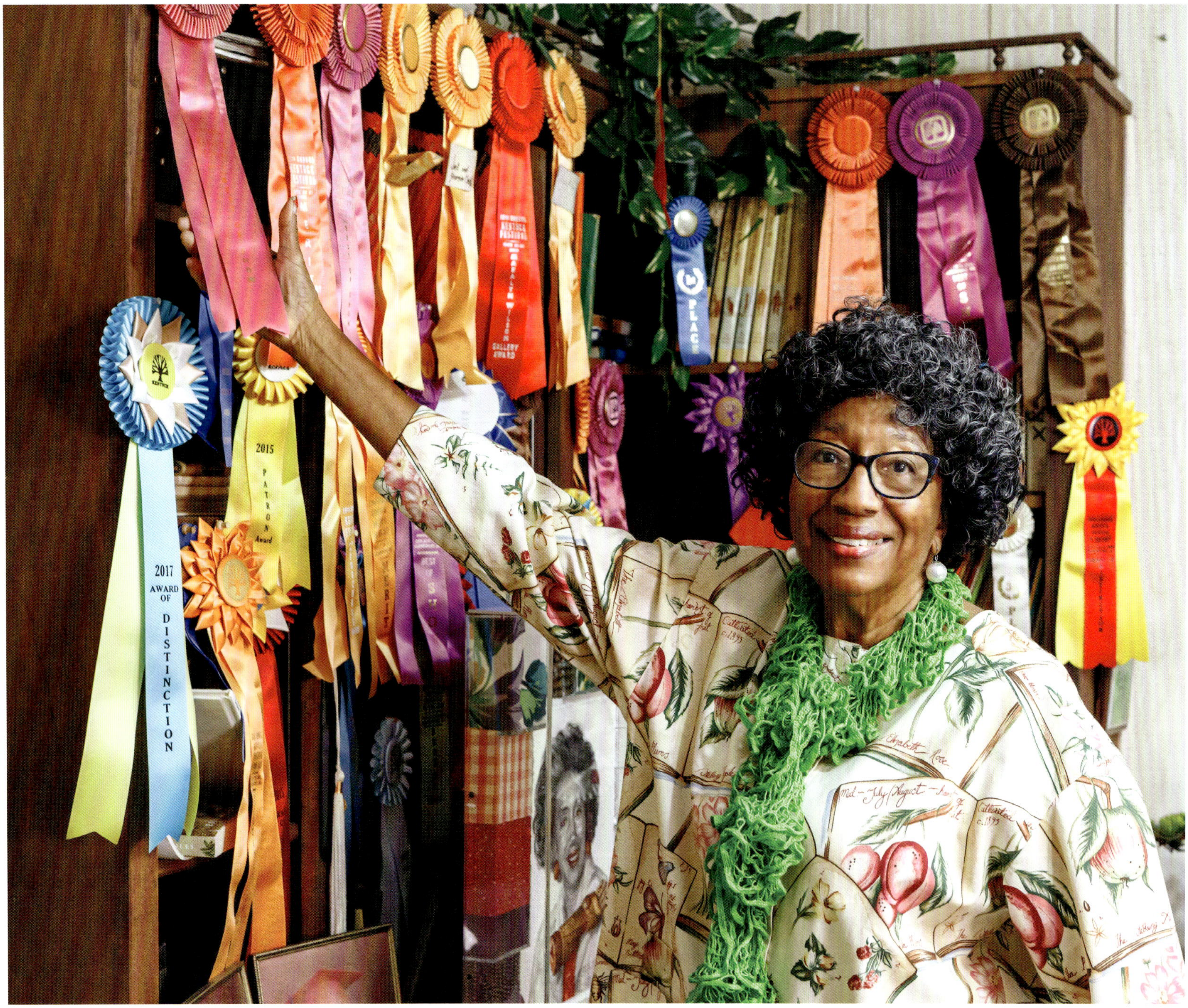

The previous two pages show a detail of one of Yvonne's early patchwork quilts.
Above: A wall of ribbons and accolades from an incredible artistic career. Photo by Dave Walker.

INTRODUCTION

Yvonne Wells, the Storyteller

Teresa Duryea Wong

I'm on a mission to make the artist Yvonne Wells a household name. This book, which highlights thirty-four of her quilts in the International Quilt Museum permanent collection, is part of that mission. The entire collection of thirty-four quilts is featured here in stunning detail, including the never-before-seen backs of many of these quilts.

At the time of this writing, the IQM has some eleven thousand quilts and textile objects in its collection that span centuries and hail from around the entire globe. Yvonne Wells is the most represented artist in the entire collection. This statistic is an astounding testament to her incredible vision as a folk artist and her career as a prolific and ingenious quiltmaker. Since her first quilt in 1979, Wells has made well over five hundred quilts. And the numbers continue to rise because she still has stories to tell.

She was born on December 26, 1939, as one of nine children born to a Presbyterian minister and an elementary school teacher. Growing up, art, and especially quilts, were not present in her life. Instead, her parents emphasized reading and education, church and family. Wells was a self-described tomboy who went on to become a physical education teacher for thirty-five years in the Tuscaloosa, Alabama, school system. As a student, she excelled at sports, especially track and softball, and even had dreams of competing at the Olympics.

Wells has lived most of her life in Tuscaloosa. Her husband of sixty years, Livingston Nathaniel Wells, passed away in 2020, yet he lives on in her art. You will most definitely find a patch of one of his shirts, possibly cut up with or without his knowledge, or maybe even one of his socks, tucked into one of Wells's artsy creations. There are also bits of clothes and stories from her two children, four grandchildren, and three great-grandchildren among the unusual and unexpected materials she expertly manipulates into her textile creations.

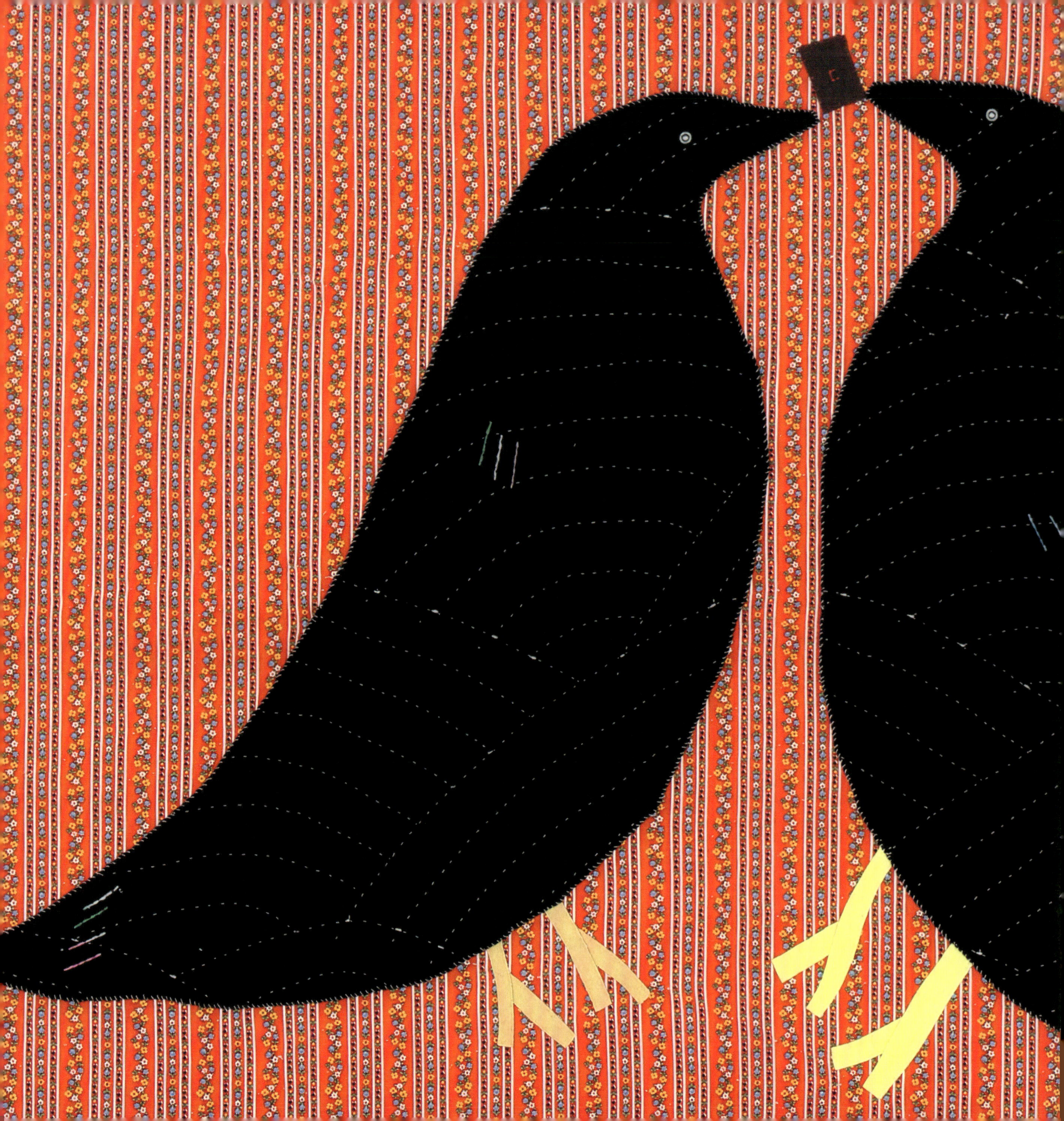

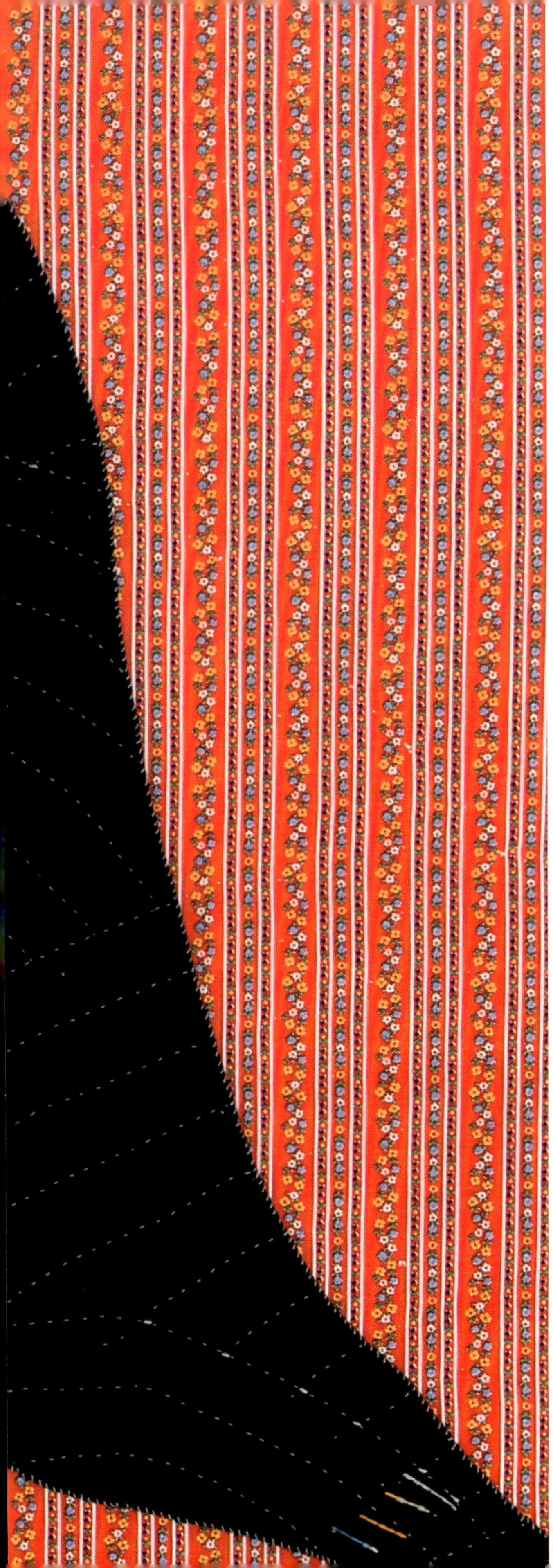

Lovers with a Broken Heart (1987), detail.
Lovers with a Broken Heart (1987), detail. Photo by Teresa Duryea Wong.
Following pages: Wells in front of (from left to right) *Three Wise Men* (2017), *Me Mask* (1993), and *Breaking the Glass Ceiling* (2017). Photo by Dave Walker.

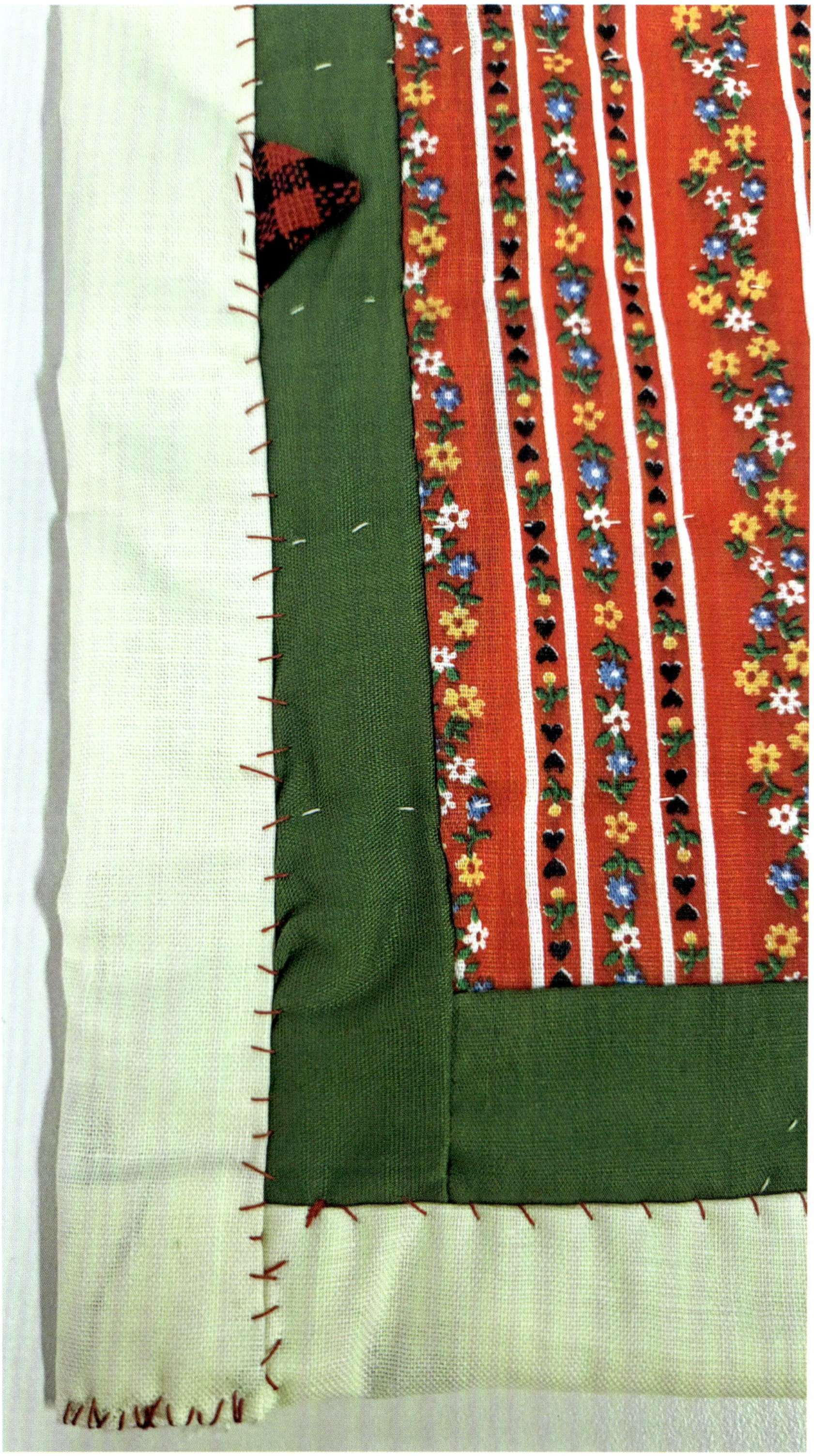

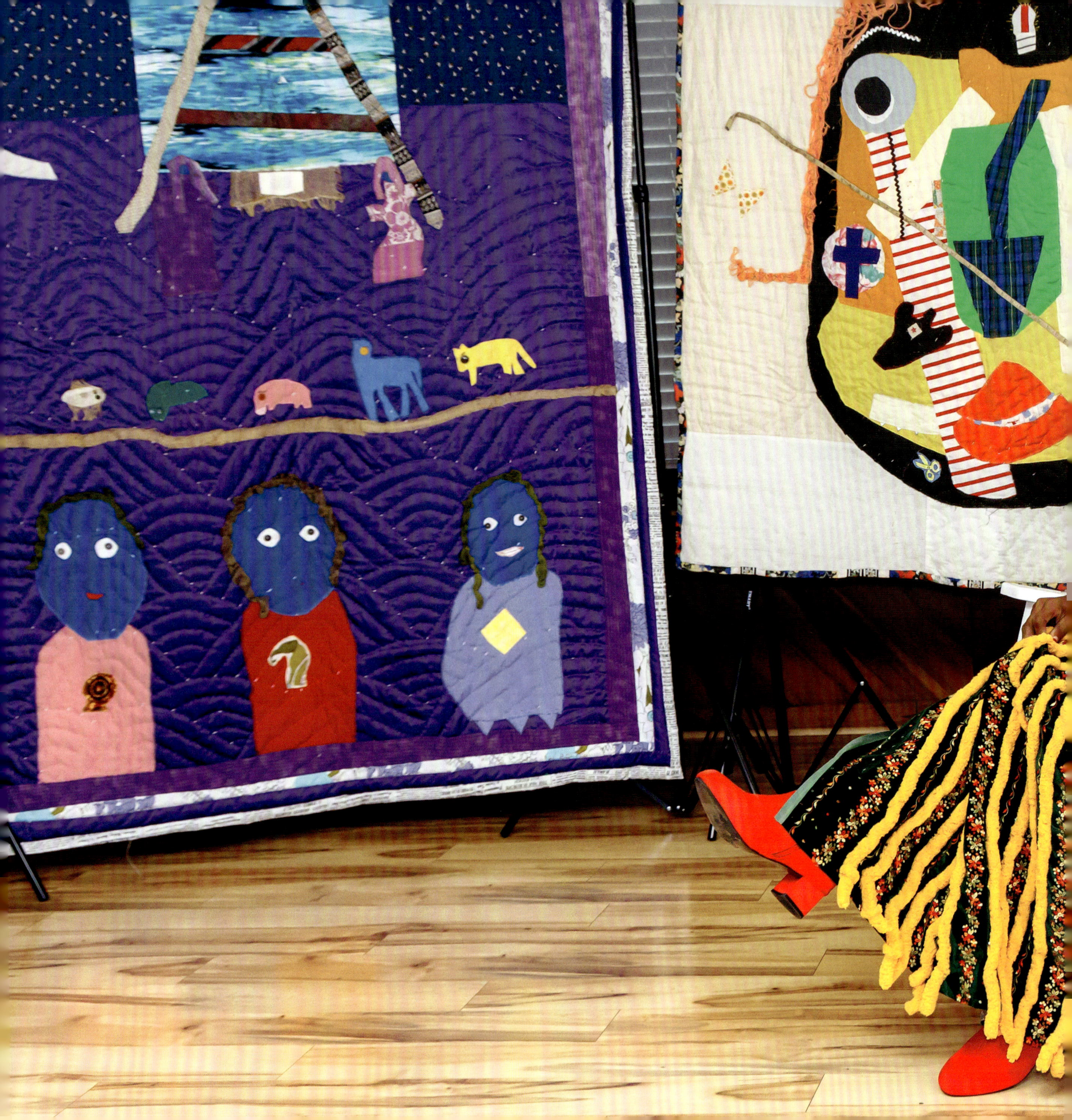

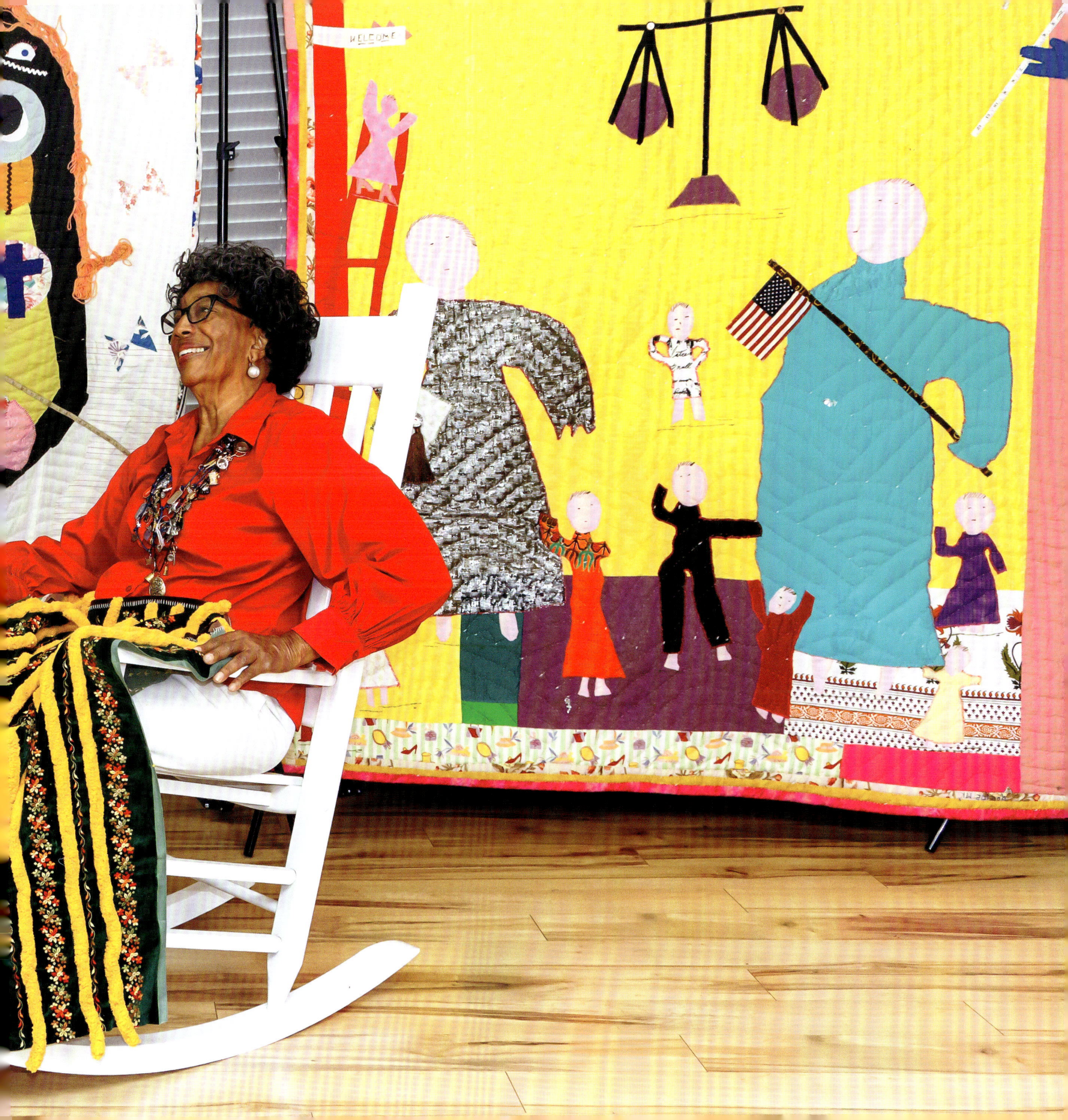
WELCOME

Even their drawings. In fact, the two goats butting heads in *Seven Deadly Sins: Sloth* were drawn by her grandson.

At the time she began her teaching career in 1962, Alabama's schools—and most schools in the South—were segregated. Wells was later part of a group of schoolteachers and administrators who ushered in desegrated schools, and she eventually found herself in a new role teaching both Black and white students together. Her experience of a being a Black woman in the South who has witnessed the Jim Crow era and the birth of the Civil Rights Movement has left an indelible mark on her view of the world. Occasionally that view plays out in her artistic expression in powerful ways as evidenced in her quilts *The Mother Ship* and *Yesterday: Civil Rights in the South.*

Sharbreon Plummer, PhD, has researched and written extensively on the role of Black quilters in the South, and her essay *Place and Purpose: Black Quilt Traditions in the South* adds more depth and complexity to this history and Wells's place as a quiltmaker within this larger community.

Besides these sociopolitical themes, Wells's faith also plays a significant role in her art. She is a devout Christian and longtime member of Tuscaloosa's Brown Memorial Presbyterian Church. She often recreates Bible stories, including in *Noah's Ark* and *Moses Receiving the Ten Commandments.*

One of her signature elements in her quilts is the inclusion of small, triangular patches, often in sets of three. The triangles, Wells explains, are "my little friends." They represent the Trinity: the Father, Son, and Holy Ghost. Sometimes the entire triangle appliqué is stitched down on all sides, but in other examples, only one side of the triangle is attached to the quilt so that if you were to touch it, you could lift the triangle like a flap.

Wells's most obvious, and at the same time abstract, use of the triangles is in her large quilt titled *The Red Quilt*, which has not three, but four triangles arranged just slightly above center. Nothing else is appliquéd on this quilt, which is a rare yet stunning example of the use of minimalism to tell her story of Christianity. In addition to the triangular patches, Wells also sometimes appliqués three tiny birds to represent the Trinity. These are especially prevalent in her *Seven Deadly Sins* series (see detail image on page 107).

As part of our decision for this book regarding the locations in which to photograph Wells to best represent her life and her status as a world-class artist, it was imperative to include a portrait of Wells inside her church. This building and its congregation are as much a part of Wells as her needle and thread.

The role of Black artists who had no role models is expertly explained in Kyra E. Hicks's essay *Vision Without Precedent: Harriet Powers and Yvonne Wells*. Hicks is a quilt expert and the author of an important history of

Pieced Diamonds (c. 1980–1987), detail.

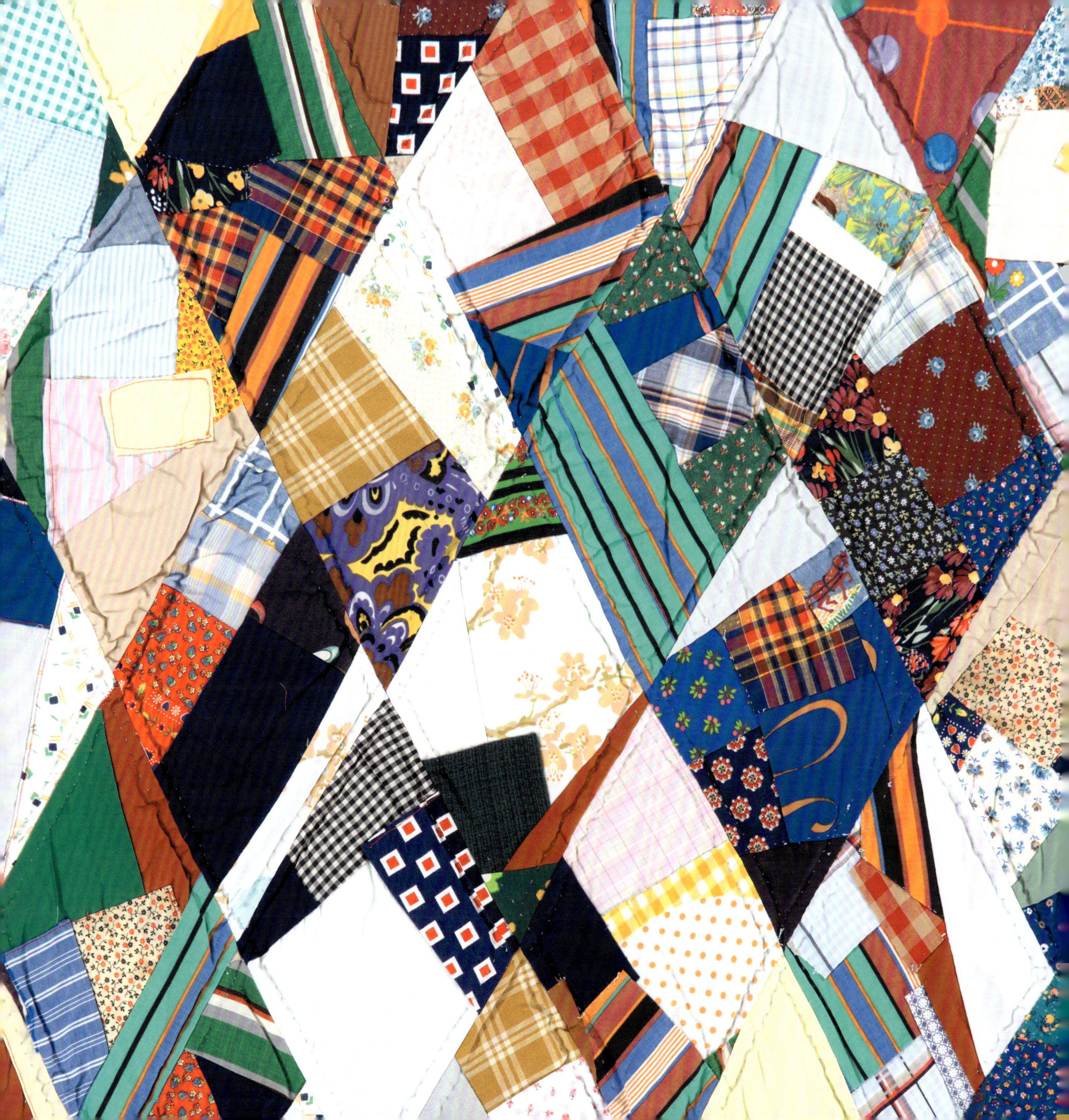

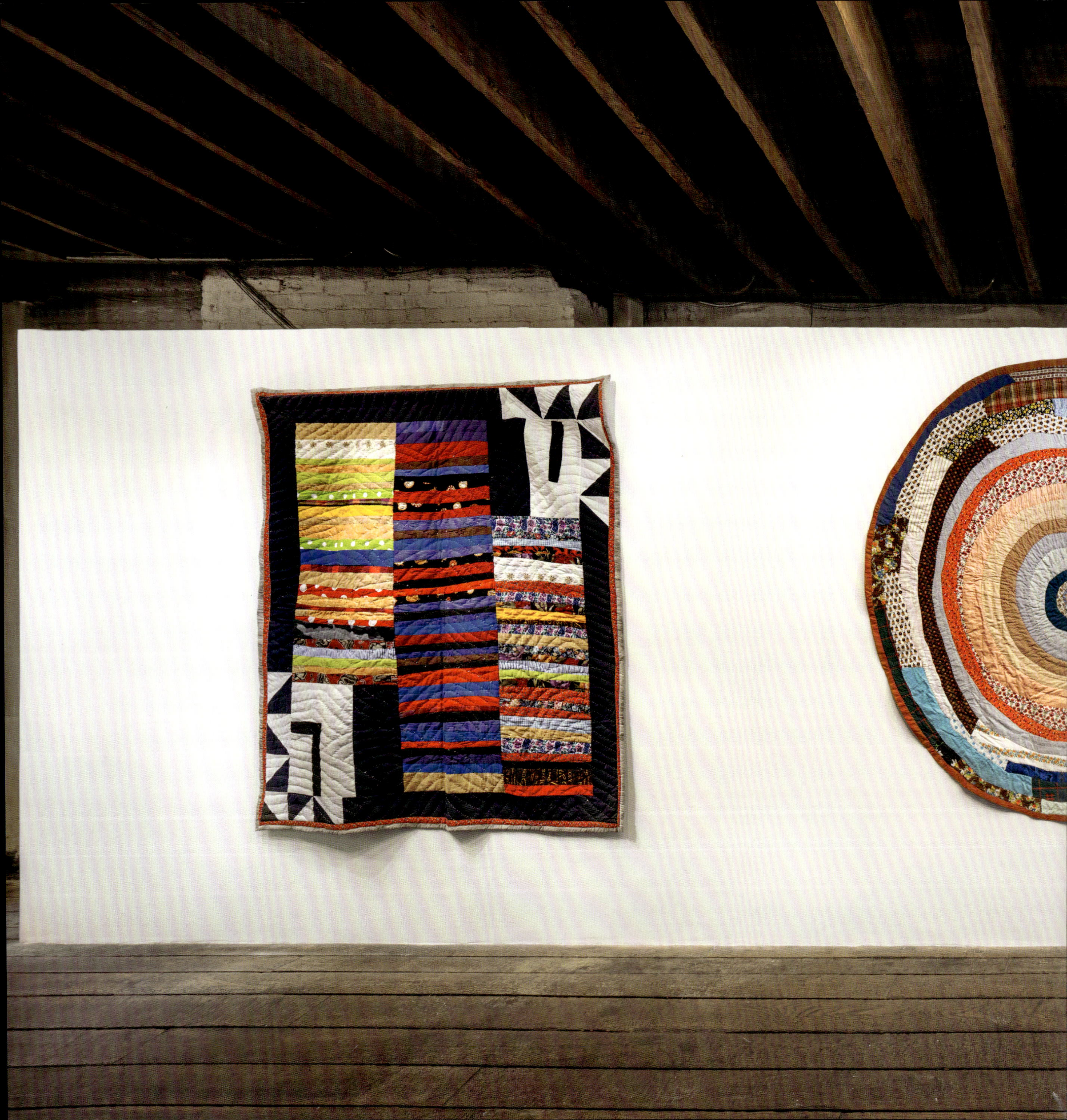

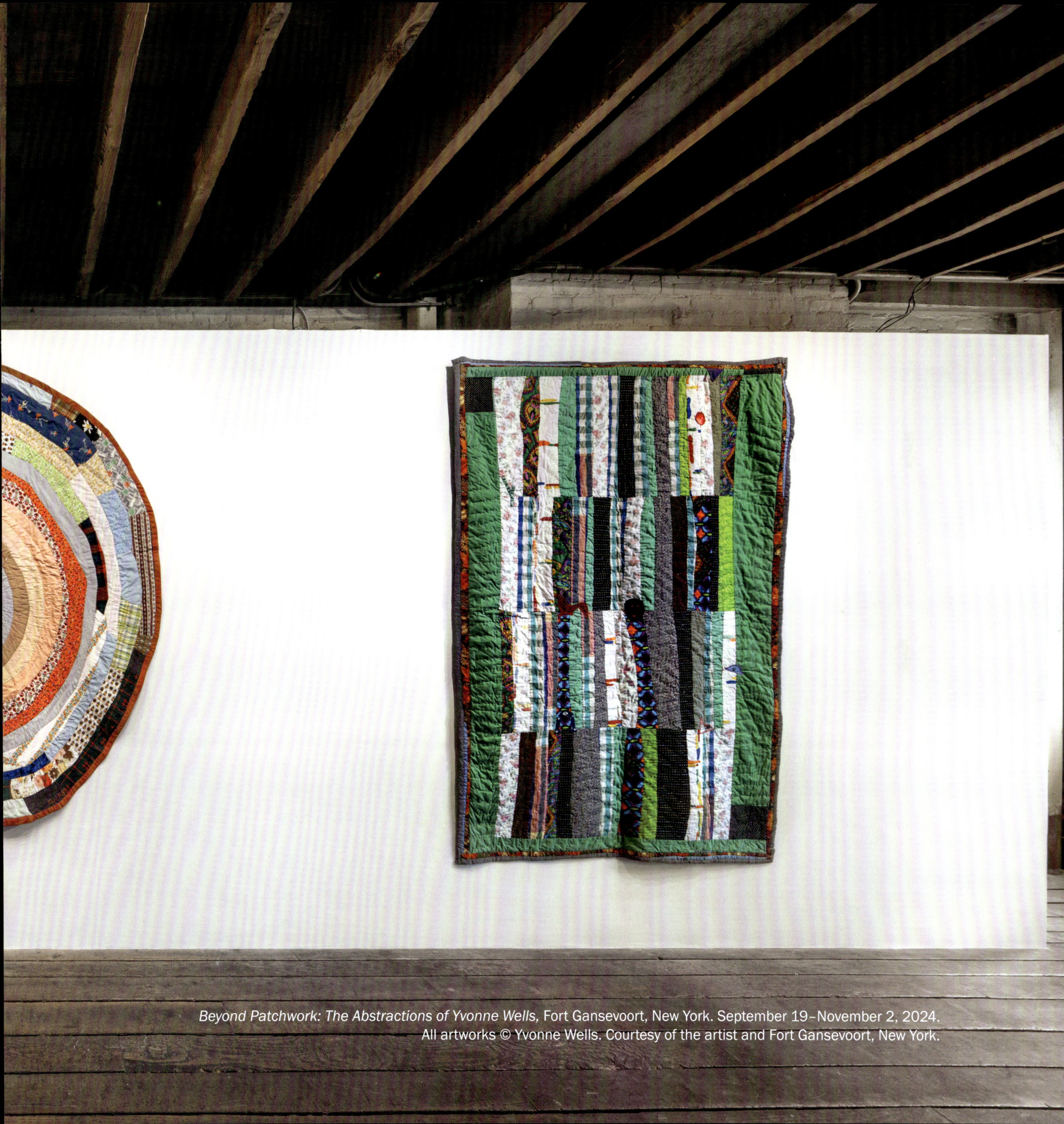

Beyond Patchwork: The Abstractions of Yvonne Wells, Fort Gansevoort, New York. September 19–November 2, 2024.

the famed quilter Harriet Powers, a formerly enslaved woman who went on to become one of America's most famous quilters. This essay offers a deep dive into the similarities between Powers's biblical figures and Wells's, especially in the depictions of the Crucifixion these two artists both created.

One of the beautiful things about art is that it is open for interpretation. If a work of art inspires a viewer to study it long enough, the viewer will eventually reach their own assessment, their own story. That's what art does for us. It allows a moment to expand our mind to create a narrative of our own. And the viewer's interpretation may be completely different from what the artist had in mind.

Going Home is a classic example of this idea. When I first saw this quilt, I was immediately riveted by the simple imagery that communicated such strong ideas and questions. I had no idea who made it or why. But the aesthetic pulled me in, and I was hooked. The first narrative I invented for this work of art was to think about which bird, or birds (which I also assumed were substitutes for humans), were going home. Was it the one bird heading downward who was going home? Or was it the three birds flying upward who were going home? Was the one bird a loner, or was he cast out? Or was he running away from home? And does home mean heaven? The fact that my imagination conjured so many thoughts and possibilities kept me studying this piece of art for quite some time.

A decade later, I had several opportunities to meet Wells and hear her describe this quilt in her own words. In *Going Home*, Wells explained to me, the patches of purple in the bottom right corner represent the arms of Christ. The lone bird is returning to righteousness. Her original intent is now blended with my own imaginary narrative, and together the two stories enrich my appreciation for this artwork.

Hearing an artist's explanation is priceless. That's why in this book, Wells describes the intricacies of her most brilliant series of quilts, the *Seven Deadly Sins*, in her own words. She explains the dense imagery in each quilt and how these larger-than-life characters came about, and why.

Stacy Morgan, PhD, is a folk art expert and professor at the University of Alabama who authored a catalogue raisonné, *The Story Quilts of Yvonne Wells* (University of Alabama Press, 2024), in partnership with Wells. His assessment of Wells's *Seven Deadly Sins* is that this series of seven extremely large quilts is the crown jewels of Wells's entire body of work. They are masterful expressions of a serious subject, with larger-than-life characters. Each one is executed with unconventional materials, and each quilt exudes a sense of whimsy that makes their difficult message more palatable.

The *Seven Deadly Sins* series was created between December 2004 and March 2006. In 2023 they entered the permanent collection of IQM.

Moses Receiving the Ten Commandments (1987), detail.

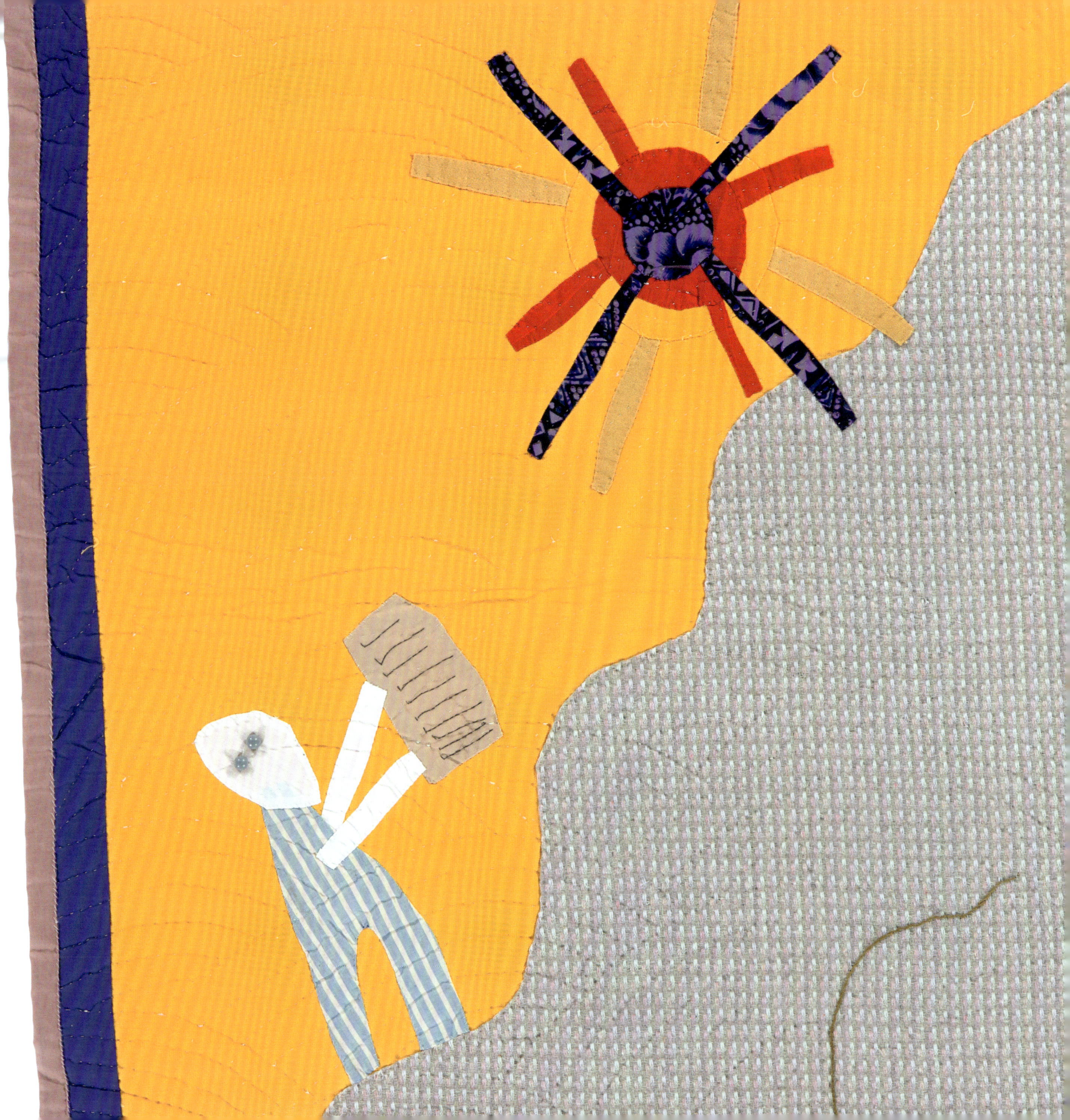

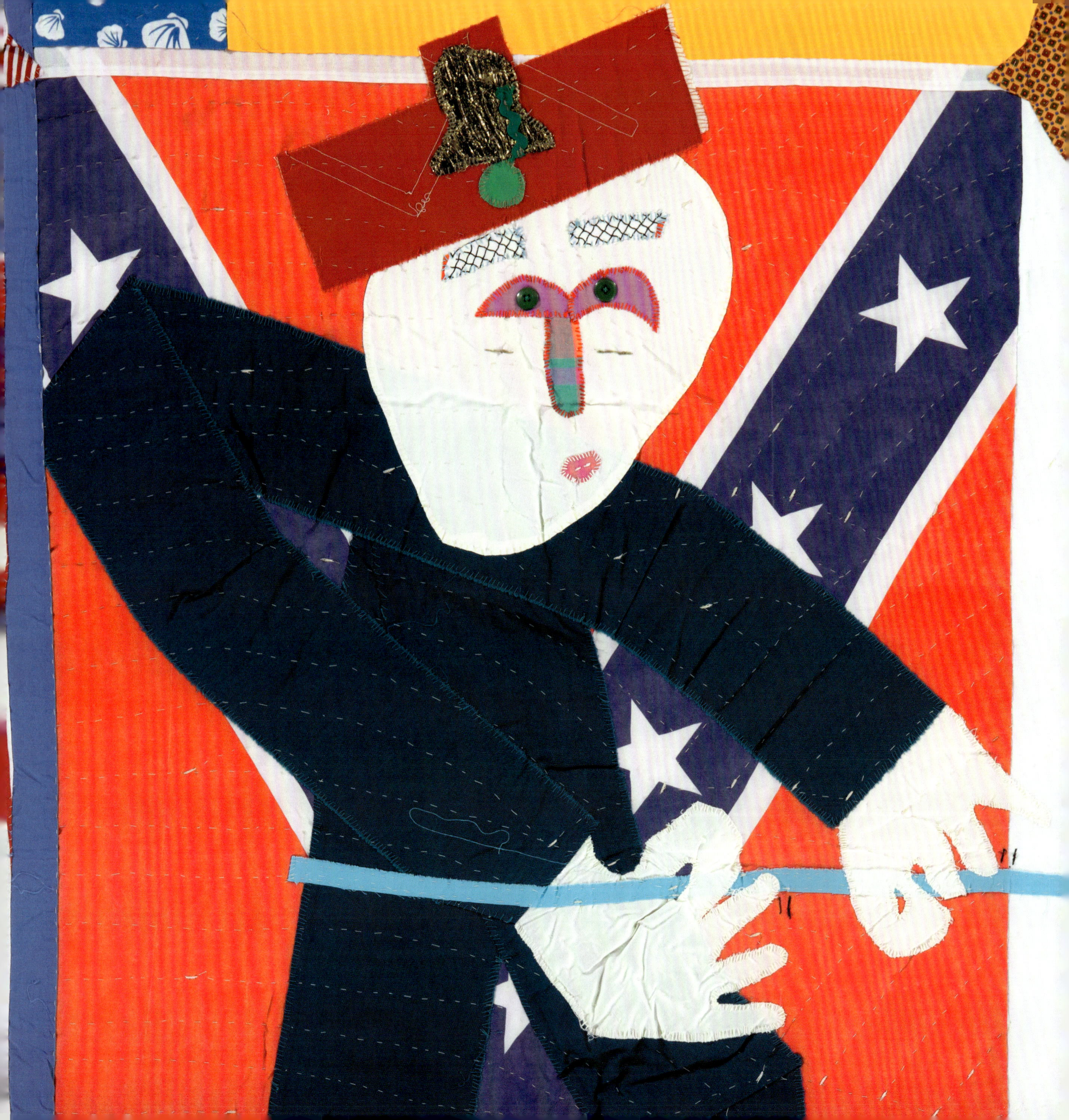

The decision to acquire this series was an important milestone, both for the quilts themselves as well as for the museum. When Wells finished these seven artworks, she made the bold decision that if they were ever exhibited, then the entire set must be shown together. And not just together, but they must also be exhibited in the correct order according to her interpretation of their order in the Bible, starting with *Lust* and ending with *Pride*. Additionally, she would never agree to sell one quilt from the series alone. They were a set and must remain a set. Now, the seven masterworks are together and protected, and forever in the home of the perfect caretaker who will carefully preserve these quilts and dutifully maintain the artist's stipulations for future generations.

Alongside these serious religious and social justice messages, Wells is also an artist who captures an incredibly wide swath of American culture in a way that is both entertaining and unforgettable. For example, she has depicted Marilyn Monroe, Elvis Presley, Ruth Bader Ginsberg, and even Aunt Jemima. In recent years, she was inspired to tell the story of Danica Patrick, the most successful female race car driver in American history. *Lady Race Car Driver* is also part of the IQM collection.

Everyday moments also become incredible works of art in Wells's hands. For example, she was inspired to make *The Gossip Quilt I* after imagining two neighbors leaning over a fence and gossiping. Her delightful interpretation of that moment takes the shape of long-stemmed flowers with a gentle lean, their blooms taking the shape of heads. In the bottom corner is the sun, not yet fully risen.

Wells came late to quilting. She was in her forties when she became fully immersed in this artform. She is completely self-taught, and her vision is wholly innate. In 1985 she was encouraged to show her quilts for the first time at the Kentuck Festival of the Arts, where she was awarded Best of Show. She went on to win five additional Best of Show awards at Kentuck in 1990, 1991, 1995, 1997, and 2004. She has gone on to win many other top awards at other venues around the country. She has participated in dozens of group exhibitions and has had numerous solo exhibitions. Her work is included in several prestigious museum collections including the Smithsonian African American Museum of History and Culture in Washington DC and the Montgomery Museum of Fine Arts in Montgomery, Alabama. She is represented by the Fort Gansevoort Gallery in New York City, where her quilts are dispersed to collectors everywhere.

What sets Wells's art apart is her unparalleled originality. She has a sophisticated artistic vision, yet her technical skills are improvised, and this mix enables a masterful blend that captures the viewer's attention and makes her quilts unforgettable. For example, she sometimes quilts the three layers of her quilts together using fishing line or even dental floss.

The Greeting (2000), detail.

Plain old thread just doesn't fit her needs, and frankly she needs something strong enough to hold some of her quirky objects in place, such as thick fake fur, a burlap potato sack, heavy curtains, or even parts of a screen door. These unconventional materials seem almost natural in a quilt by Yvonne Wells. In fact, when asked why she cut up her sweater and turned it into hair, or why she added a motorcycle flying out of a basket of money, or why she attached a grown man's vest to a quilt, Yvonne Wells has a timeless reply. "It tells my story."

ΔΔΔ

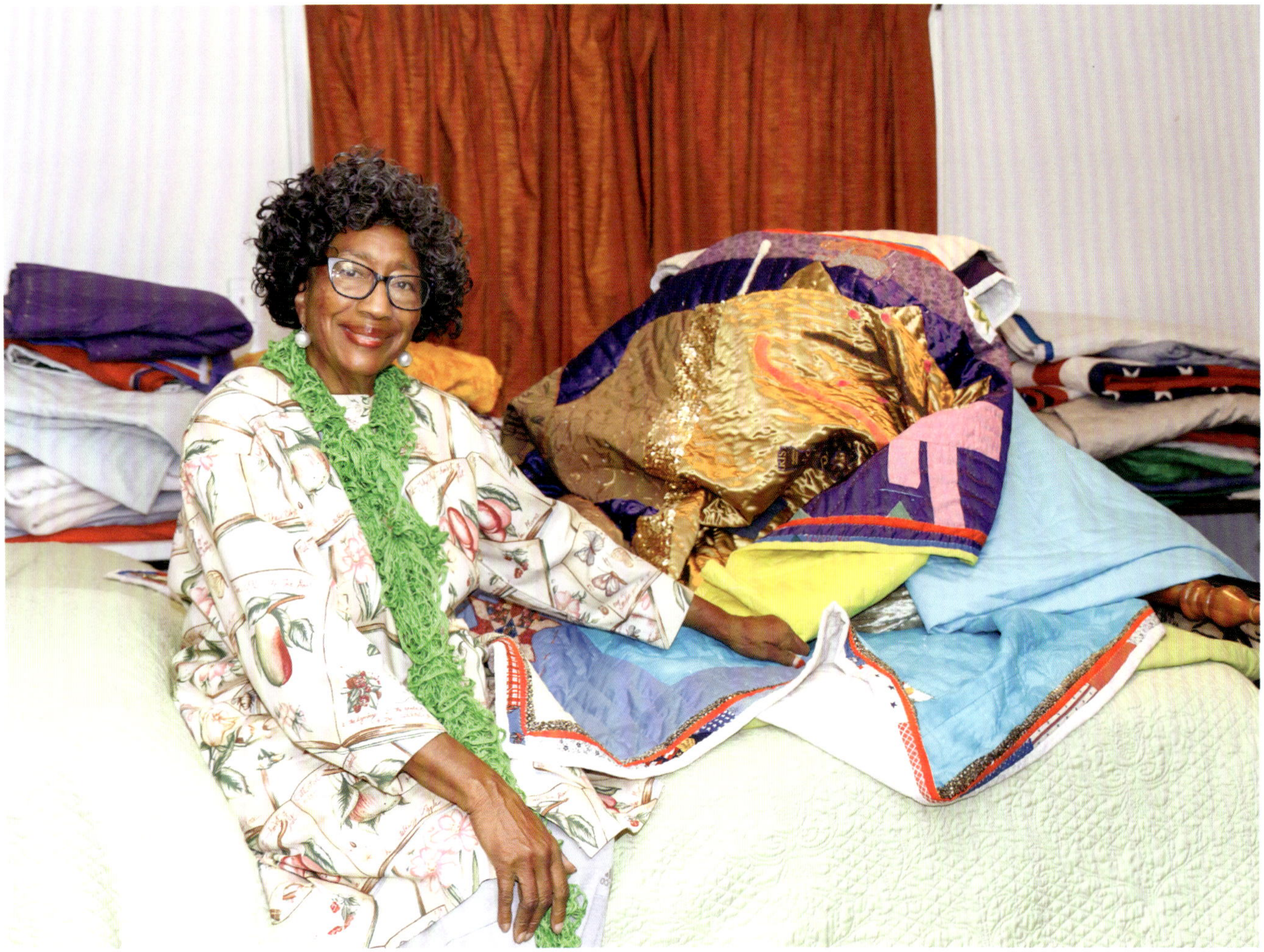

Wells in her Tuscaloosa home where some of her quilts are stored.
Right: *The Gossip Quilt I* (1987).

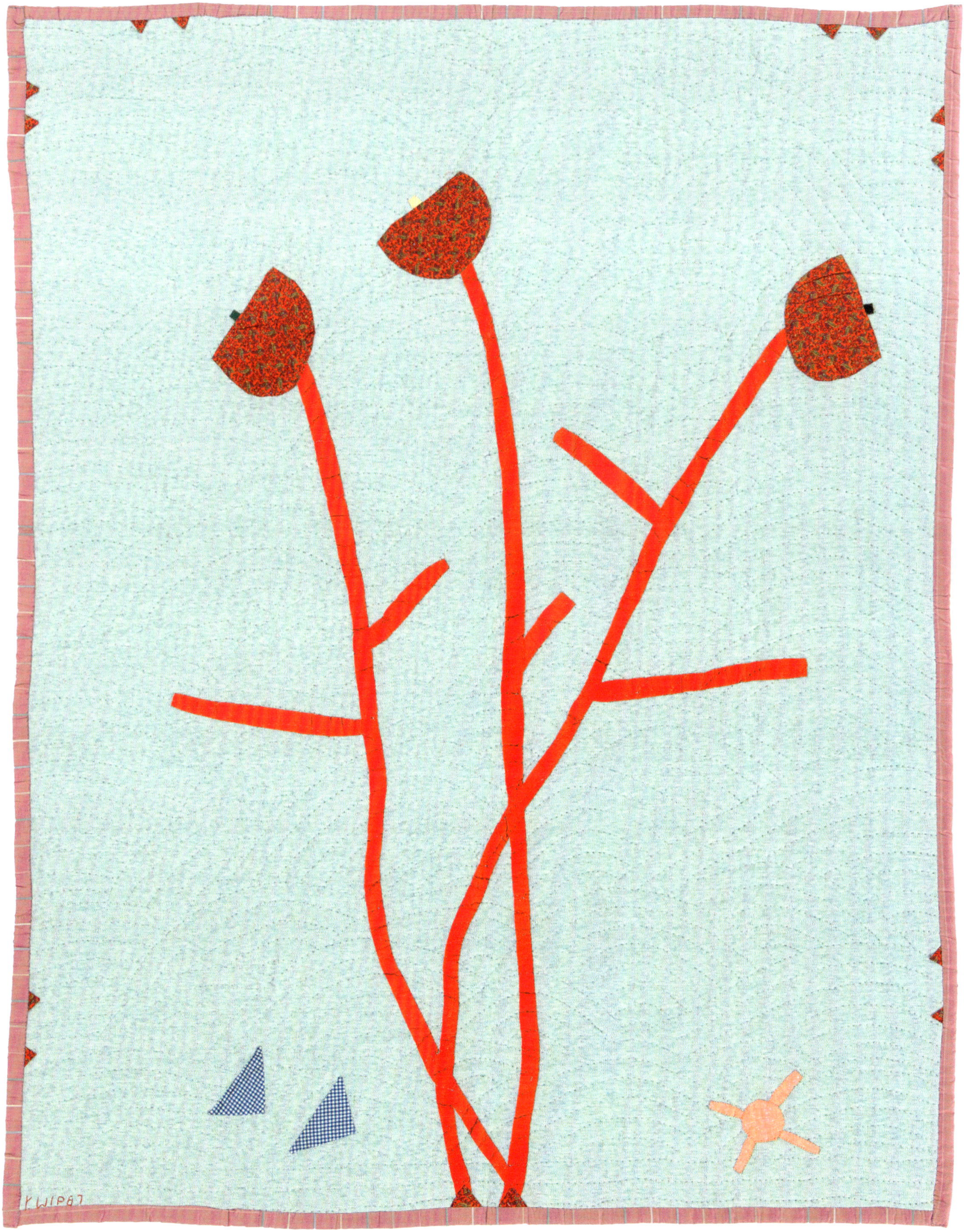
YWIP87

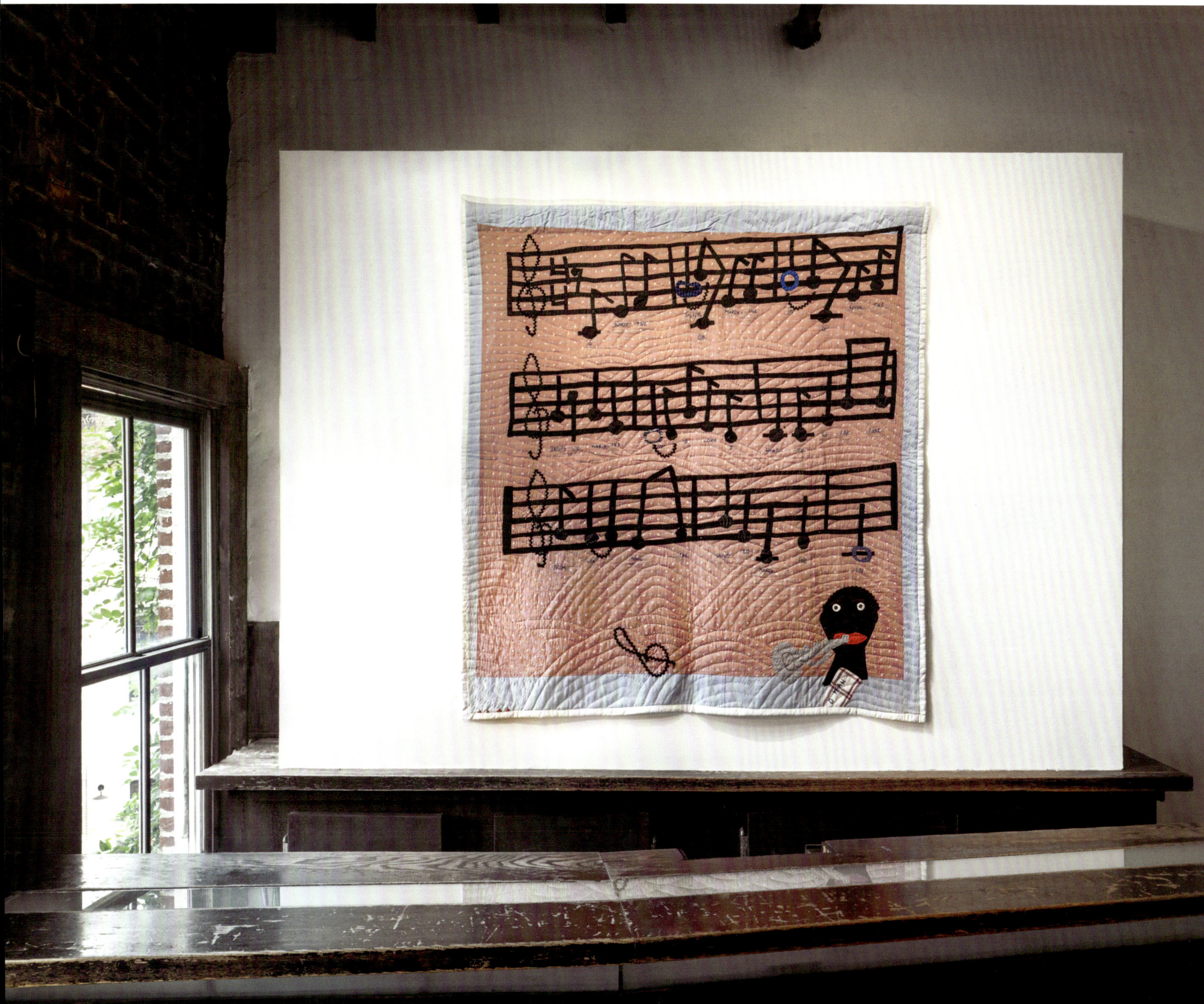

Yvonne Wells: Play The Hand That's Dealt You, Fort Gansevoort, New York, June 8–August 12, 2023. All artworks © Yvonne Wells. Courtesy of the artist and Fort Gansevoort, New York. Right: Yvonne Wells in front of *Marilyn Monroe* (2004).
Page 44: *Going Home* (1987), detail. Page 45: Traditional diamond quilt detail. Page 46: *First Dark* (1987), detail. Page 47: *Seven Deadly Sins: Wrath* (2004), detail.

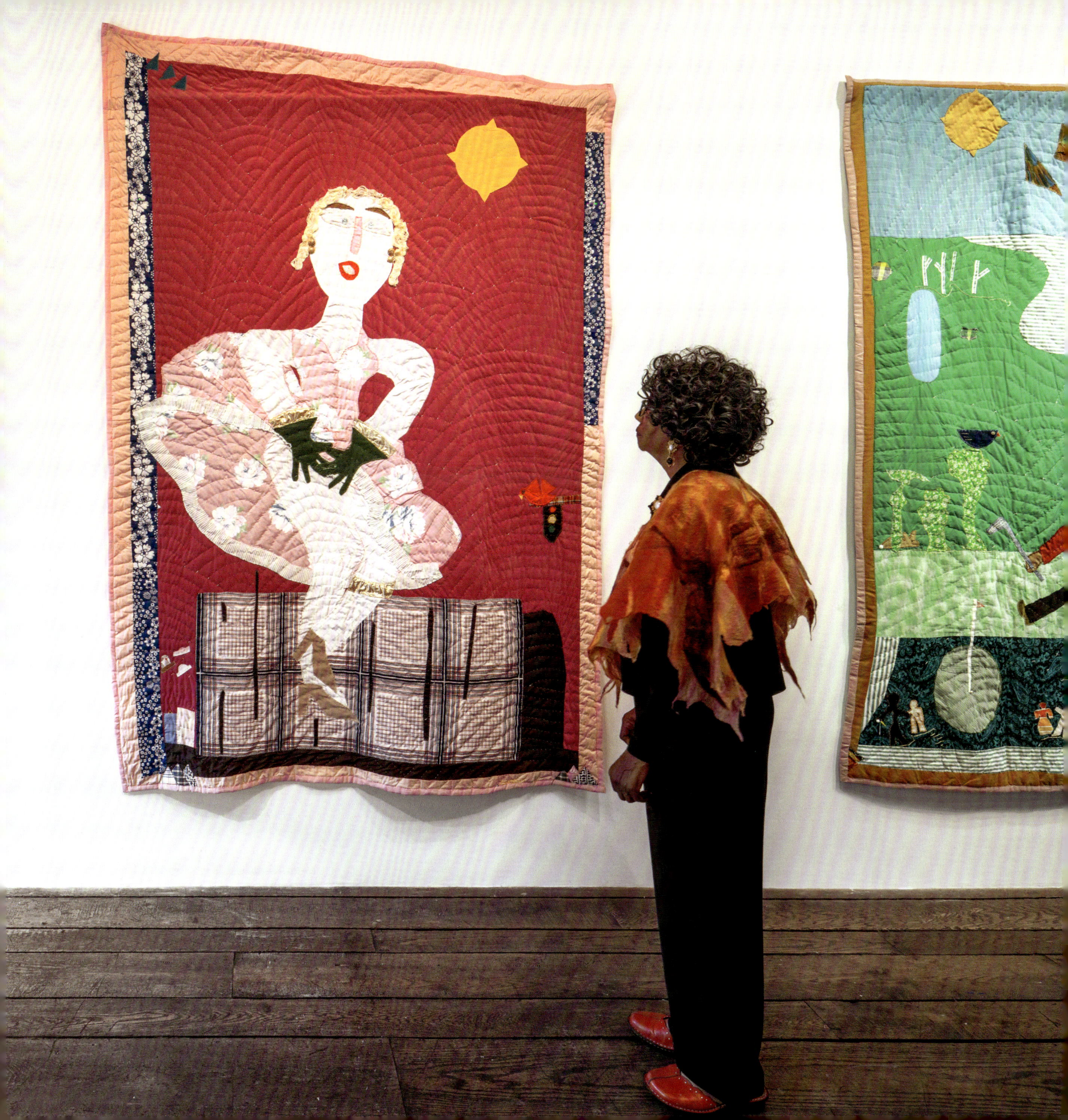

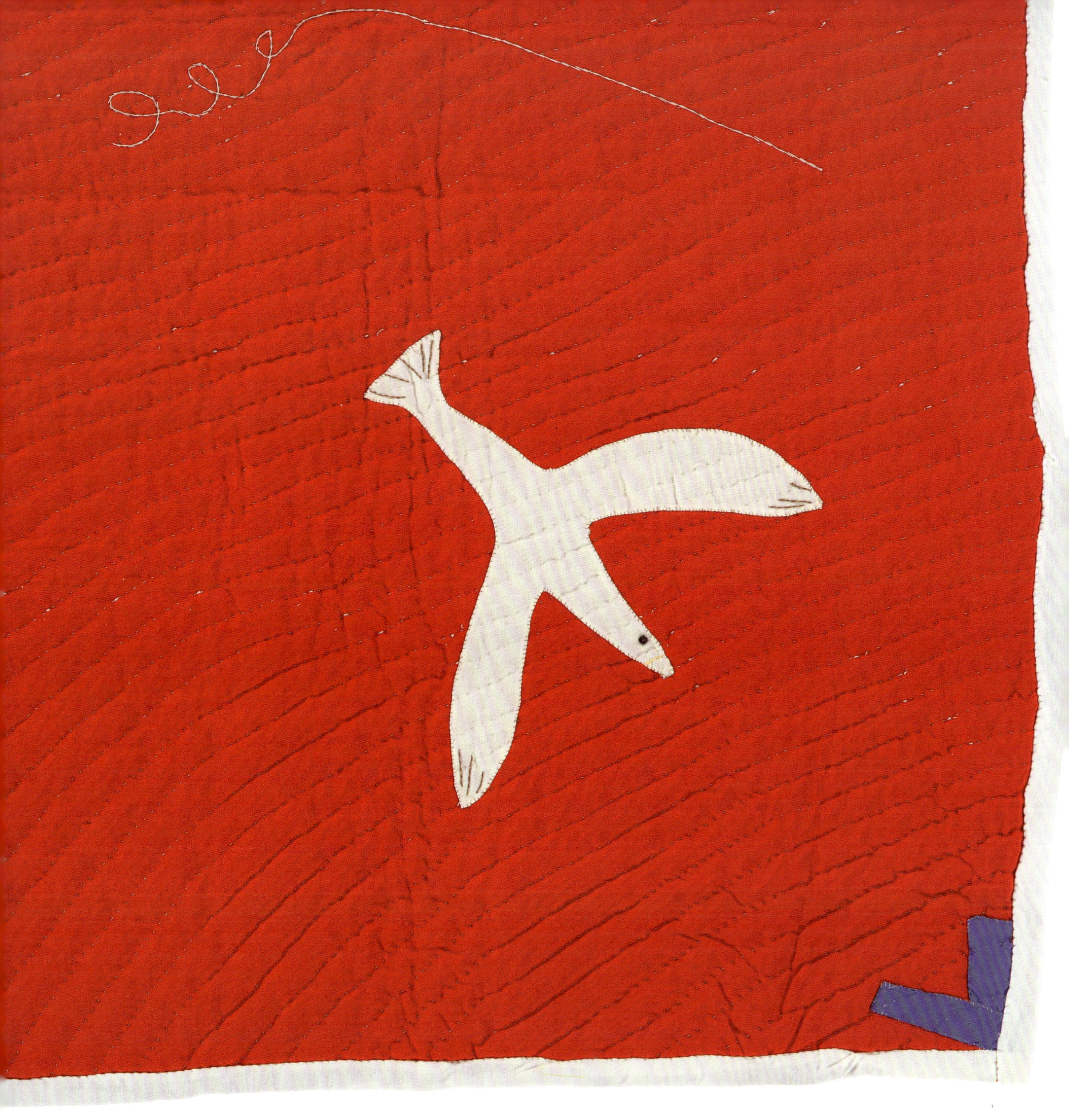

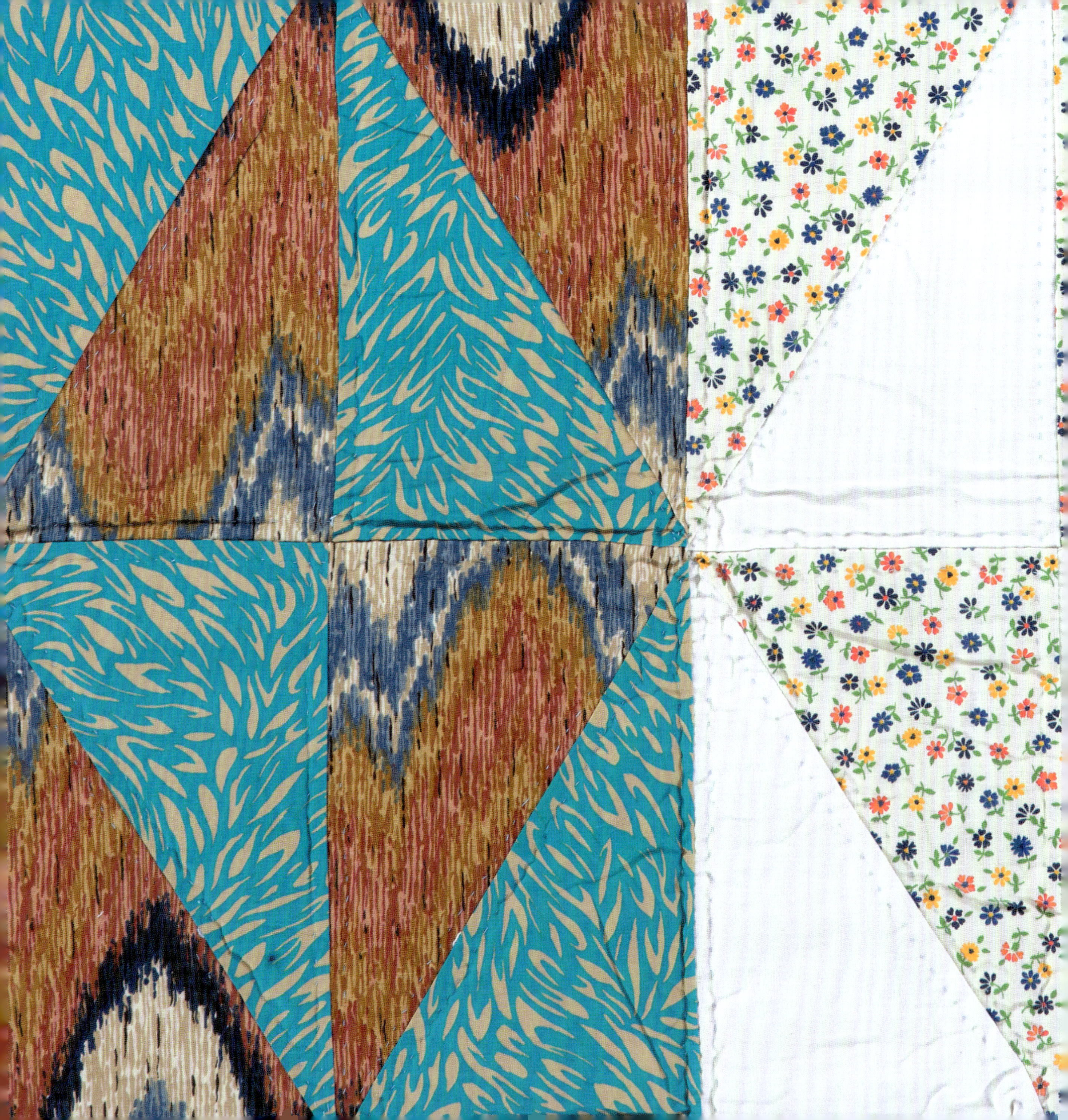

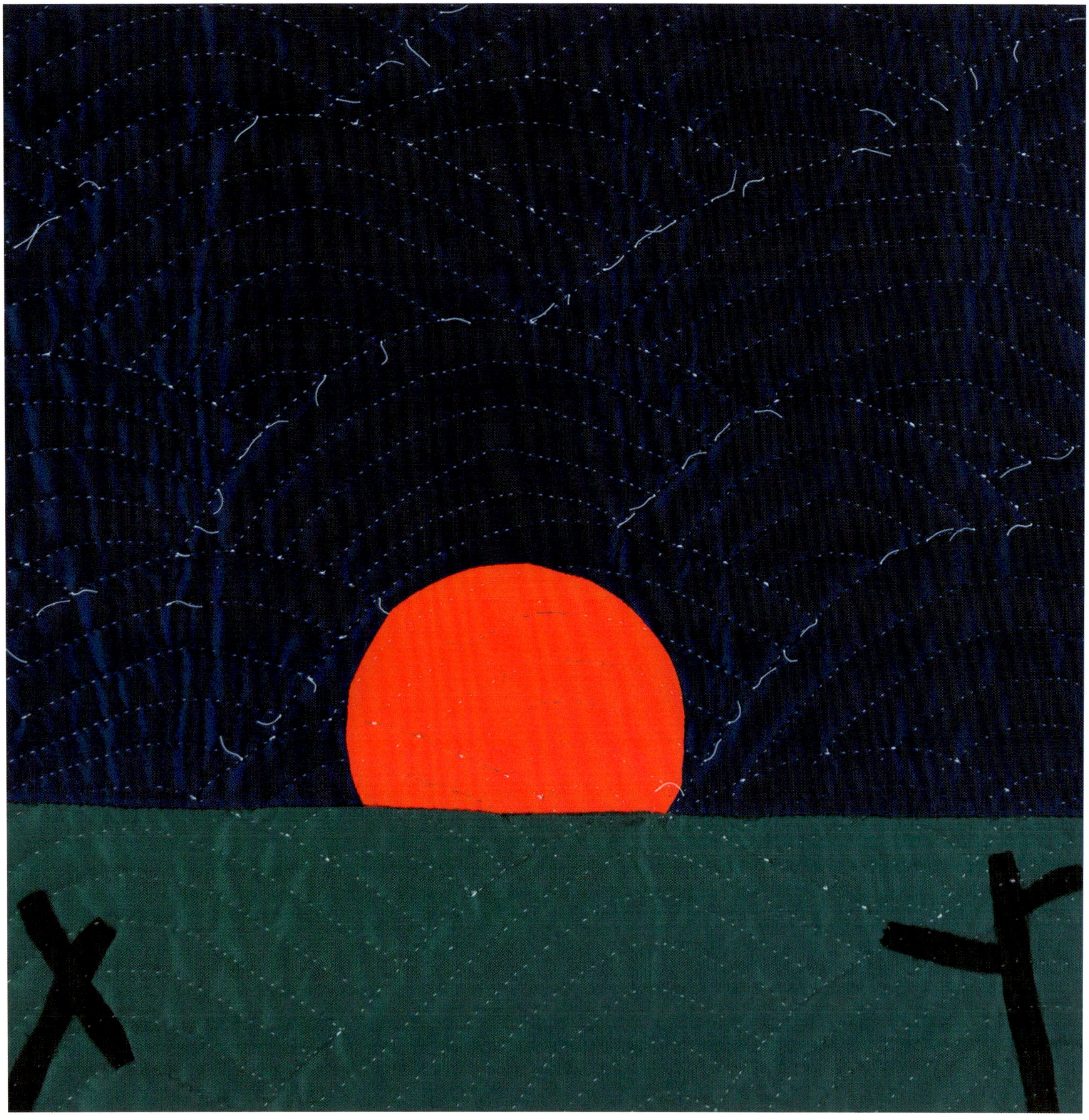

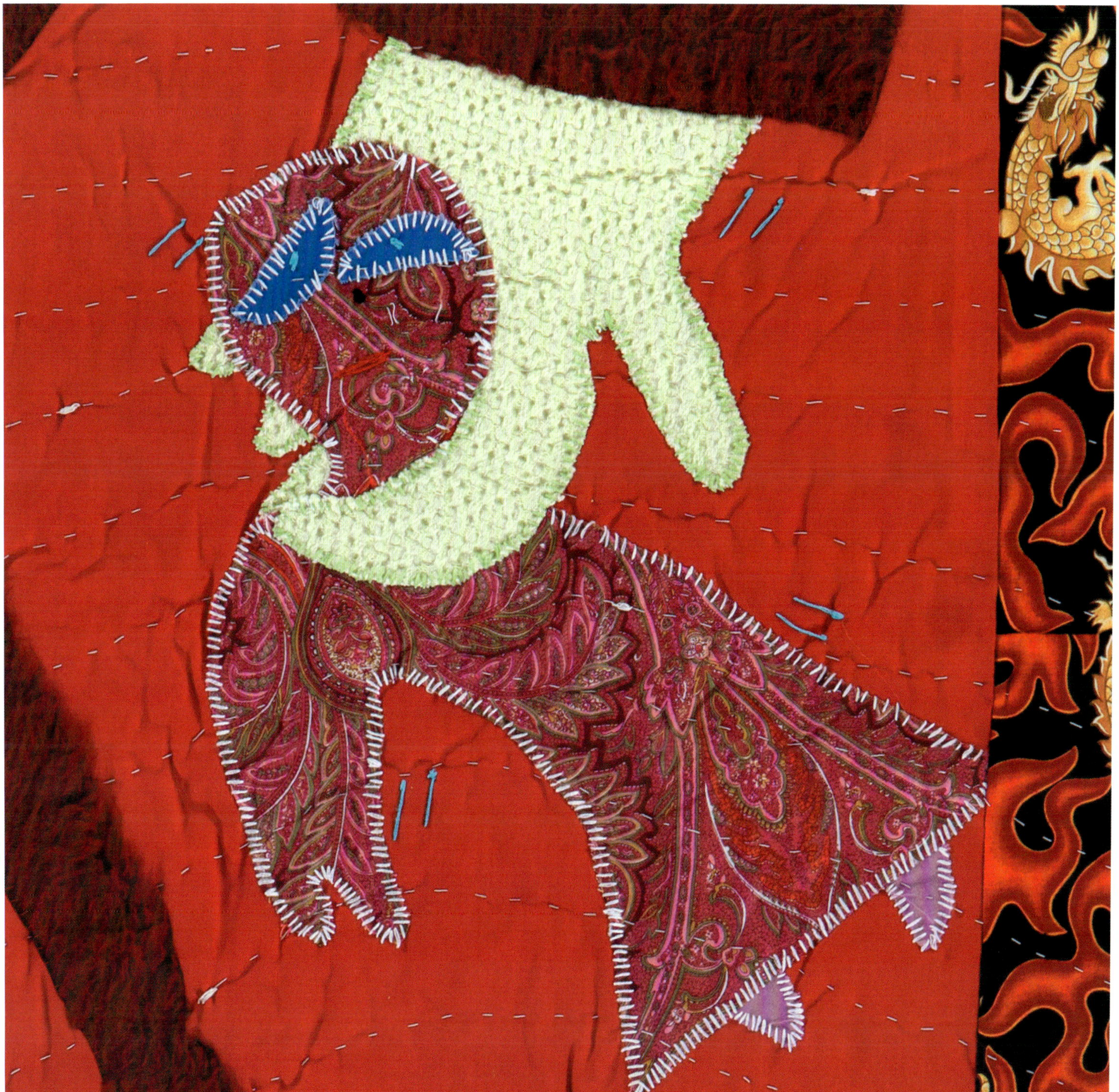

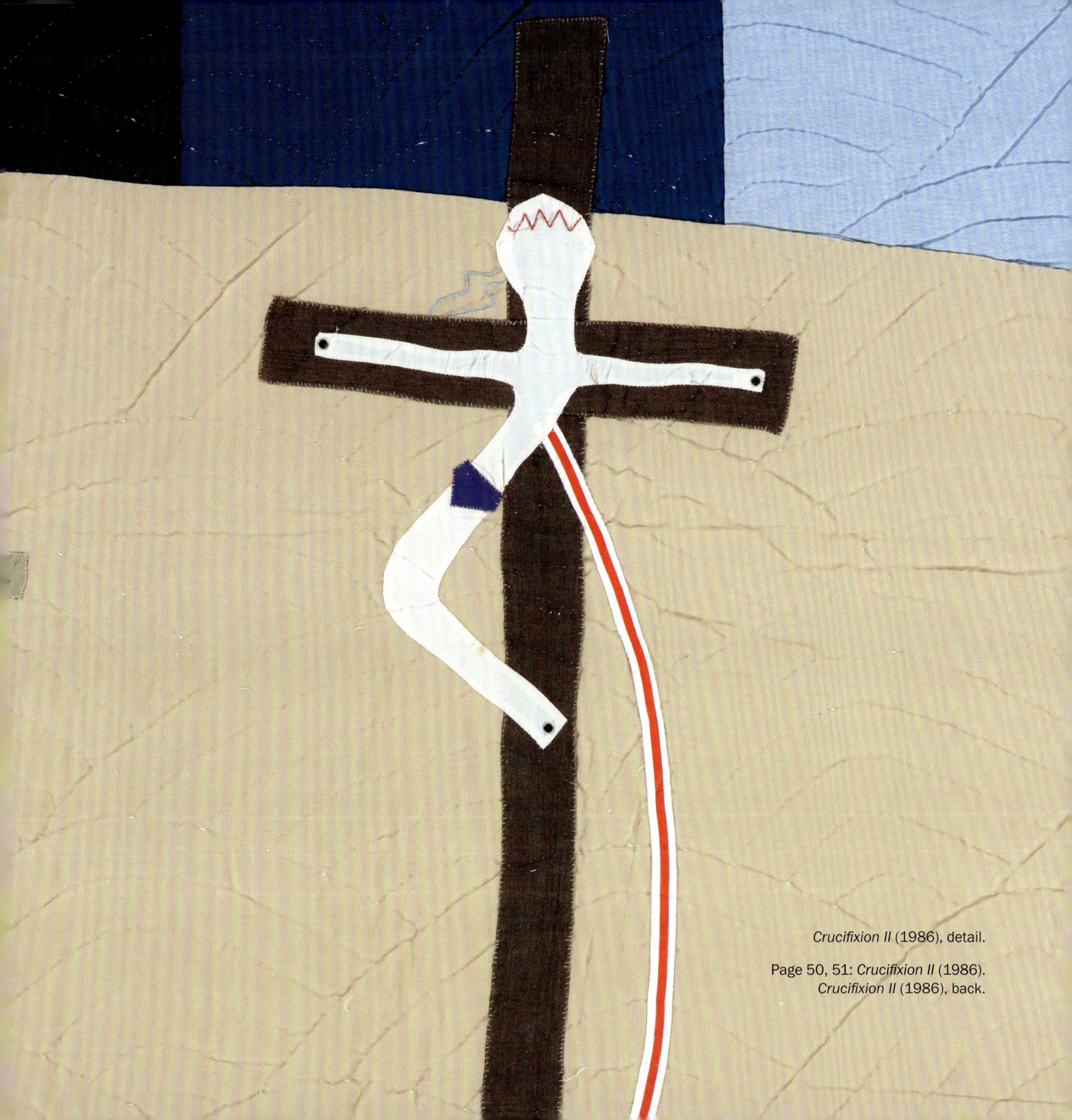

Crucifixion II (1986), detail.

Page 50, 51: *Crucifixion II* (1986).
Crucifixion II (1986), back.

Vision Without Precedent
Harriet Powers and Yvonne Wells

Kyra E. Hicks

My grandfather, George W. Crockett Jr. (1909–1997), lived to see my early quilting efforts. And as I thought about renowned quilters Harriet Powers and Yvonne Wells, a quote from my granddad kept intruding. I interviewed him in 1990 for a school assignment. He had recently retired from the United States House of Representatives, having served six terms. He said, "I've got to stop now at the age of eighty. I can't run for the Senate. I can't even *consider* running for the presidency; I'm too old. But if I were fifty or forty, goodness knows that would be within my sphere of hope."

I never imagined that my granddad, a Black man, aspired to be president of the United States. There were no references. In fact, a student named Barack Obama was just completing his final year at Harvard Law School. Likewise, there were no Faith Ringgold, Bisa Butler, or Yvonne Wells to serve as references for Harriet Powers, a creative nineteenth-century quilter who would later be known as the mother of African American quilting.

Harriett Angeline Powers was born enslaved on October 29, 1837, in Madison County, just outside Athens, Georgia, on a farm owned by John and Nancy Lester.[1] She lived with her mother, also an enslaved woman, according to the 1850 Madison County, Georgia, slave census.

In 1855 Harriet (using the popular spelling) married Armstead Powers, who was enslaved by James Nunn on a farm about ten miles from Harriet.[2] Their son Alonzo recalled that his parents lived apart in the early years of their marriage. He shared that his father could face physical punishment of "twenty-five licks" from slave patrollers if he was caught visiting his mother without permission.[3]

The Powerses had nine children, including Amanda Powers Witcher (c. 1855–1918), Alonzo Powers (c. 1860–1942), Nancy Powers (c. 1866–unknown), Lizzie Powers (c. 1868–unknown), Marshall Powers (c. 1873–1943), and James Powers (c. 1877–1879). Three of the children survived to adulthood.[4]

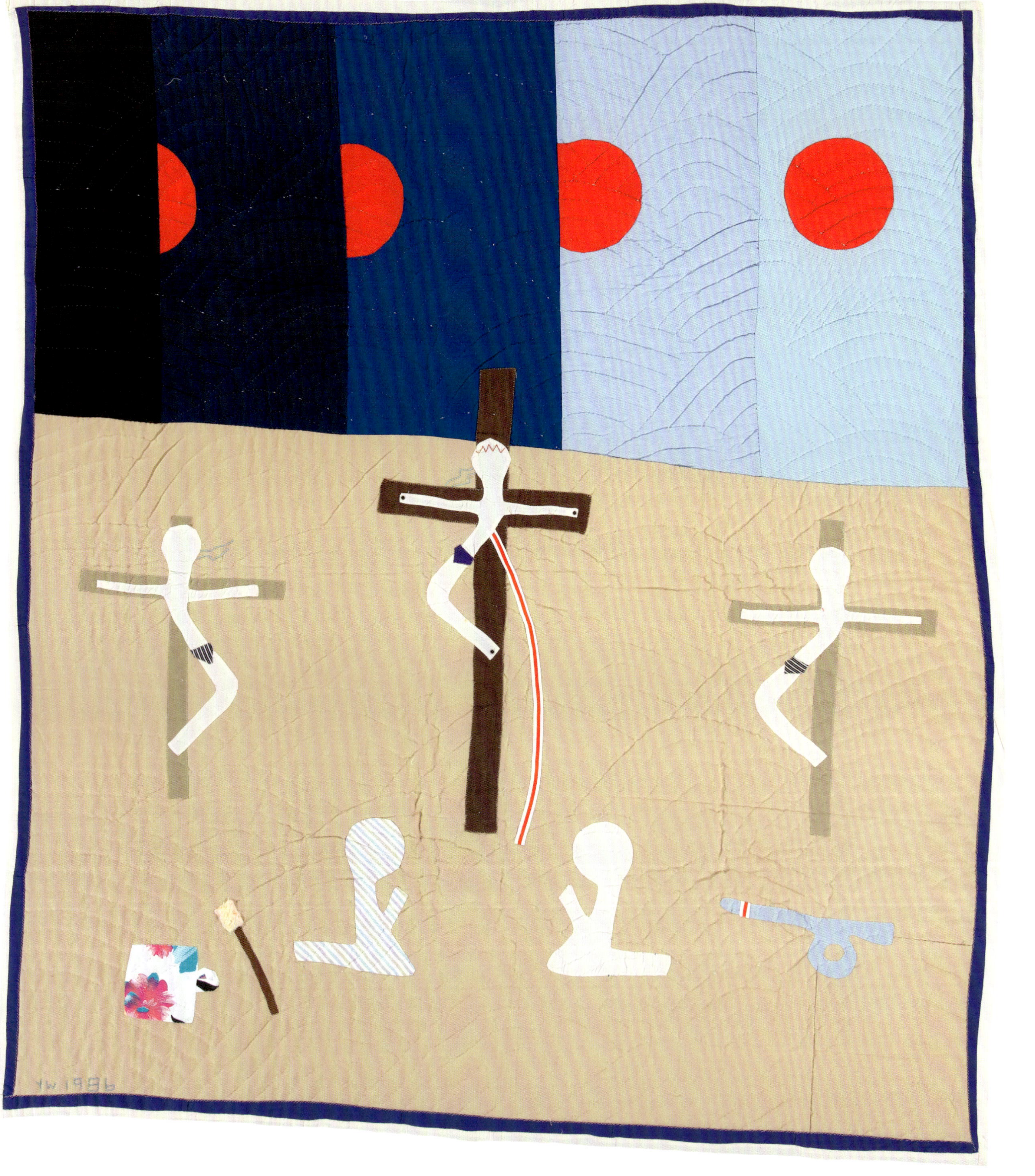
YW 1986

> "Mrs. Powers and Mrs. Wells share remarkable parallels. Both are Southern Black women whose strong religious faith are, at times, reflected in their quilts . . . Each is a storyteller using cloth. Their quilts earned awards at local fairs—Mrs. Powers at the Athens Colored Fair of 1887, and nearly a century later, Mrs. Wells at the Kentuck Festival of the Arts in 1985. Neither followed anyone else's patterns; instead, their unique artistic vision flowed from their own imaginations."
>
> —Kyra E. Hicks

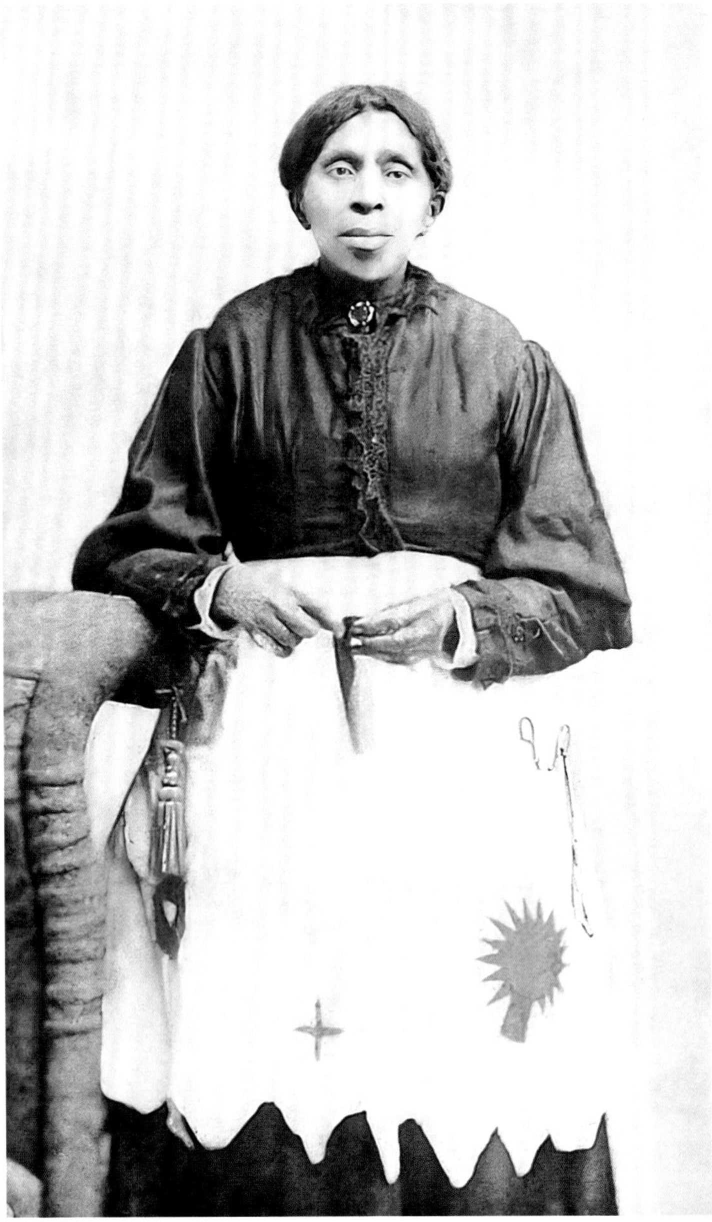

Harriett Angeline Powers was born enslaved on October 29, 1837. This portrait of her was captured c. 1896–97. Photograph by Charles F. McDannell (c. 1867–1916), Athens, Georgia. Image enhanced by D. Tarhoni in 2023. Digital cleaning enabled the scissors in Mrs. Powers's pocket to become more visible. The scissors were a tool central to her quiltmaking. Photo courtesy of Kyra E. Hicks.

The adult children married and collectively had about twenty children. Some of Harriet and Armstead's grandchildren stayed in Georgia, and others later moved and raised families in Alabama, Illinois, New York, Pennsylvania, Tennessee, and Virginia.

The first time on record that Harriet Powers publicly exhibited a quilt was twenty years after the Civil War. In November 1886 the first annual Colored Fair opened at the Athens, Georgia, fairgrounds. The *Weekly Banner-Watchman* reported that the women's department at the fair housed "a great many very pretty quilts and homemade bed covers."[5]

Visiting the Colored Fair was Jennie Smith, a twenty-eight-year-old local art teacher from the private all-girls Lucy Cobb Institute. She was mesmerized by Harriet Powers's Bible-themed quilt on display and sought to purchase the extraordinary story quilt.

The *Bible Quilt*, now owned by the Smithsonian National Museum of American History in Washington DC, was composed of eleven appliquéd blocks, each featuring a well-known Bible story, including Adam and Eve naming the first animals; a dove descending from Heaven following the baptism of Jesus by his cousin John the Baptist; Judas Iscariot surrounded by thirty pieces of silver; the Last Supper; and a bleeding Christ crucified with two thieves.

Miss Smith wrote about the *Bible Quilt* and quiltmaker in 1891:

> In one corner there hung a quilt which "captured my eye" and after much difficulty I found the owner, a negro woman who lives in the country on a little farm whereon she and her husband make a respectable living.
>
> She is about sixty five years old, of a burnt-ginger cake color, and is a very clean and interesting woman, who loves to talk of her "old miss" and her

> life "'fo de war."
> The scenes on the quilt were biblical, and I was fascinated.
> I offered to buy it, but it was not for sale at any price.
> After four years Harriet sent me word that I could buy it, if I wanted it.
> Alas! My financial affairs were at a low ebb, and I could not purchase.
> Last year I sent her word I would buy it if she still wanted to dispose of it.
> She arrived one afternoon in front of my door in an ox-cart, with the precious burden in her lap encased in a clean flour sack, which was still further enveloped in a crocus sack.
> She offered it for ten dollars, but I only had five to give.
> After going out and consulting her husband, she returned and said "ownin ter de hardness of de times, my ole man 'lows I'd better teck hit," and not being a new woman, she obeyed.
> After giving me a full description of each scene with great earnestness, and deep piety she departed, but has been back several times to visit the darling offspring of her brain. She was only in a measure consoled for its loss when I promised to save her all my scraps.[6]

The first time I learned that Jennie Smith purchased the *Bible Quilt* for just five dollars I was livid, though I later learned she was indeed in a financial bind.[7]

More importantly, I came to understand how rare the preservation of a quilt by a formerly enslaved woman, along with first-person documentation, was. Mrs. Powers's quilt and the written descriptions of the quilt blocks may have been lost to history had the purchase by Miss Smith not happened, or if Mrs. Powers's unique vision in designing a story quilt as early as the 1880s had not captured the attention of those who saw her creations.

Jennie Smith organized a display of her Lucy Cobb Institute art students' work in the Women's Building at the 1895 Cotton States and International Exposition held in Atlanta, Georgia. Nearly eight hundred thousand individuals attended the exposition during its four-month run. She also arranged for the *Bible Quilt*, which she now owned, to be displayed in the Negro Building. Among the dignitaries visiting the Negro Building were President Grover Cleveland (1837–1908), who spent an afternoon touring exhibits there, and Booker T. Washington (1856–1915), founder of the Tuskegee Institute.

The *Bible Quilt* was so unusual in design that reporters wrote about the quilt in articles syndicated across the nation. One article included descriptions of three outstanding quilts in the Negro Building: a white muslin quilt featuring a coffee tree in full bloom by Martha Ricks, who stitched an identical quilt for Queen Victoria; a large quilt featuring the entire text of the Lord's Prayer appliquéd in blue fabric by Mrs. A. S. Scroggins, who also appliquéd her name in equally large letters; and the *Bible Quilt* pronounced as a "gem of the collection . . . simply indescribable, but is alone worth the trip to Atlanta to see."[8] These three quilts were also captured in stereographs by the B. W. Kilburn Company of Littleton, New Hampshire.

Mrs. Lorene Curtis Diver (1846–1922) of Keokuk, Iowa, visited the exposition with her husband, James. Mrs. Diver sought permission to photograph the *Bible Quilt* and hired a local professional for the task. She wrote the description of each block on the back of the large sepia-colored reproductions.[9] Mrs. Diver was so enamored with the Bible Quilt that she sought out Jennie Smith to purchase the quilt, but no sale. Mrs. Diver later corresponded with Harriet Powers, who replied in a January 1896 letter where she described her life.[10]

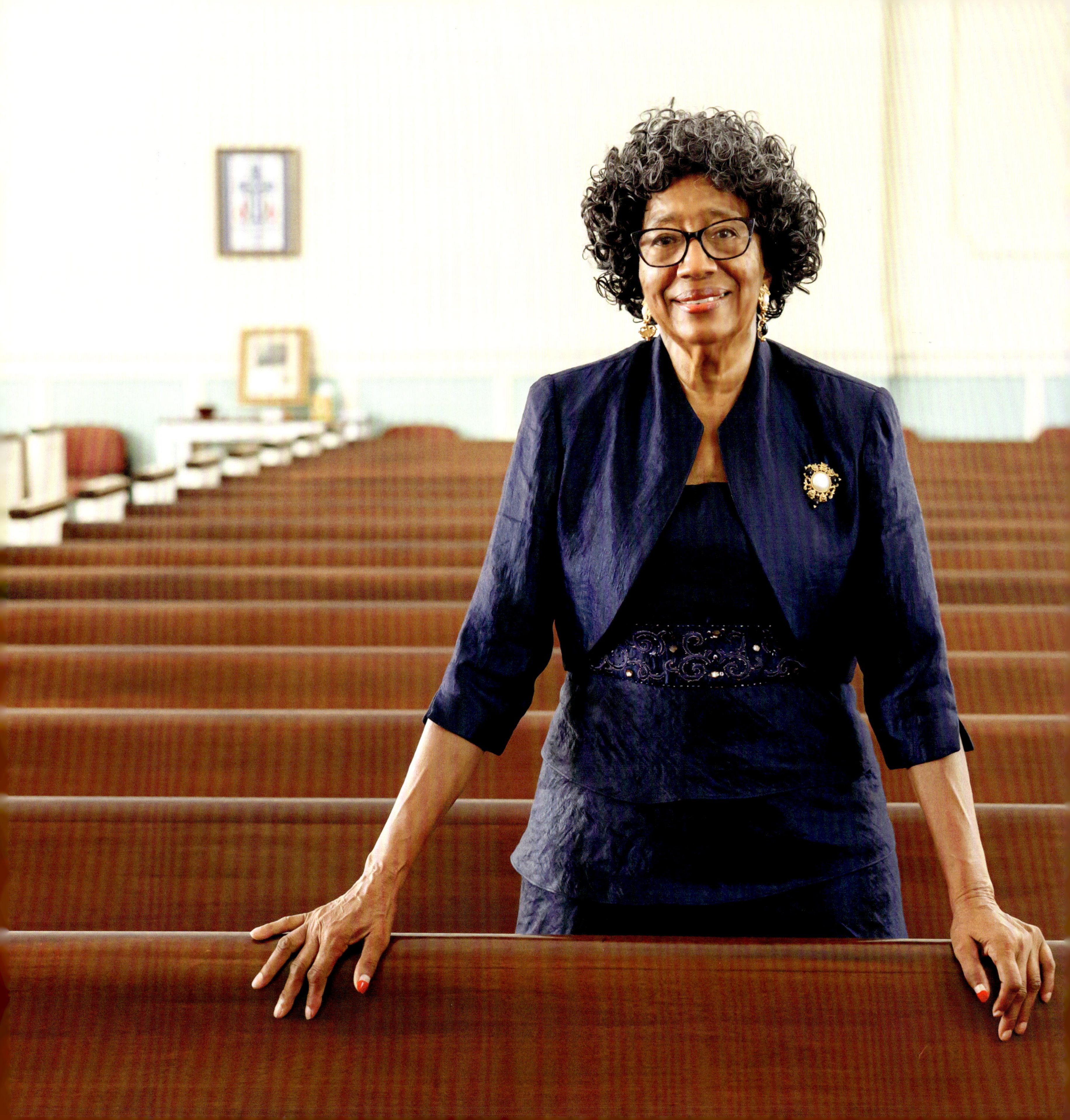

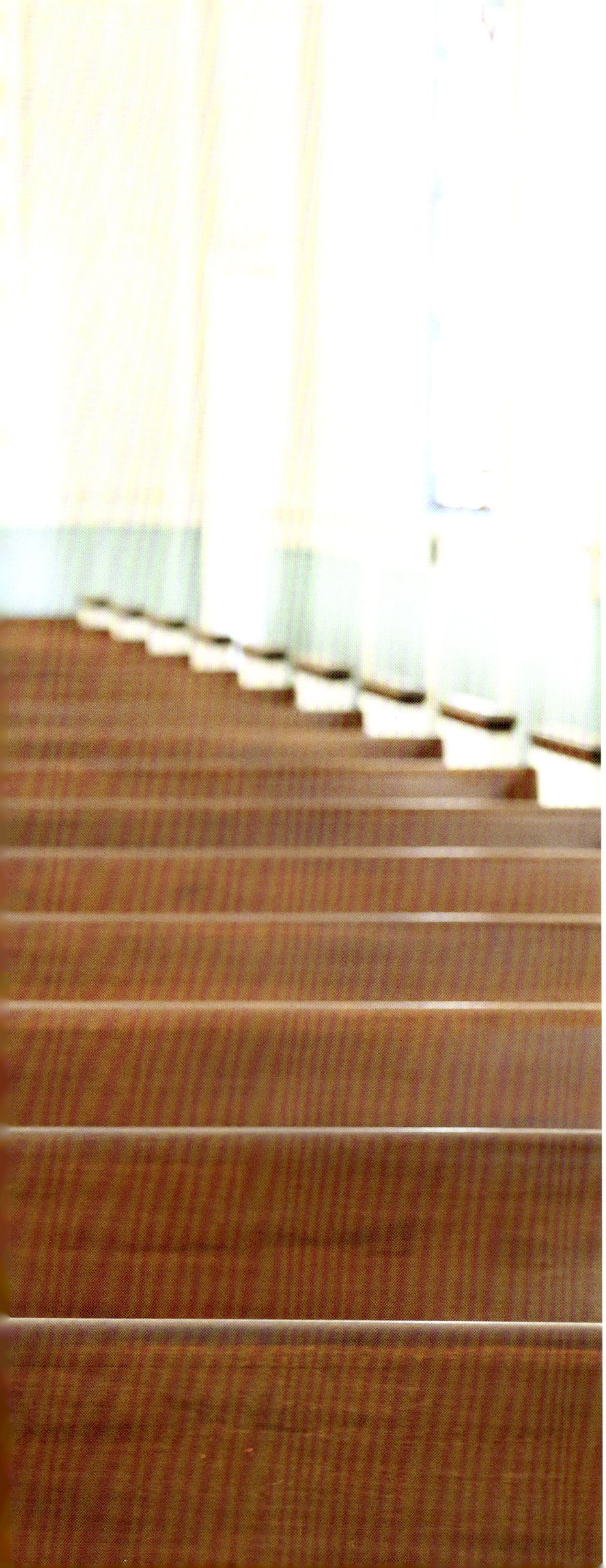

Yvonne Wells was born on December 26, 1939, as one of nine children born to a Presbyterian minister and an elementary school teacher. She has lived most of her life in Tuscaloosa, Alabama. She is a devout Christian and longtime member of Tuscaloosa's Brown Memorial Presbyterian Church. Wells often incorporates religious topics in her art, especially scenes from the Bible, including the *Crucifixion*, *Noah's Ark*, and *Moses Receiving the Ten Commandments*, and most importantly, her masterful series of the *Seven Deadly Sins*. Photo at Brown Memorial Presbyterian by Dave Walker.

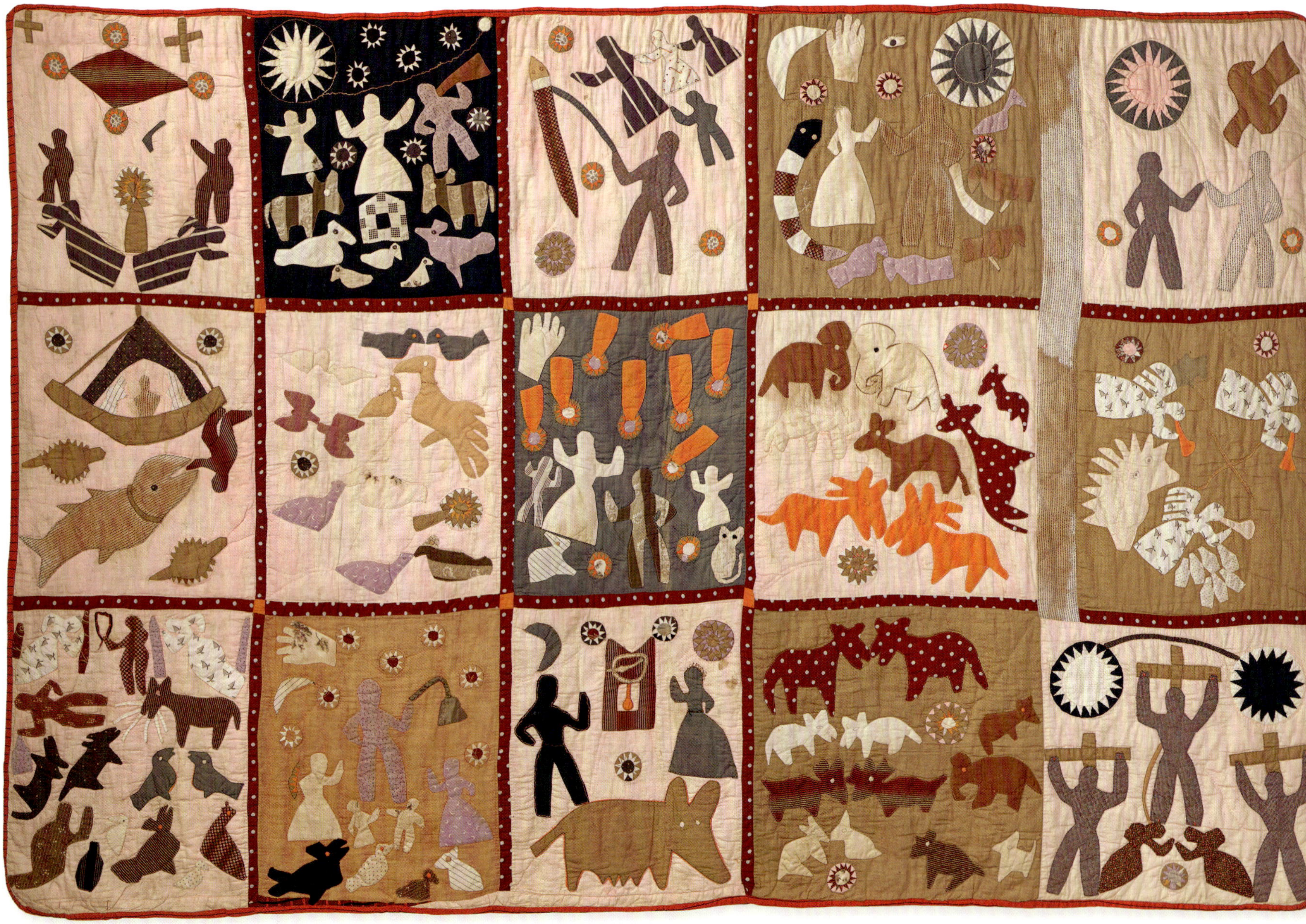

Harriet Powers, American, 1837–1910
Pictorial quilt. American (Athens, Georgia), 1895–98
Cotton plain weave, pieces, appliquéd, embroidered, and quilted. 175 x 266.7 cm (68 7/8 x 105 in.)
Museum of Fine Arts, Boston. Bequest of Maxim Karolik. 64.619 Photograph © 2026 Museum of Fine Arts, Boston.

She shared that she learned to read at the age of eleven and that she was married to Armstead and was the mother of nine children. She was a member of Mt. Zion Baptist Church and enjoyed reading the Bible. She also described stitching a quilt of 4,050 diamonds in 1872. She also wrote that a star quilt she created won a prize at the Athens Colored Fair of 1887, and she described making two religious based quilts: *Adam and Eve in the Garden of Eden* (which we call the *Bible Quilt* now) and another one featuring the Lord's Supper (whereabouts unknown today). Mrs. Powers also sent a carte de visite of herself by the Athens photographer Charles F. McDannell. Mrs. Powers demonstrated her self-assurance in this letter—especially when she closed the missive by writing, "This I Accomplish, Harriet A. Powers." There is no evidence (yet) that a quilt sale between Mrs. Divers and Mrs. Powers took place.

However, representatives from Atlanta University saw the *Bible Quilt* on display at the exposition and sought to commission a quilt by Mrs. Powers for the Reverend Dr. Charles Cuthbert Hall (1852–1908).[11] Dr. Hall was vice president of the Board of Trustees at Atlanta University, a college founded in 1865 to educate African Americans. The quilt was likely presented to him in New York during his appointment as president of the Union Theological Seminary.

Mrs. Powers stitched what has become known as the *Pictorial Quilt*, a fifteen-block pieced and appliquéd quilt featuring both biblical stories and natural phenomena. The Bible-related blocks reference individuals such as Adam and Eve, Job, John the Baptist, Jonah, Moses, and Christ crucified alongside two thieves.

In 1960 Rev. Basil Hall (1888–1979), the eldest son of Dr. Charles Hall, brought the *Pictorial Quilt* to the Museum of Fine Arts, Boston, where textile curator Adolph Cavallo (1943–2011) considered it for acquisition. Cavallo was amazed by the sixty-two-year-old quilt. He shared, "I had never seen a quilt like that. The richness of her imagination was fascinating, so touching, so sweet, so human. Even the Crucifixion [block] had a great deal of feeling."[12]

Art collector and major museum donor Maxim Karolik (1893–1963) was, according to Cavallo, "absolutely charmed" by the quilt and went on to purchase the quilt, along with handwritten cards describing the quilt blocks and a carte de visite of Mrs. Powers, as a gift for the museum.[13]

Mrs. Powers possessed a unique creative vision, stitched quilts from her own imagination, and shared that vision with others through exhibitions and correspondence. She even provided photographs of herself to those who sought information about her and her quiltmaking.

My grandfather had no role model to guide his desire to run for the presidency of the United States. Likewise, Mrs. Powers, a formerly enslaved woman, likely had no model for becoming an artist. Yet two of her story quilts, attributed to her hand, have survived independently and now reside in major museum collections, recognized today by people all over the globe. She is rightly called the mother of African American quilting.

Yvonne Wells is, without doubt, a daughter of Harriet Powers.

Mrs. Powers and Mrs. Wells share remarkable parallels. Both are Southern Black women whose strong religious faith is, at times, reflected in their quilts. In their lifetimes, each has been a wife, mother, grandmother, and great-grandmother. Even their family ties echo one another—Mrs. Powers was the mother of nine children, while Mrs. Wells was one of nine children. Each is a storyteller using cloth. Their quilts earned awards at local fairs, Mrs. Powers at the Athens Colored Fair of 1887, and nearly a century later, Mrs. Wells at the Kentuck Festival of the Arts in 1985.

Neither followed anyone else's patterns; instead, their unique artistic vision flowed from their own imaginations. Their artistic output, however, differs greatly: Mrs. Powers stitched at least five quilts—four described in her letter to Lorene Diver and the *Pictorial Quilt*—while Mrs. Wells has created over five hundred quilts.[14] Finally, each also had someone who helped bring their work to wider audiences—Jennie Smith for Mrs. Powers, and Robert Cargo, the late influential folk art dealer in Tuscaloosa, Alabama, for Mrs. Wells.

I was inspired to teach myself to quilt in 1991 after visiting the Taft Museum's exhibition *Stitching Memories: African-American Story Quilts*. I had never attended a quilt exhibit nor seen such a powerful collection of narrative quilts. Among them was a quilt depicting Melrose Plantation by Clementine Hunter (1886–1988). Works by Nora Ezell (1917–2007) and Faith Ringgold (1930–2024) were the first quilts with words I had ever seen. And then there was the *Crucifixion* quilt (1986) by Mrs. Wells.

The Crucifixion is a theme that both Mrs. Powers and Mrs. Wells turned to in their quilts. Mrs. Wells's first story quilt was the *Crucifixion*, and she would go on to make two more versions in 1986 and 1987.[15] Both women told the story of Christ's final hours in fabric, depicting Jesus on the cross and bleeding from his side. Each included two criminals also sentenced to death, and each used the sky or the sun to mark the passage of time that fateful day. Both women placed Mary, the mother of Jesus, alongside Mary Magdalene kneeling at the foot of the cross. The Crucifixion stands as an iconic image for both quilters, and in the case of Mrs. Wells, it has become a signature work.

Just as my granddad dared to imagine possibilities that had once been unthinkable, Harriet Powers stitched without precedent, creating story quilts that have become a pillar in African American quilting traditions. Nearly a century later, Yvonne Wells, following her own vision rather than anyone else's pattern, has built a body of work now celebrated in major exhibits, collected by patrons and museums, and even gracing Hallmark greeting cards![16] From my granddad's unspoken hope of the presidency to Mrs. Powers's groundbreaking quilts and Mrs. Wells's renown, each reminds us all that vision can precede example—and that sometimes, we become the very role models we once lacked.

ΔΔΔ

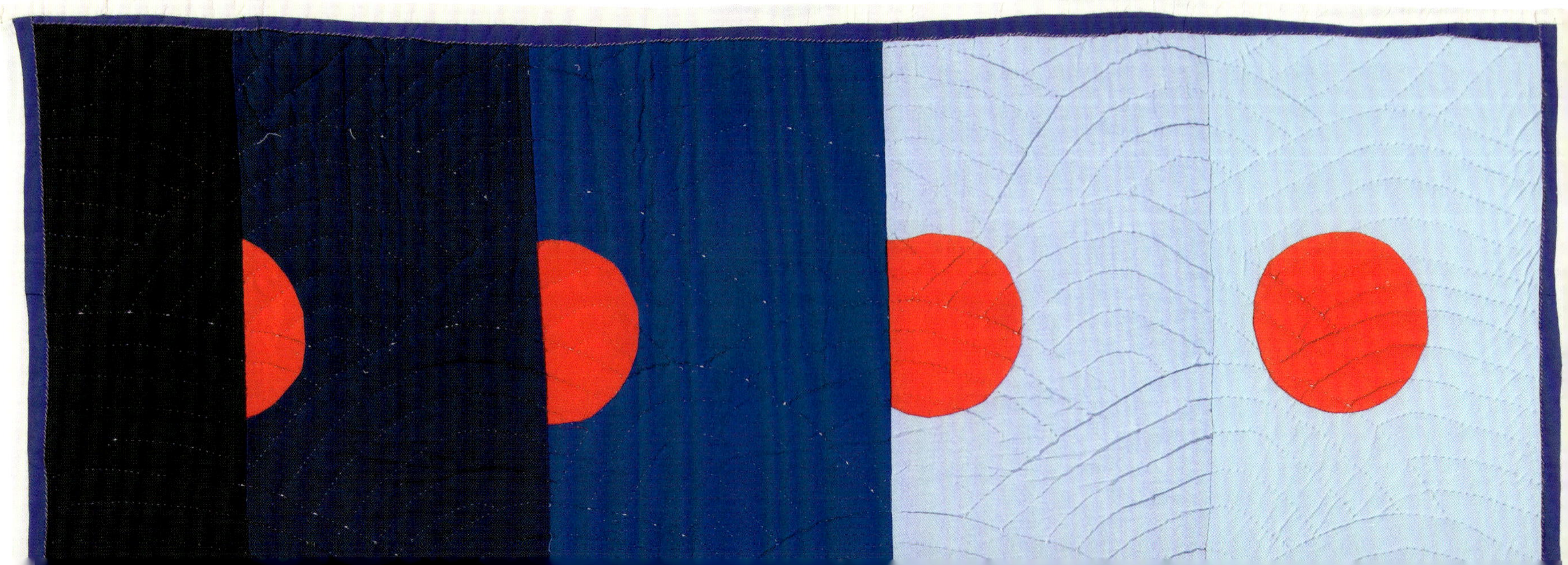

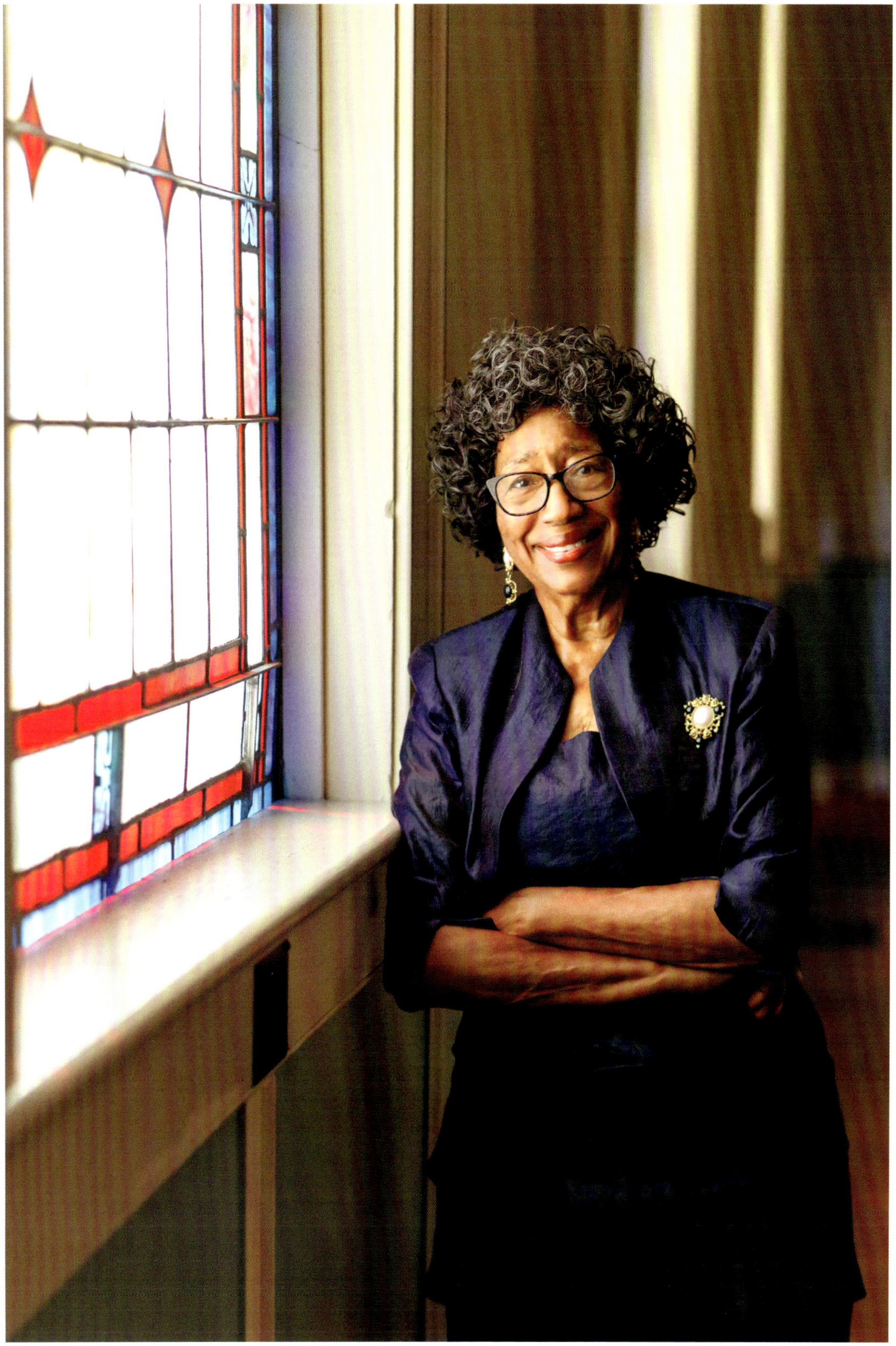

Right: At Brown Memorial Presbyterian, Tuscaloosa, Alabama. Photo by Dave Walker. Left: *Crucifixion* (1986), detail.

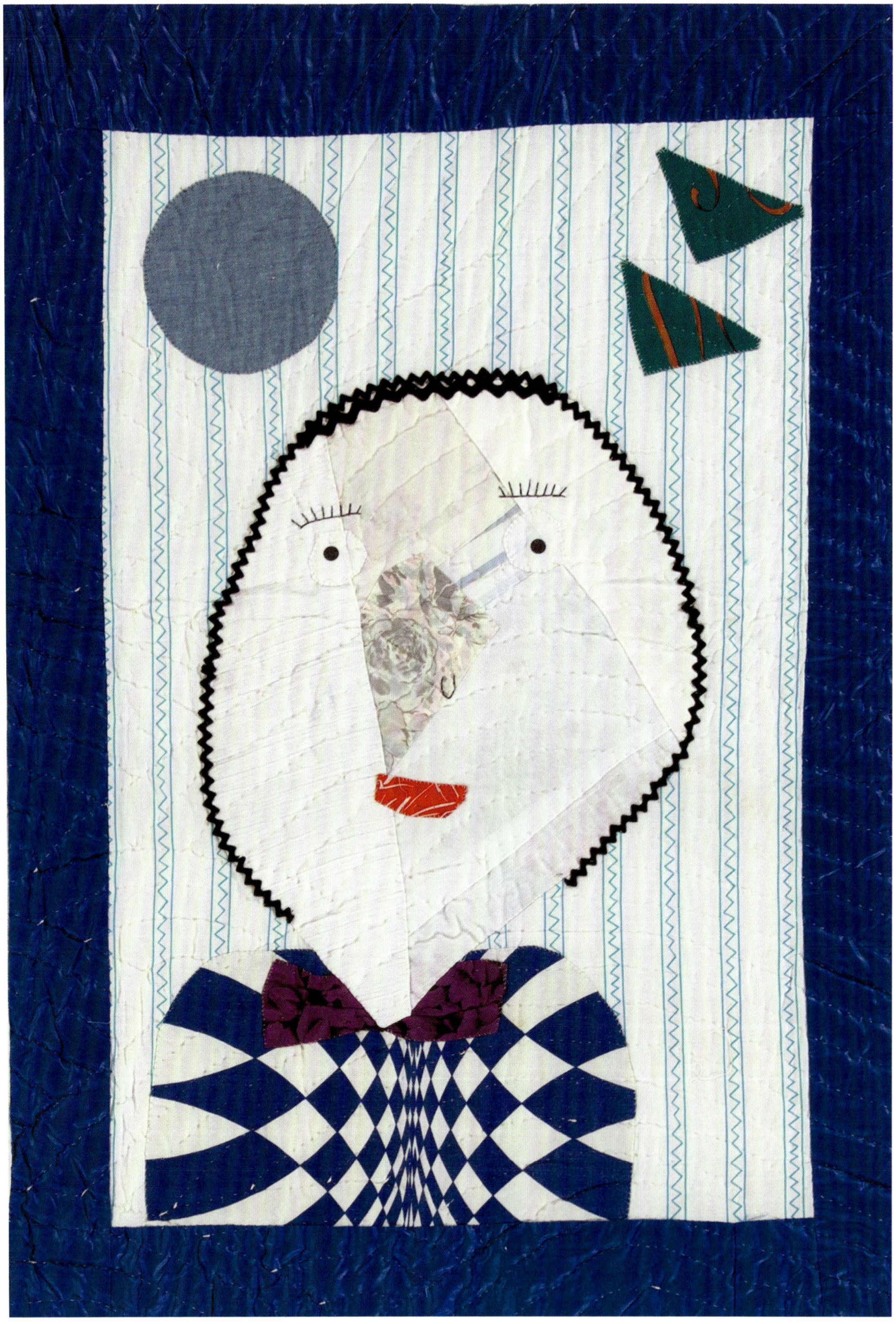

Left: *Ugly Faces* (1990), detail. Right: Wells's box of "stuff." Photo by Dave Walker.

“My process was on the floor around a whole lot of stuff. . . . Out of a box, or a suitcase I had there. And I would collect fabric material that I would buy, and I would find, and people would give to me. We had carpet on the floor, so that’s where I worked. I would put down pieces that I thought would go with what I am seeing, and I would start from there.”

—Yvonne Wells

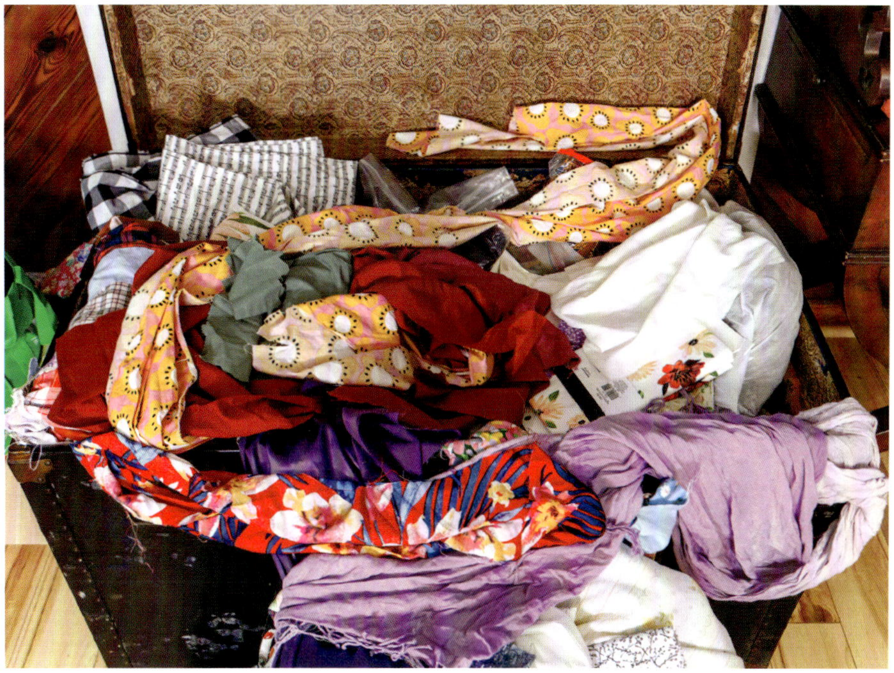

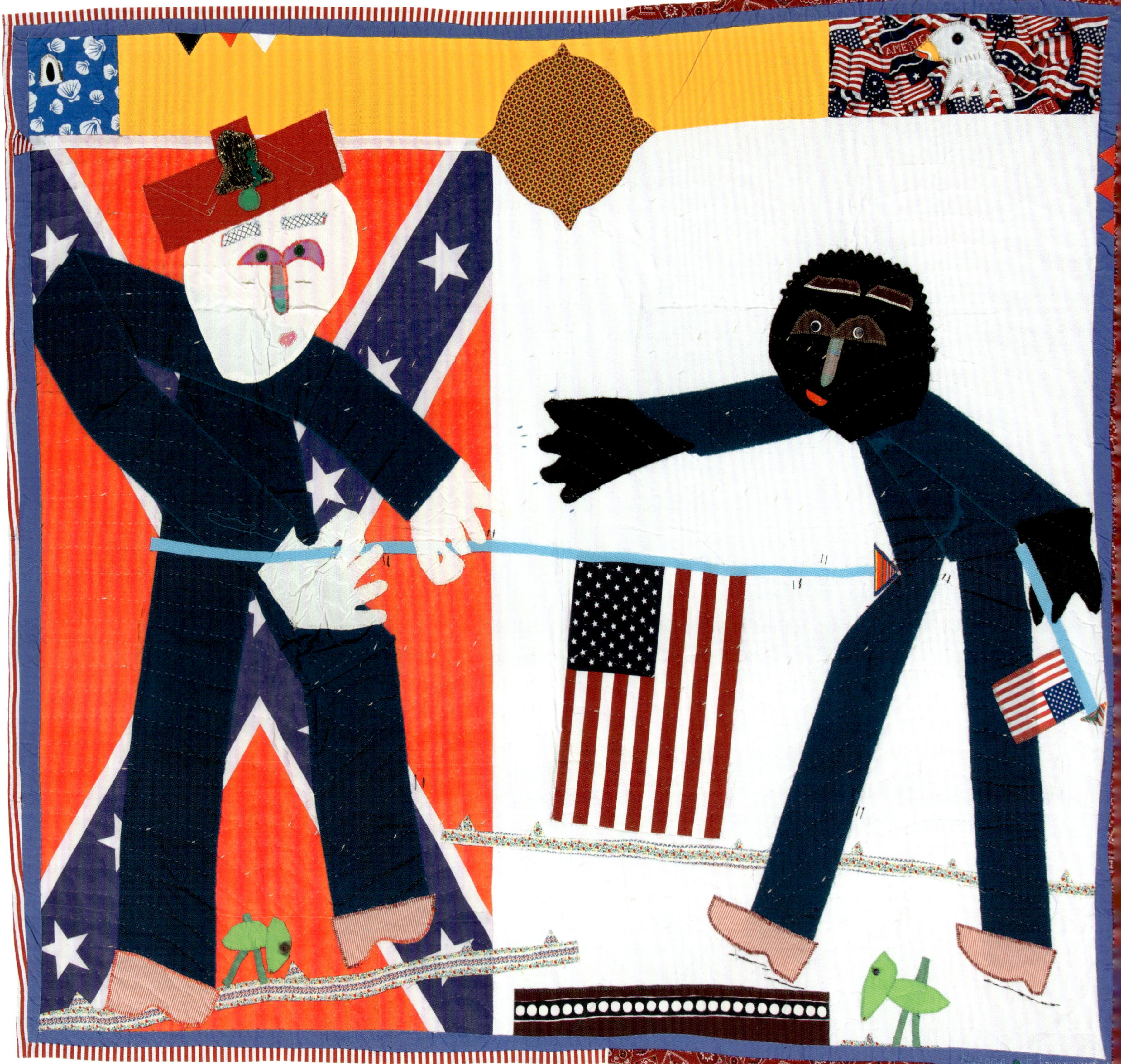

QUILT TRADITIONS

Place and Purpose
Black Quilt Traditions in the South

Sharbreon Plummer

The tradition of quilting in the American South is more than a folk or craft tradition. It's a living archive that speaks to aesthetics of place and history, especially for Black women. For these quilters, cloth speaks to a sense of identity and a legacy of making that spans across generations. Both firsthand narrative and research have shown that, among Black women, networks of beloved community joined together to establish quiltmaking traditions that allowed them to sustain themselves and one another. As a result, we now have women like Yvonne Wells—an Alabama-born, self-taught quilter—who continue to steward this centuries-long tradition that is inseparable from the visual and material culture of the South.

Early quilting in the South was shaped by rhythms and demands of everyday life. For Black people, particularly in the Antebellum South, economic exploitation and necessity were dueling pressures that shaped how quilts came into being. As cotton grew into a primary commercial crop in the region, so did the amount of labor shouldered by those who were enslaved on plantations. Black women were subjected both to this labor and to the responsibility of sewing-related tasks such as garment construction and quilting. Plantation mistresses had their own demands for support, with enslaved women often working on more elaborate spreads for the plantation home and covers in preparation for winter.[1]

Concurrently, personal quilt practices were also developed in response to the needs of the Black plantation community and individual family units. Quilts created outside of the oversight of plantation owners was a means of creating both external and internal warmth, while also developing an aesthetic that is now revered.

Left: *The Greeting* (2000). Page 64: *The Greeting* (2000), back. Page 65: *The Greeting* (2000), detail.

"The state of Alabama has been prominent in many chapters of the story of Black quilting. . . . It is in that same rich soil that someone like Yvonne Wells emerges—not inheriting a familial quilting tradition in the sense of having been taught as a child, but still shaped by the same tenets and environment that inspired her predecessors."

—Dr. Sharbreon Plummer

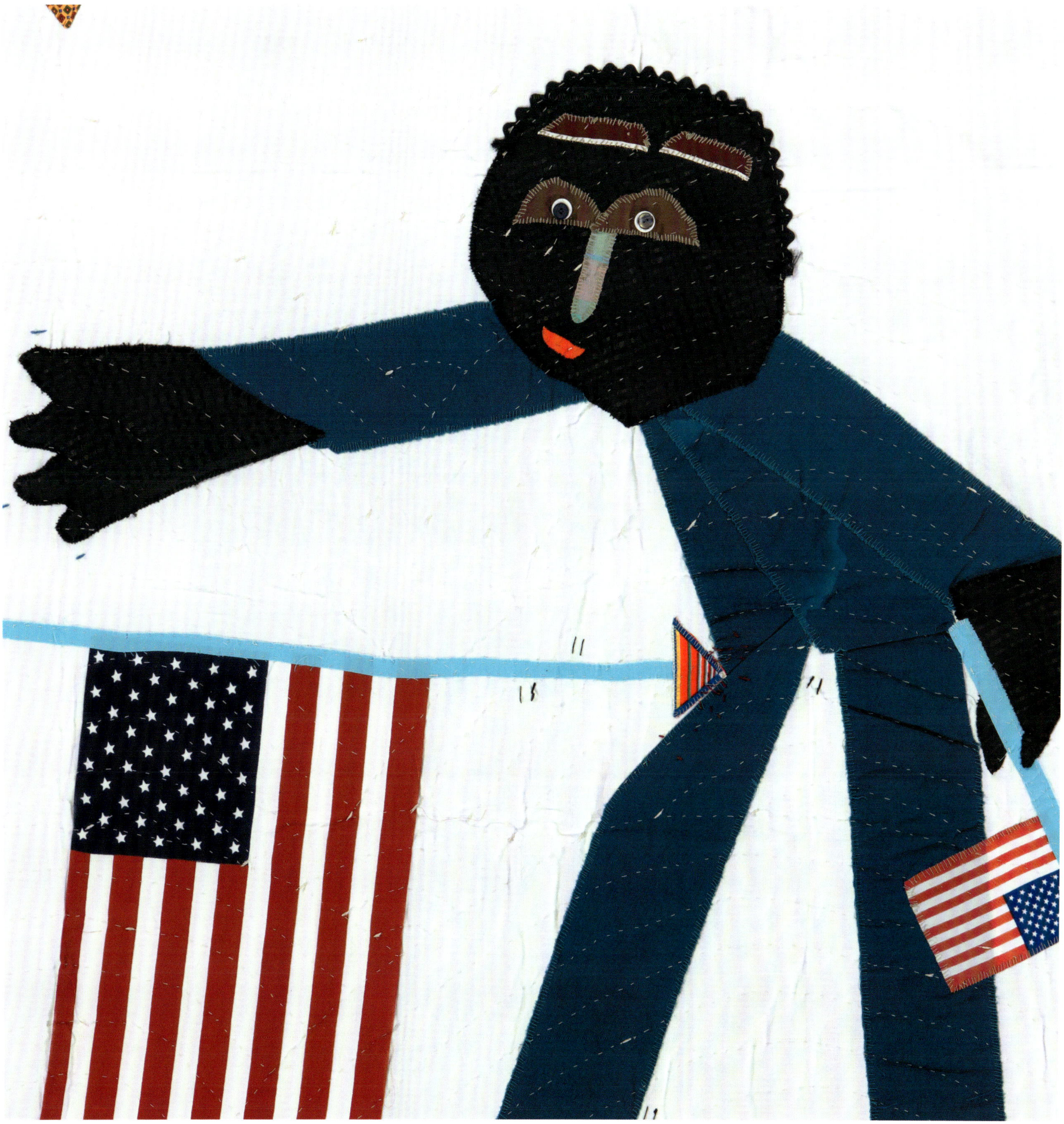

The tradition of patchwork and reuse was born out of their reinterpretation of whatever was serviceable. Scraps, old clothing, feed sacks, and other remnants were methodically pieced into utilitarian items that reflected the material culture of the time.

Overlapping those practical origins is also a community aesthetic. Quilt parties, or "quiltings," allowed for a conflation of creativity and skill between community members.[2] The sharing of patterns and materials between mothers, grandmothers, and neighbors was a means of both collective labor and visual experimentation. Over time, these teachings informed some of the most appreciated aspects of quilts created by Black quilters from the nineteenth and twentieth centuries. From the imperfect geometry of intuitive piecing to appliquéd shapes derived from nature and the observations of the built environment, these ideas and techniques connect to the visual culture that binds many Black Southern quilters together. It is through this "vernacular" that we learn about the artistic values and priorities of Black quilters. Their boldness of aesthetic choices (e.g., contrast, balance, color, and texture) took priority over the politics of correctness and Americana perfection upheld by their white counterparts.[3]

The state of Alabama has been prominent in many chapters of the story of Black quilting. The women of Gee's Bend have drawn global attention through their approach to improvisation and interconnectedness as a community. The Freedom Quilting Bee, founded during the Civil Rights era, united women quilters in cooperative economic work, using quilts as commerce and mutual aid in support of social justice. Other Alabama quilters like Mozell Benson and Nora Ezell gained notoriety for their nontraditional and narrative quilts. It is in that same rich soil that someone like Yvonne Wells emerges—not inheriting a familial quilting tradition in the sense of having been taught as a child, but still shaped by the same tenets and environment that inspired her predecessors.

While many Black quilters learned in family or community contexts, many are also self-taught. Self-taught quilters like Wells often pair memory and observation with their own internal vision and storytelling. For example, she recalls seeing her mother make utility quilts that were "made in the morning and used that night," while she herself did not begin quilting until the age of forty.[4]

To interpret Wells's work amid this lineage, it is important to interrogate recurring aesthetic features in Southern Black quiltmaking and how she aligns or diverges. While there is no comprehensive definition for how these works are formed, there are a number of facets and characteristics that hold prominence within the region and among quilters that reside in it.

One form that flourished among Black Southern quilters is the story or pictorial quilt. In these works, quiltmakers move beyond abstract motifs to narrative forms and symbolism. When words were not always available or suitable as a form of expression, a needle and thread could convey one's innermost thoughts. Popular artifacts such as Harriet Powers's

Raggedy Andy (1982–83), detail.

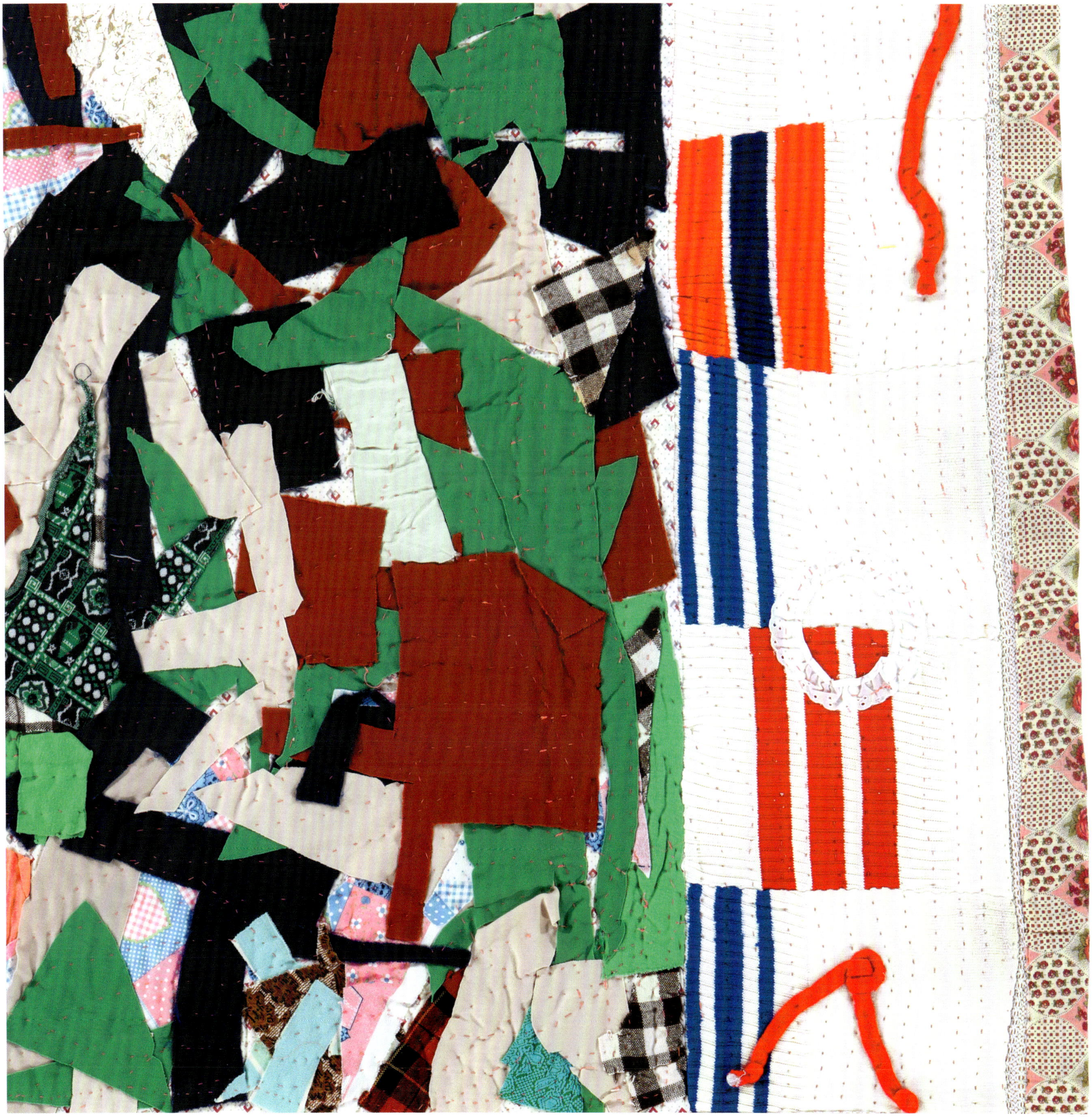

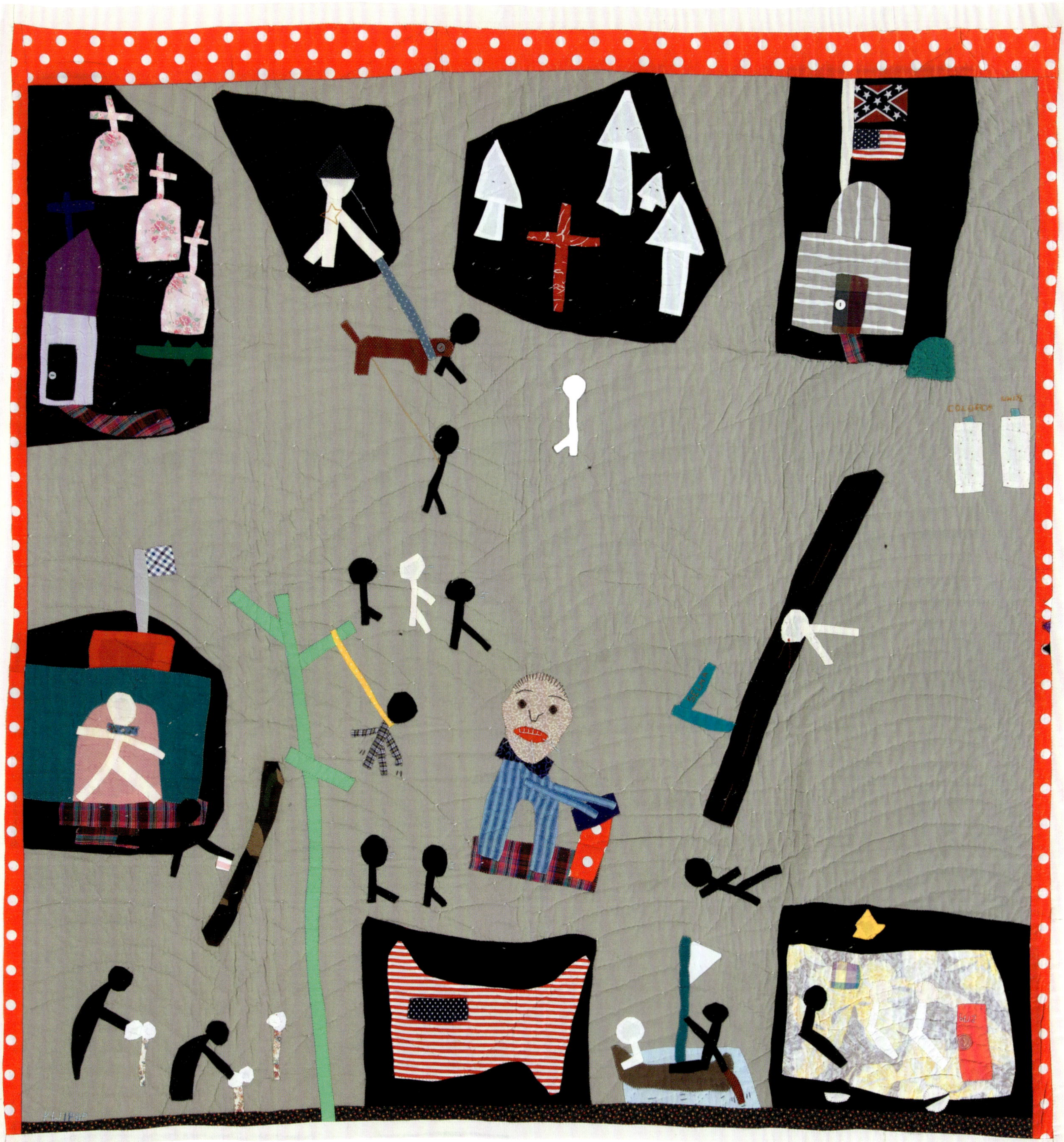

Bible Quilt demonstrate how embedding themes like Bible stories, personal history, and spiritual allegory have held cultural significance for centuries.

Wells, too, draws from biblical imagery and the memorialization of daily life and history, particularly the Civil Rights Movement. For instance, quilts like *Yesterday: Civil Rights in the South* bring together simplistic shapes and symbols (akin to the forms employed by Powers) to capture vignettes of a complex story—in this instance, the activism of Dr. Martin Luther King Jr. and the tension of the local political climate that surrounded his efforts.[5]

Many have also argued that improvisation is a defining characteristic of Black Southern quiltmaking.[6] It is believed by some that this form of abstraction connects to cultural retentions that are embedded within Black quilters of the diaspora. However, just as Black quilters are not a monolith, neither is their creativity. Strip piecing and other abstract patchwork was a form of adaptability—often to either material circumstances or access. Another way to consider improvisation is to explore what shapes a quilter's eye and approach to building harmony in the midst of competing design choices. Unfortunately, early Black quiltmakers in the South did not always receive that level of consideration. Women like Wells, who are able to exercise their voice in a self-assured way, embed improvisation with added depth. Statements such as "the materials I use have their own stories and histories . . . the quilts talk to me, and I listen," point to a relationship to material that is deliberate and shaped by intention and careful observation.[7]

While she admittedly says she will use "anything [she] can stick a needle in" (following the lineage of repurposing), she is methodical in her design choices. Improvisation, in her and many others' hands, is not an act of happenstance. Instead, it is the use of a developed eye to create calculated disorder. As she states, "The more disorganized I am, the better the quilt comes out. It gives me time to think and see what this piece says to me and see what the shape looks like, and it has a conversation with other quilts."[8]

Boldness could also be referenced as a preference for Black quilters in the region. Across generations, quilters have expressed themselves through contrasting colors and unexpected fabric combinations to create works that are visually striking. When the world around them sought to suppress their voice and self-expression, Black quilters found freedom in the work of their hands. Artists such as Anna Williams, Hystercine Rankin, Sarah Mary Taylor, and Cleola McFarland are but a few examples of quilters within the South whose artistic experimentation resulted in distinct styles of making that are still recognizable today. Wells embodies the same spirit of boldness in her own making. Not one to be confined to one style or material, one quilt could combine abstracted and figurative forms with lace and screen wire to tell a single story.

Yesterday: Civil Rights in the South (1989), detail.

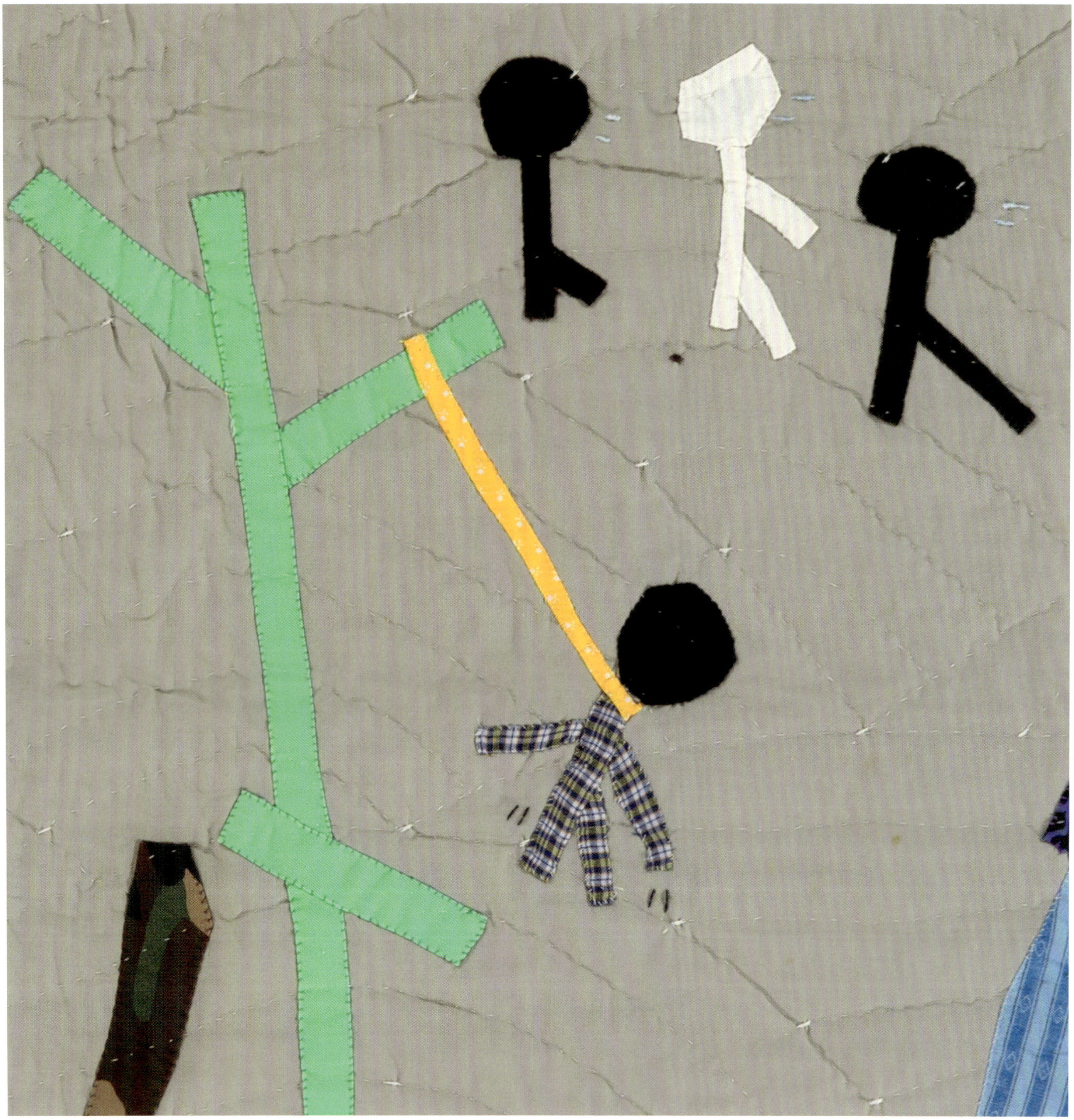

In conclusion, to map Black quilt history in the South means uncovering a living, breathing tradition. While quilting's relationship to Black history may reach back to a distant past, its impact and influence are still at play in a contemporary way. Quilts developed for necessity—through communal and family traditions—seeded the blooming of independent, self-taught voices that can now fully embrace their place as artists.

However, it is imperative that we never lose sight of how these practices are shaped by a place and stories that should be revered and preserved. Yvonne Wells occupies an essential place in this tradition. Though she later stepped into her visual inheritance, she embraced all of the influences around her to innovate a style all her own—one that derives from cultural influence but is led by what's in her heart.

ΔΔΔ

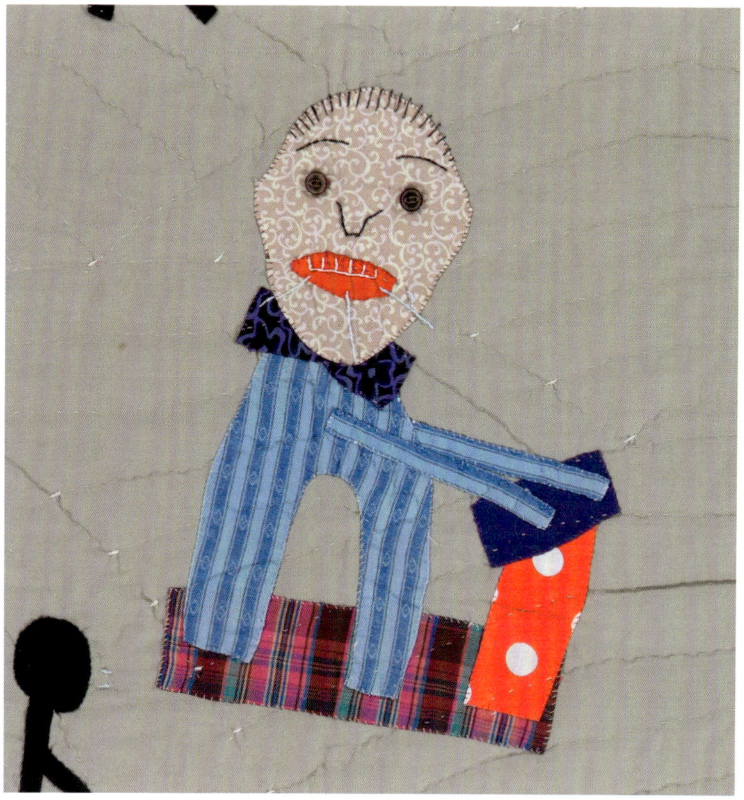

Yesterday: Civil Rights in the South (1989), details.

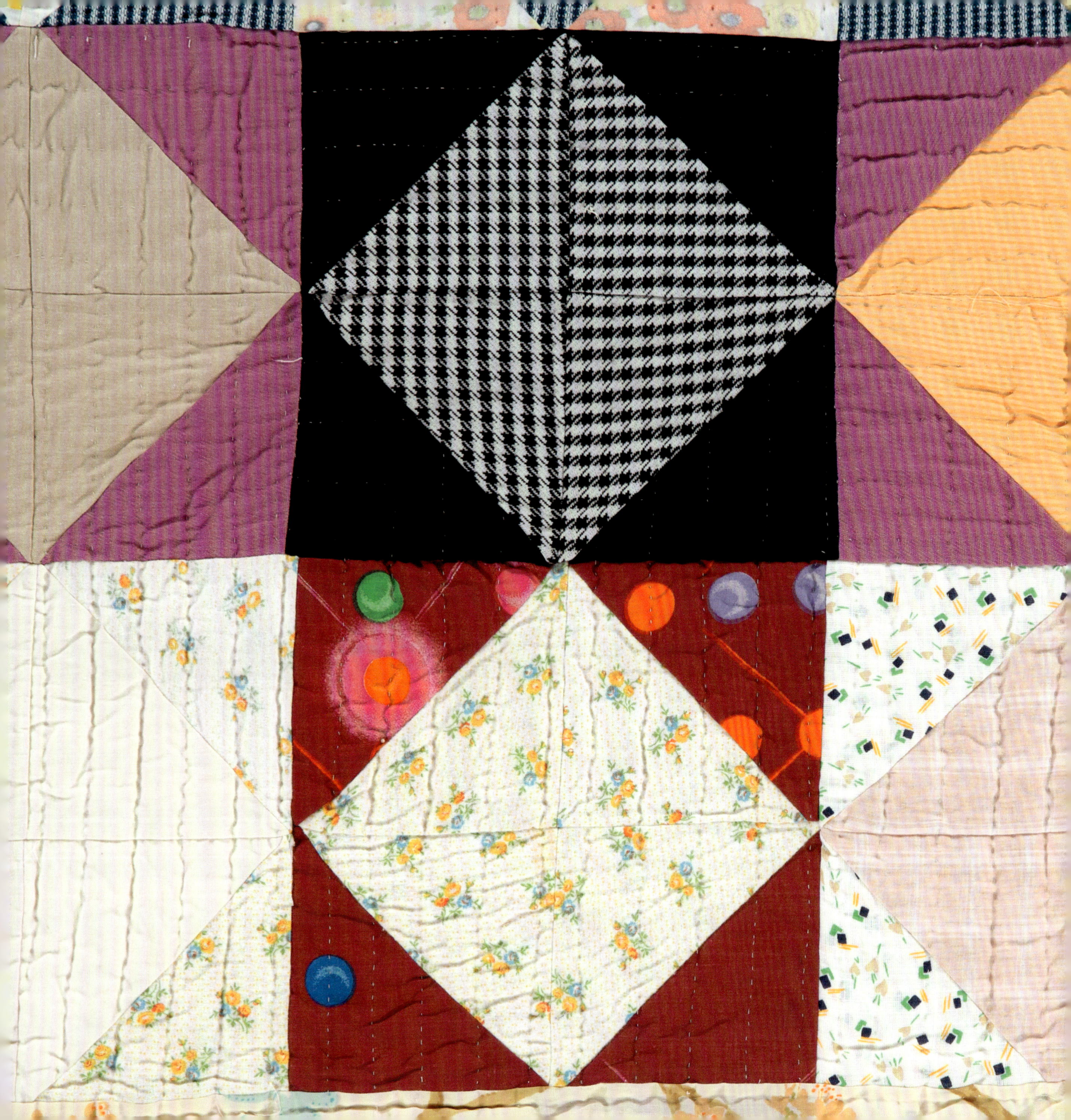

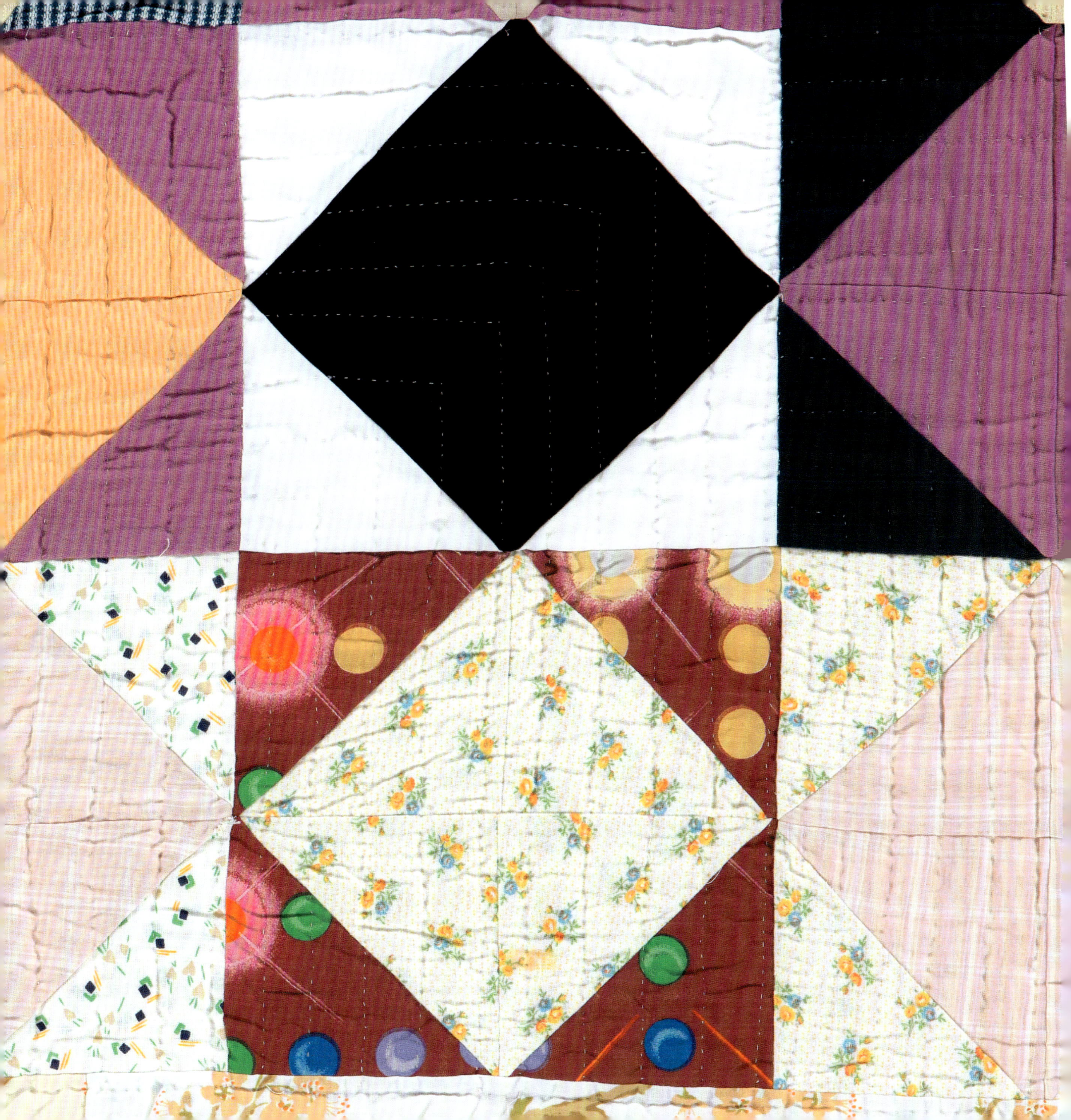

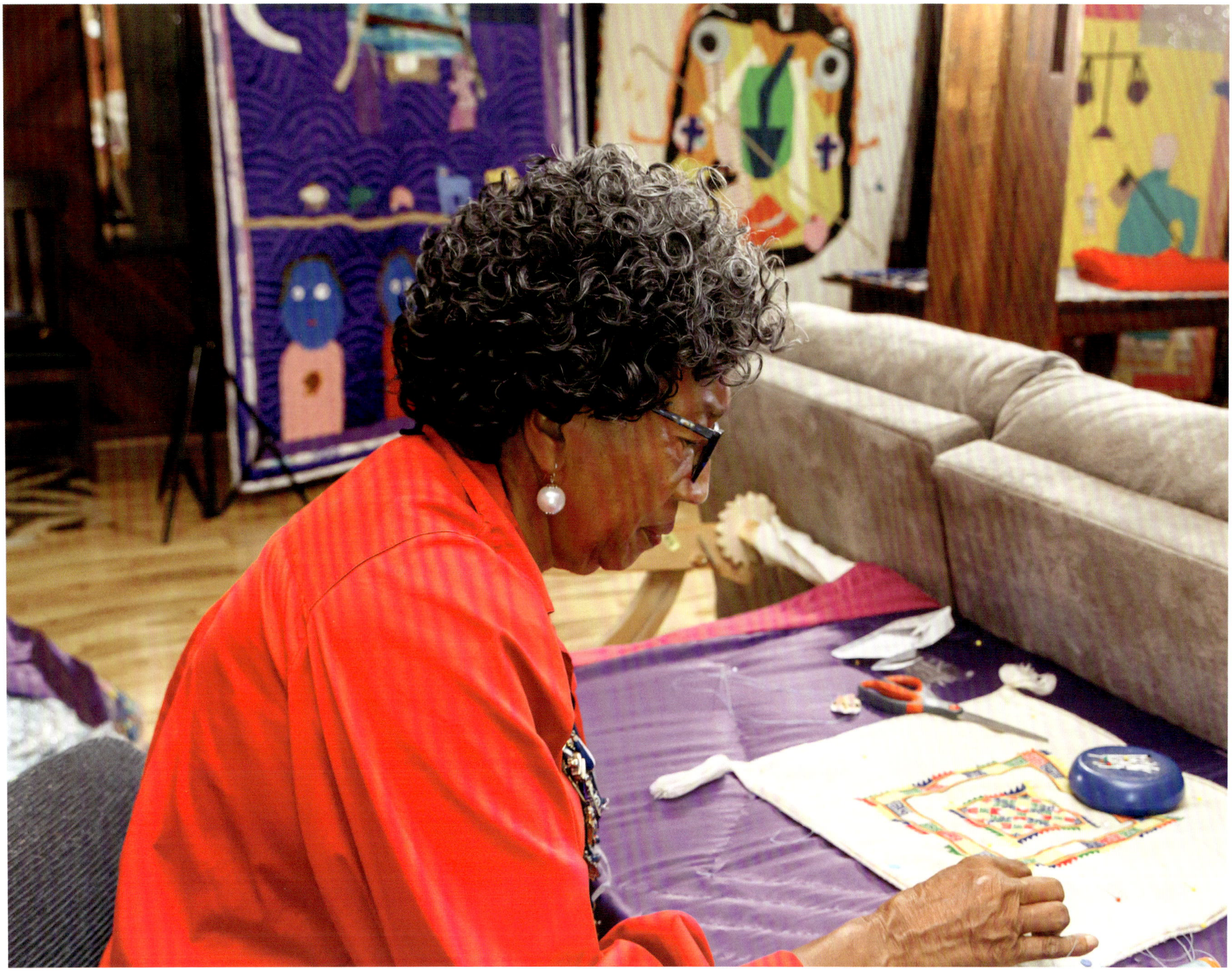

Previous pages: Detail of a traditional quilt. Above: Wells at work in her home. Photo by Dave Walker.
Right: *Double Stars* (1980s), detail.

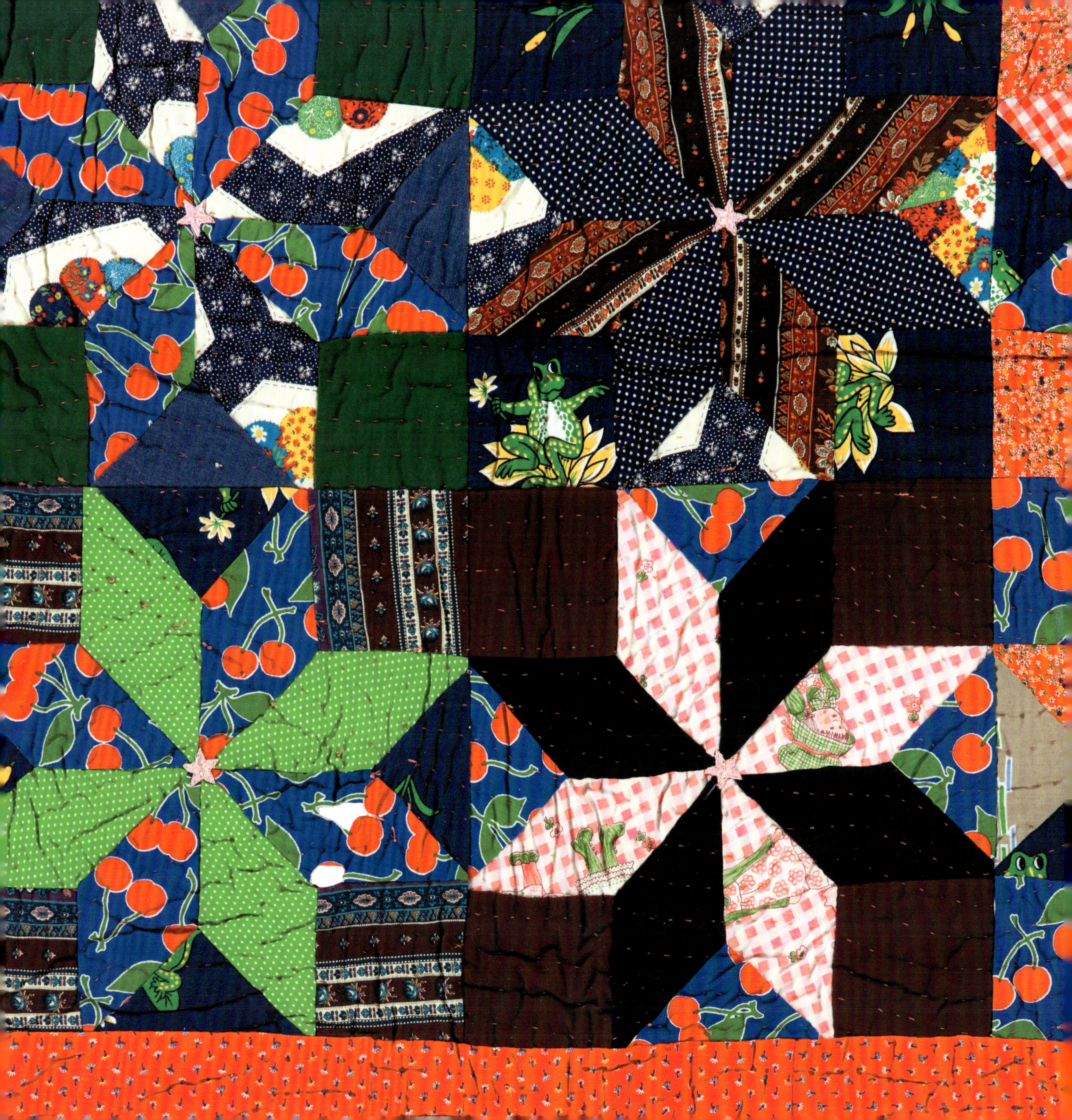

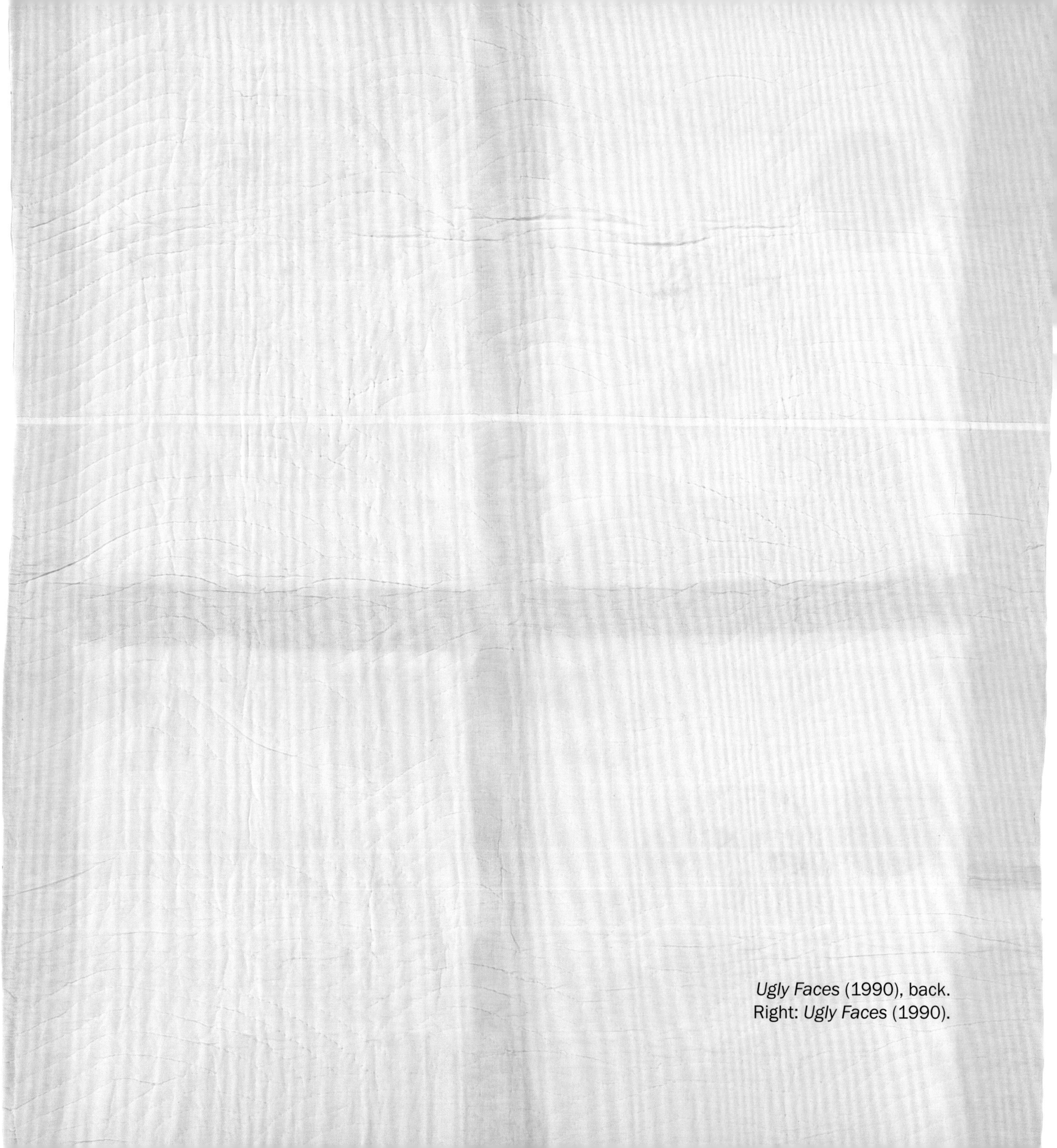

Ugly Faces (1990), back.
Right: *Ugly Faces* (1990).

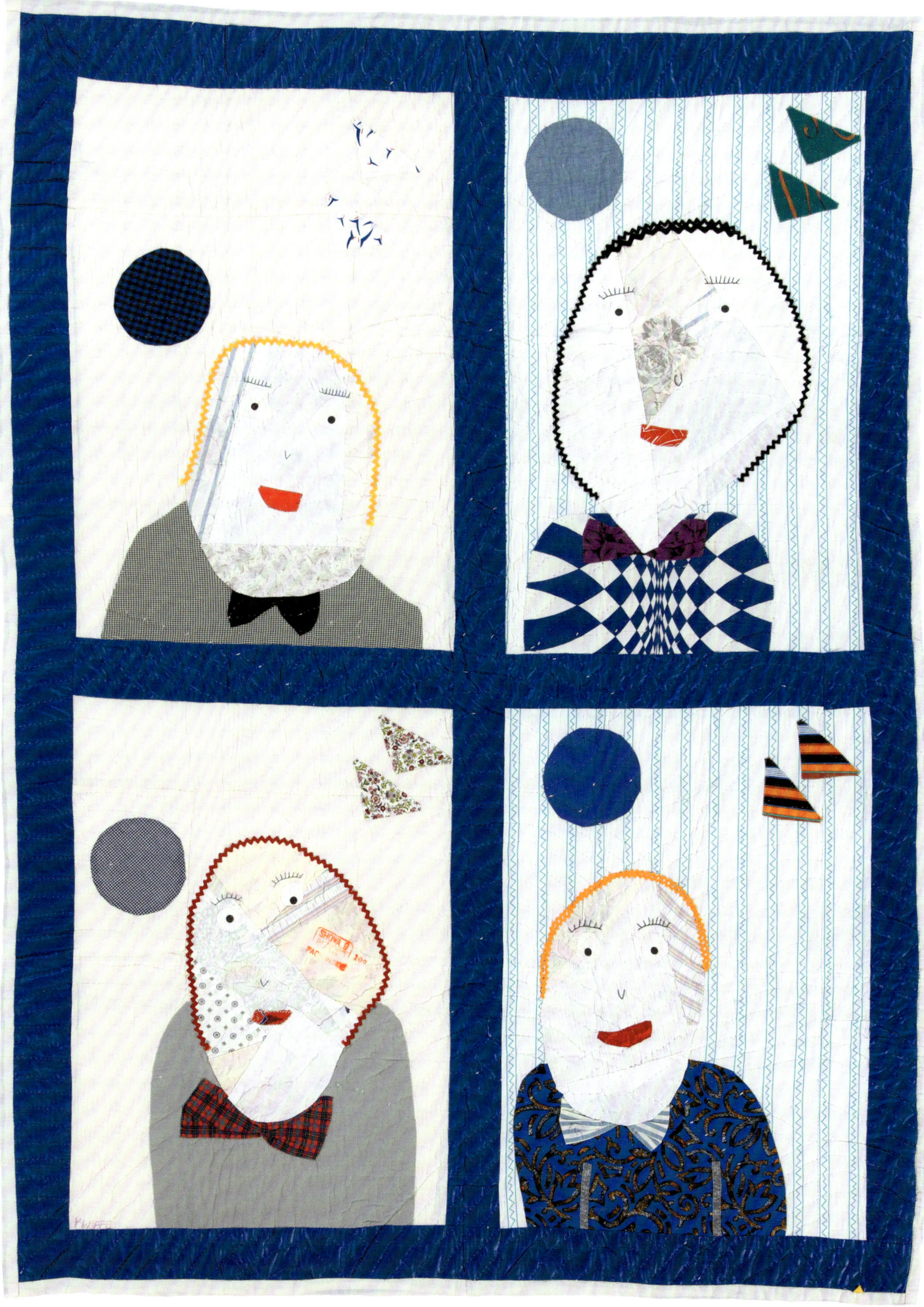

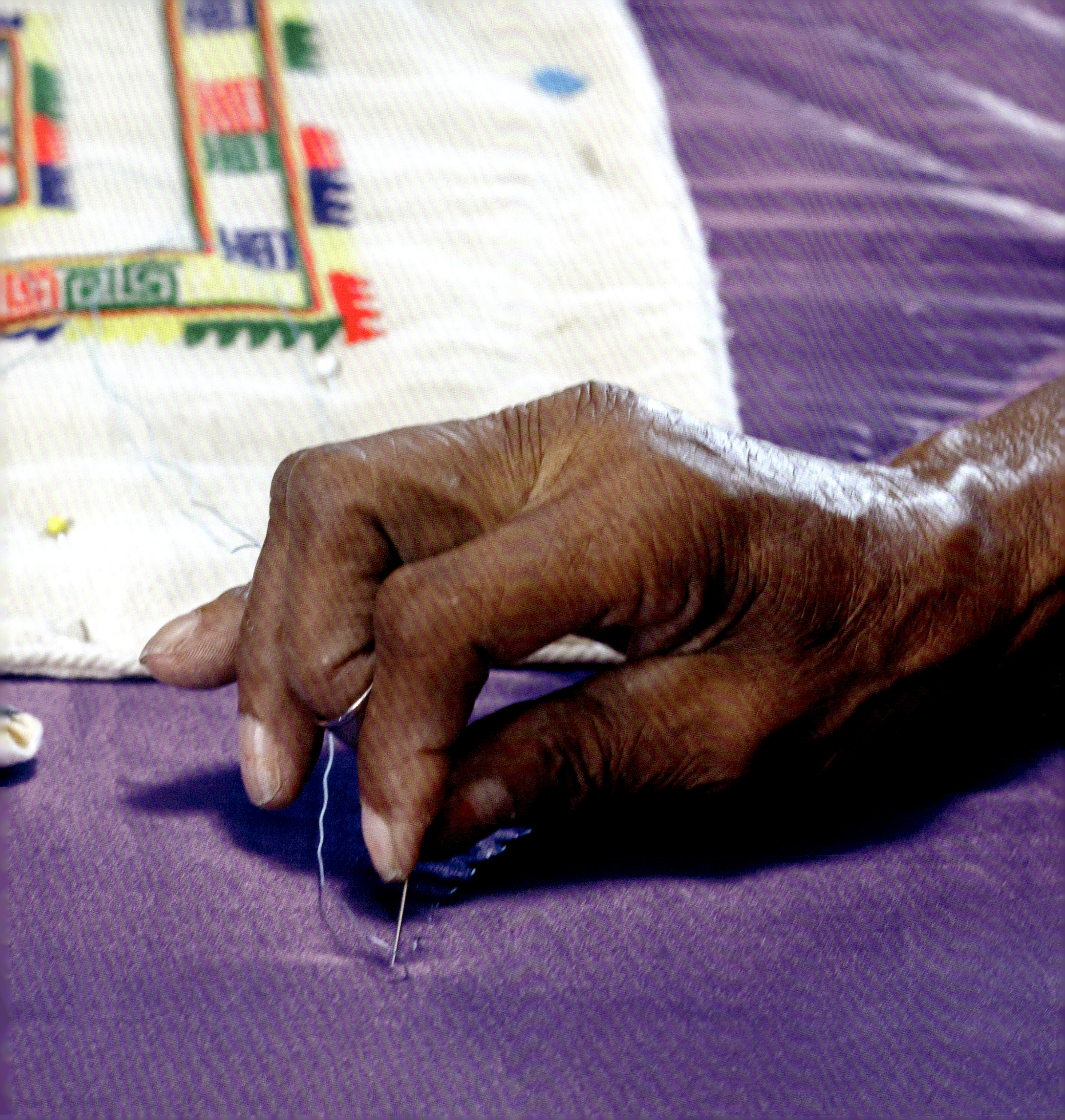

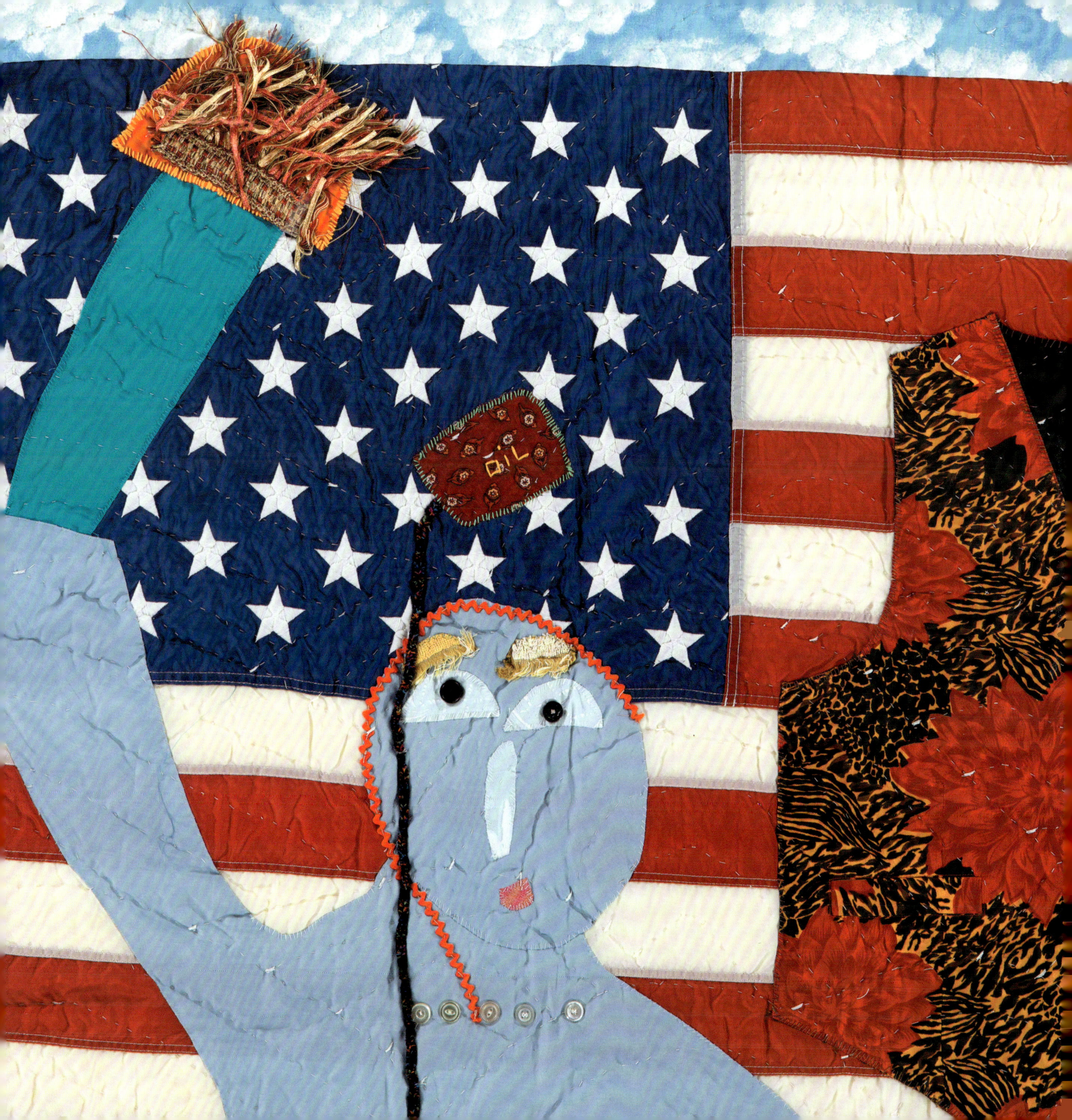
OIL

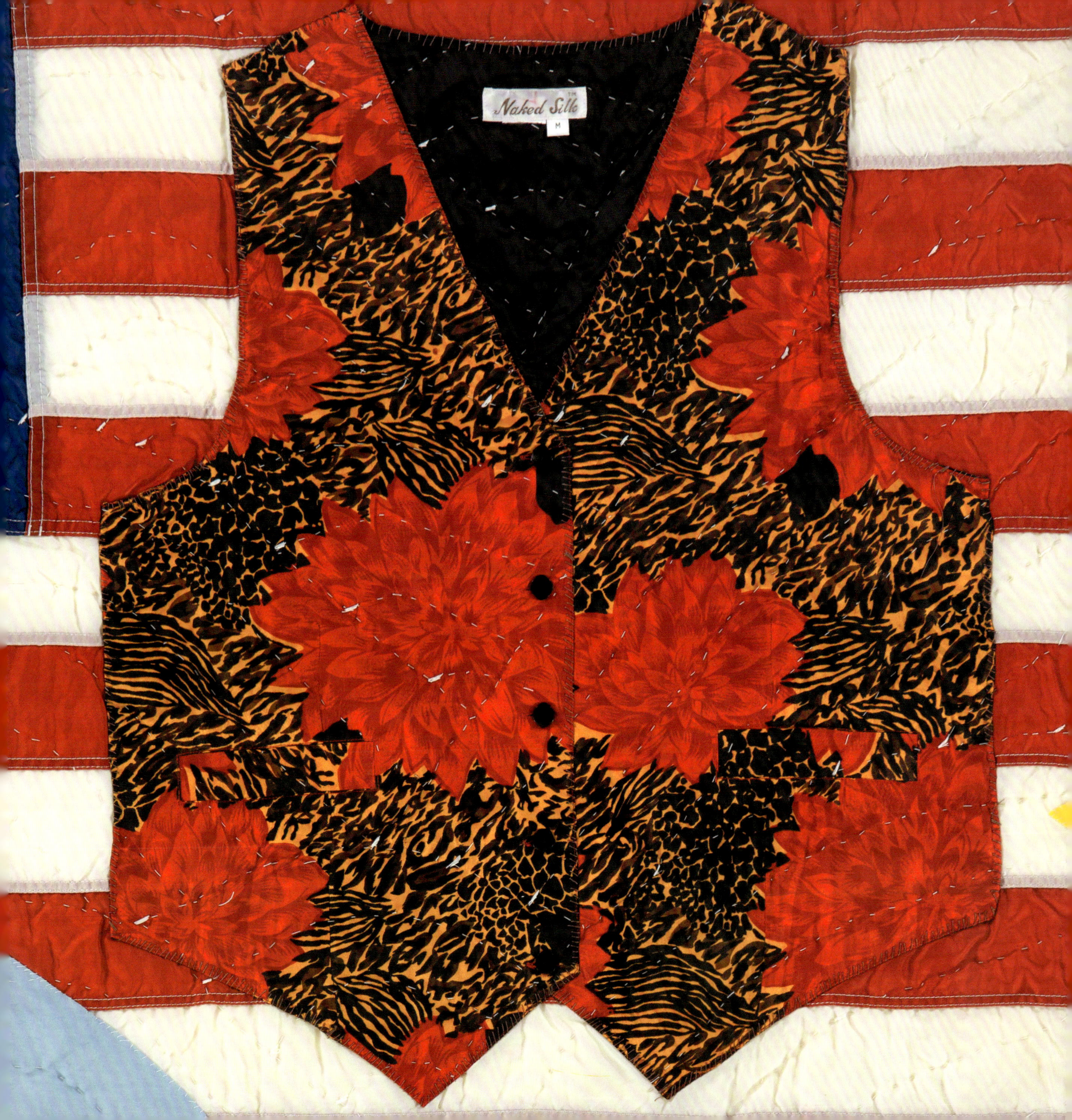
Naked Silk
M

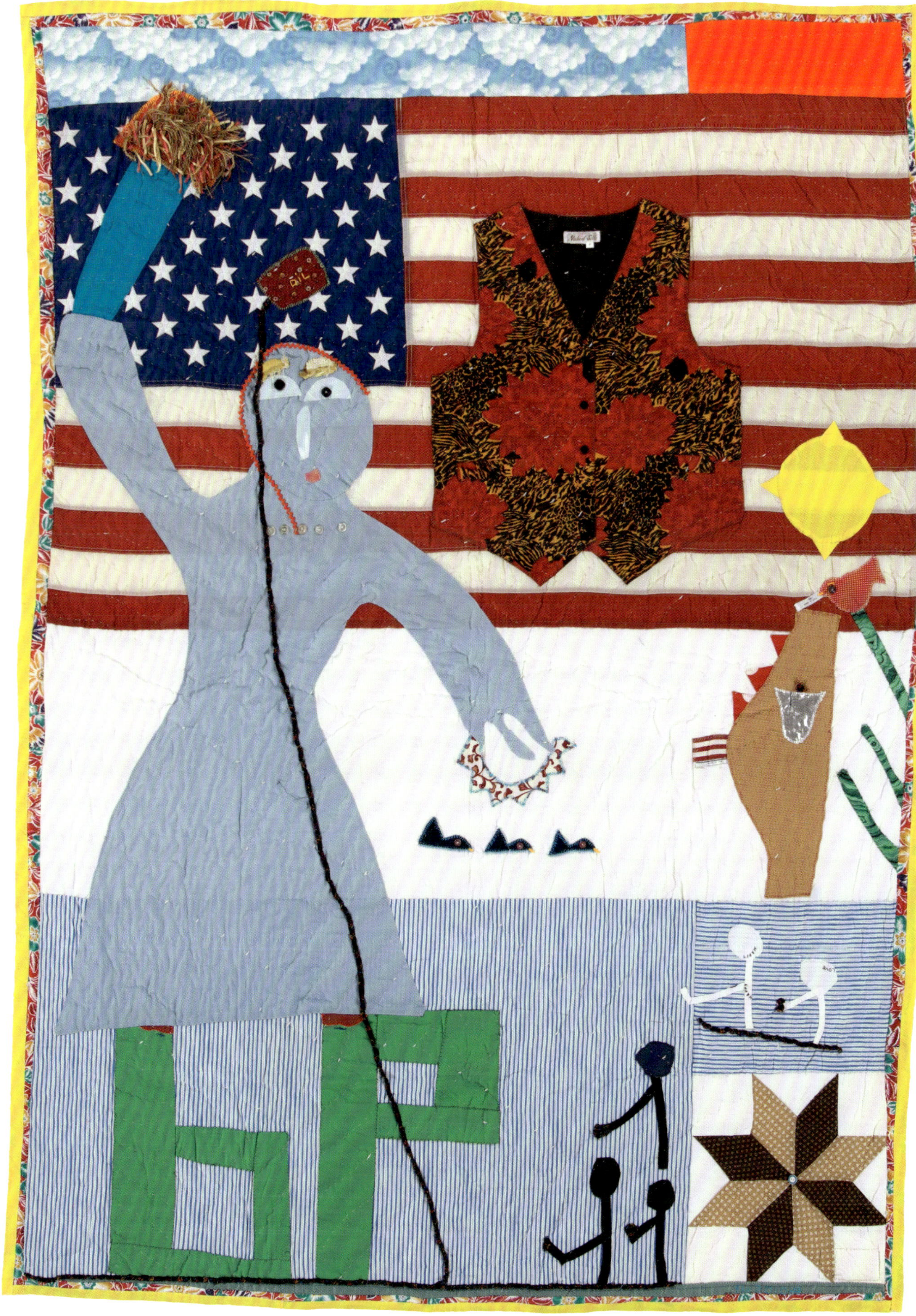

Page 78: Wells with needle and thread. Photo by Dave Walker. Page 79: *Invest in America (BP Oil Spill)* (2010), detail.
Page 80: Wells incorporates an entire vest in her *Invest in America* quilt.
Right: Invest in America (BP Oil Spill) (2010).

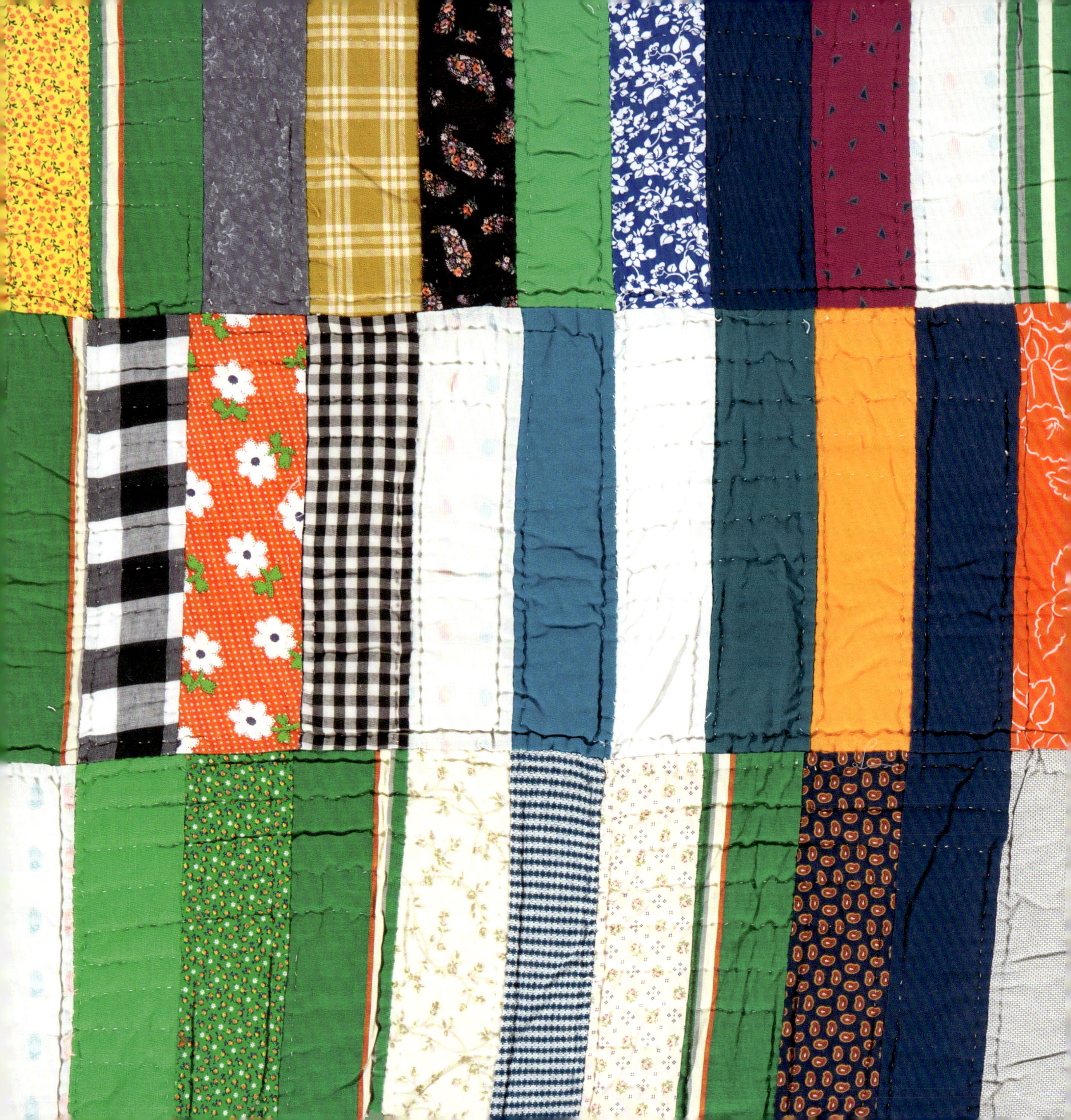

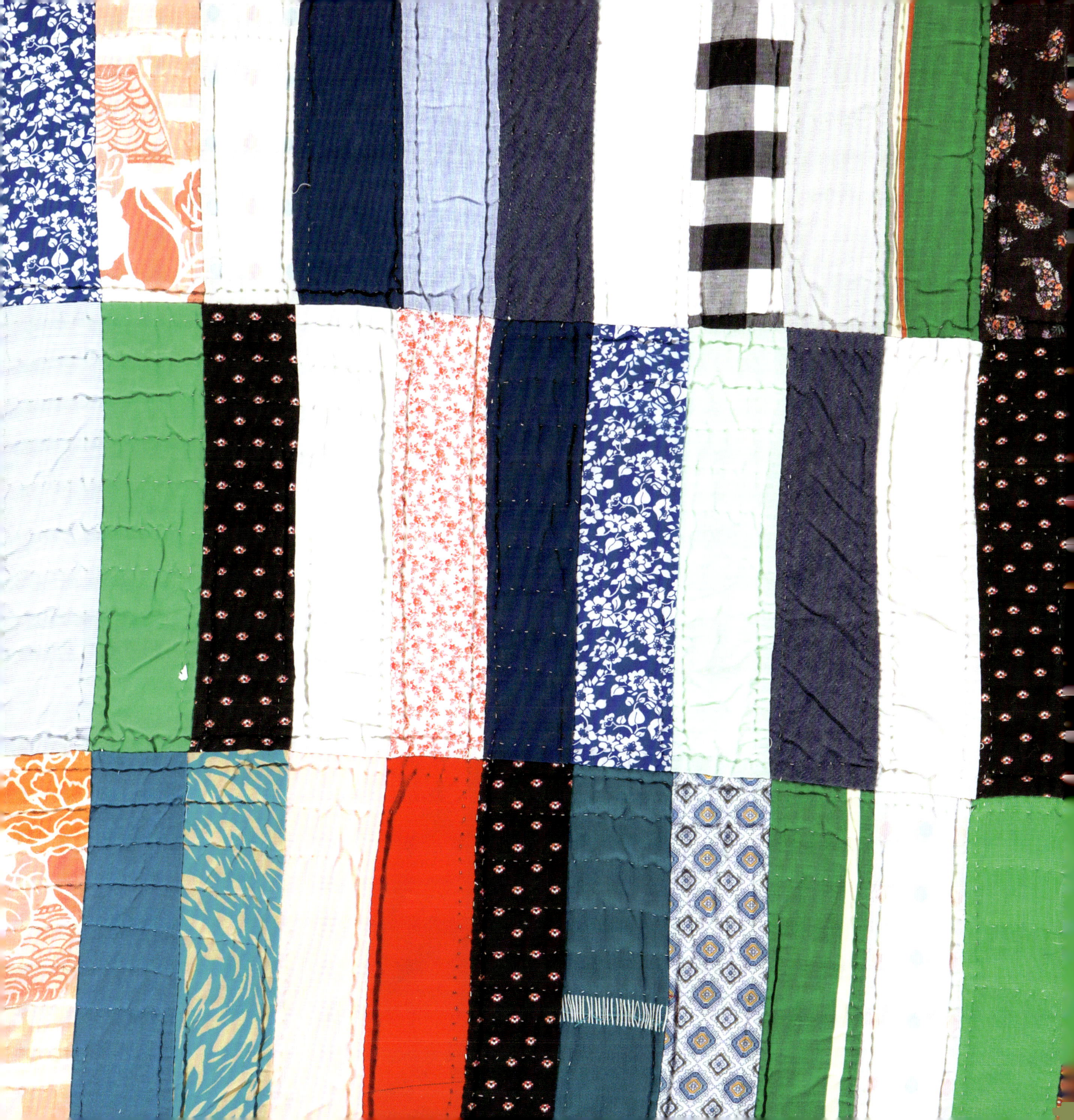

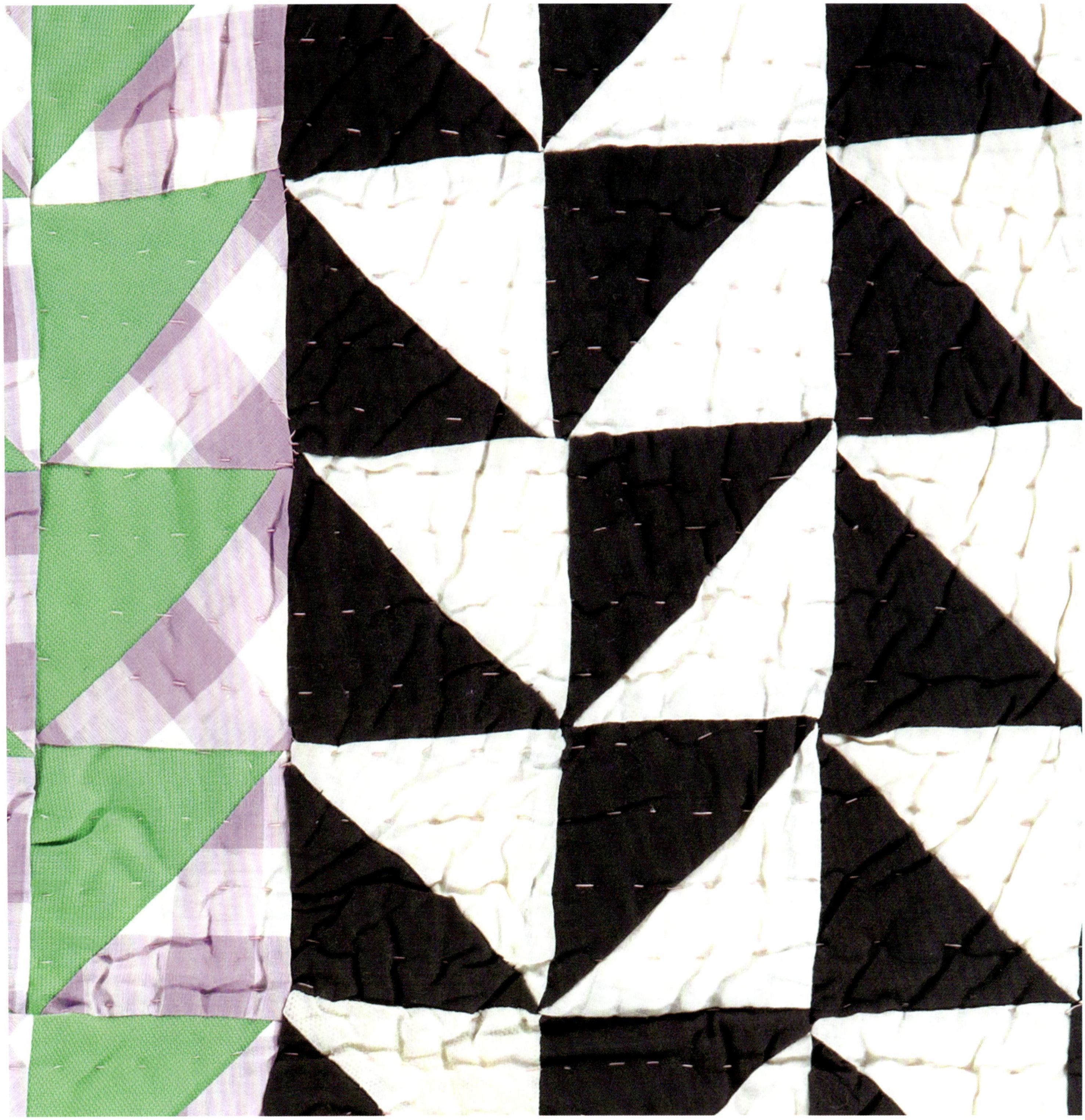

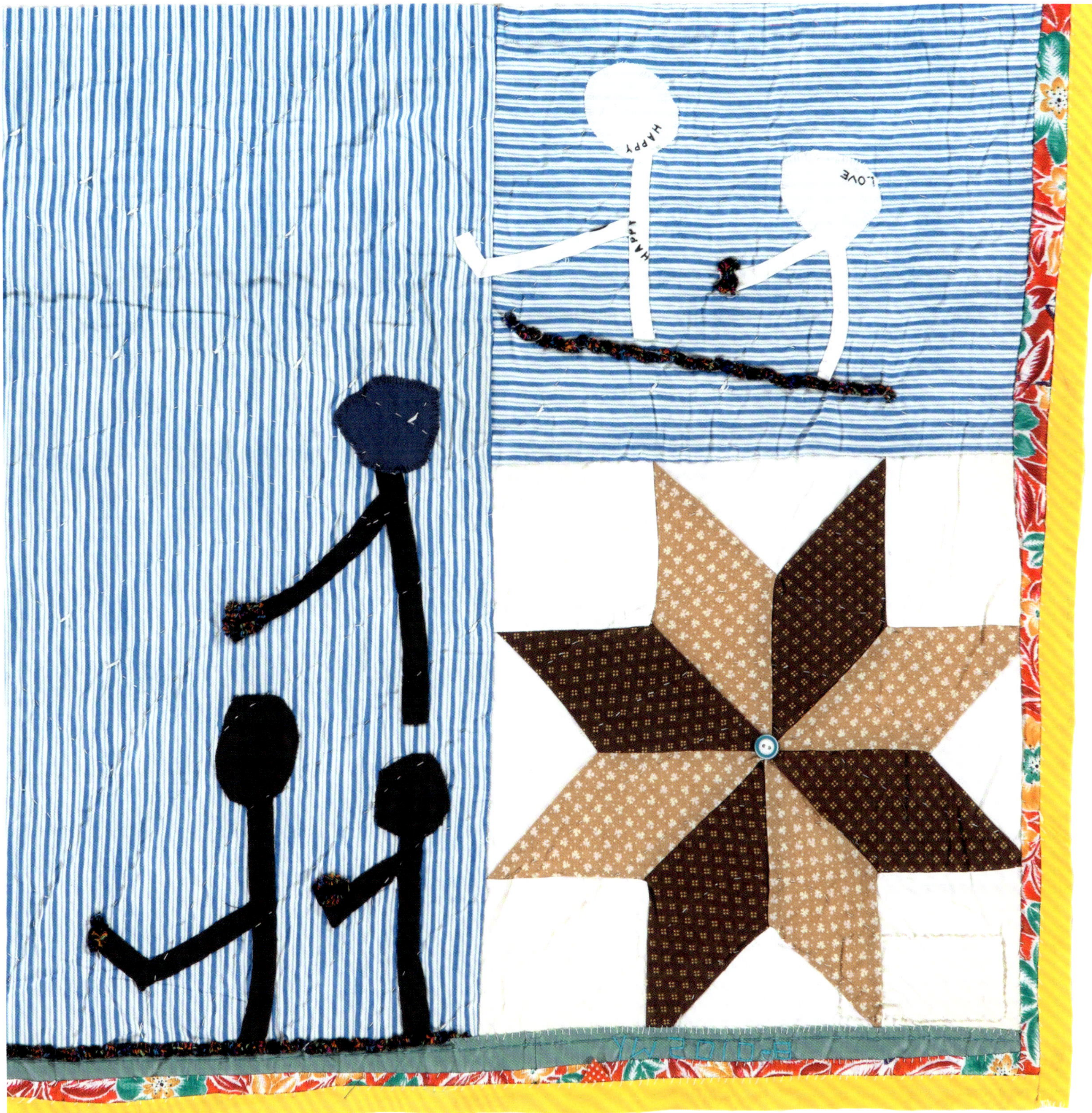

Pages 82, 83, 84: Traditional quilt details. Above: *Invest in America (BP Oil Spill)* (2010), detail.

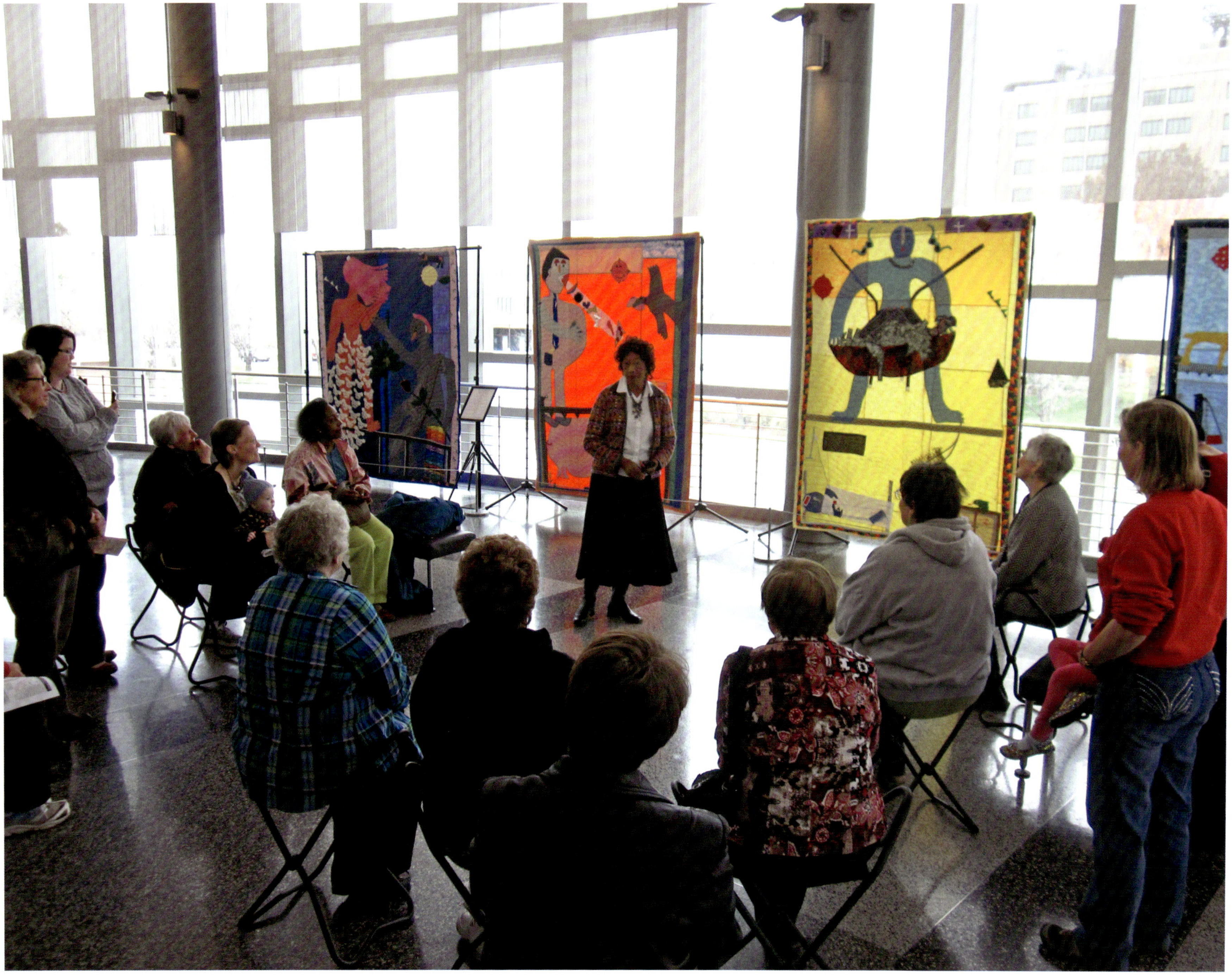

In 2011 the IQM displayed a solo exhibition of Yvonne Wells's work titled *Yvonne Wells: Quilted Messages*. While those quilts were on view in the museum's gallery, Wells also allowed the IQM to host a pop-up exhibition of a new series she had recently completed, the *Seven Deadly Sins*, shown here in the lobby area as Wells treats visitors to a special presentation.

SEVEN DEADLY SINS

These seven quilts entered the permanent collection of IQM in 2023.

The seven deadly sins are a collection of vices that are prevalent teachings in Christianity. Christians believe that partaking of these vices can lead one astray and, ultimately, to a life separate from God.

Yvonne Wells created her *Seven Deadly Sins* series between December 2004 and March 2006. The artist has ordered the sins in a particular order, and she maintains that if the group of quilts is ever to be exhibited, the quilts must be shown in this order. The order is lust, gluttony, greed, sloth, anger, envy, and pride. The first quilt in the series she made was *Anger*.

The series is often considered the crown jewel of Wells's body of work due to the larger-than-life characters, the shift from stick figures to fully formed humans and animals, the use of curved body parts, and her signature unconventional materials. There are multiple repetitive symbols in the series. For example, three tiny birds are seen in each quilt, and these represent the Christian Trinity: the Father, Son, and Holy Ghost. The sun or moon is always depicted with four points that represent north, east, south, and west.

Each sin is visualized according to a specific color and animal that is traditionally associated with that vice.

ΔΔΔ Lust is dark blue, and the animal is the cow.
ΔΔΔ Gluttony is orange, and the animal is the pig.
ΔΔΔ Greed is yellow, and the animal is the frog.
ΔΔΔ Sloth is light blue, and the animal is the goat.
ΔΔΔ Anger is red, and the animal is the bear.
ΔΔΔ Envy is green, and the animal is the dog.
ΔΔΔ Pride is lavender, and the animal is the horse.

On the following pages, each quilt is described in Wells's own words.

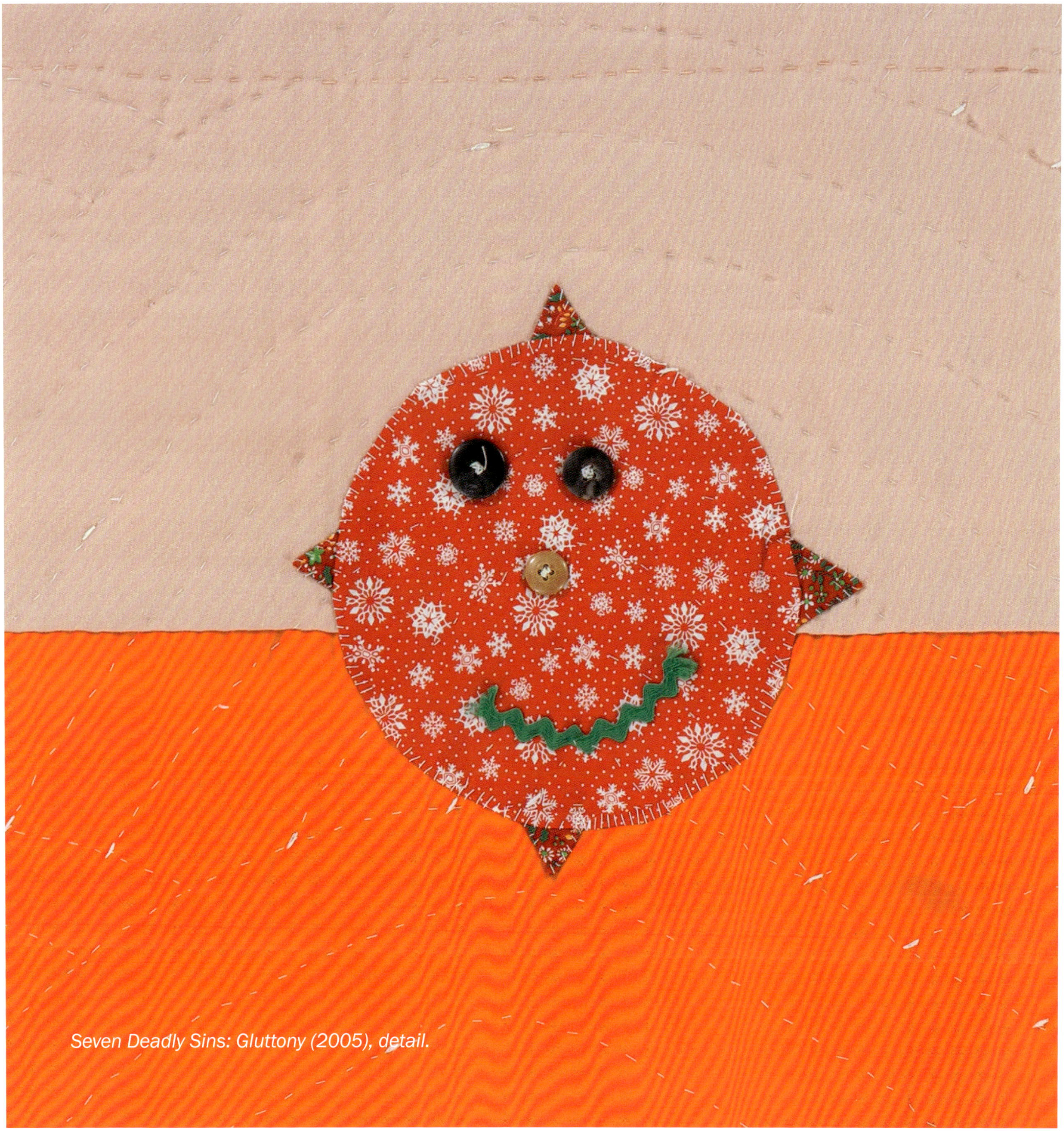

Seven Deadly Sins: Gluttony (2005), detail.

"The *Seven Deadly Sins* emerges on the whole as more spirited than somber, and more pleasurable for the viewer than 'preachy.' Beyond its virtues as compelling art, the presence of these lighthearted moments within the quilts arguably make the series more effective as a vehicle for conveying serious points to viewers. . . . After all, as the adage most often attributed to playwright George Bernard Shaw puts it, 'If you're going to tell people the truth, you'd better make them laugh.'"

— Stacy Morgan
Coauthor: *The Story Quilts of Yvonne Wells*[1]

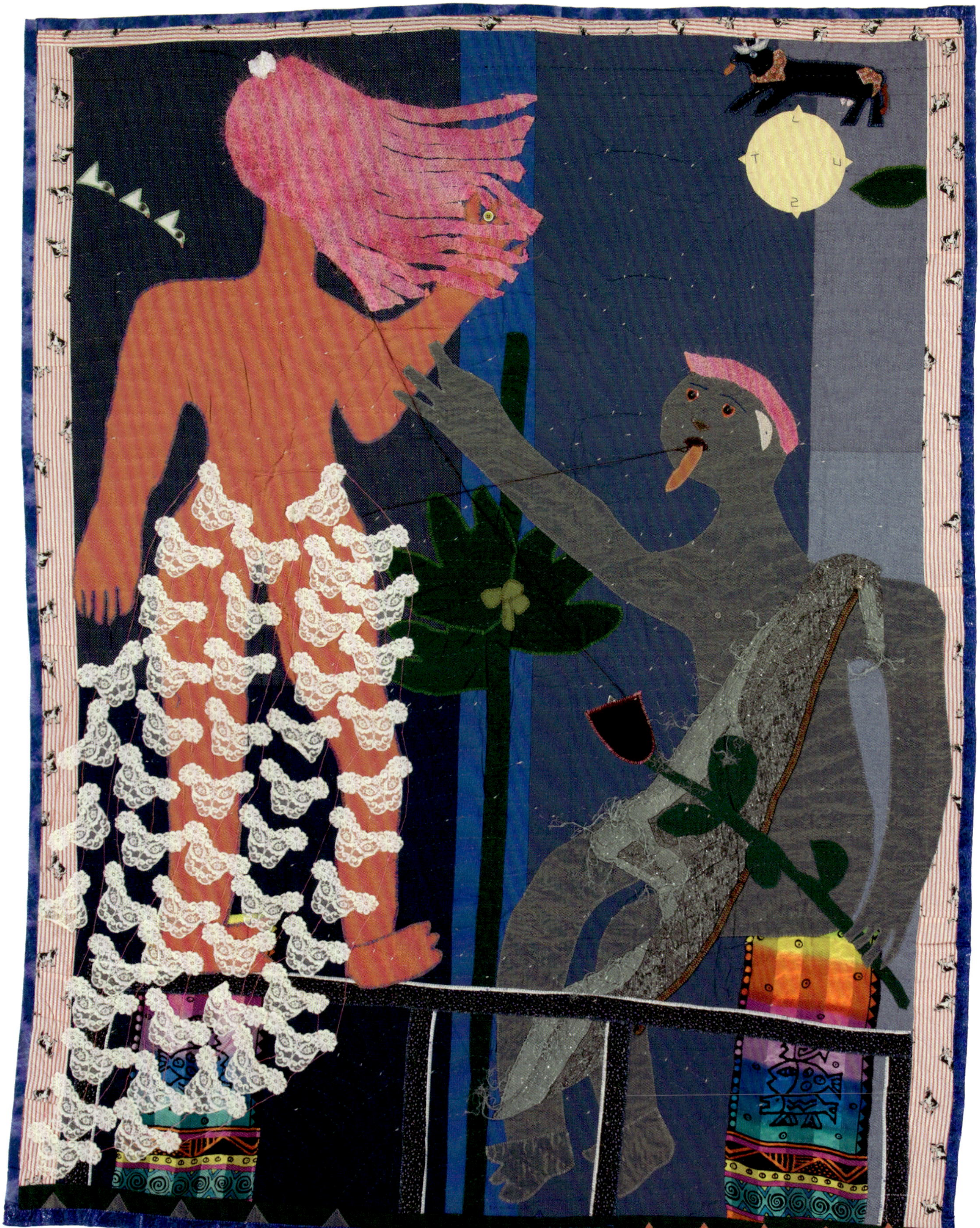

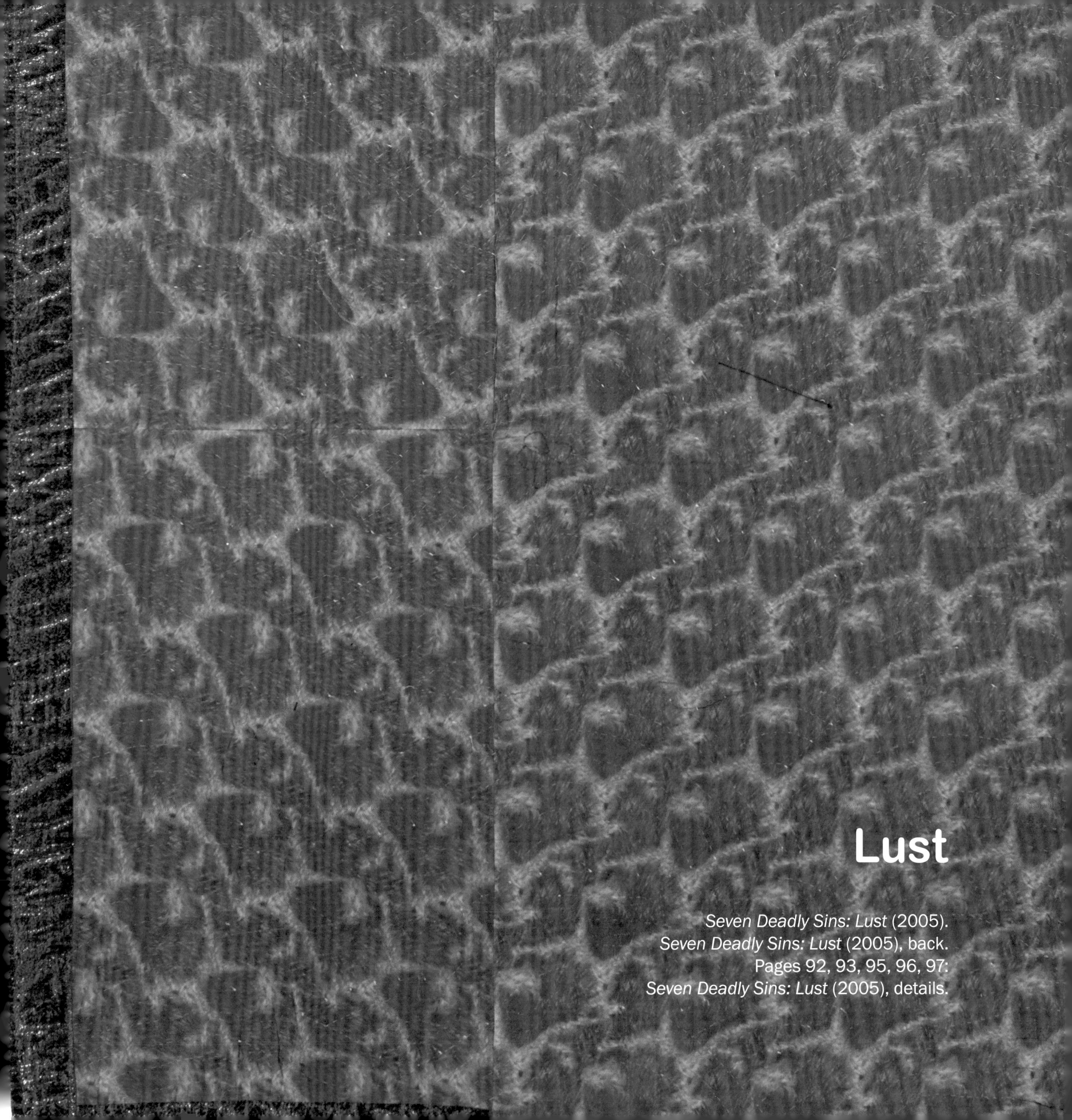

Lust

Seven Deadly Sins: Lust (2005).
Seven Deadly Sins: Lust (2005), back.
Pages 92, 93, 95, 96, 97:
Seven Deadly Sins: Lust (2005), details.

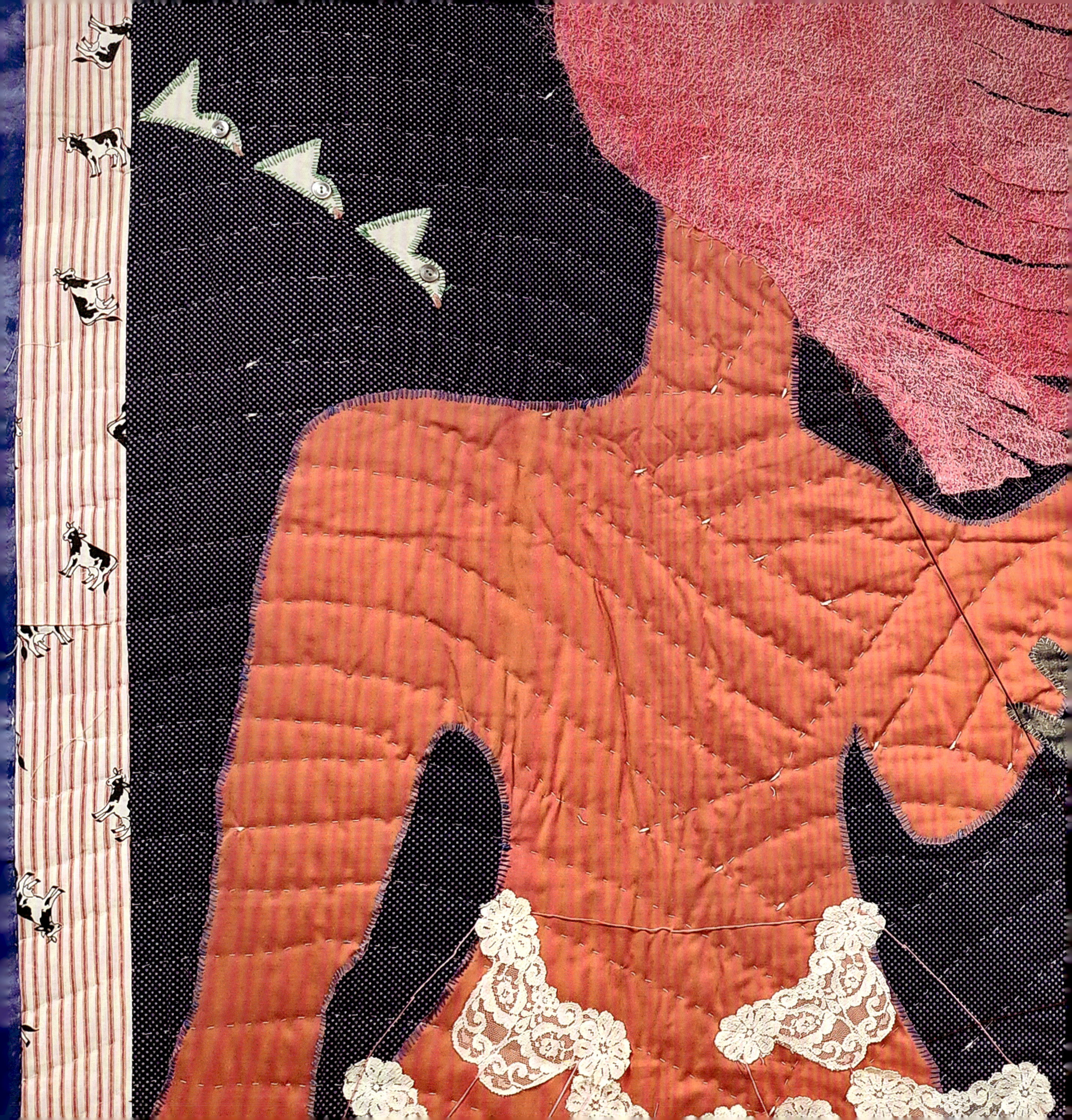

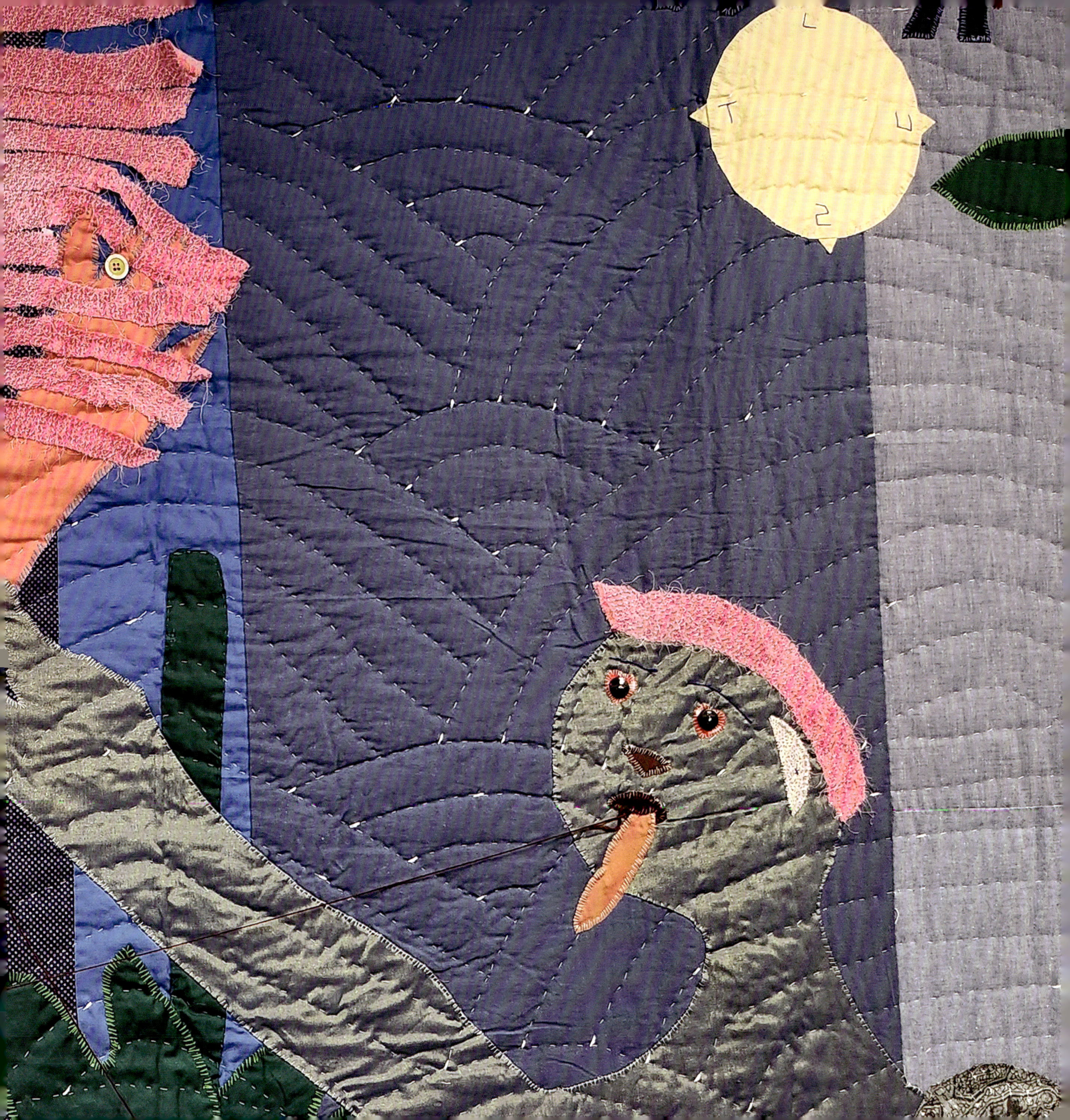

Lust

This is the first in the series of the *Seven Deadly Sins*, and it's called *Lust*, which is the least of all of the seven sins. I never thought lust would be the least of all of the sins because of the title. It seems like such a serious sin.

The gentleman you see here was infatuated with this lovely lady, and he reached out to touch her hair, but he didn't quite get there. She just flipped her hair right in front of him.

I put her in a negligee. The negligee is made from curtains that Robert Cargo gave me. He said, "Yvonne, you take these. You'll know exactly what to do with them." So, I made her a negligee out of those curtains. I do buy fabric. I buy plenty of it. But I will absolutely cut up my own clothes if it fits my story. Her hair is made out of one of my sweaters. The clothing on the man is my scarf. The bench that he is sitting on, that's my scarf as well.

The color for lust is blue. The animal that represents lust is a cow. See how the cow is jumping over the moon? The letters on the moon spell out the word *lust*.

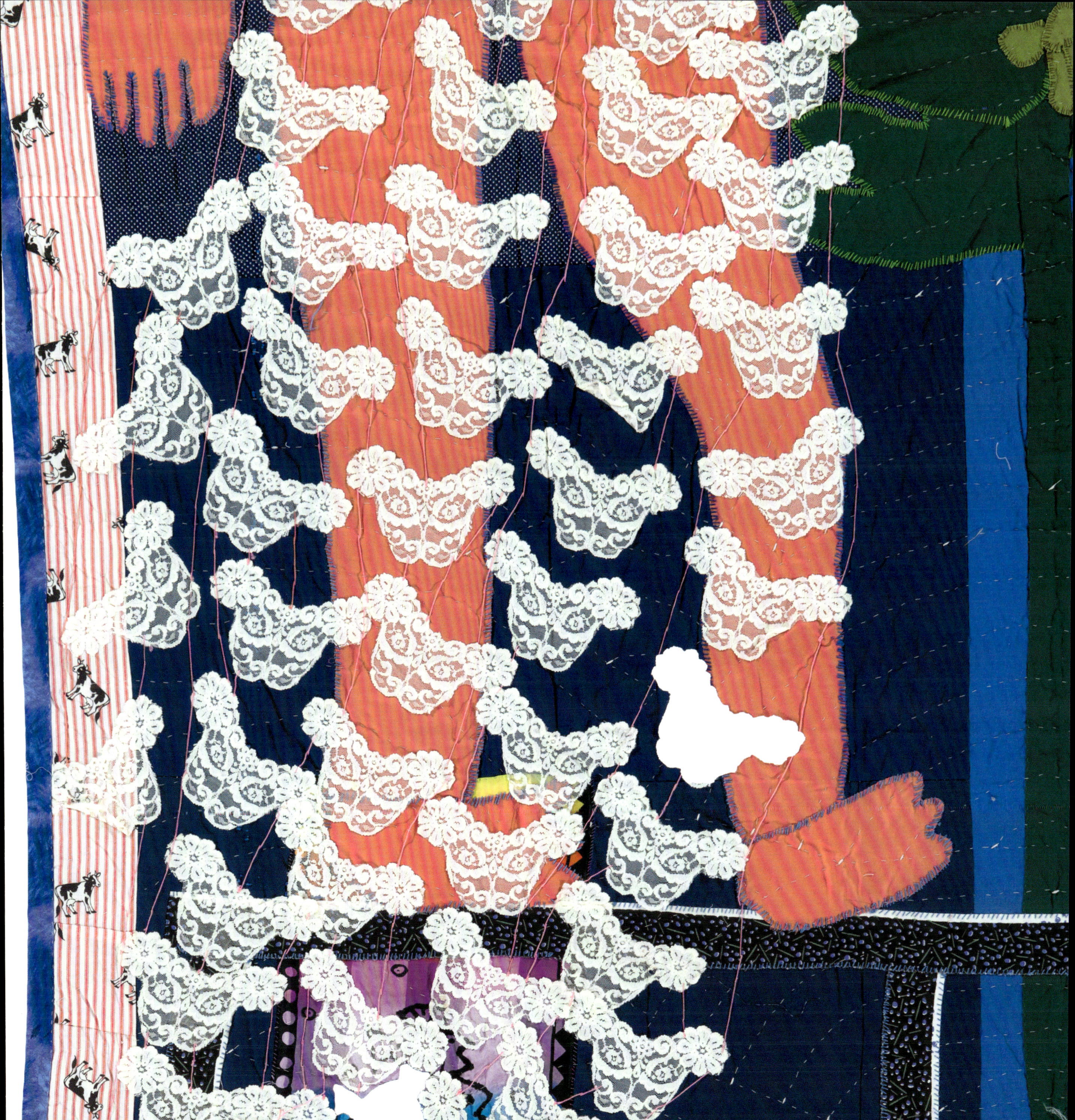

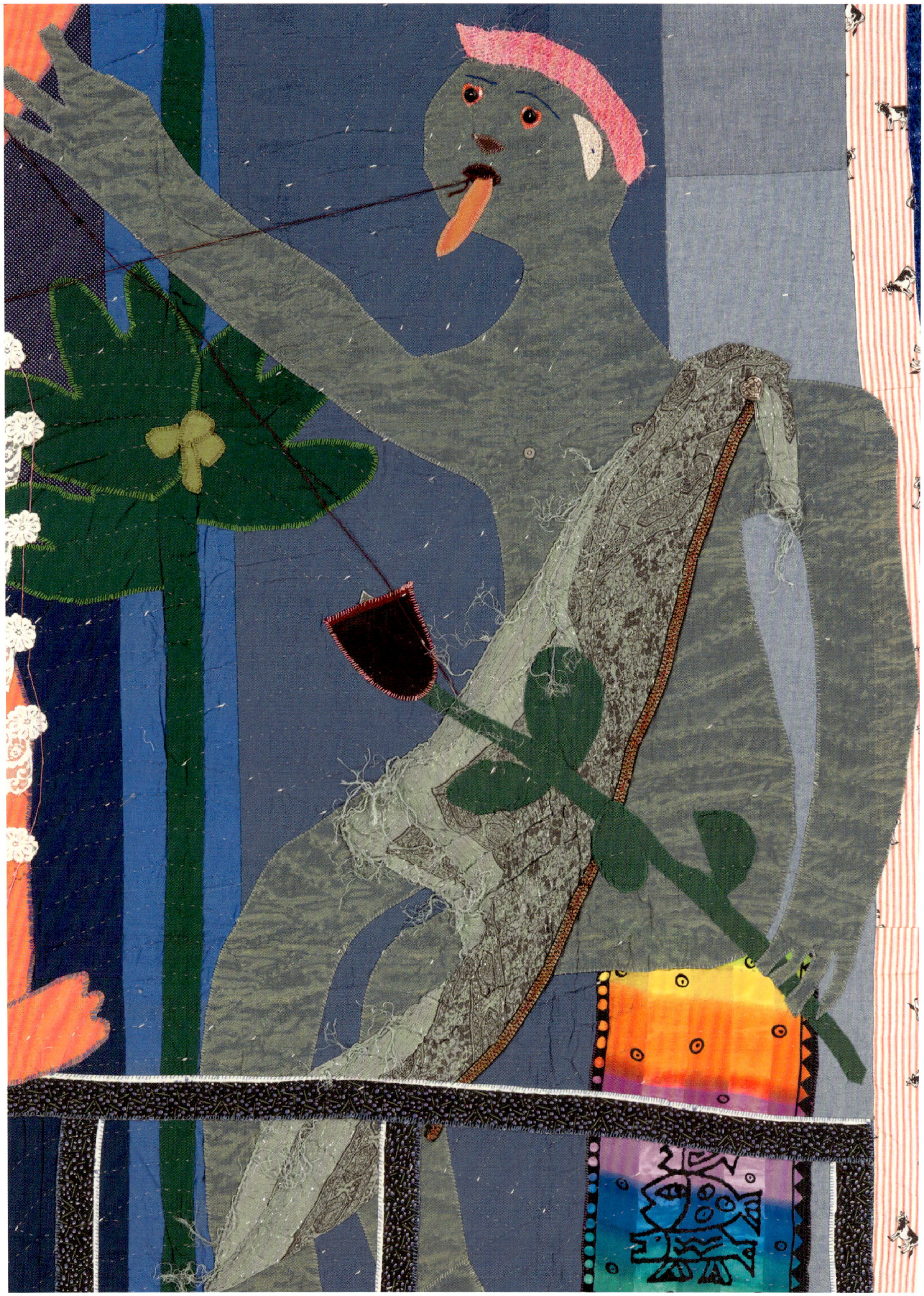

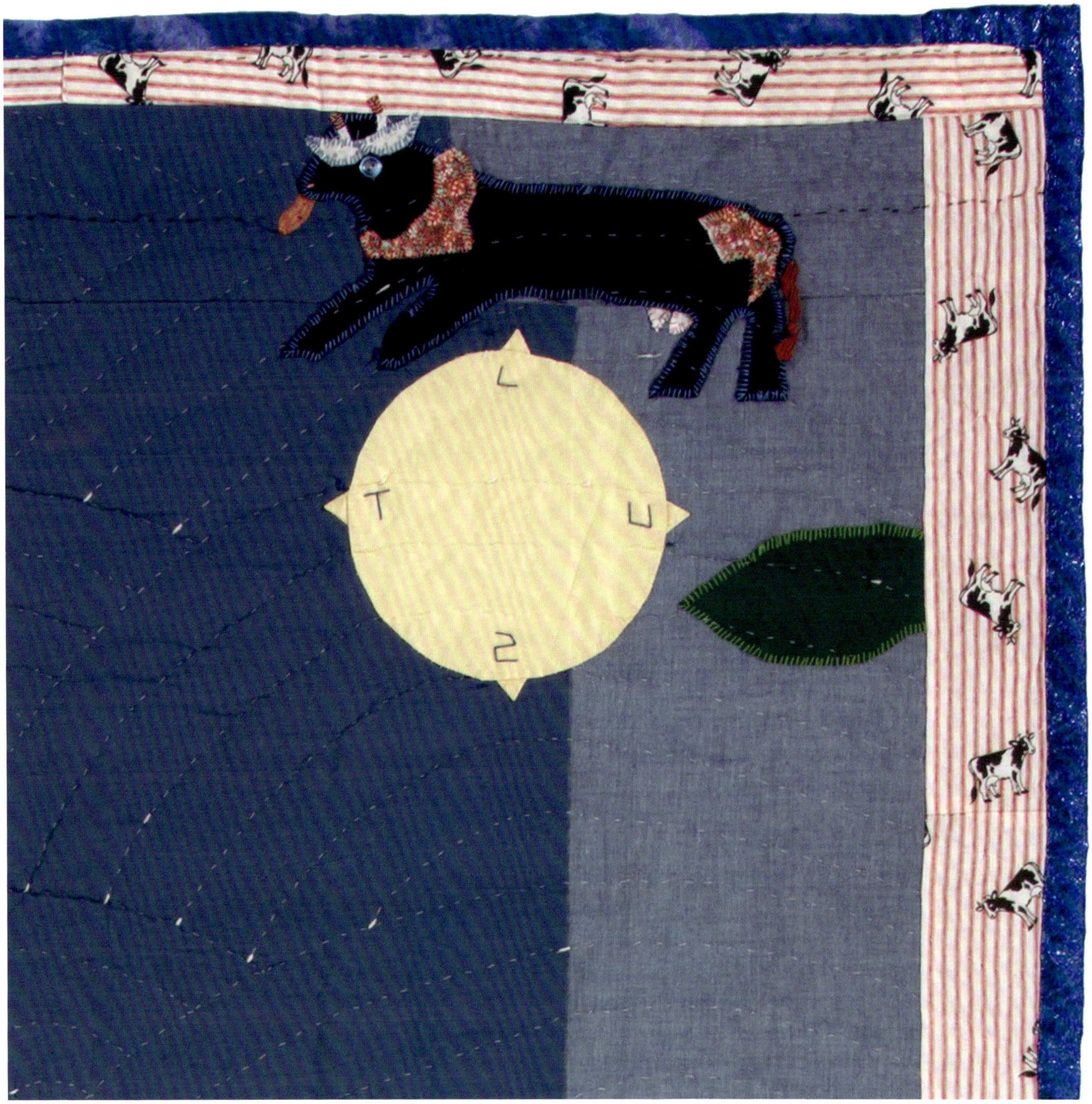

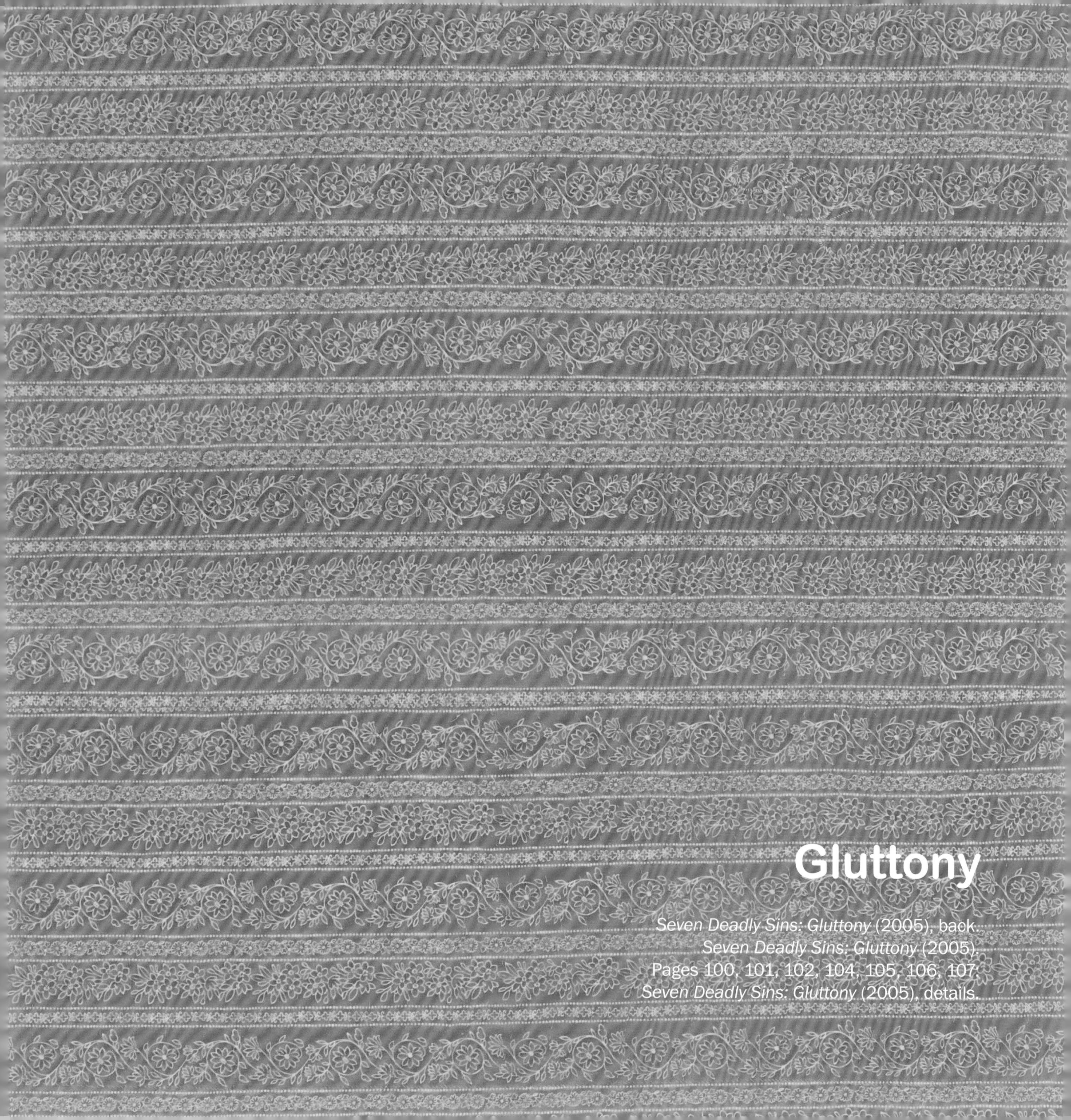

Gluttony

Seven Deadly Sins: Gluttony (2005), back.
Seven Deadly Sins: Gluttony (2005).
Pages 100, 101, 102, 104, 105, 106, 107:
Seven Deadly Sins: Gluttony (2005), details.

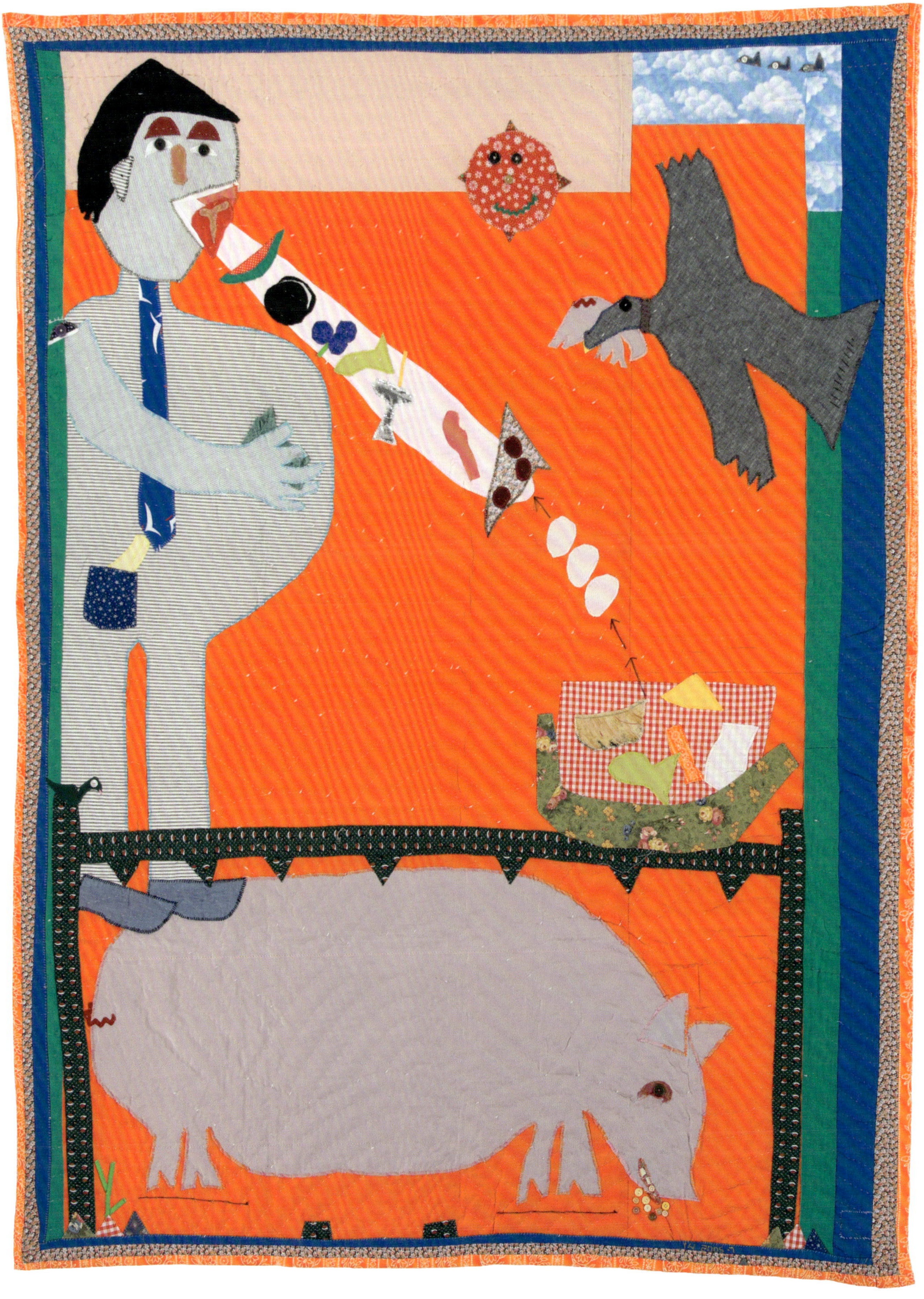

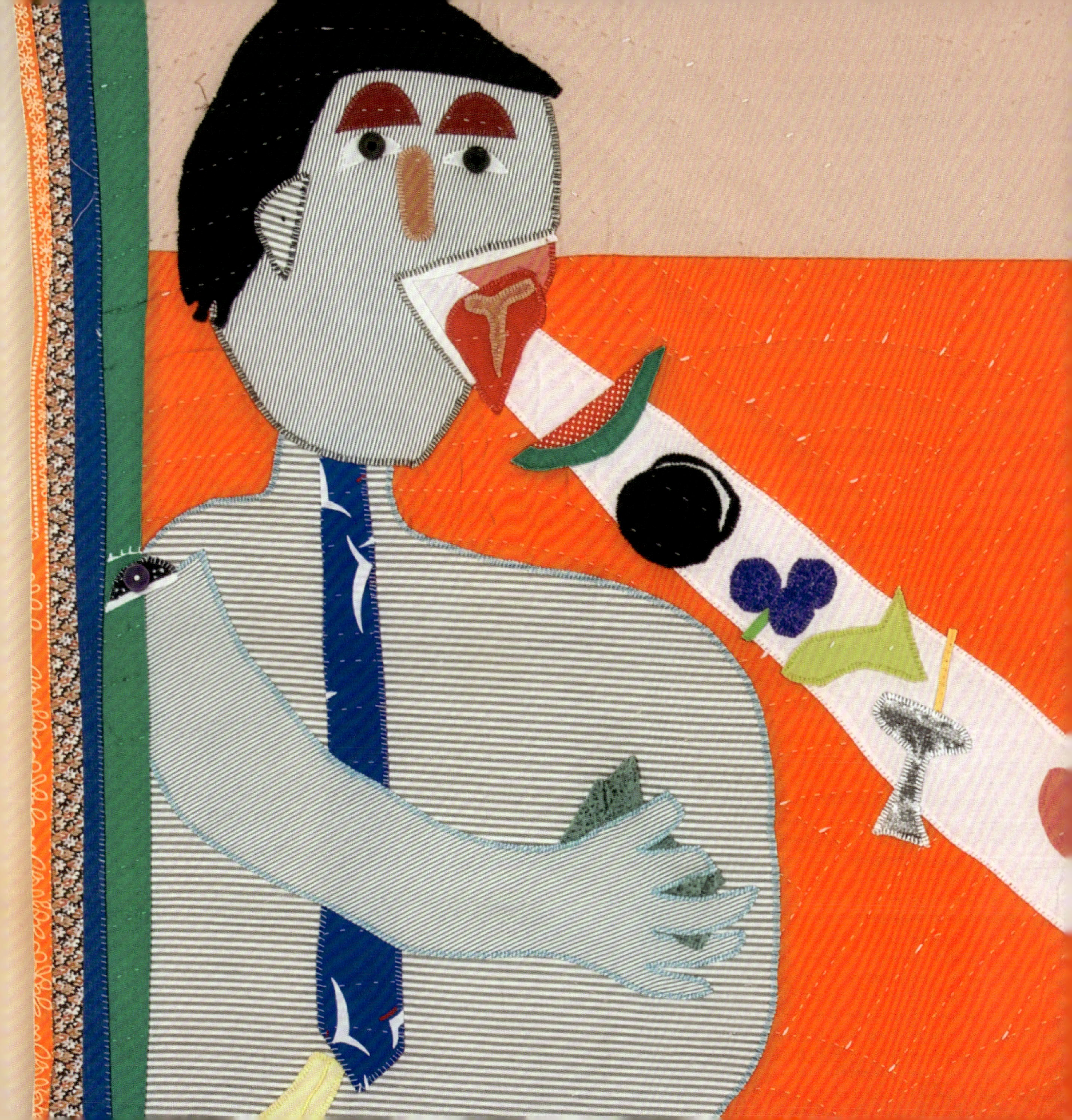

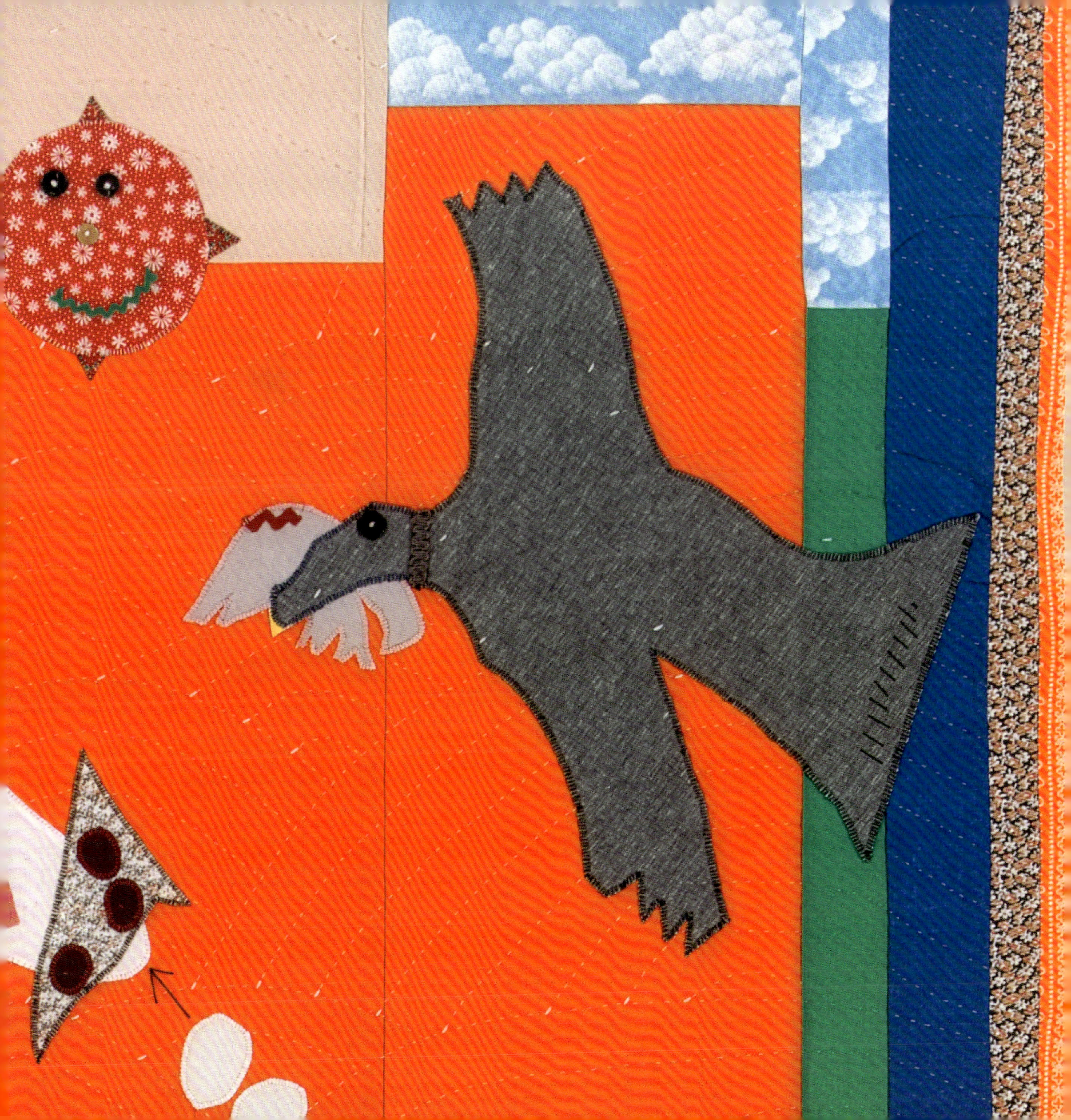

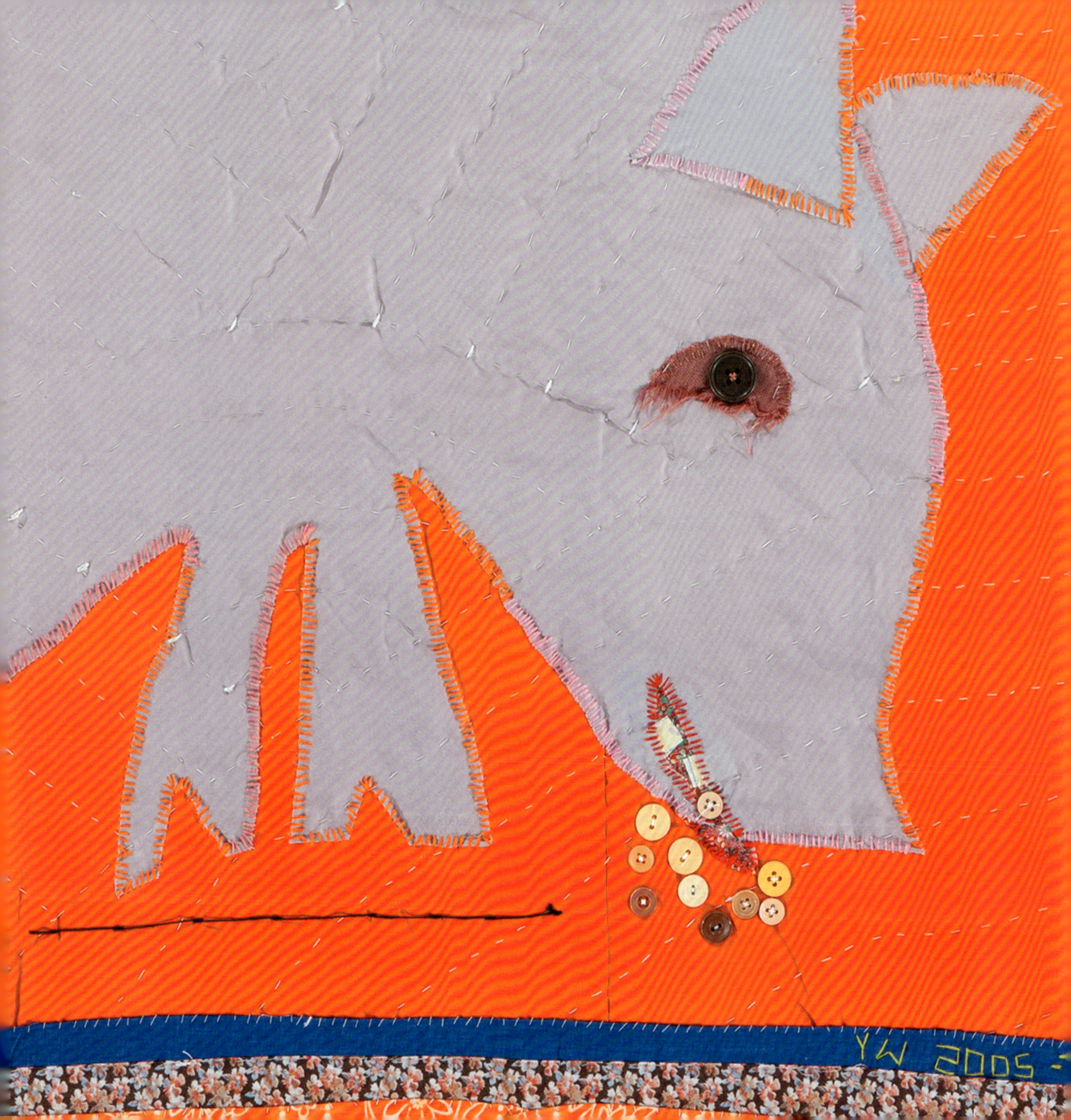
YW 2005

Gluttony

This is *Gluttony*, and it's the second sin. Gluttony means eating a whole lot of stuff. You're not supposed to eat till you throw up, but some people do. This gentleman here, he just could not stop eating. He had eggs, pizza, a chicken thigh, fish, grapes, an Oreo cookie, a slice of watermelon, and a T-bone steak. But that just wasn't enough for him, so he reached down into the picnic basket and grabbed some more food. He got more fish and bread and cheese. He was just an overeater, which is a sin.

So, the color for gluttony is orange, and the animal is the pig. You heard that expression that *you eat more than a pig* or *just pigging out*. Well, here it is.

You can see there are three birds here. I usually put those in each one of my quilts because it's just a part of me that I think belongs here. However, I didn't start putting those three birds in initially, but I felt there was something that was missing, so I added these birds. They represent the Trinity: God the Father, the Son, and the Holy Ghost.

As far as the sun is concerned, I used to put four or five rays in each sun. But I now put just four points on the sun to represent north, south, east, and west. But I do sometimes make the sun look kind of funny, and that's how this one came about.

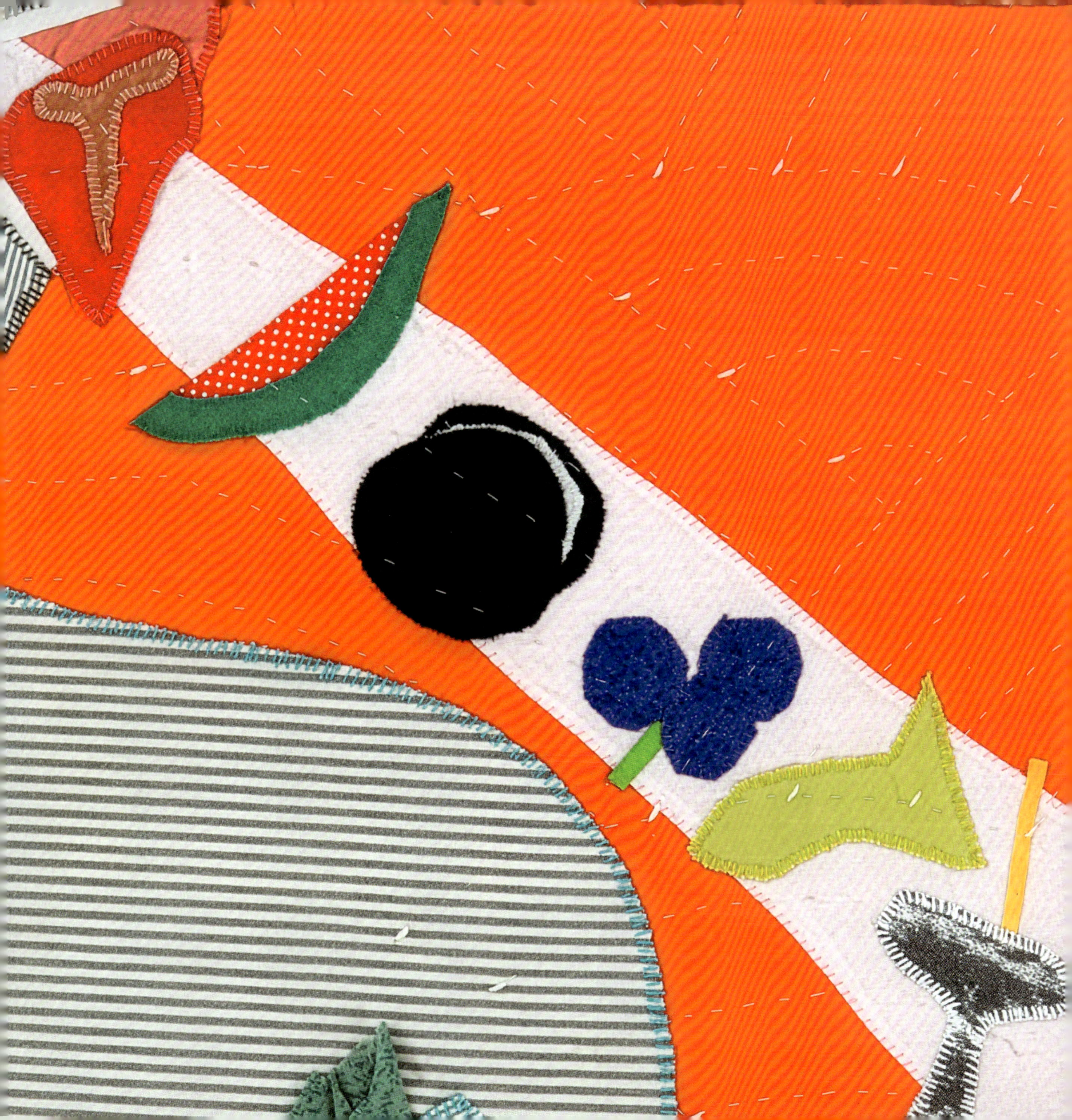

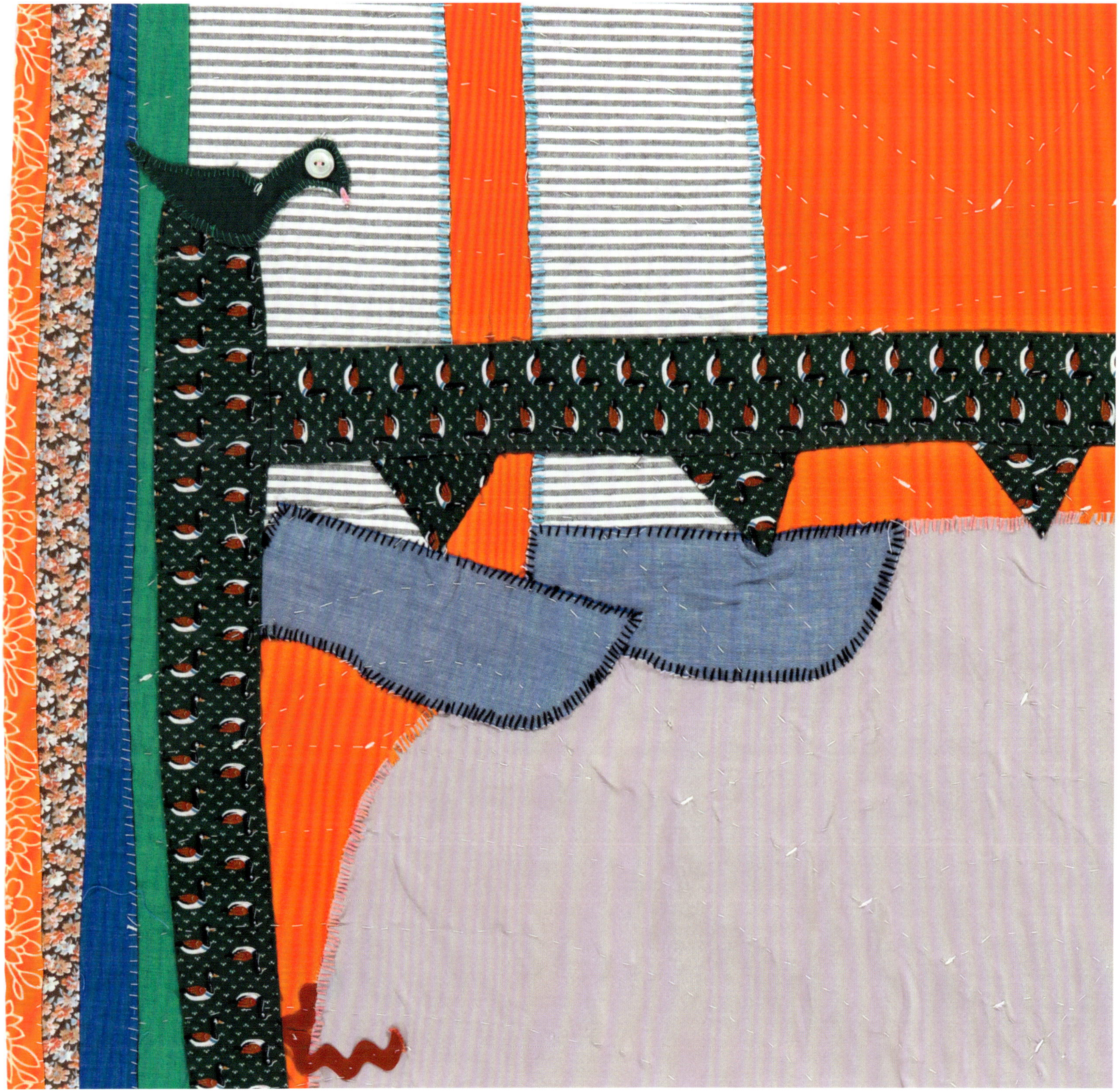

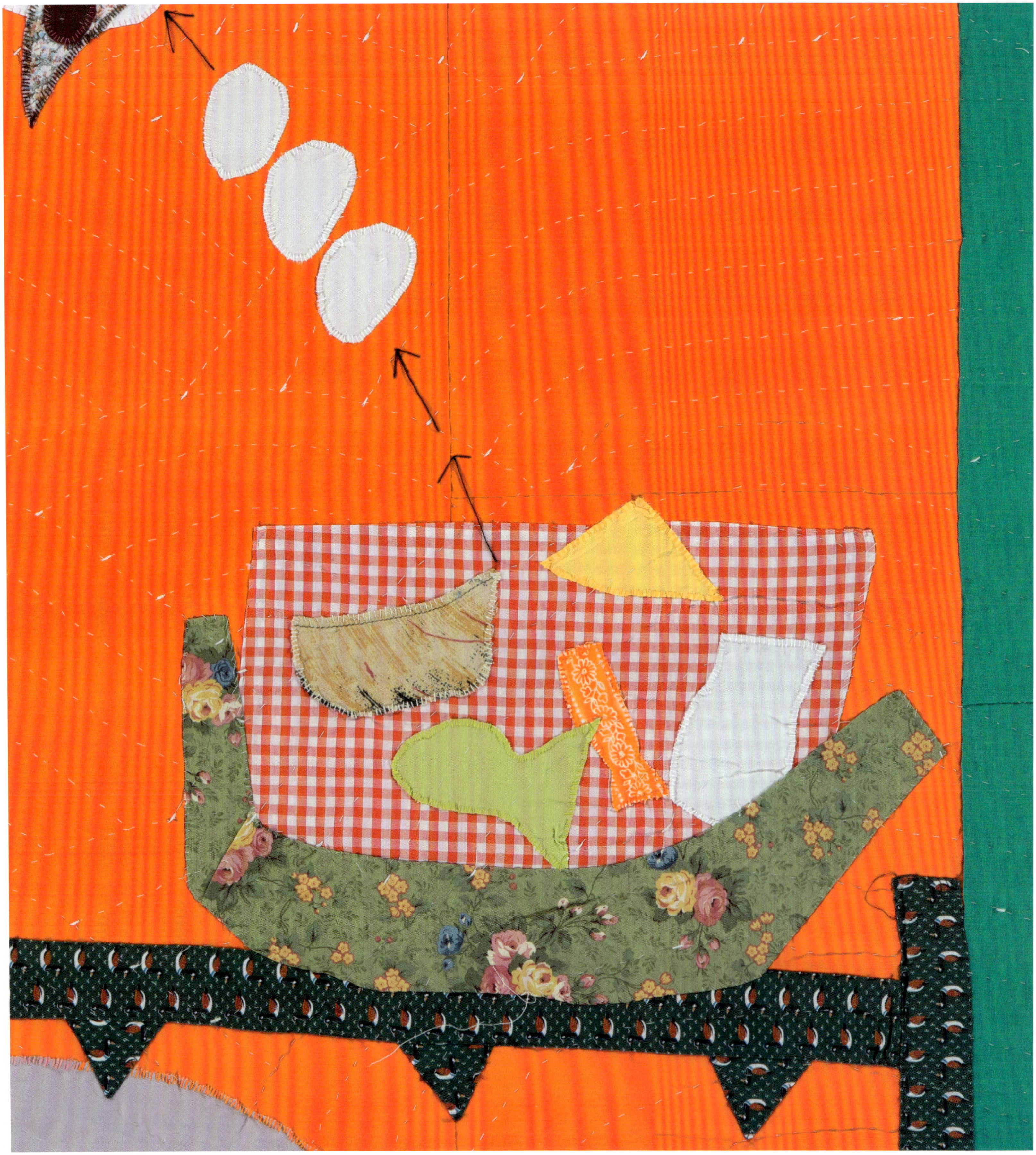

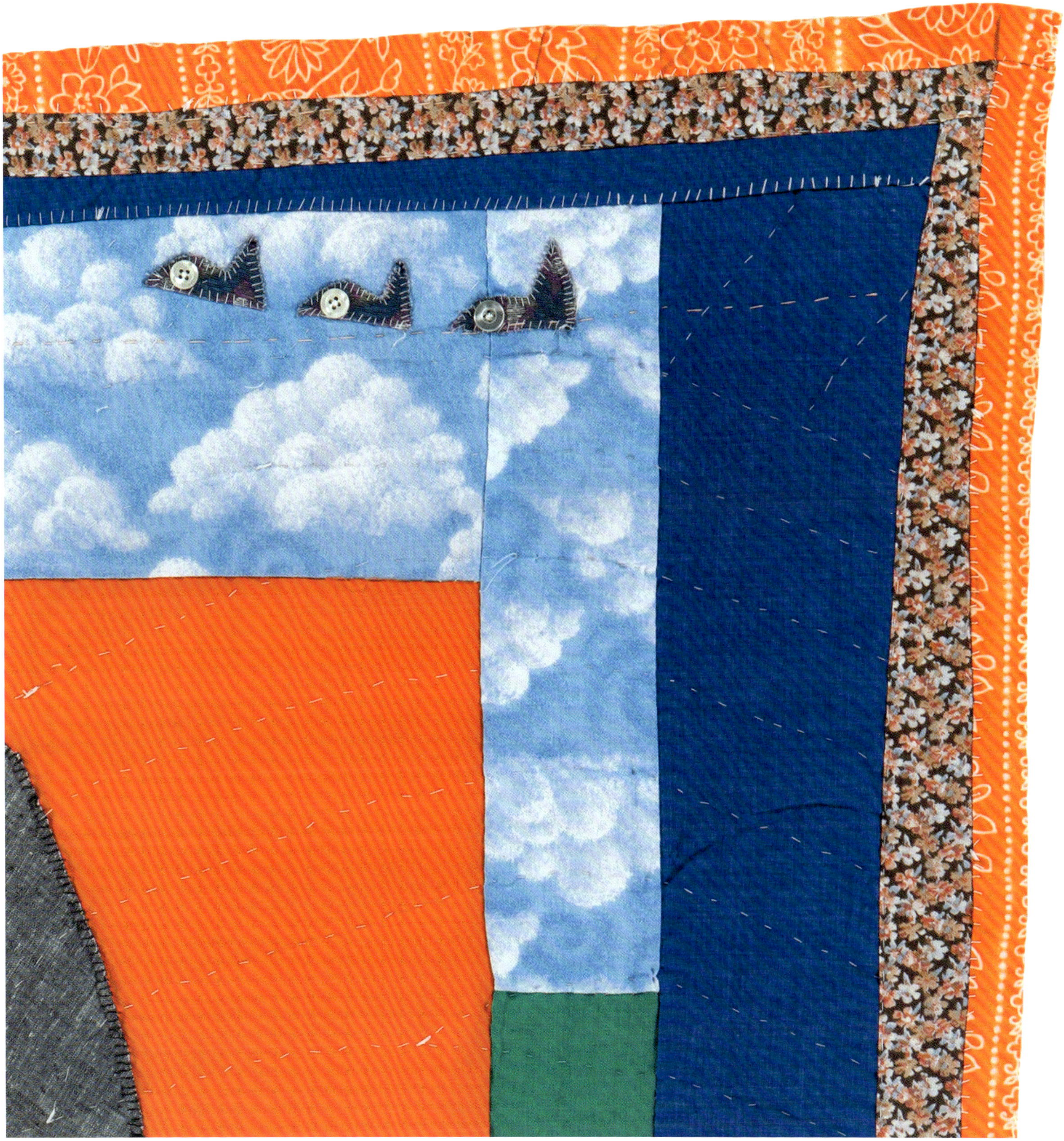

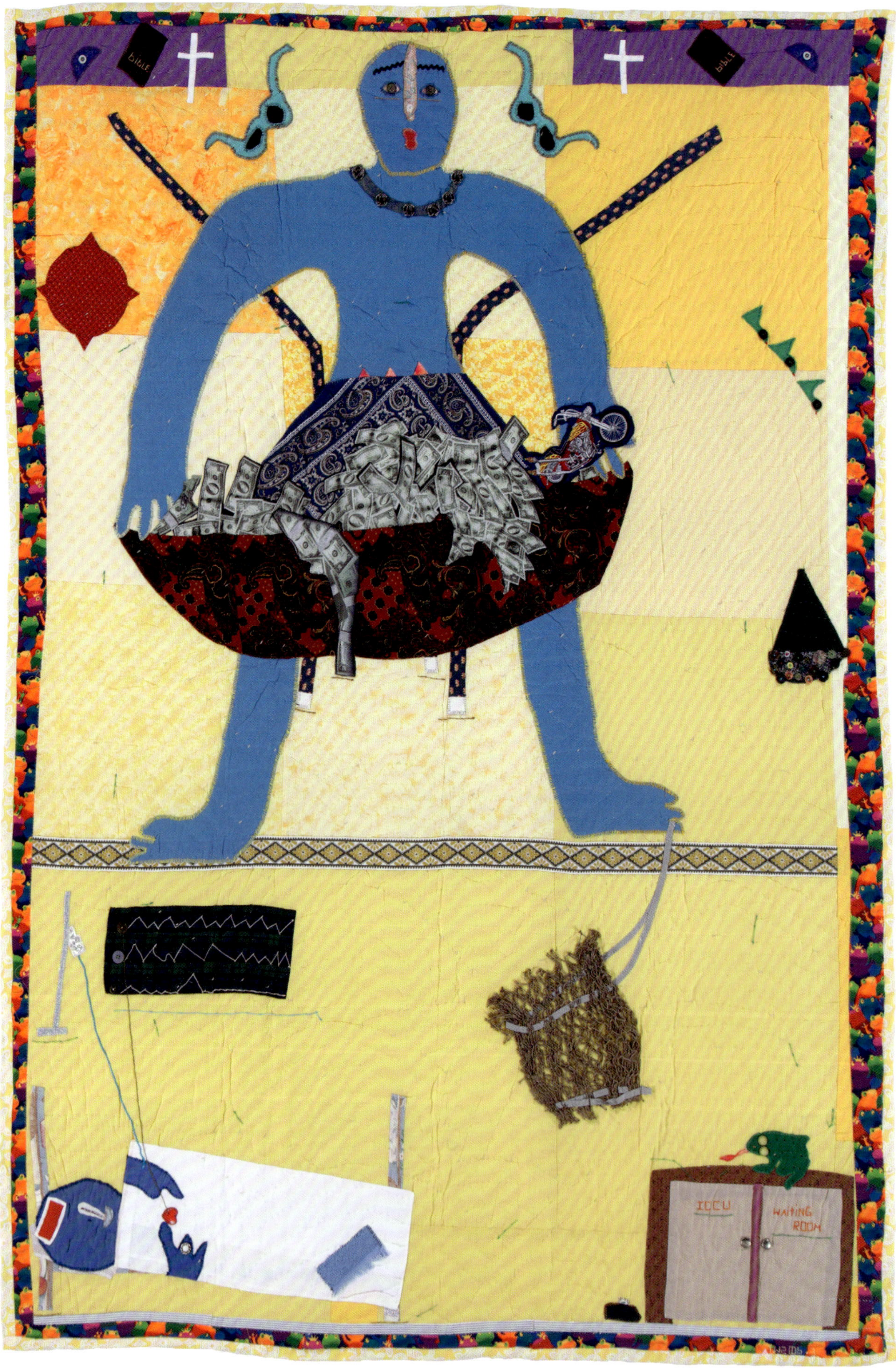
bible
bible
ICCU
WAITING ROOM

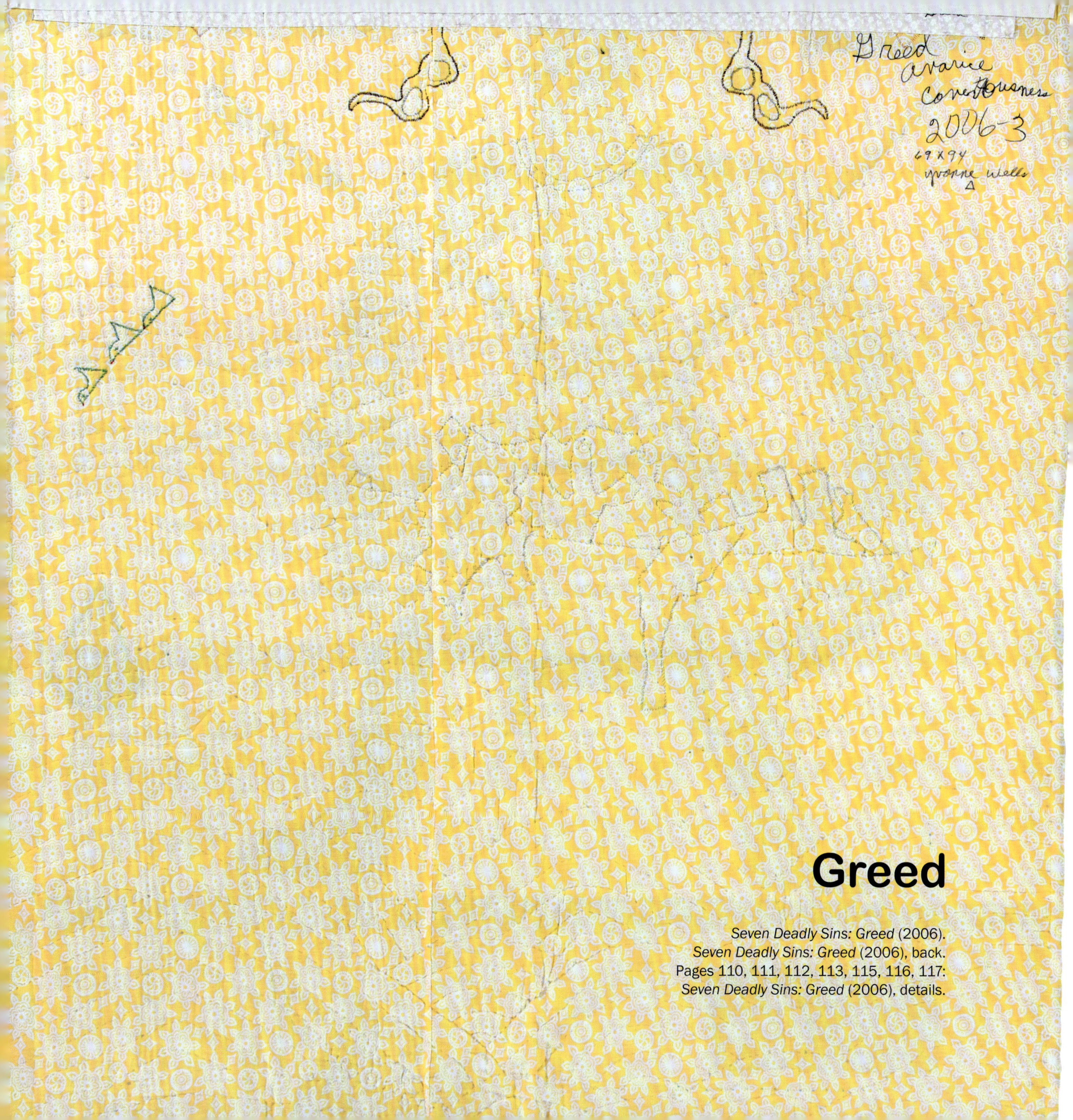

Greed

Seven Deadly Sins: Greed (2006).
Seven Deadly Sins: Greed (2006), back.
Pages 110, 111, 112, 113, 115, 116, 117:
Seven Deadly Sins: Greed (2006), details.

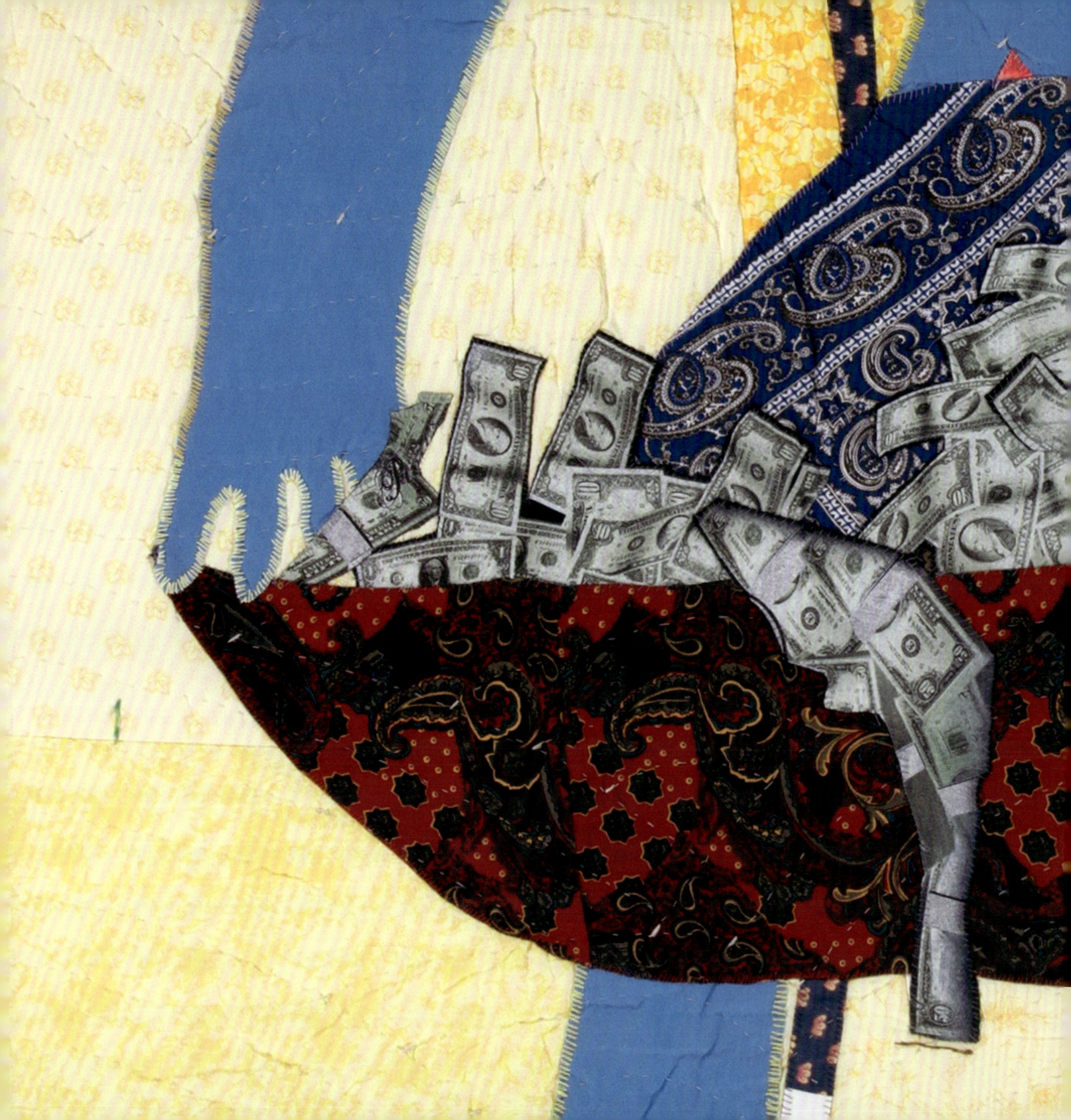

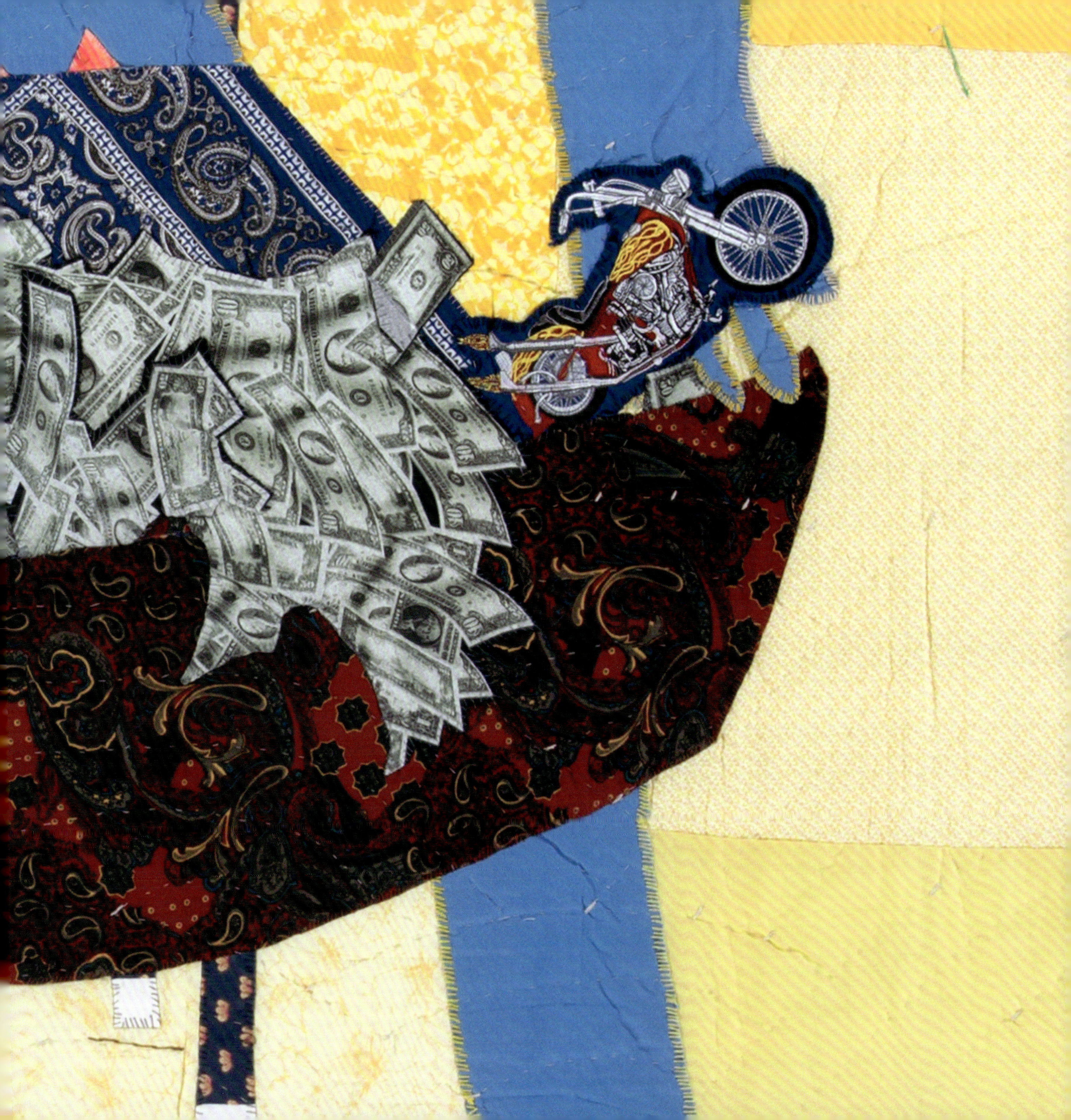

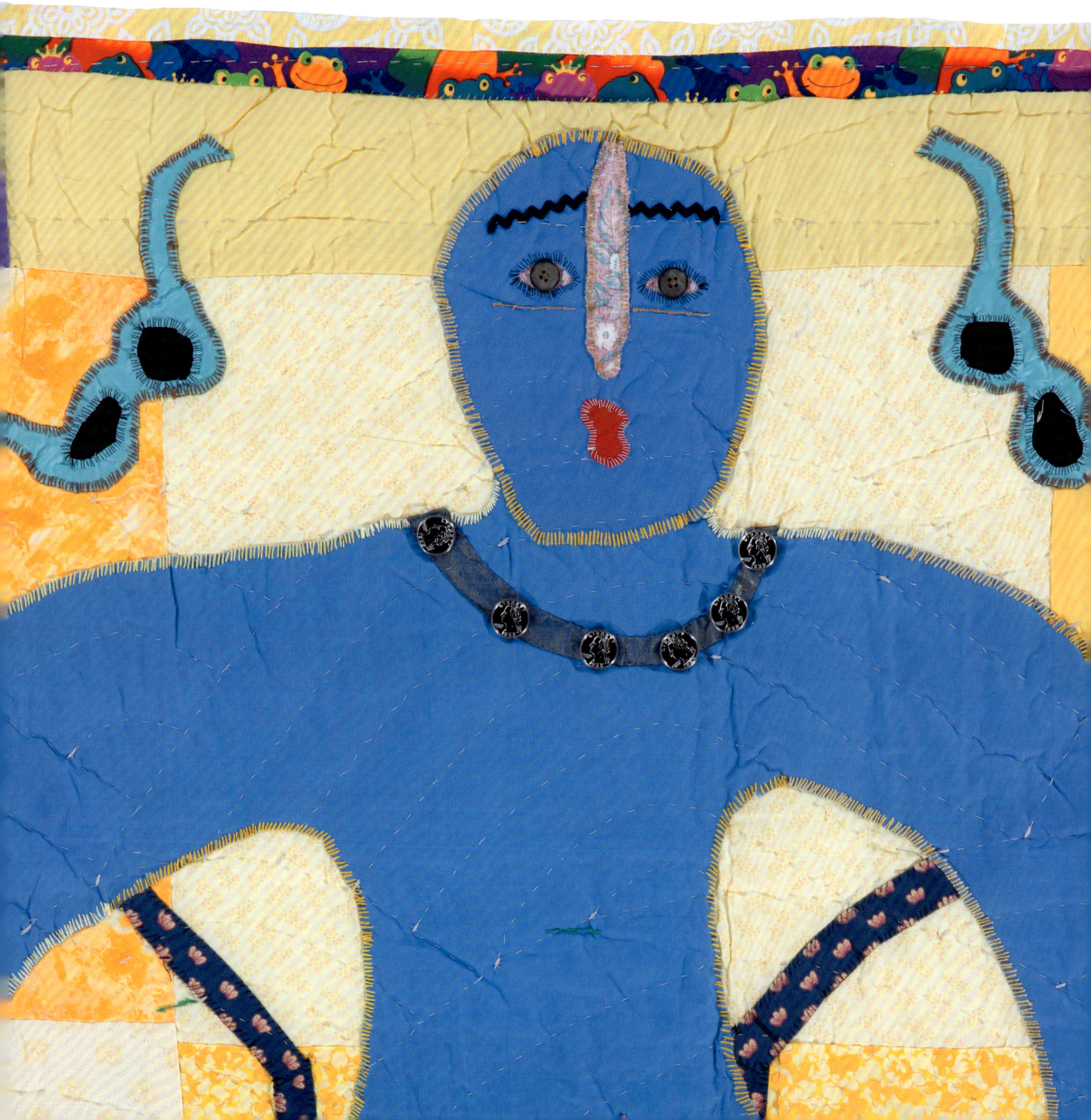

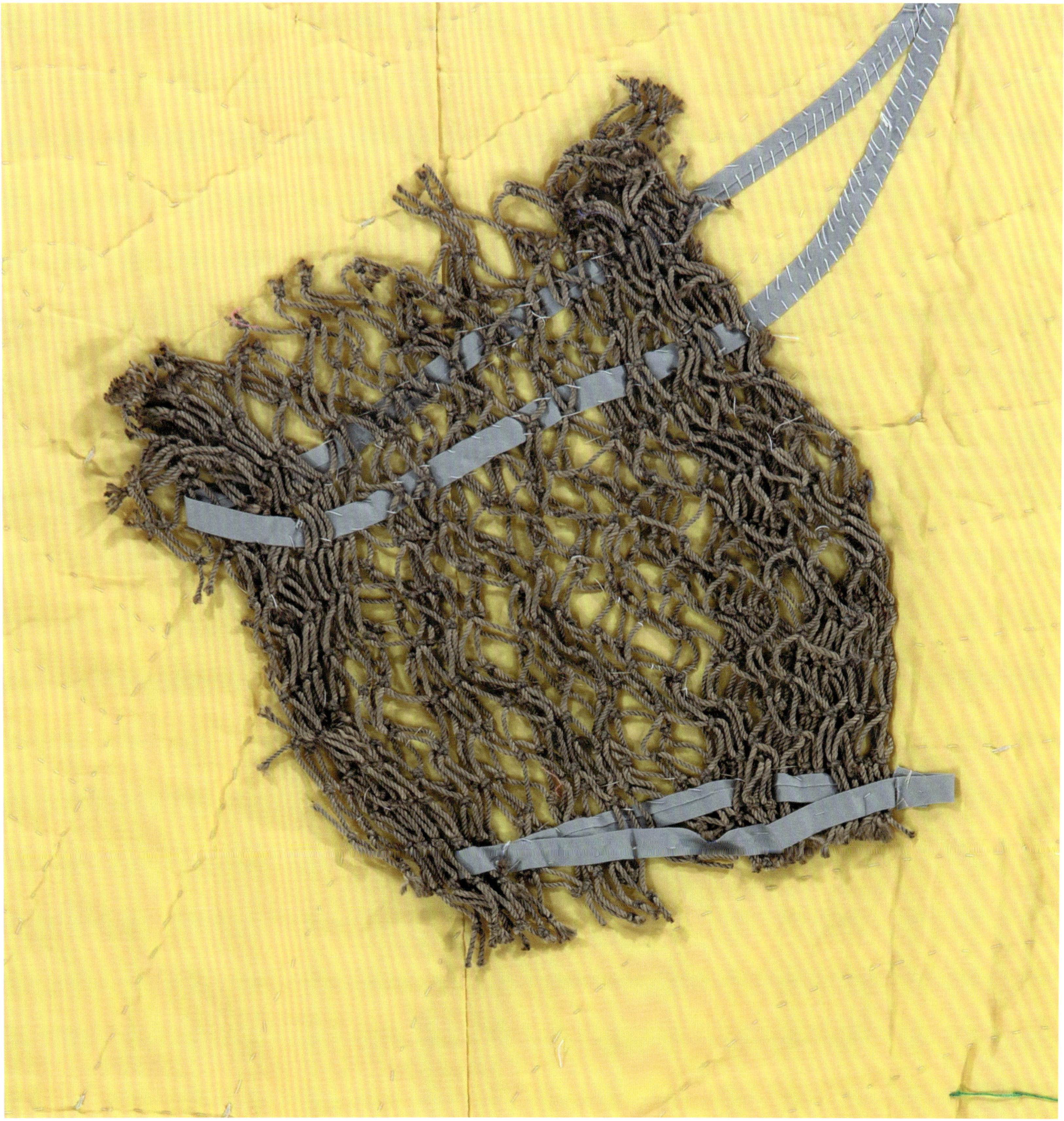

Greed

Everybody knows exactly what this quilt is about. This one is *Greed*. I went out and I found this sweater with this print of dollar bills on it, and it was perfect for my story because this man was destined to get everything that he could get his hands on. This guy is a motorcycle dude, and you can see his motorcycle coming out of his basket of money. He wants to get the money and run away fast on his motorcycle.

There's even money around this guy's neck because he wants everything that looks like money. I went out searching for that money to put around his neck. There's also a large bag here that he's hoping to fill with money. It came from an old potato sack that I had in my kitchen.

There are two pairs of eyeglasses placed on either side of him because he didn't want anybody to see him from the left or the right. He especially didn't want the Lord to see him because he knew he was wrong.

Down in the lower half of this quilt is a man who went to the hospital and sat around and waited for his loved one to die. He's sitting around in the intensive care waiting room, hoping they will die soon so he can get their money. But he was impatient. You can see I added a heart monitor. And this guy is hoping his relative will die from a heart attack or heart problems. If you look closely at the monitor, you can see heart rate lines going up and down. Eventually, the heart rate starts to get slower and slower.

Over on the right side, I also included an upside-down ice cream cone. It's upside-down because it represents death.

The color for greed is yellow, and the animal is the frog. There are also frogs in the border fabric.

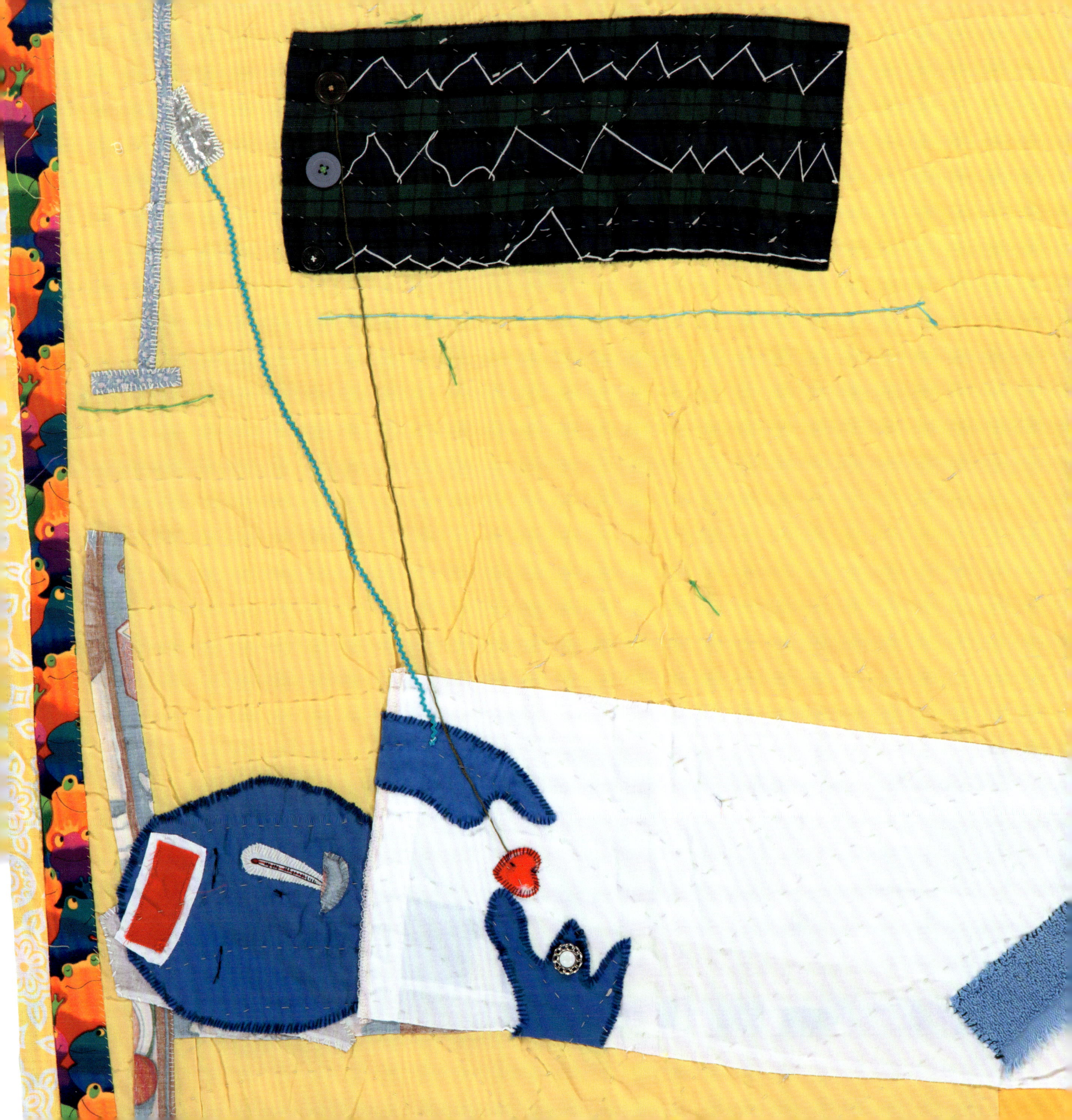

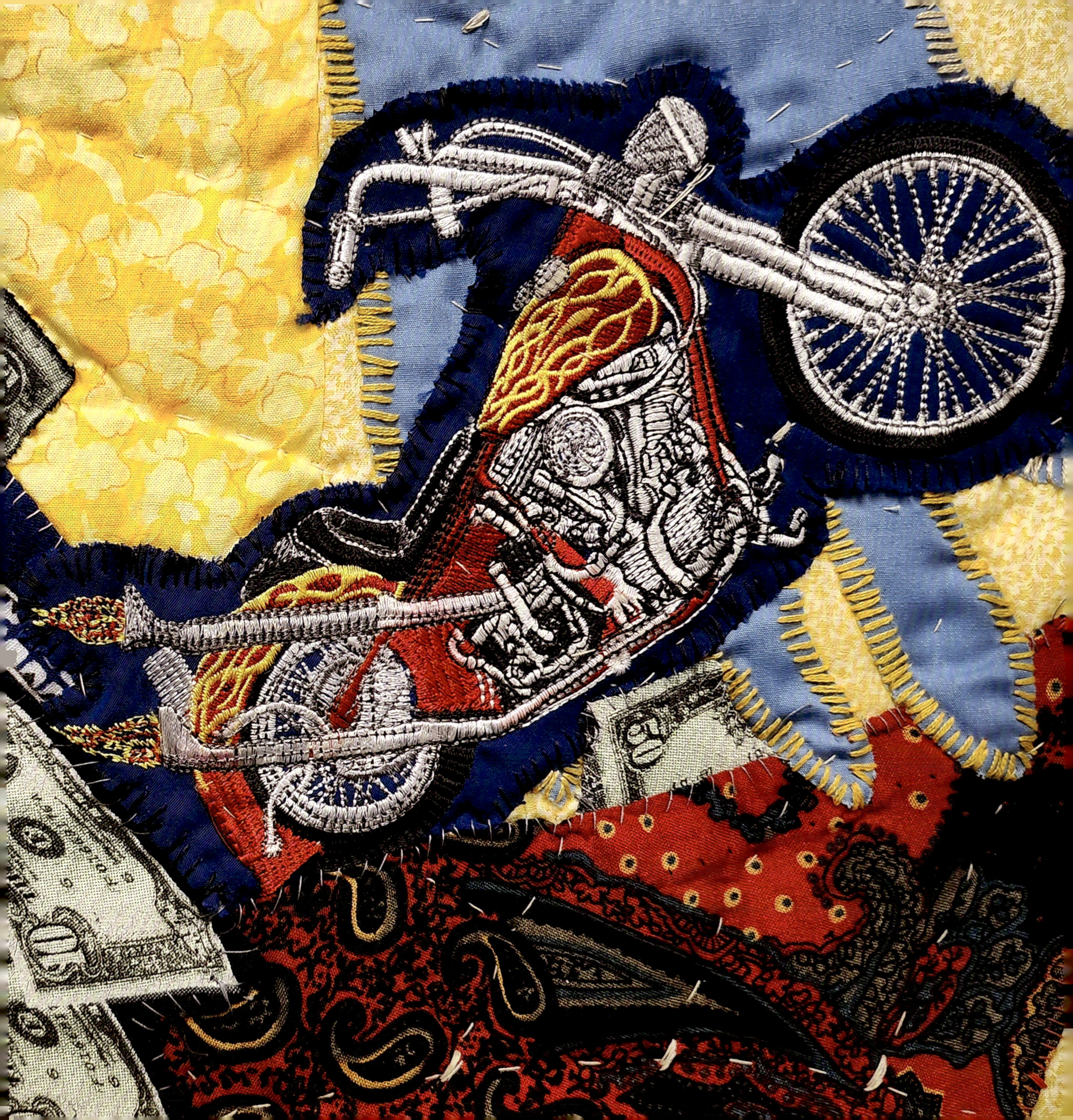

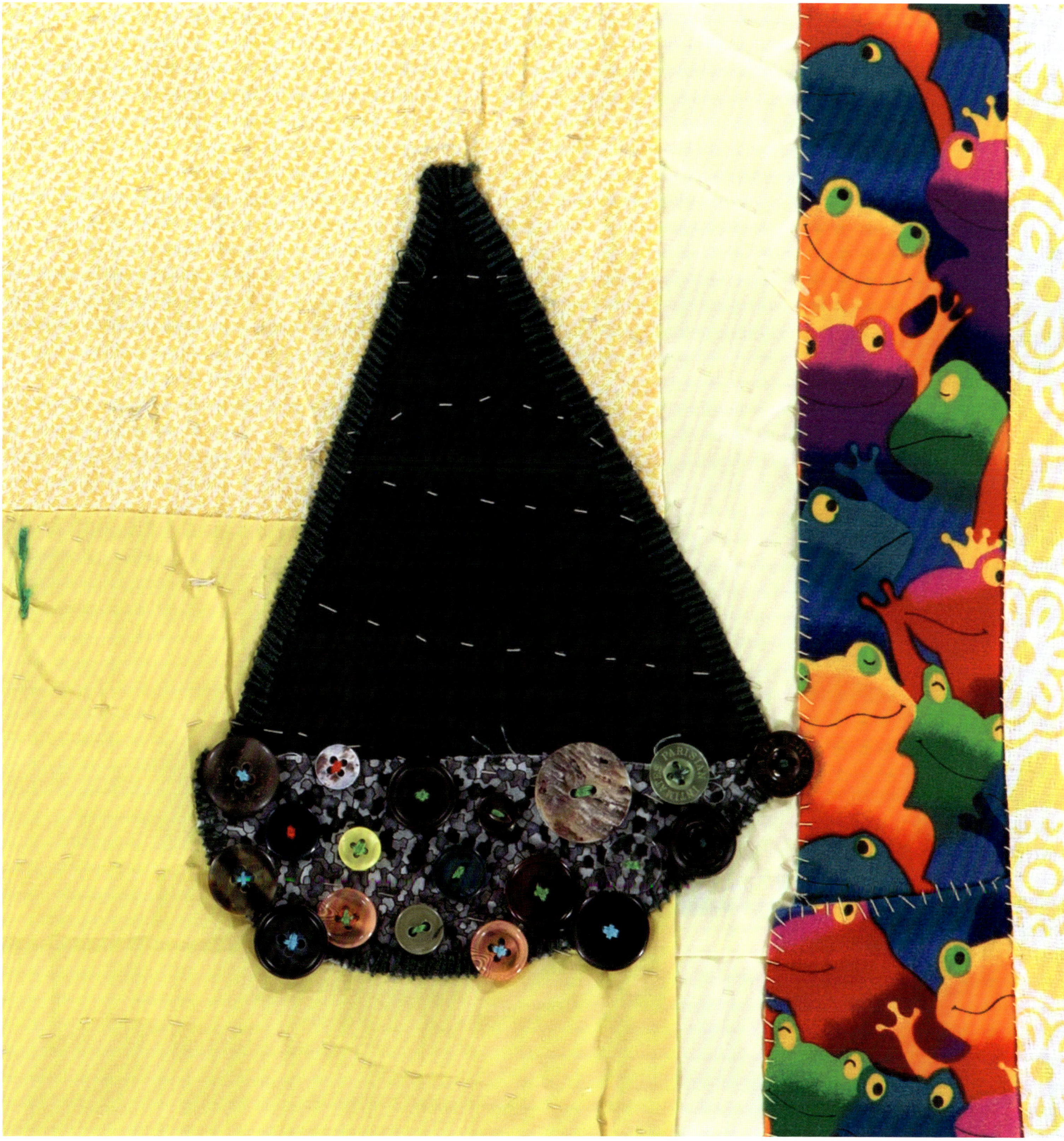

Sloth

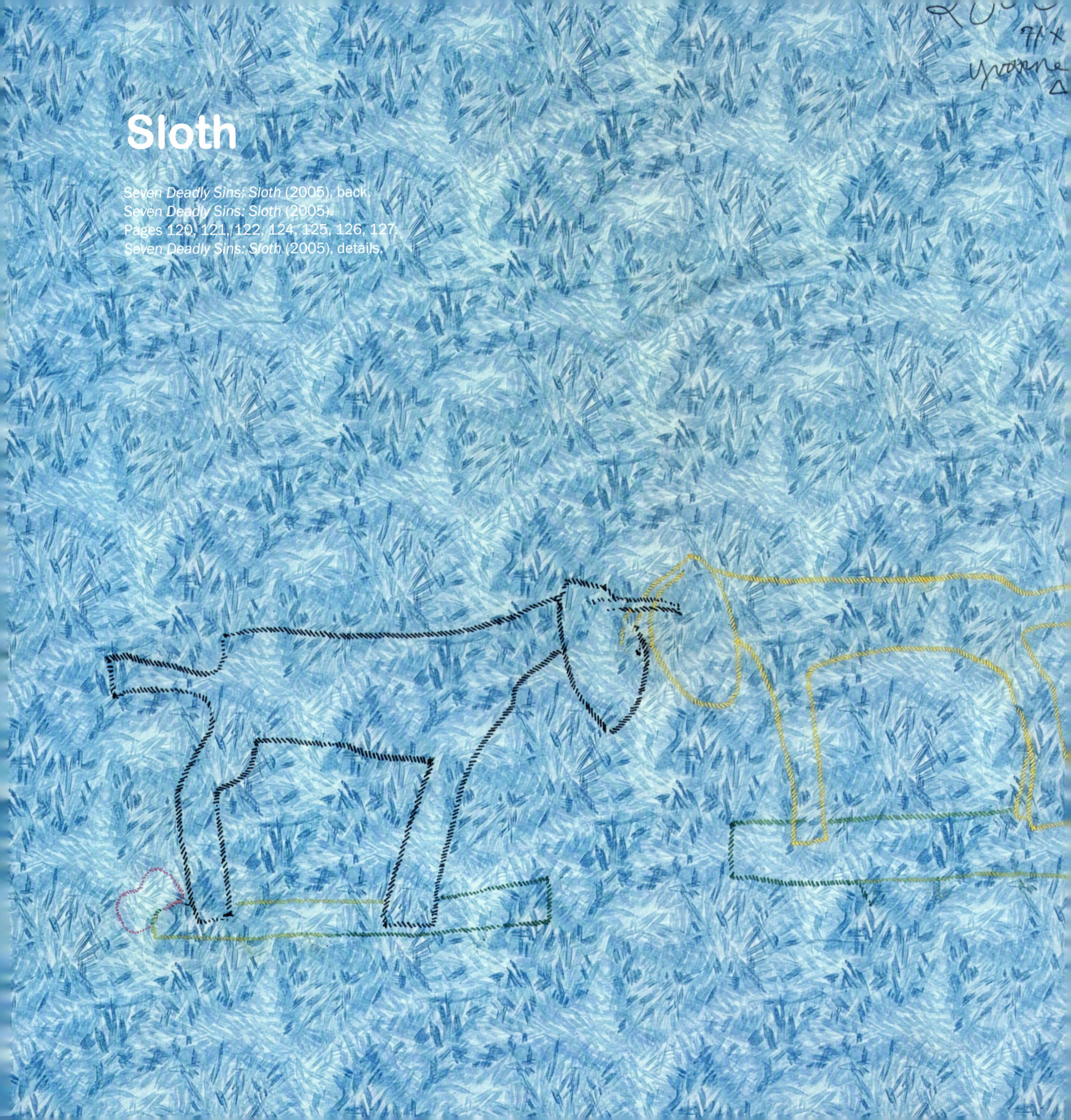

Seven Deadly Sins: Sloth (2005), back.
Seven Deadly Sins: Sloth (2005).
Pages 120, 121, 122, 124, 125, 126, 127:
Seven Deadly Sins: Sloth (2005), details.

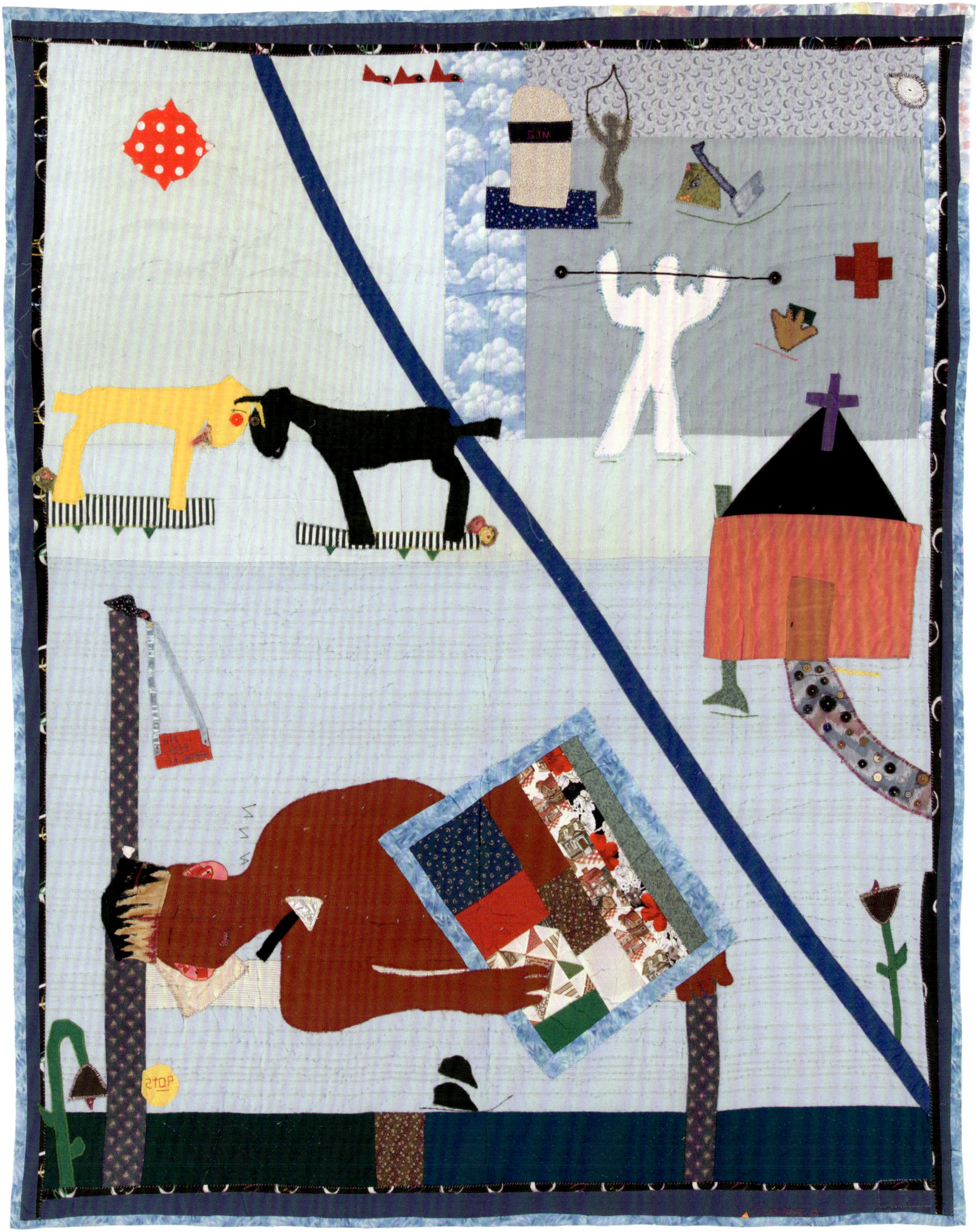
STOP

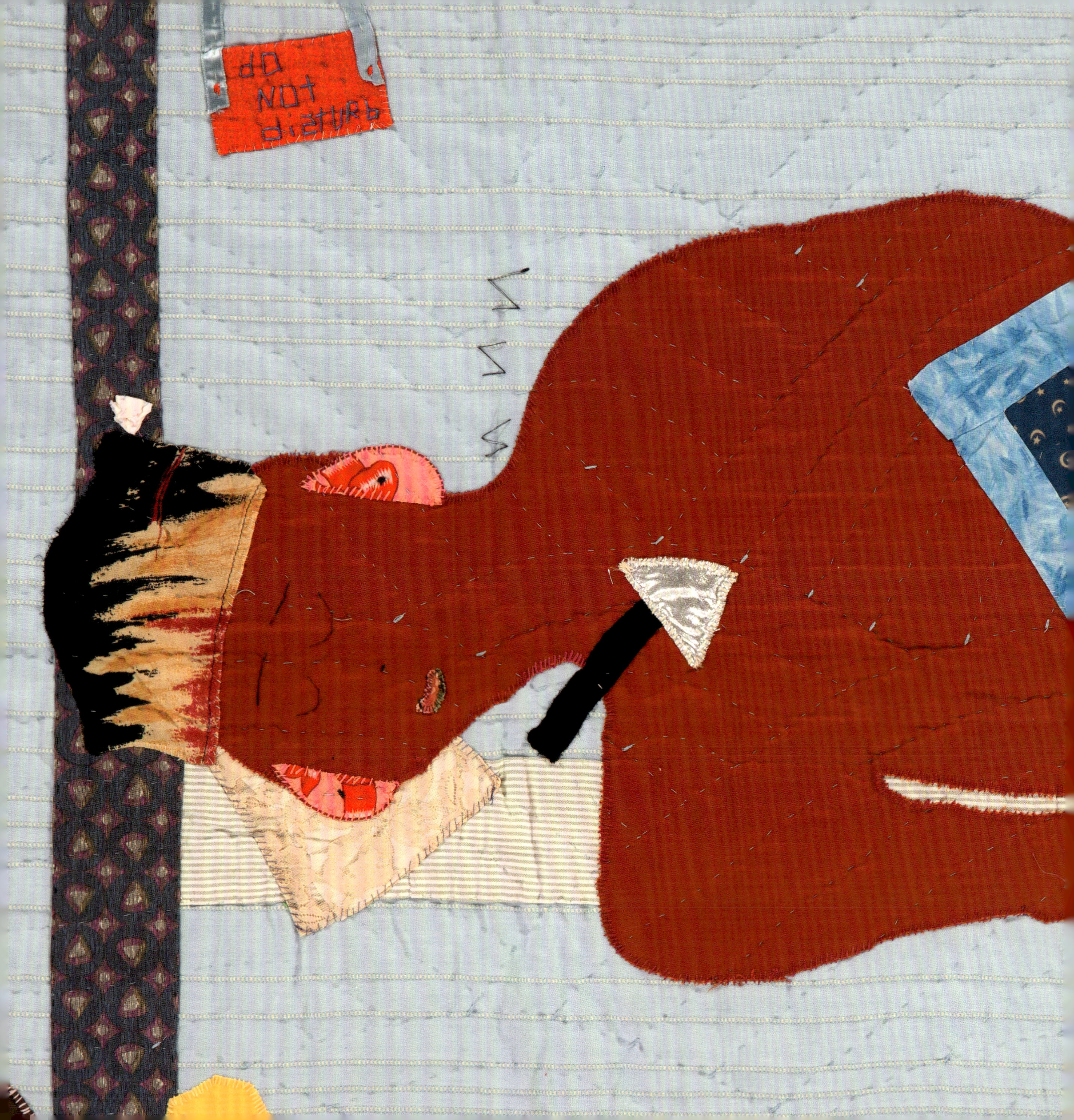
do NOT disturb

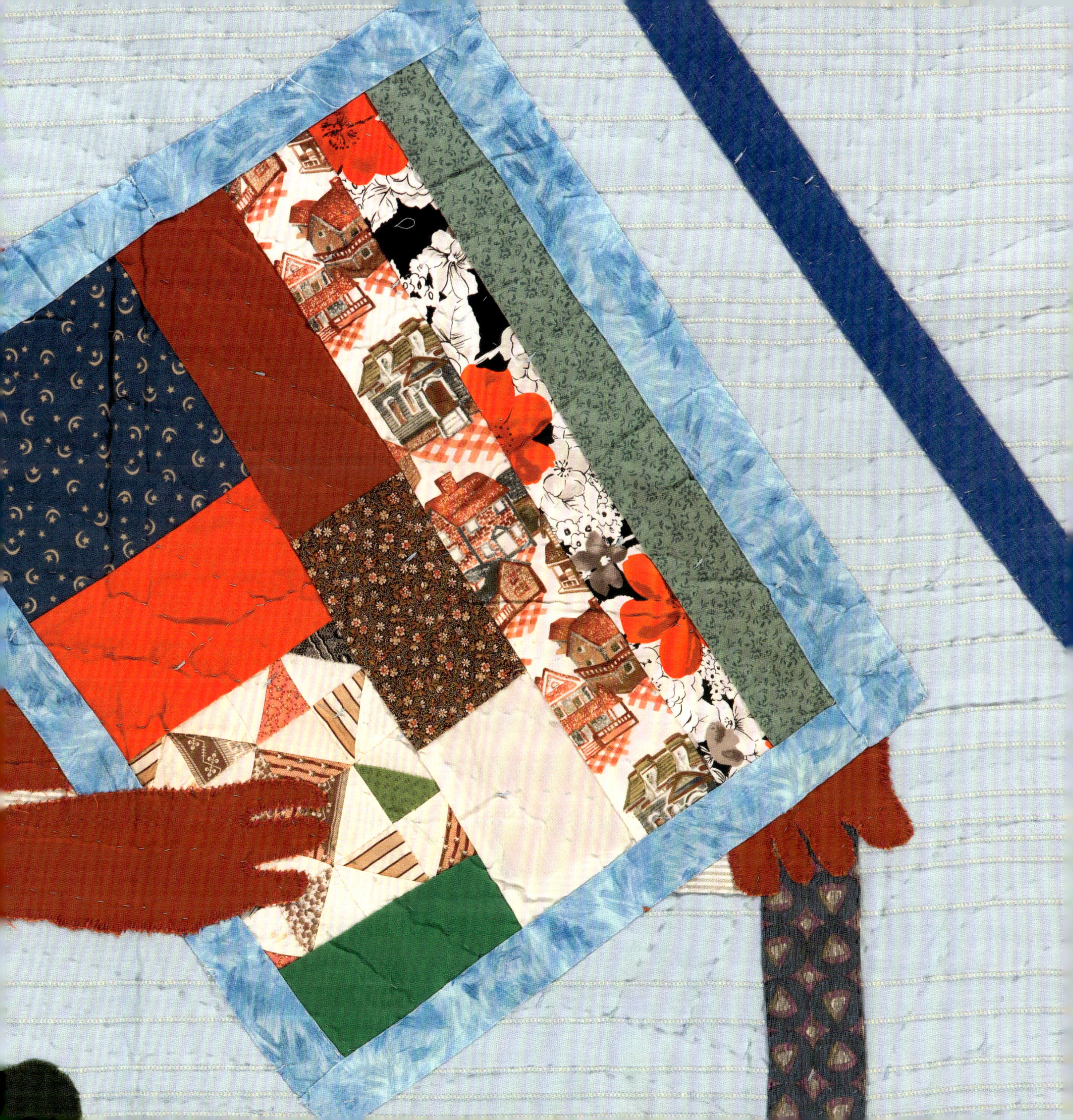

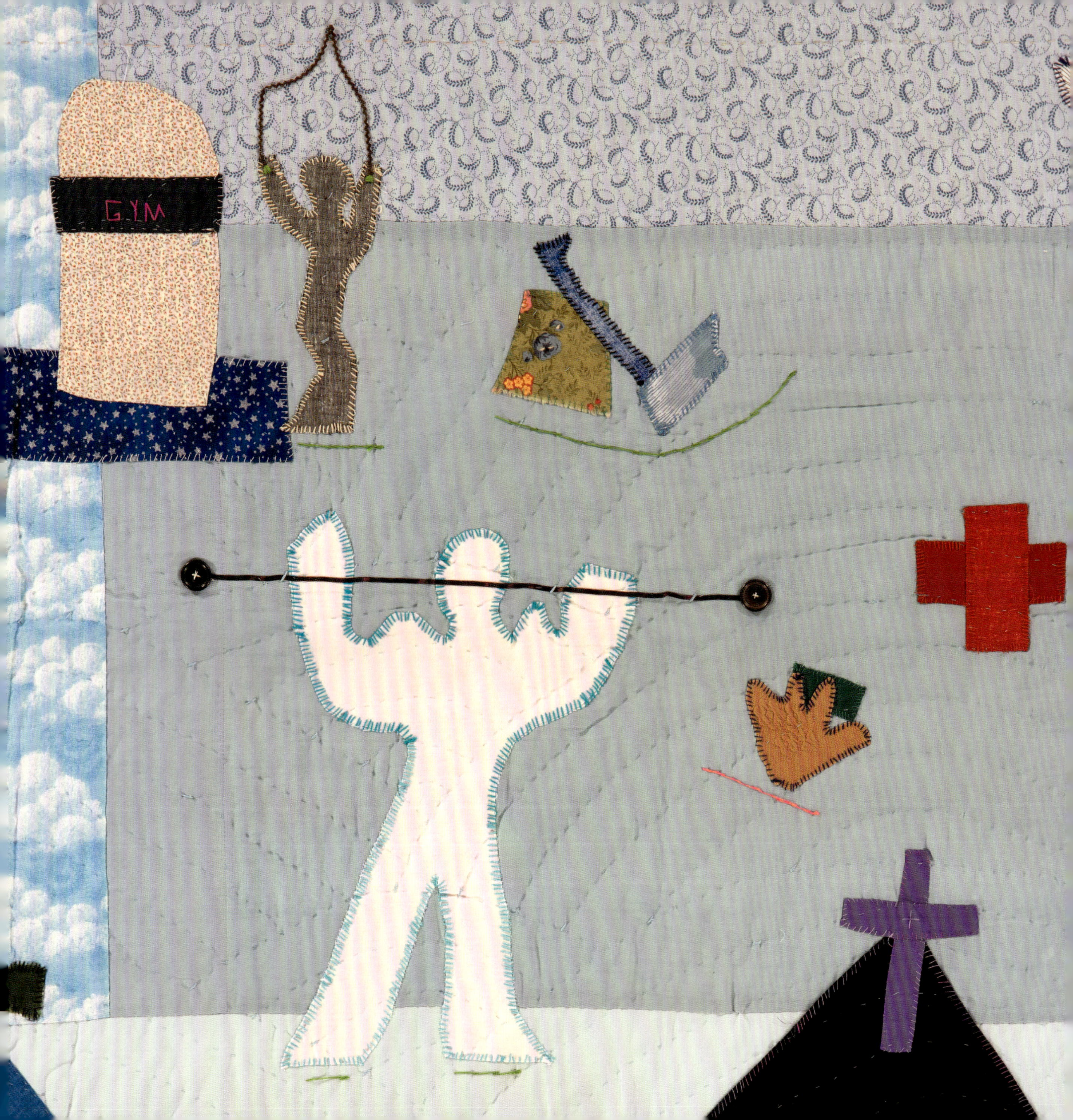
GYM

Sloth

The fourth sin in the series is *Sloth*. This one is especially sad to me because he's a very sorry guy. He just wants to sleep all the time. He put a sign on his bed that says "Do Not Disturb," and there's another sign down by his head that says "Stop." That means no one should go in the room where he's asleep because he doesn't want to be disturbed.

This guy doesn't want to go to church. He doesn't want to exercise. He doesn't want to donate to the Red Cross. He doesn't want to work. He just didn't want to do anything. He just decided to go to bed and sleep. So, I had to help him out, you know; I made a quilt and put it on him so he could go to sleep.

There is a series of *Z's* near his mouth showing he's snoozing. And you can also see that I added his chewing gum on the bedpost. I wonder, does his chewing gum lose its flavor on the bedpost at night? I don't know. But he put it there so he can get up and put it back in his mouth the next morning.

The animal for sloth is the goat, and the color is light blue. My grandson drew a pattern for these goats because I just couldn't get it right. So, I used his pattern for the two goats and cut them out.

The upper right corner is a gym. This person didn't want to exercise, right? So, I included a man lifting weights there, and above him is another guy who is active and working, and he's busy cutting down a tree.

In the corner there is a small eye, and that is the all-seeing eye of God. Actually, you'll find that same eye in quite a few of the pieces that I make. I can't make a quilt without including references to God, and I don't try.

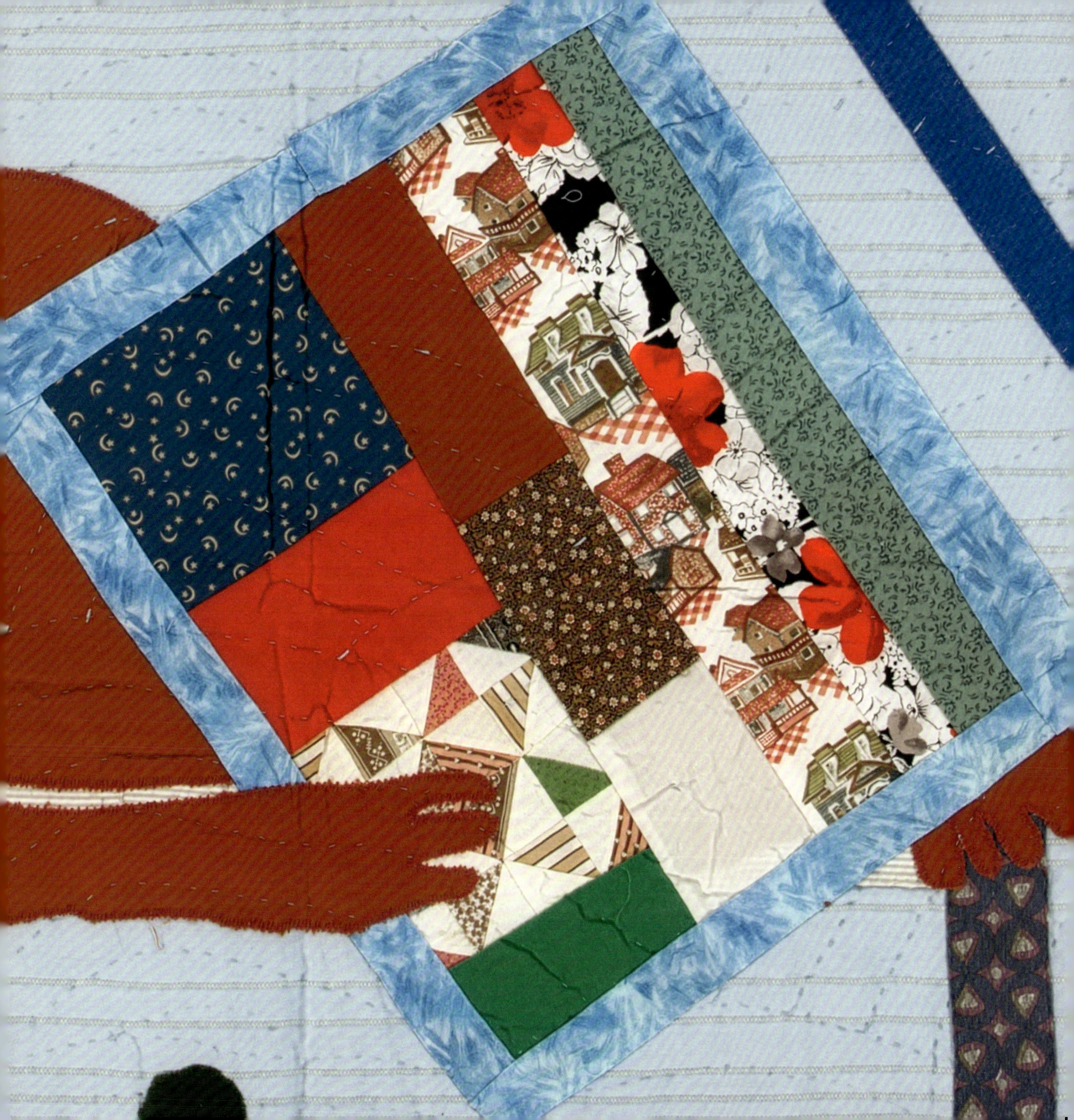

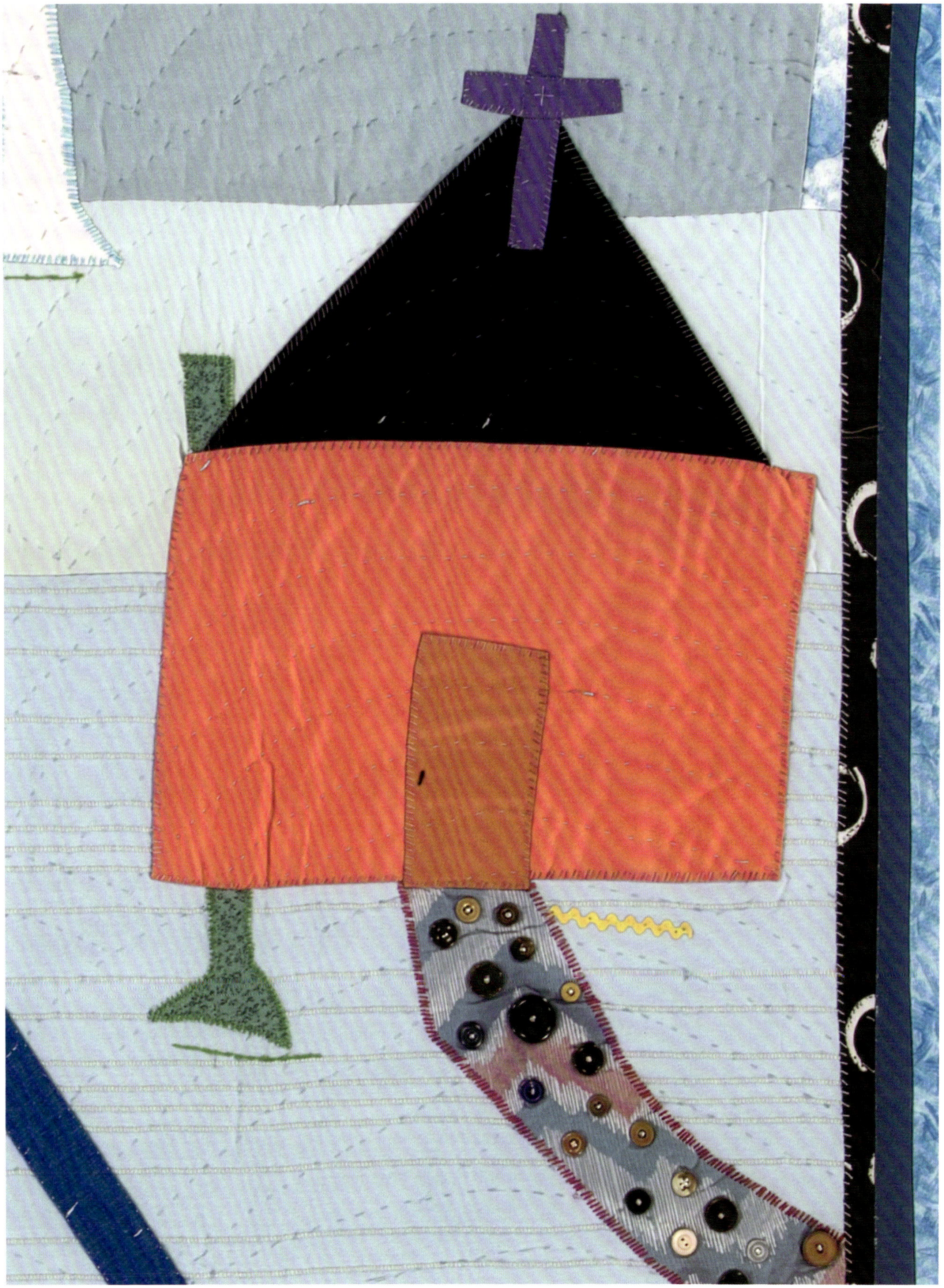

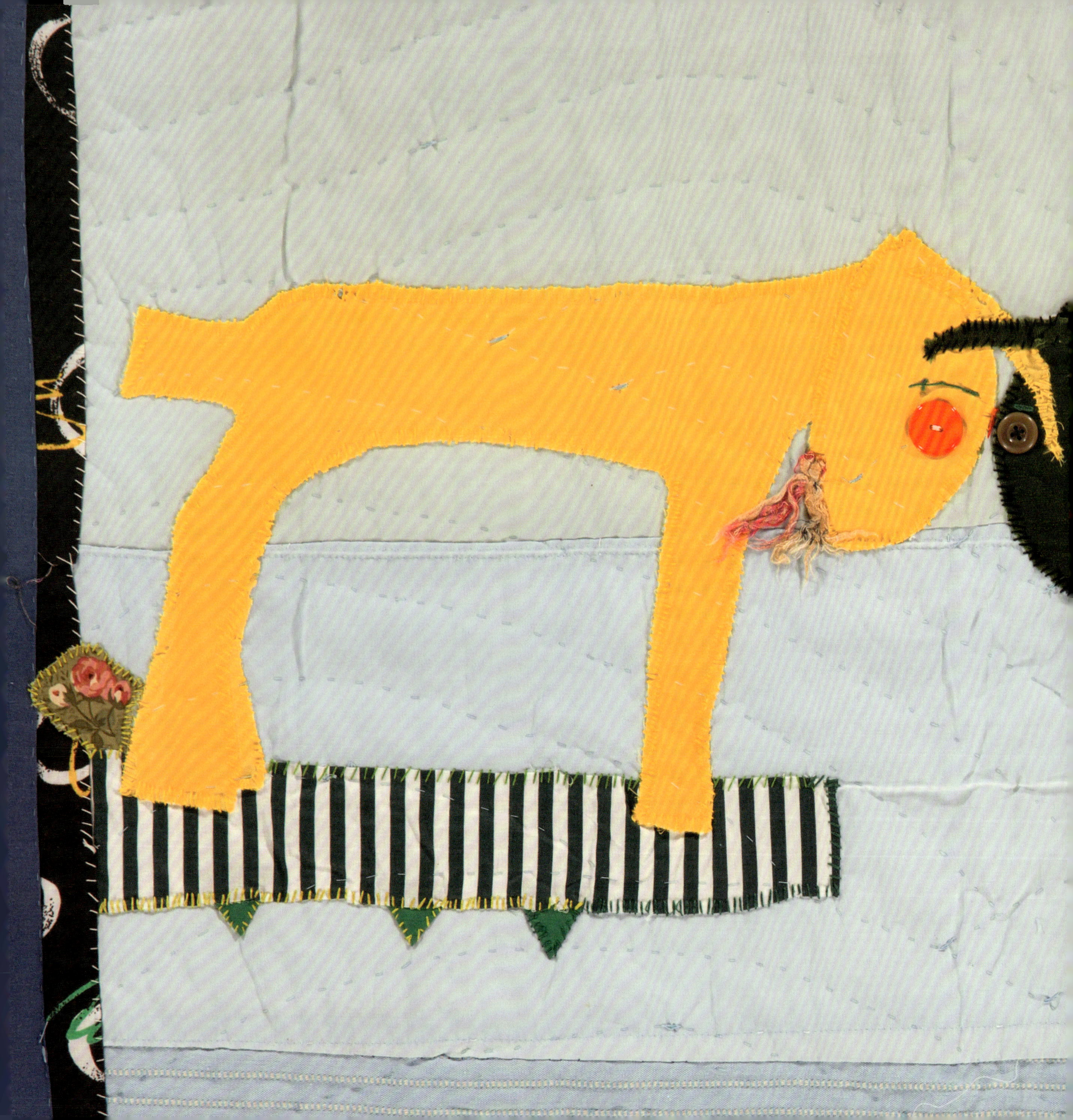

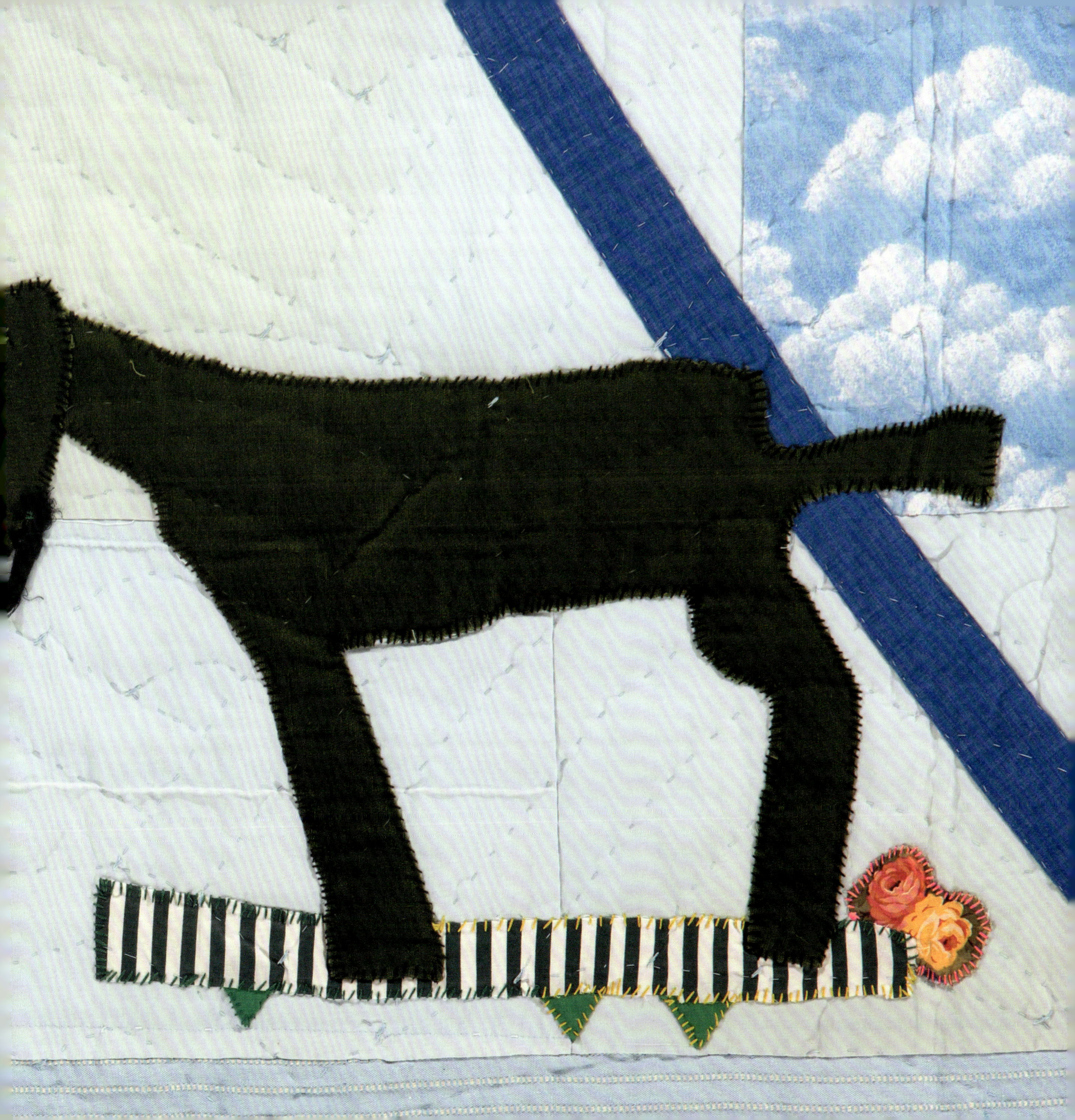

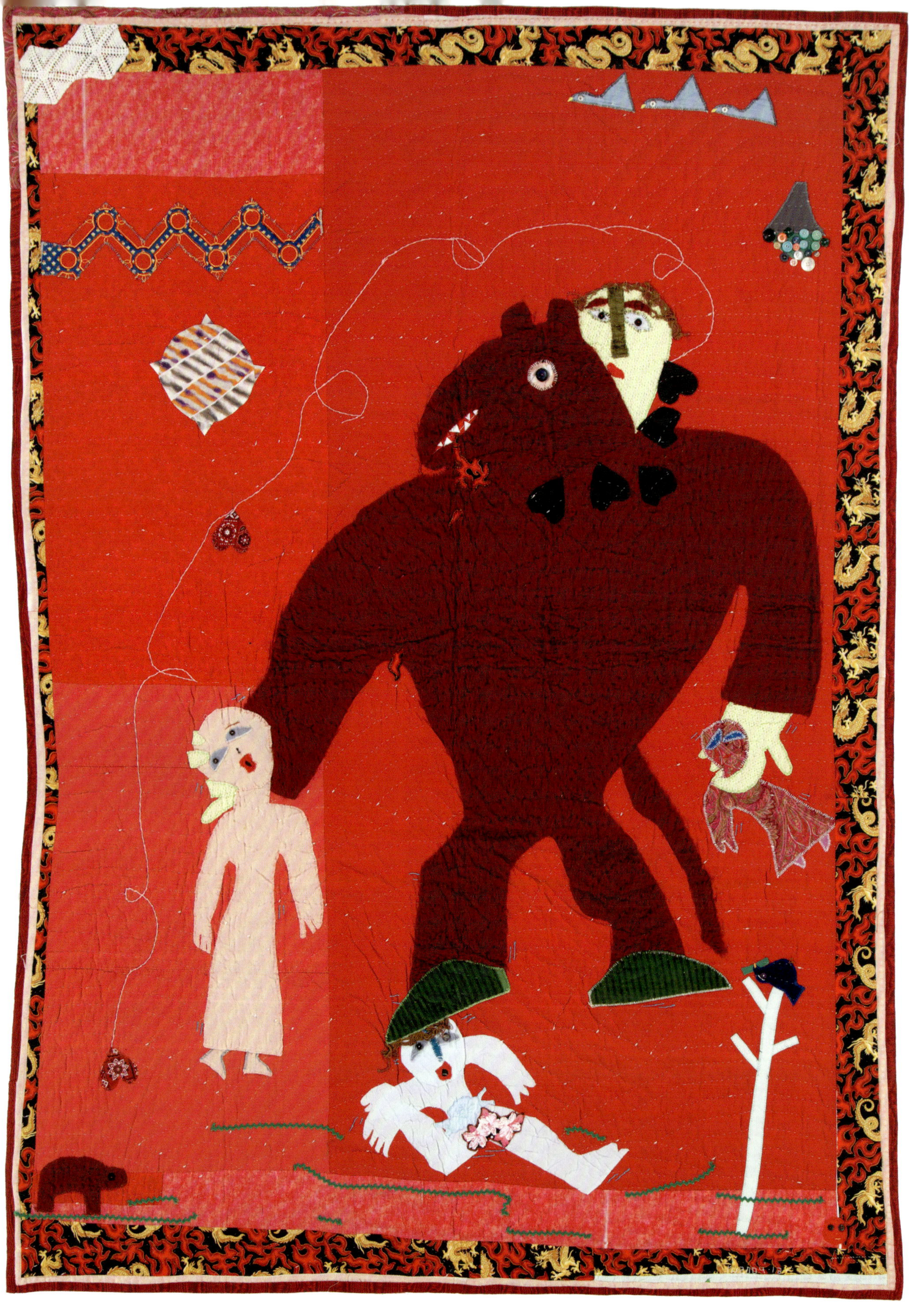

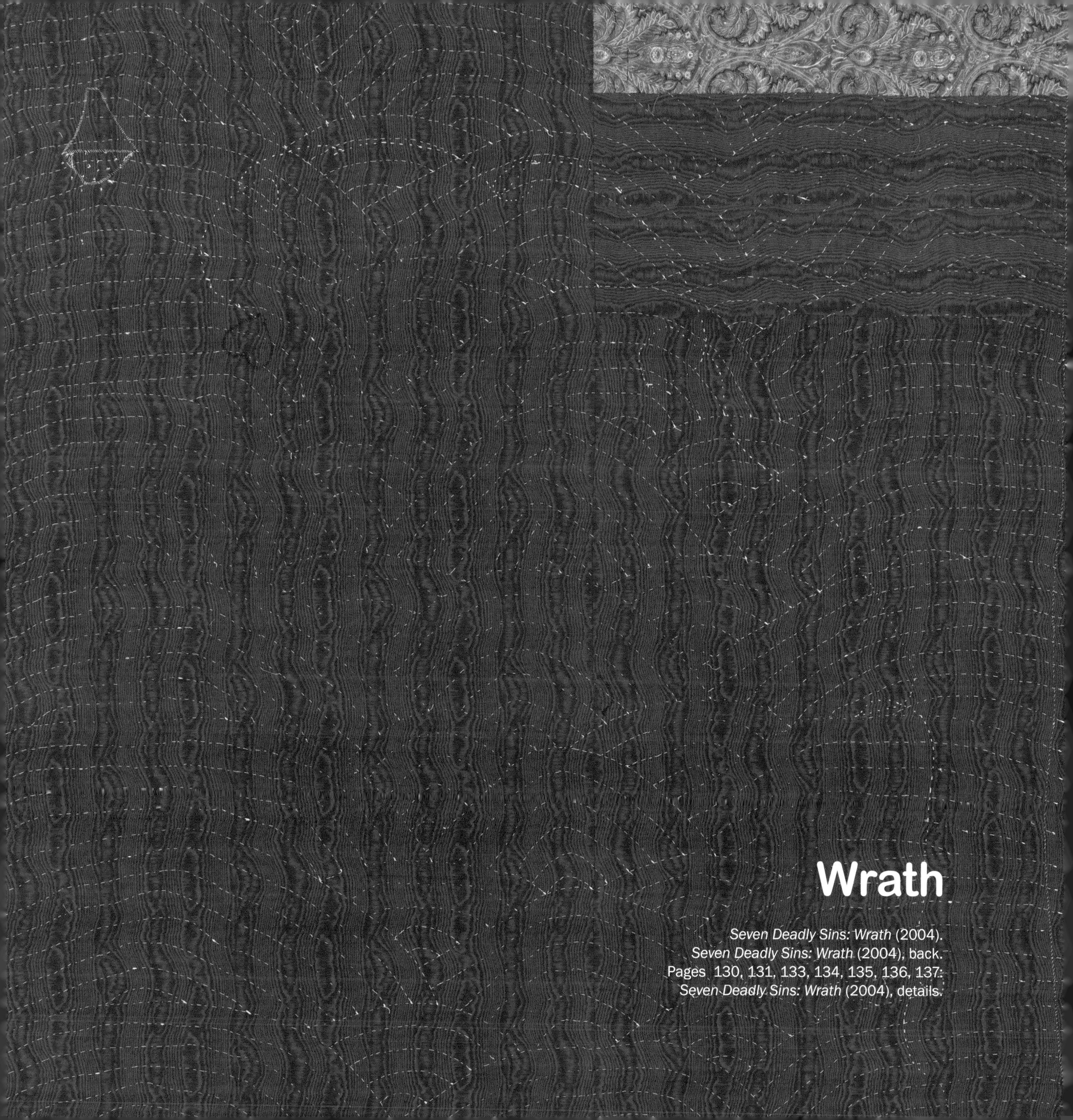

Wrath

Seven Deadly Sins: Wrath (2004).
Seven Deadly Sins: Wrath (2004), back.
Pages 130, 131, 133, 134, 135, 136, 137: *Seven Deadly Sins: Wrath* (2004), details.

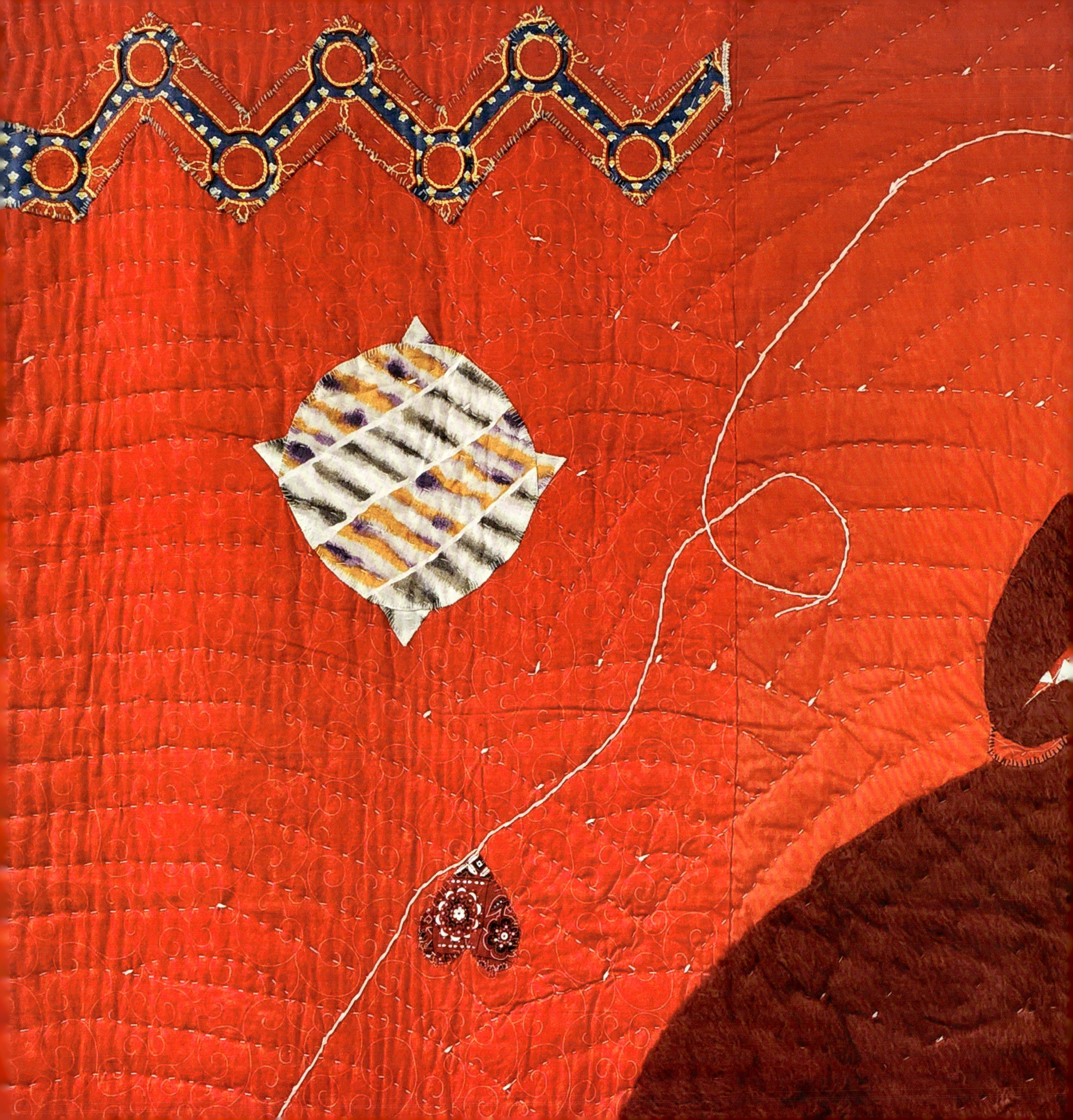

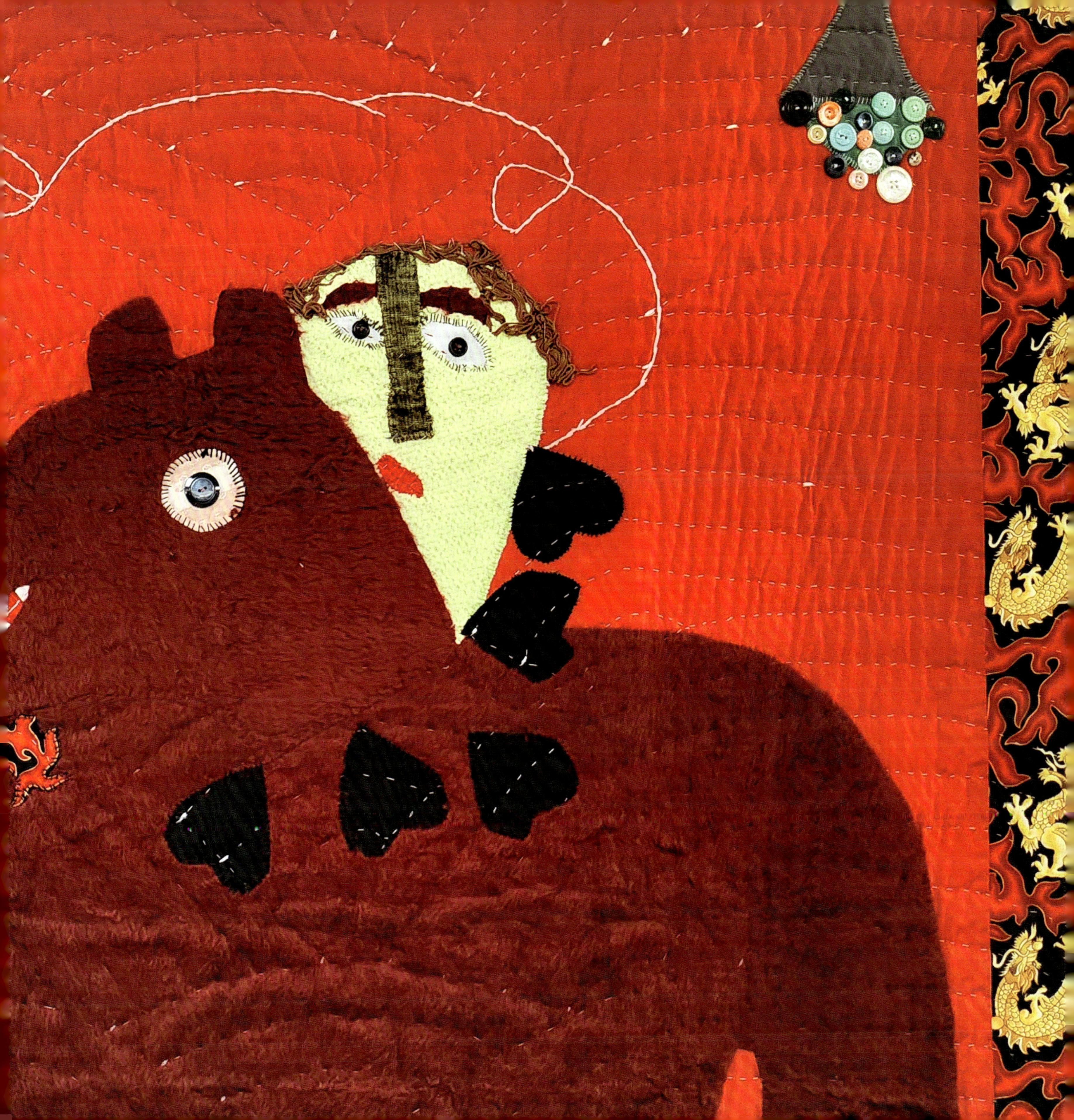

Wrath

Wrath is the first quilt in this series that I made. I don't know why I started with wrath, but I just had this vision for how it should tell my story. The animal for wrath is the bear, so I started with him. I pictured him as this really big bear, and he thinks he is the king of the castle.

The color for wrath is fire red, and I put a lot of red in this quilt, especially this red fur. I found this unusual fur to make the bear, and I was fascinated by it. I was especially grateful that I found something that I could sew through without having such a hard time.

The bear has actually transformed from a man to an animal. He has all these women here in his grasp, and he's treating them like dirt. He's shaking one and stepping on another woman. He's squeezing them too. He's doing all the wrong things to these women because they wouldn't accept his desires.

If you look around the neck of the man and the bear, there are black upside-down hearts. The black is meant to depict ugliness, and they are upside-down because his heart is all wrong. There is another upside-down ice cream cone here, and I sewed on buttons to make the ice cream. And right above the cone are the three birds that represent the Trinity.

Around the border the fabric has flames in it, and I bought this fabric because I really wanted to emulate fire. The bear is even spitting flames out of his mouth because he is so angry.

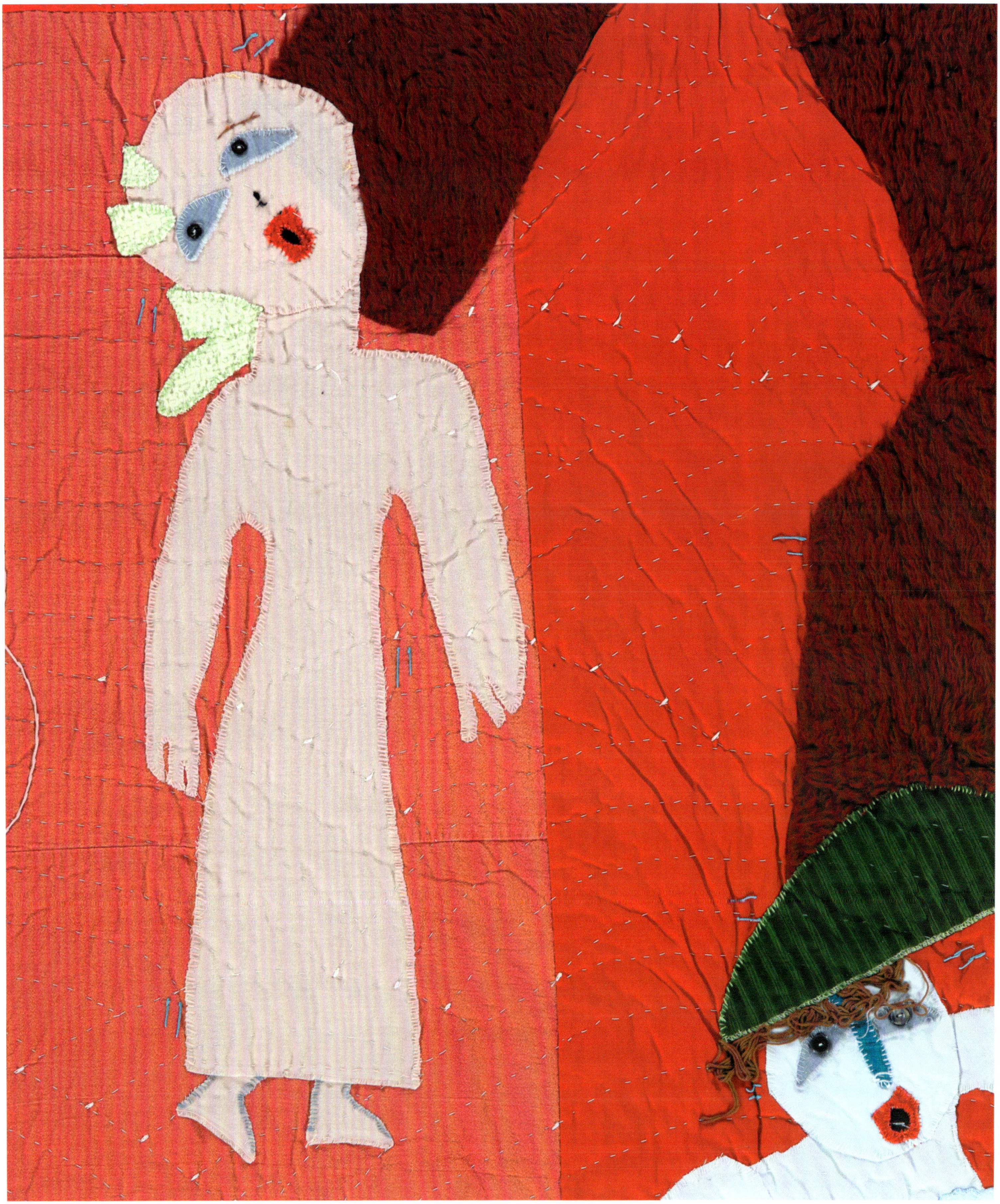

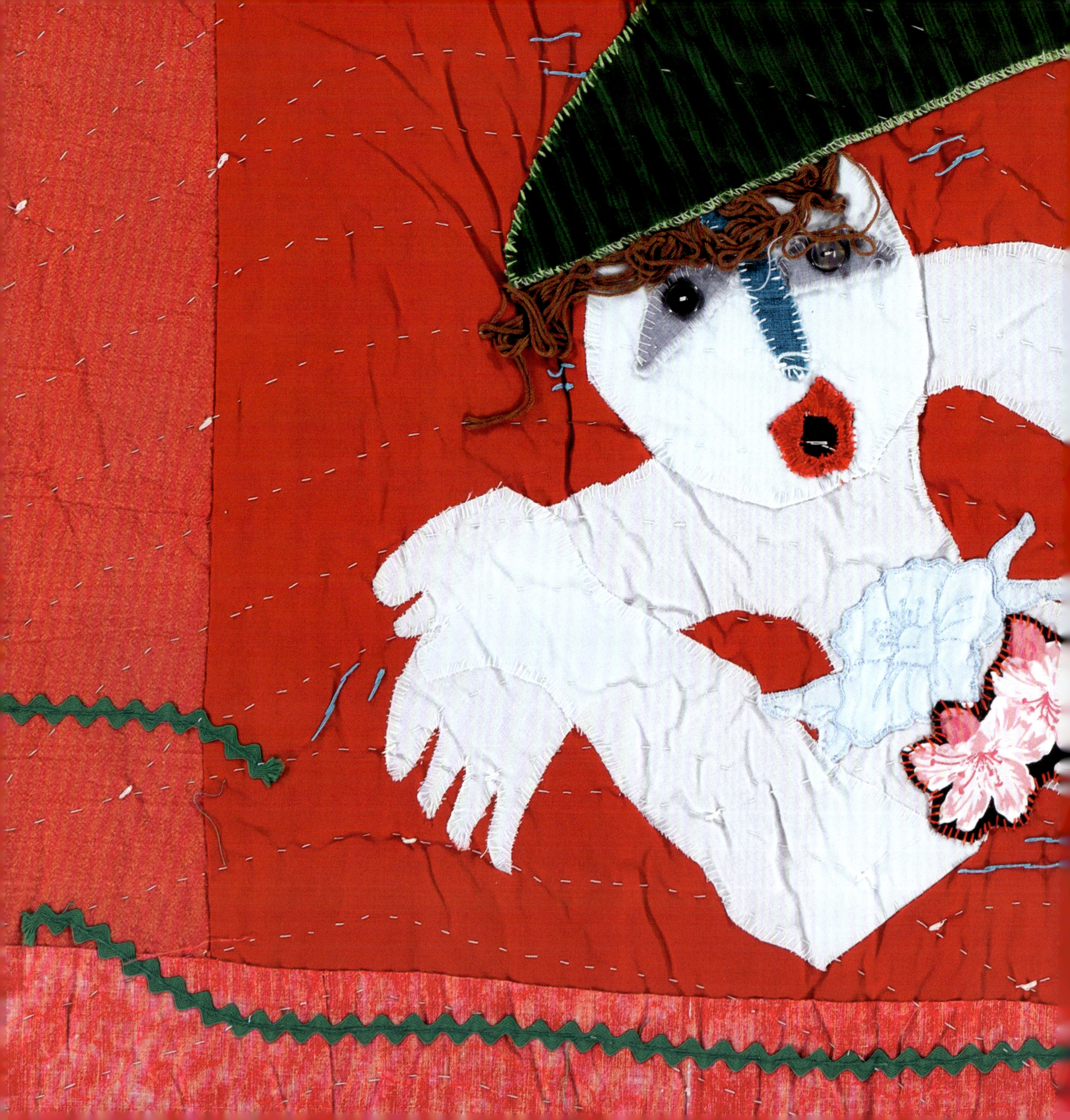

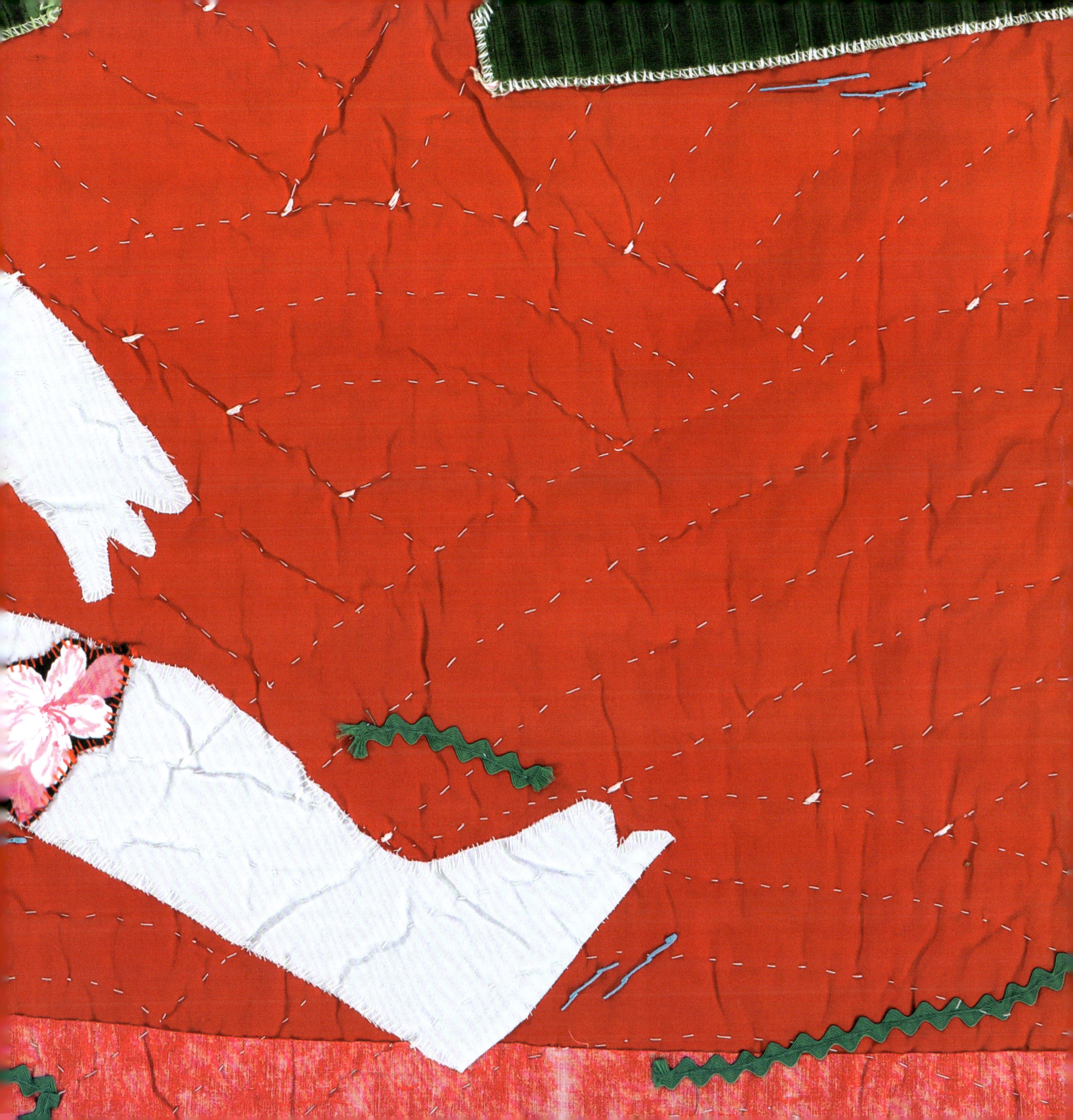

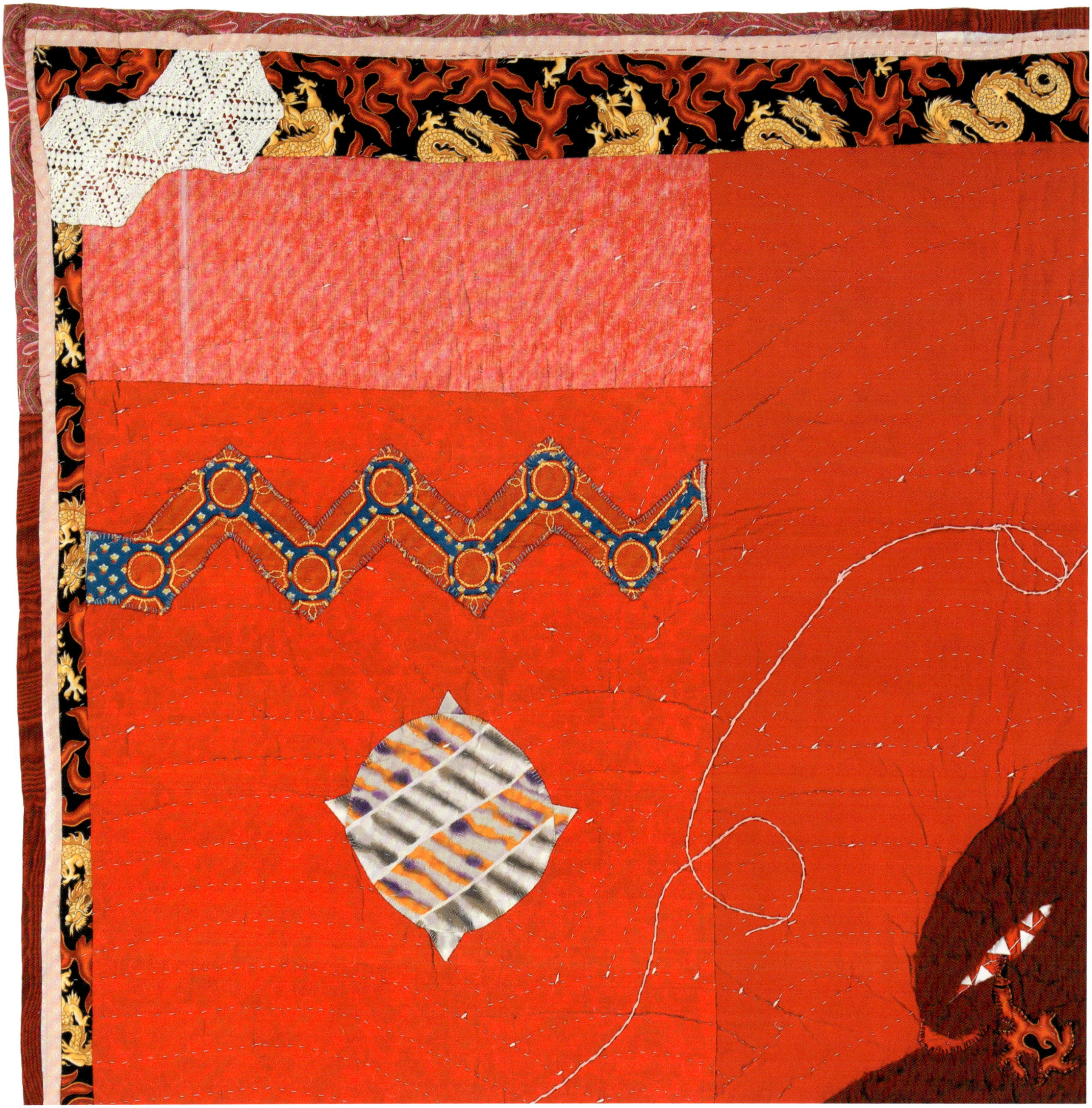

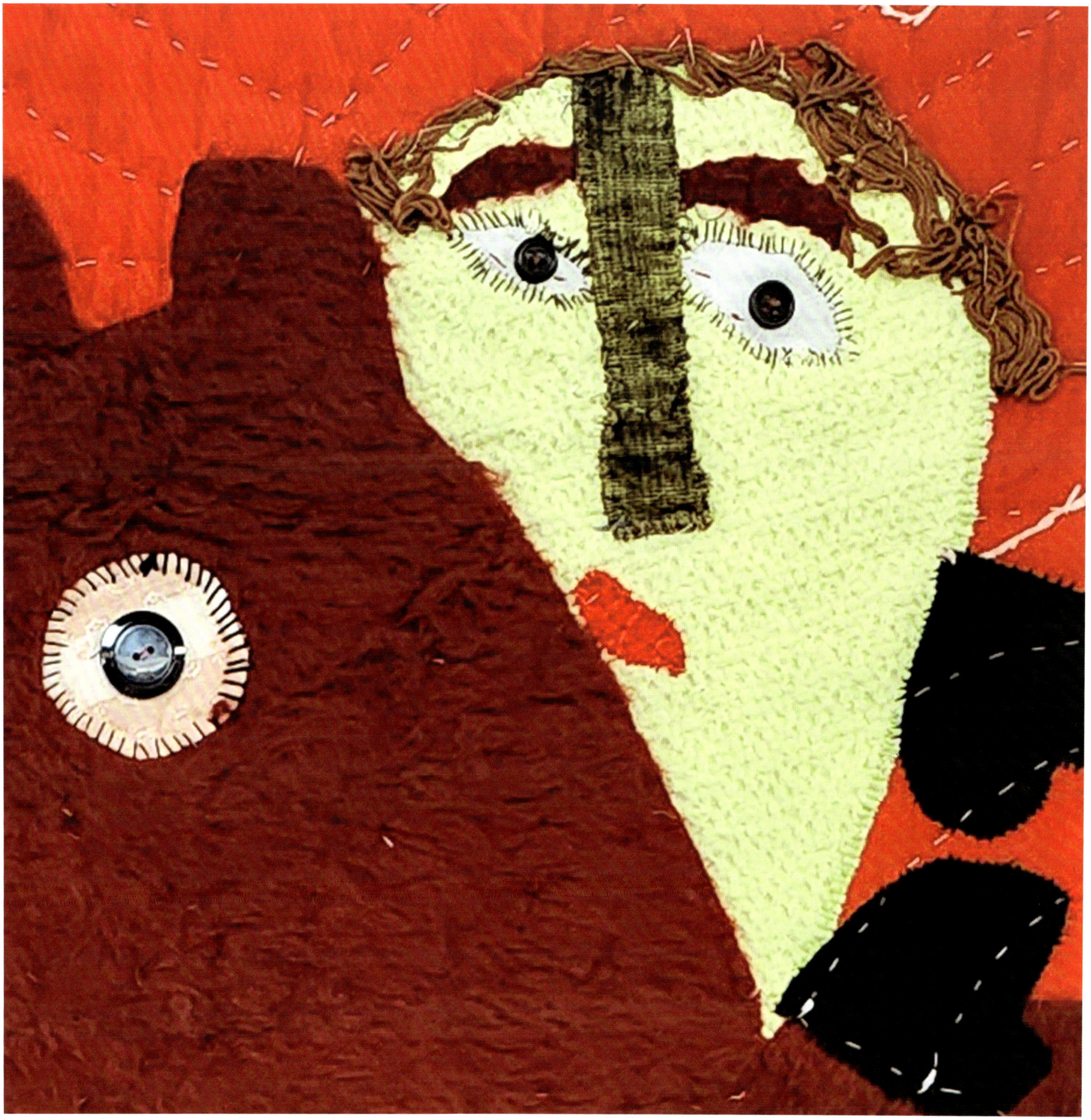

Envy

Seven Deadly Sins: Envy (2006).
Seven Deadly Sins: Envy (2006), back.
Pages 140, 141, 142, 144, 145:
Seven Deadly Sins: Envy (2006), details.

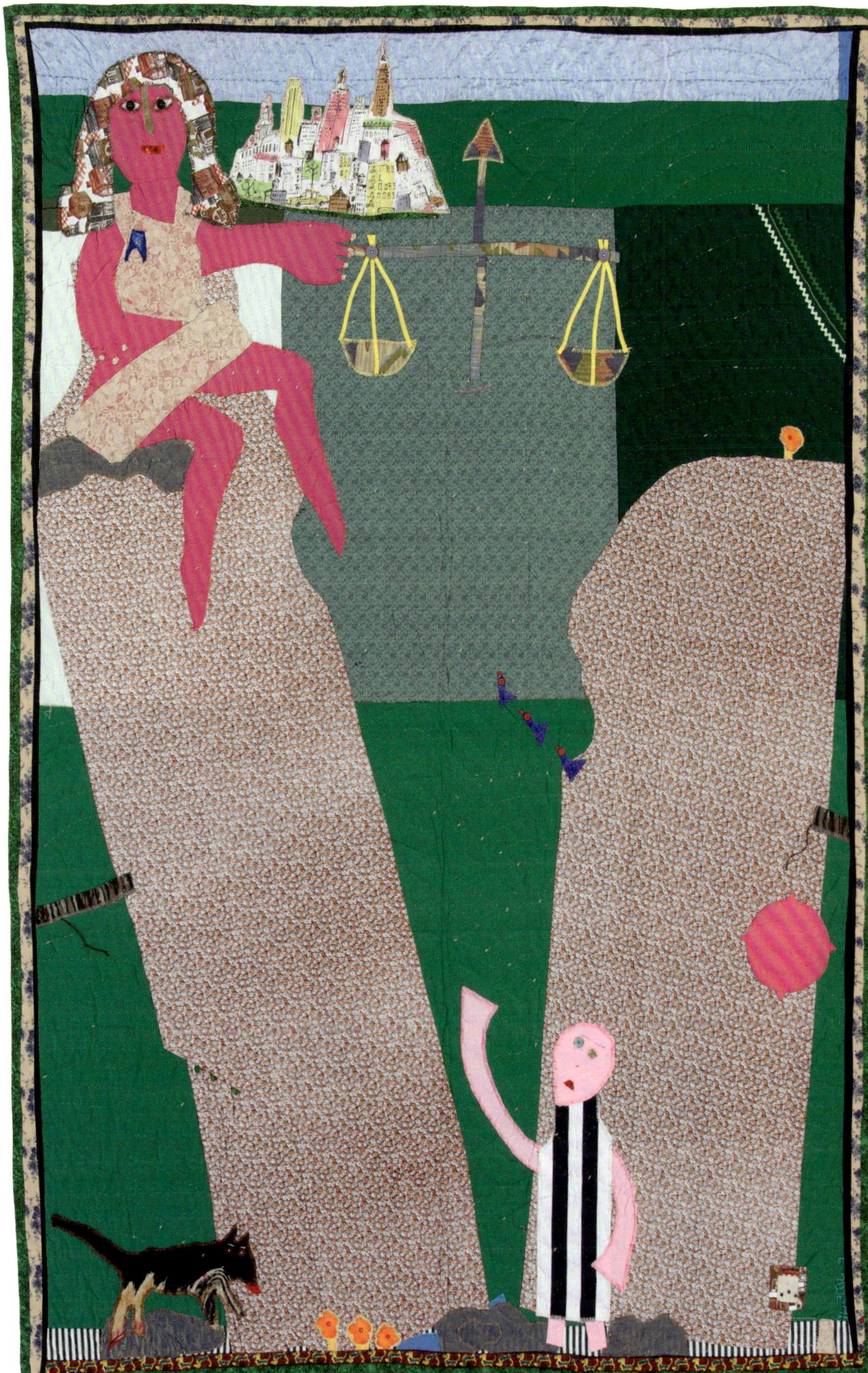

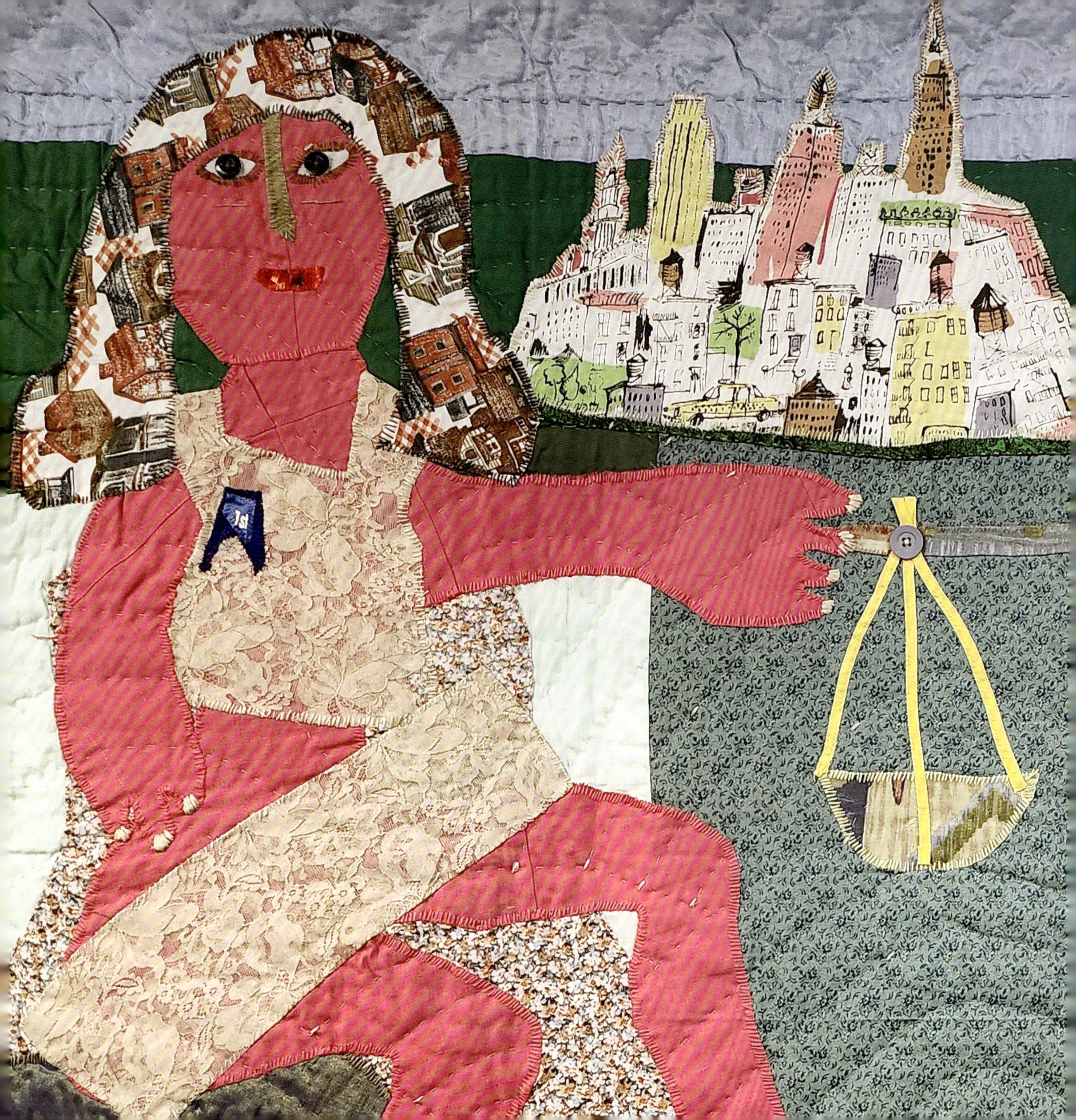
1st

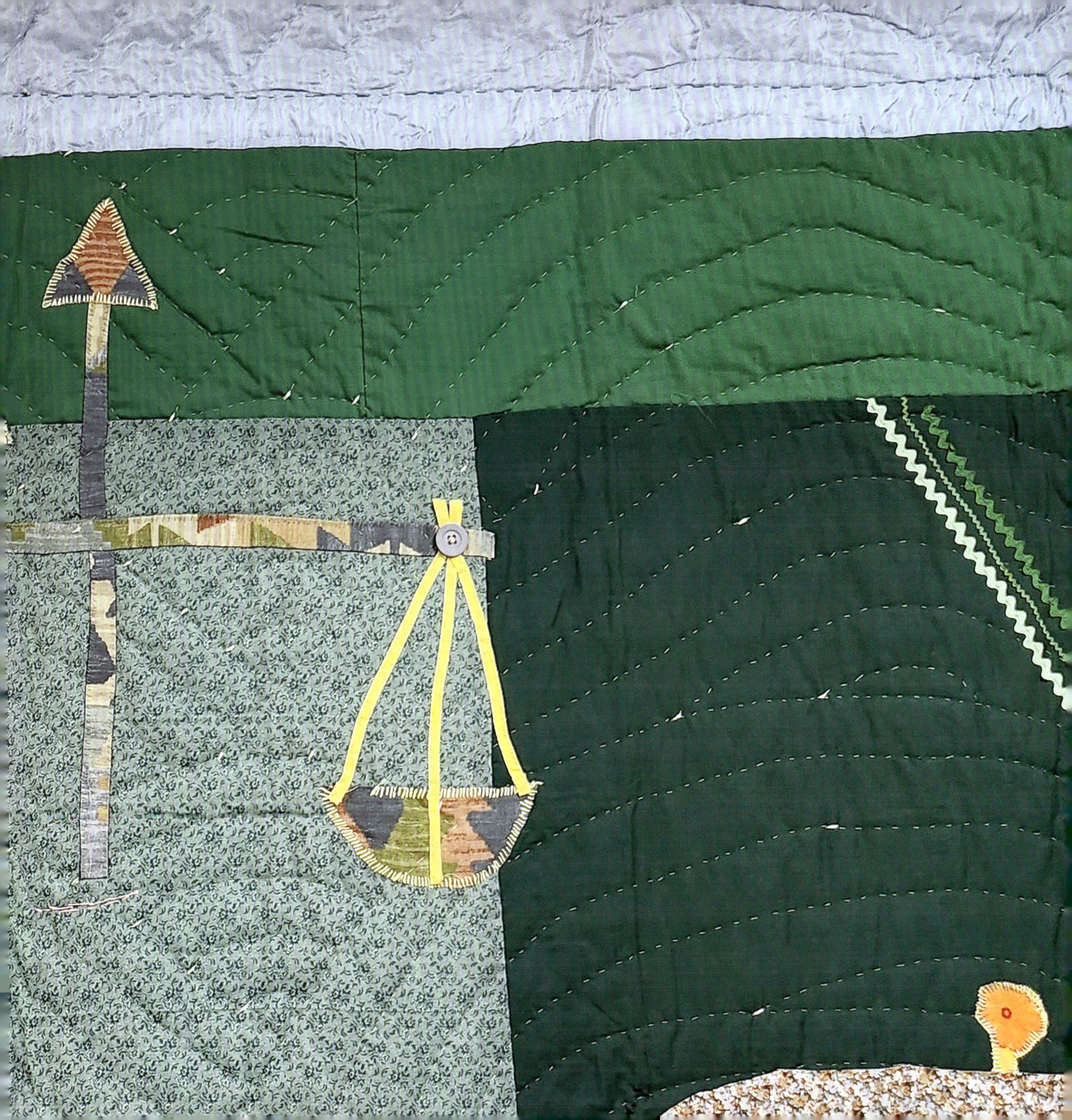

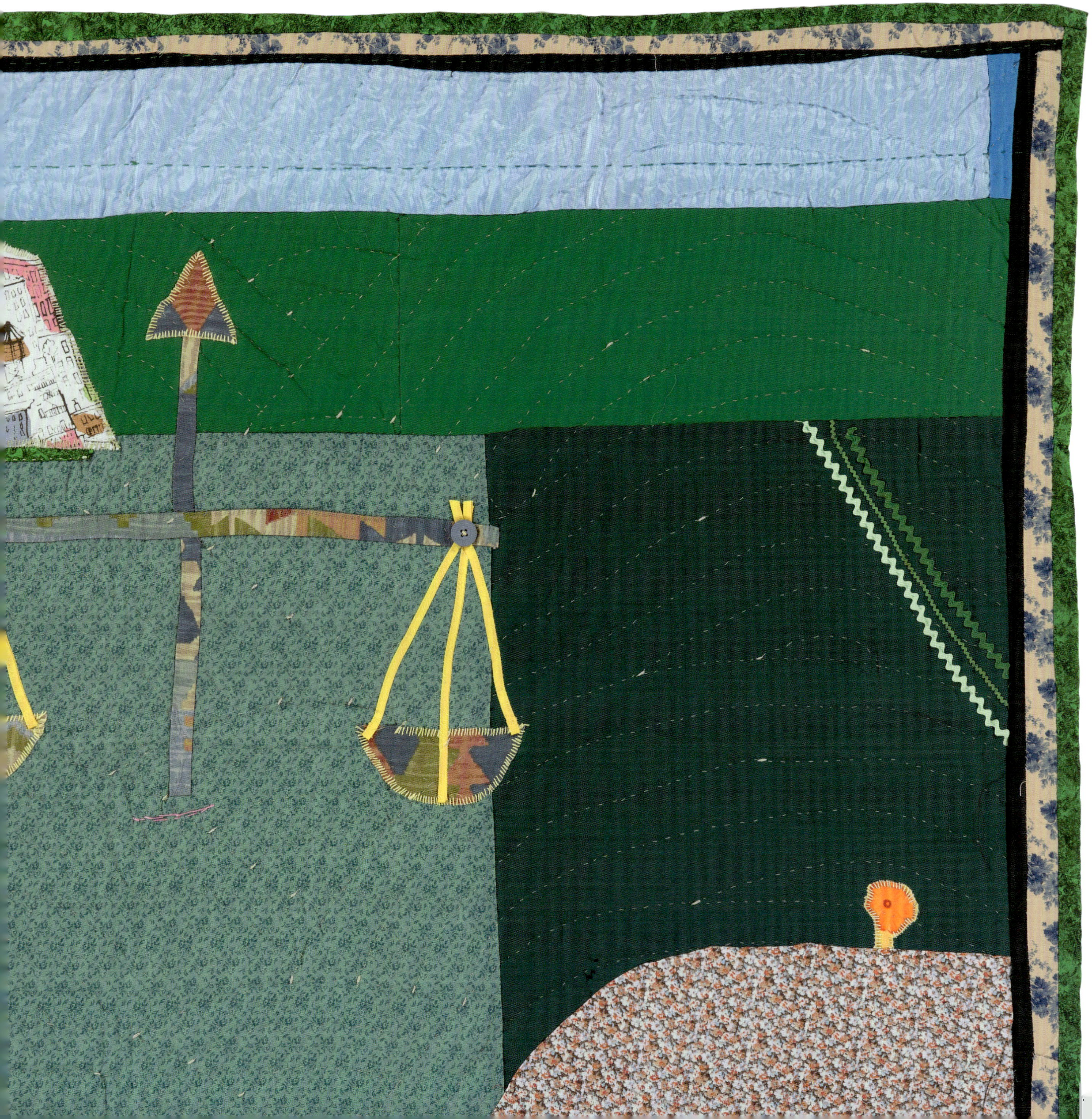

Envy

Envy is the idea that somebody else has stuff that you want, and you don't know how to get it. This lady at the bottom of the quilt is too shy to ask this beautiful woman up here how she got to her position. She's kind of sad because she's unable to ask the things she wants to know. Of course, this lady up in the sky wouldn't answer her anyway, because she is very snooty and has her nose in the air.

She's in the city of New York, sitting on a high-rise building and looking down on everyone. I made her to look like she's sitting on a mountain, and the mountain is New York. Next to her are the scales of justice. They are balanced, but in reality she knows that these scales are not actually balanced because she's on top of the world and other lady is down at the bottom.

This beautiful woman is a beauty queen, and she's wearing her first-place ribbon. Someone once told me that the woman at the bottom looked like she was wearing prisoner's clothes, but I didn't actually think of that when I created her. I just put her in stripes because she looked kind of sad and hurt and mistreated.

The color for envy is green, and the animal is the dog.

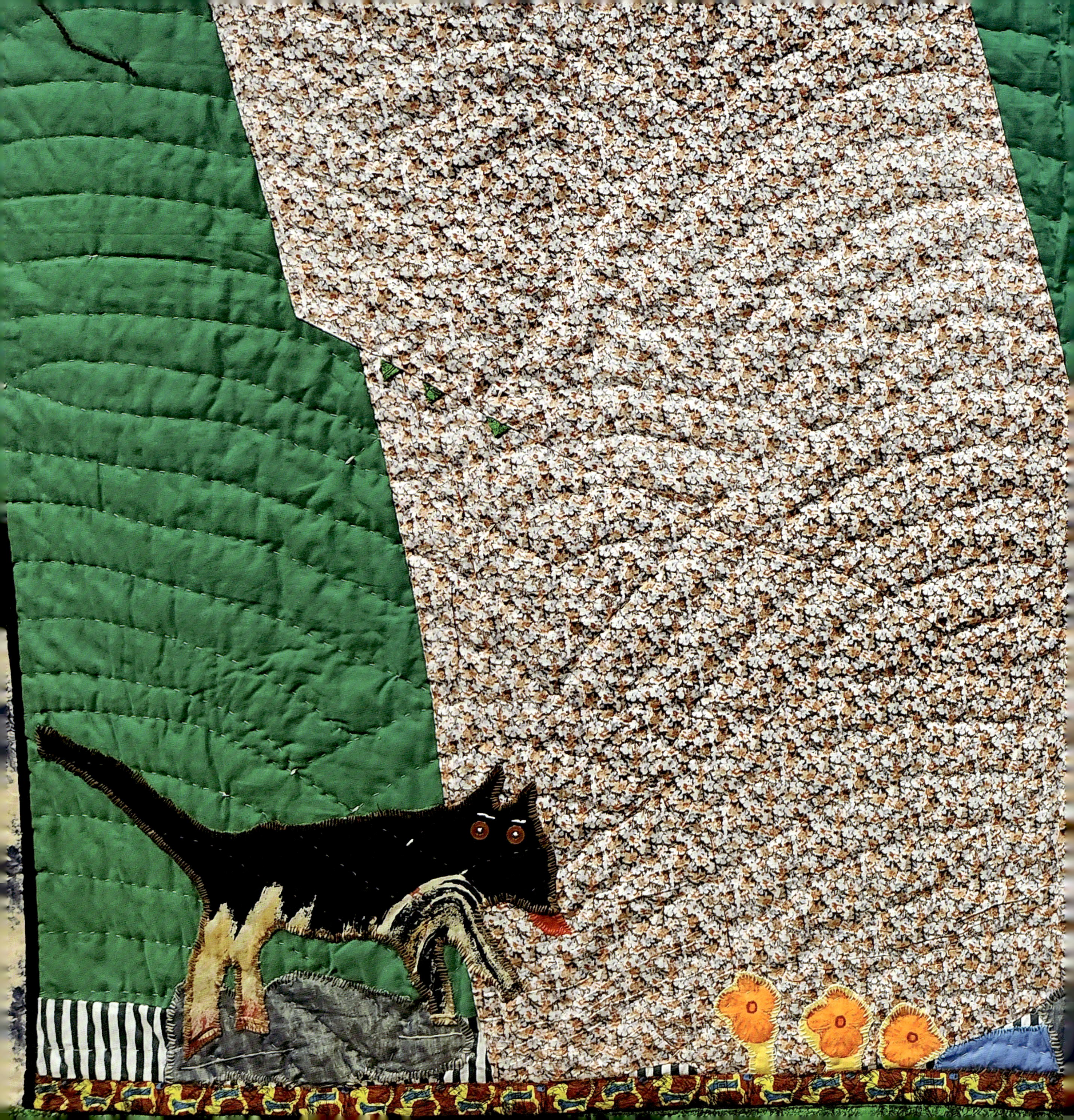

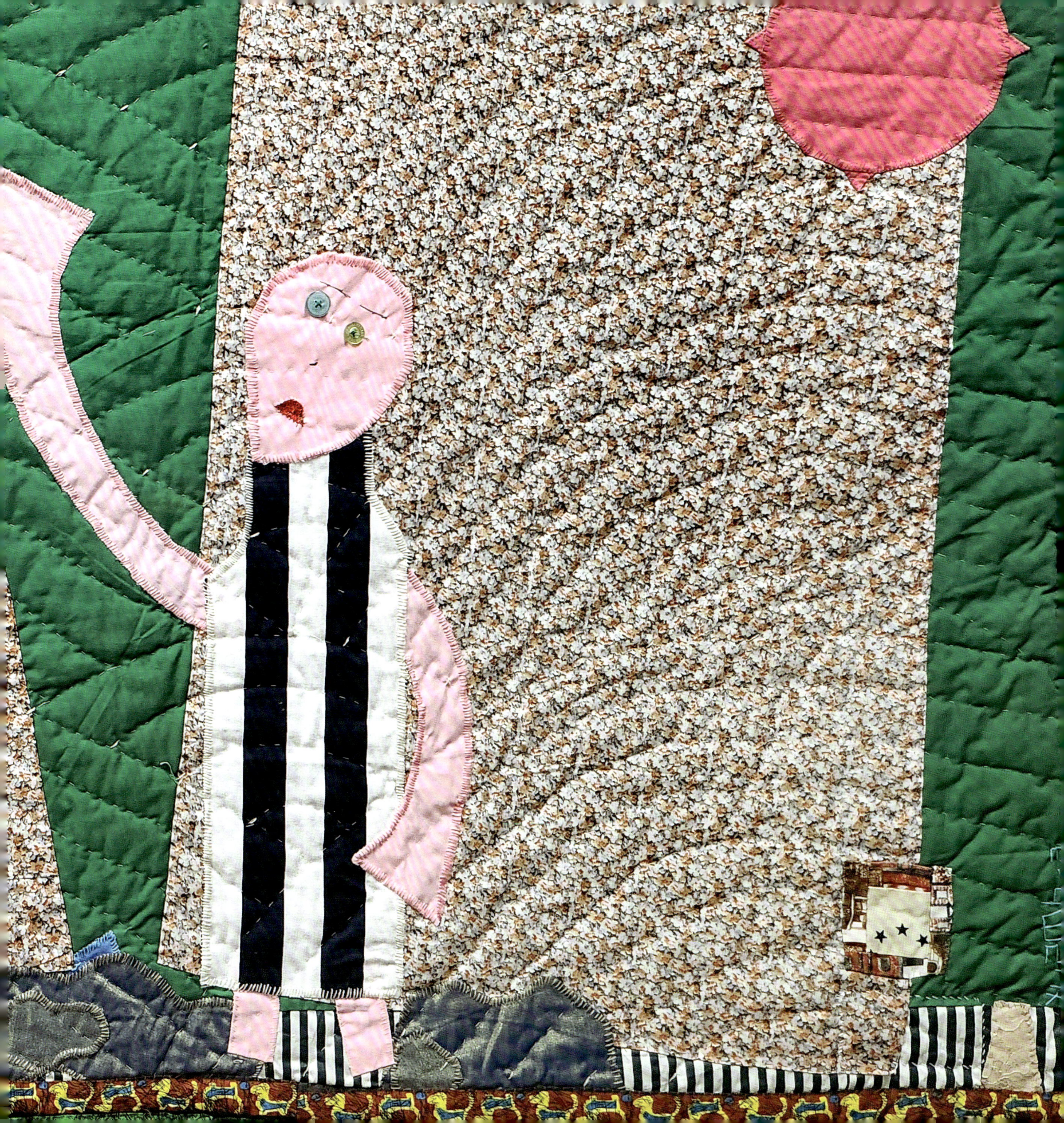

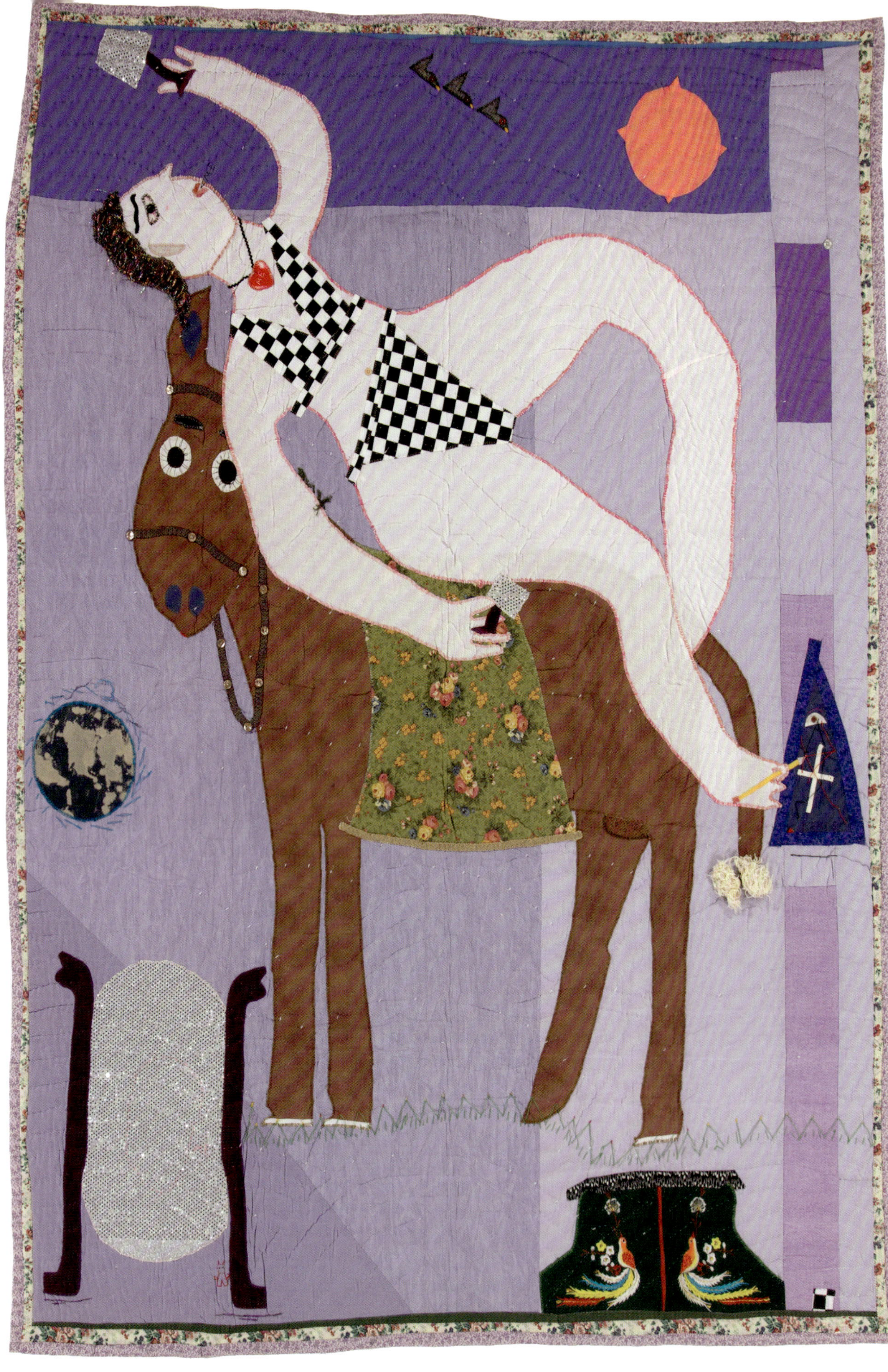

Pride

Seven Deadly Sins: Pride (2006).
Seven Deadly Sins: Pride (2006), back.
Pages 148, 149, 151, 152, 153, 154, 155:
Seven Deadly Sins: Pride (2006), details.

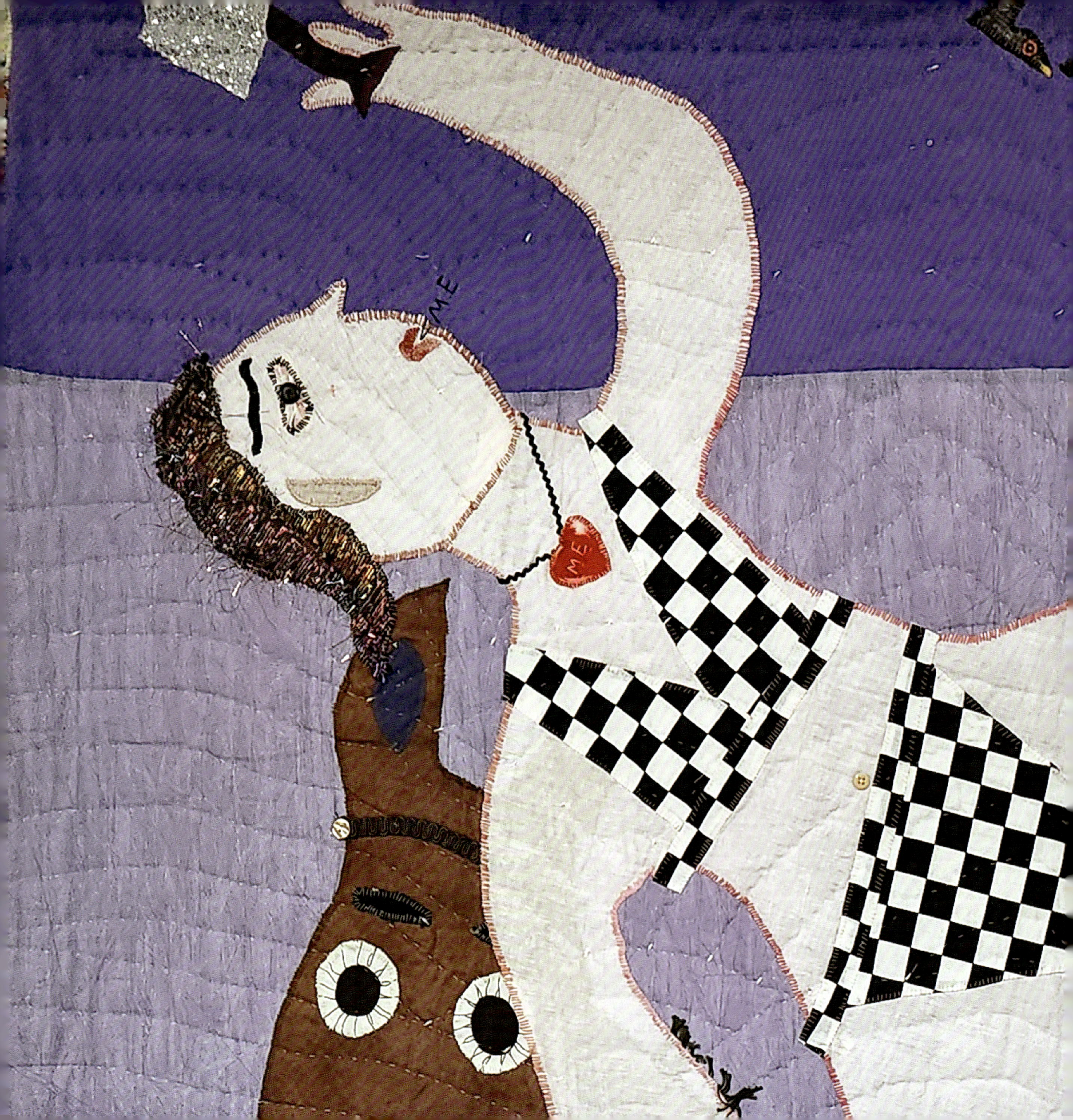
ME
ME

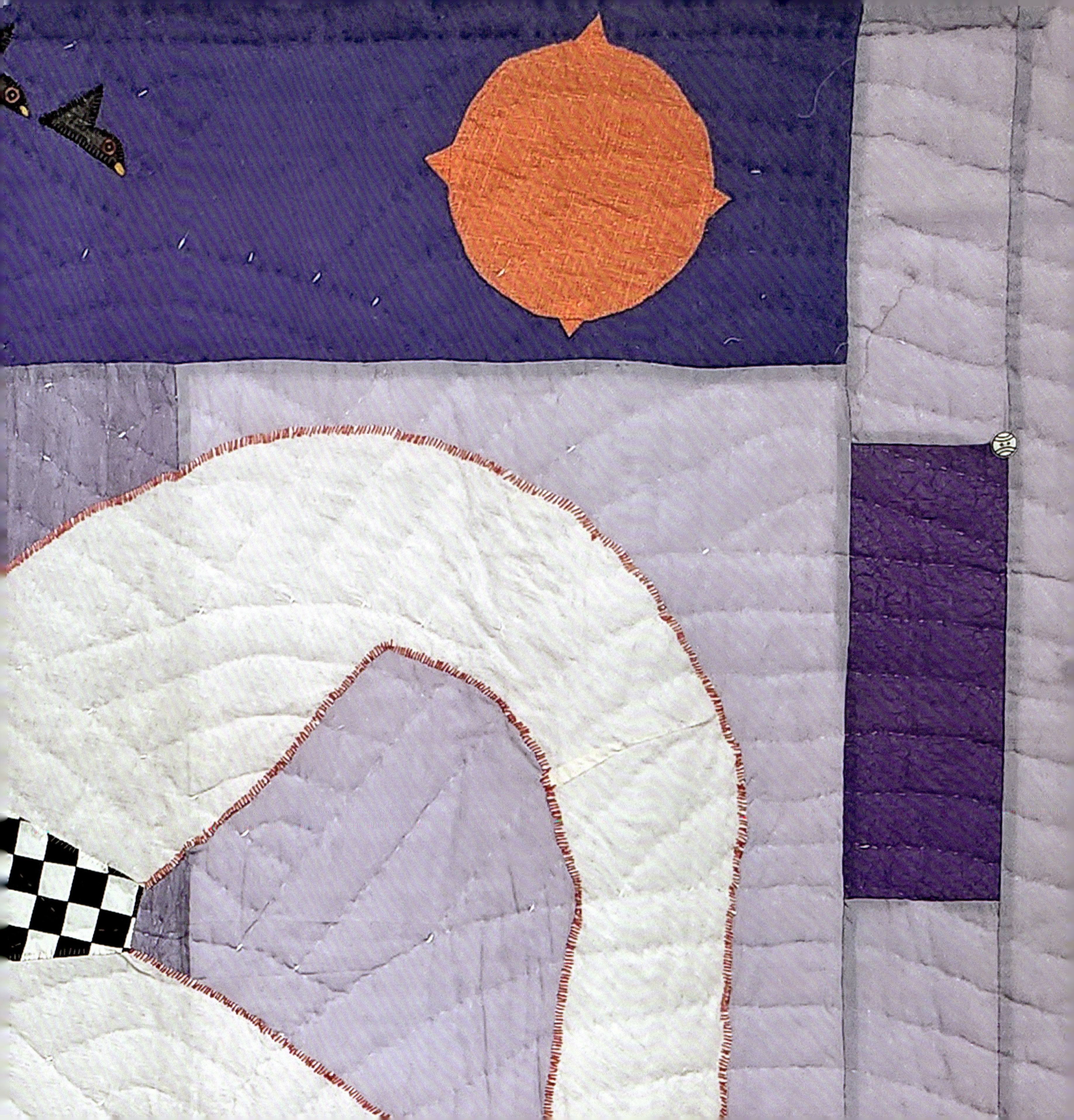

Pride

The last one in the series is called *Pride*, and it was the most difficult for me. Pride is the most deadly of all the sins, and I just wasn't sure how I would make this one at first. A prideful person is someone who thinks only of himself. This lady thinks the world only runs around her, so I included a globe of the world, and it sits over on the left side of the quilt.

She carries a mirror in her hand so that she can see herself at all times, and she likes to pat herself on the back. At the bottom of the quilt is another mirror that is standing in a frame so that when she does get off the horse, she can see her own face again right away. She likes looking at herself because she's prideful.

Around her neck is a heart necklace that says "Me." She's wearing a bikini. Originally, I wanted to put her in a yellow polka-dot bikini, but I didn't have the right kind of fabric. So, I said, "Okay, Yvonne, let's make her a black-and-white plaid bikini," and I think it came out pretty good. I'm pleased with her and also the horse she's sitting on.
She is holding a pencil in her toes, and she is scratching out the word God with that pencil. She doesn't want God to see how prideful she has become.

At the bottom on the right is a vase that is really meant as decoration. It is sitting out in the yard because I wanted to add some beauty. But also, these elaborate birds are also showing a little bit of pride because each one is looking in different directions. You know, they're all about themselves, and that's what pride is all about.

The color for pride is purple, and the animal is a horse. I love all of my quilts, but this group of the *Seven Deadly Sins* is very dear to me.

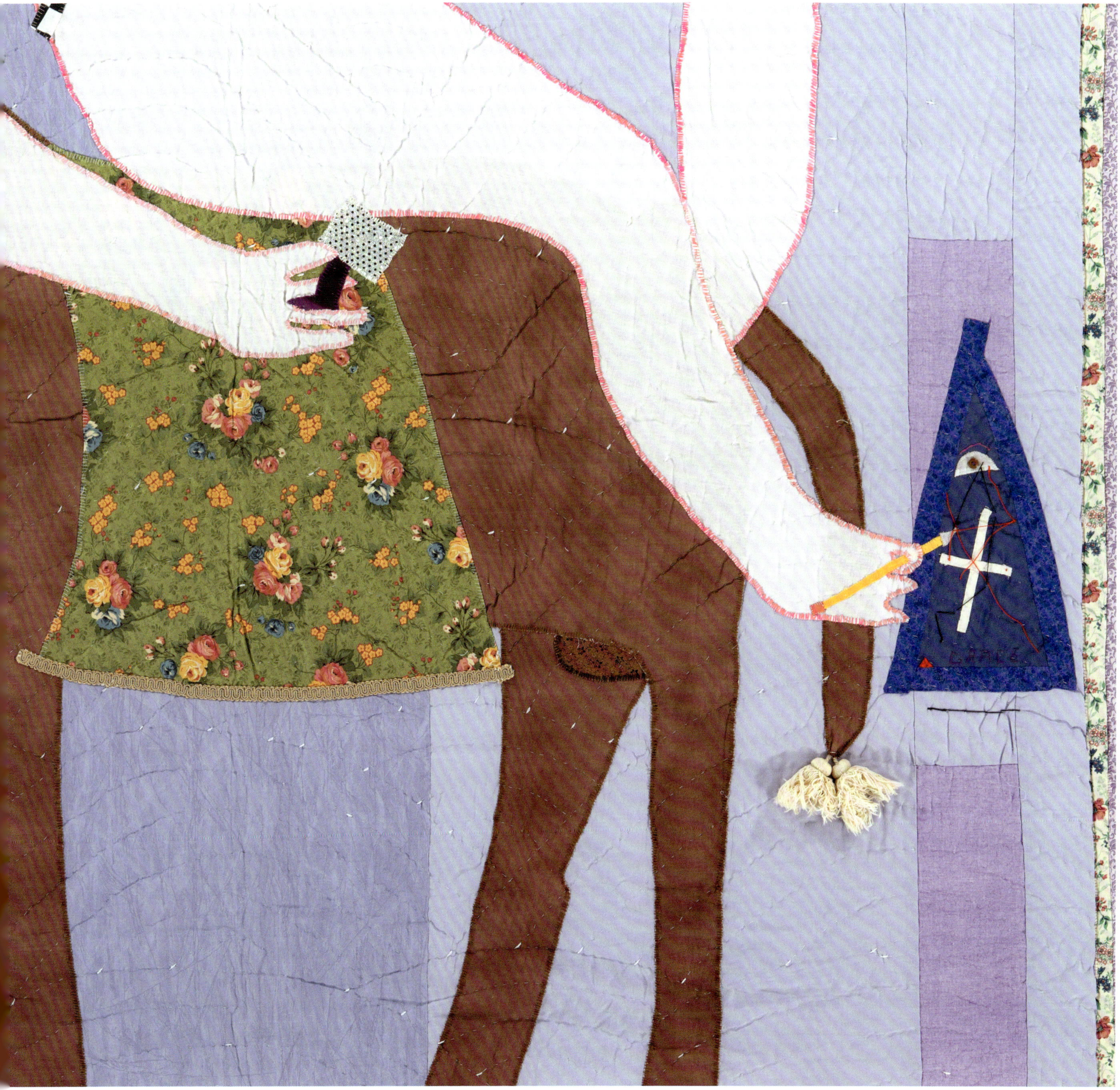

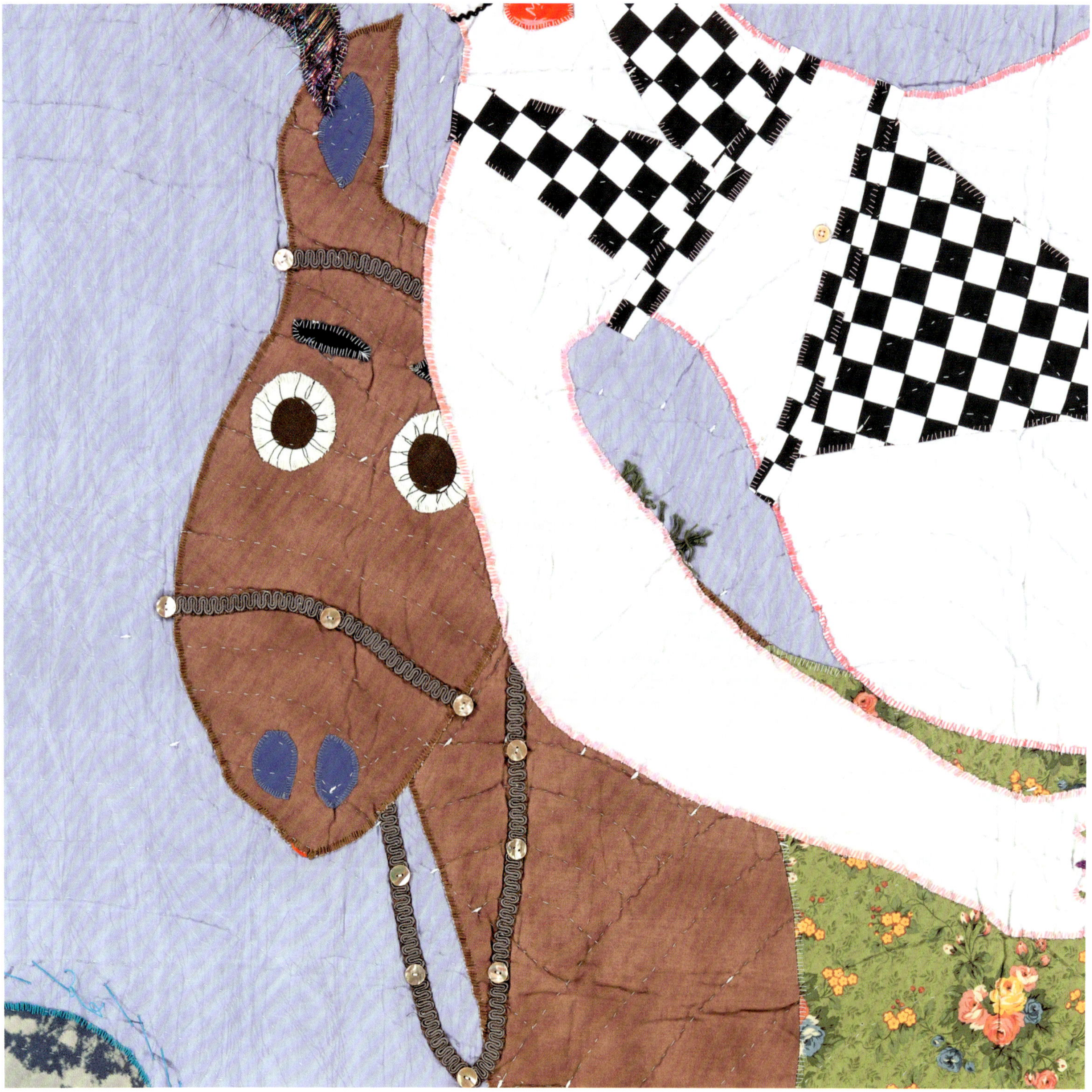

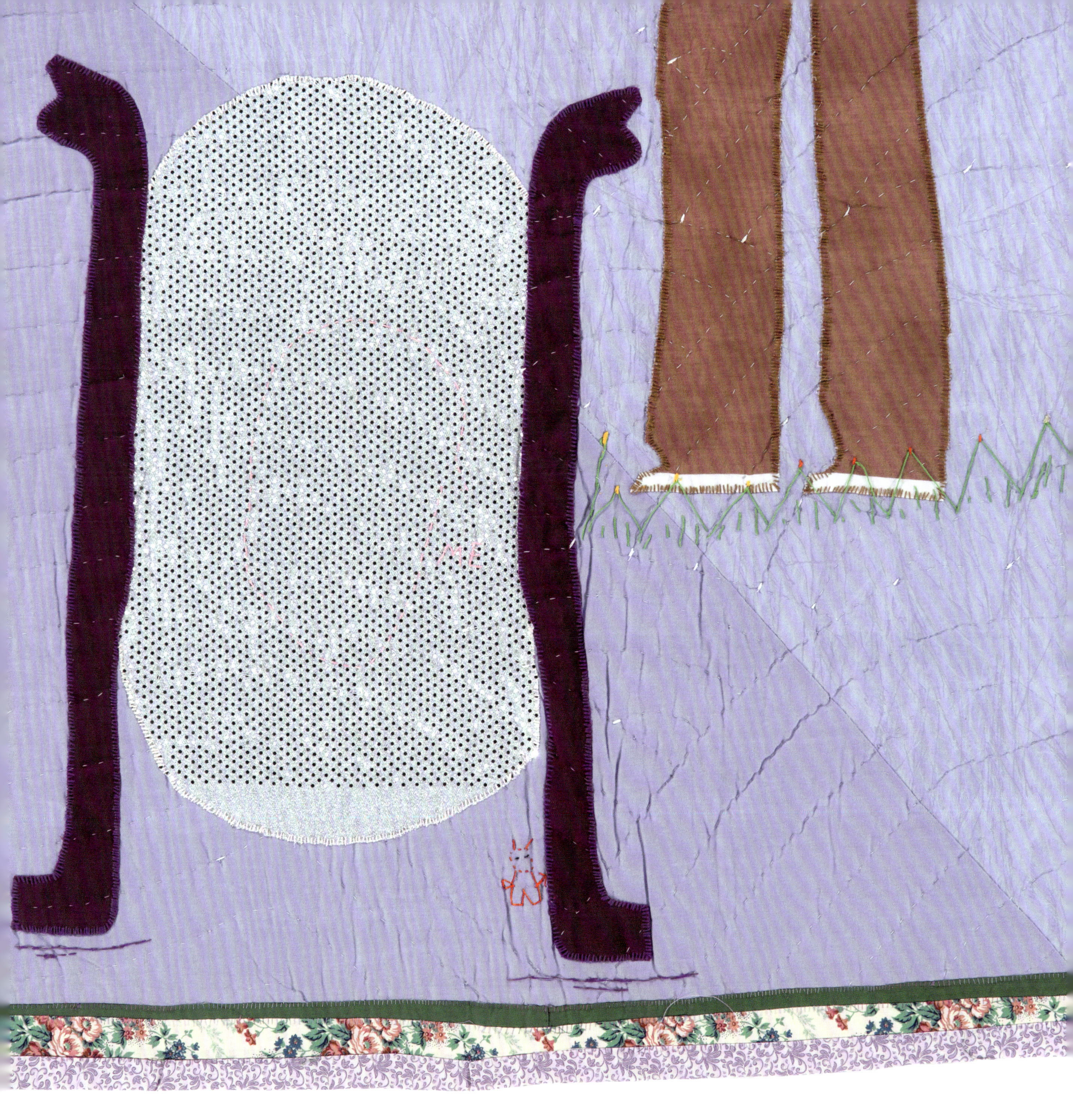
ME

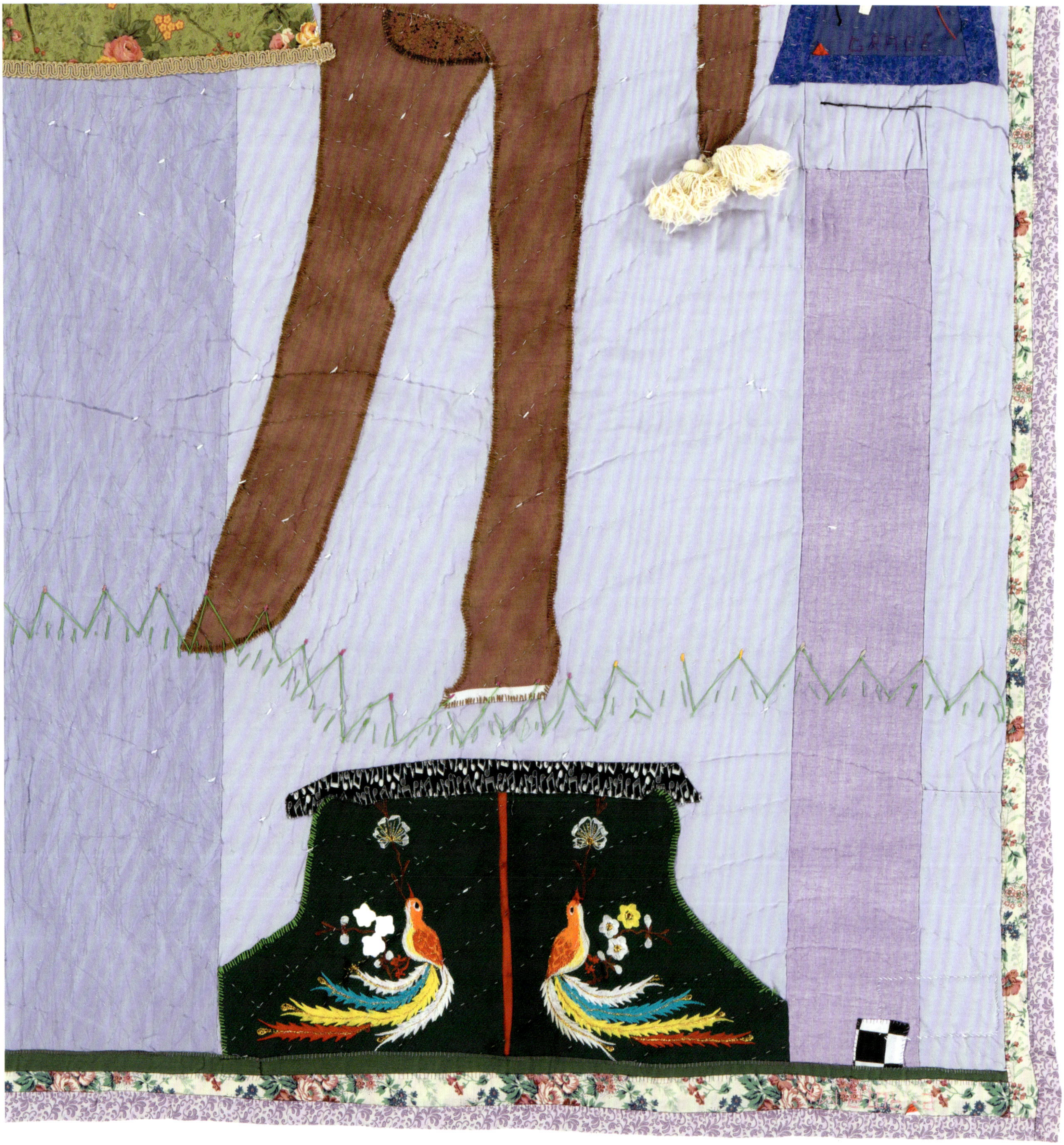
GRACE

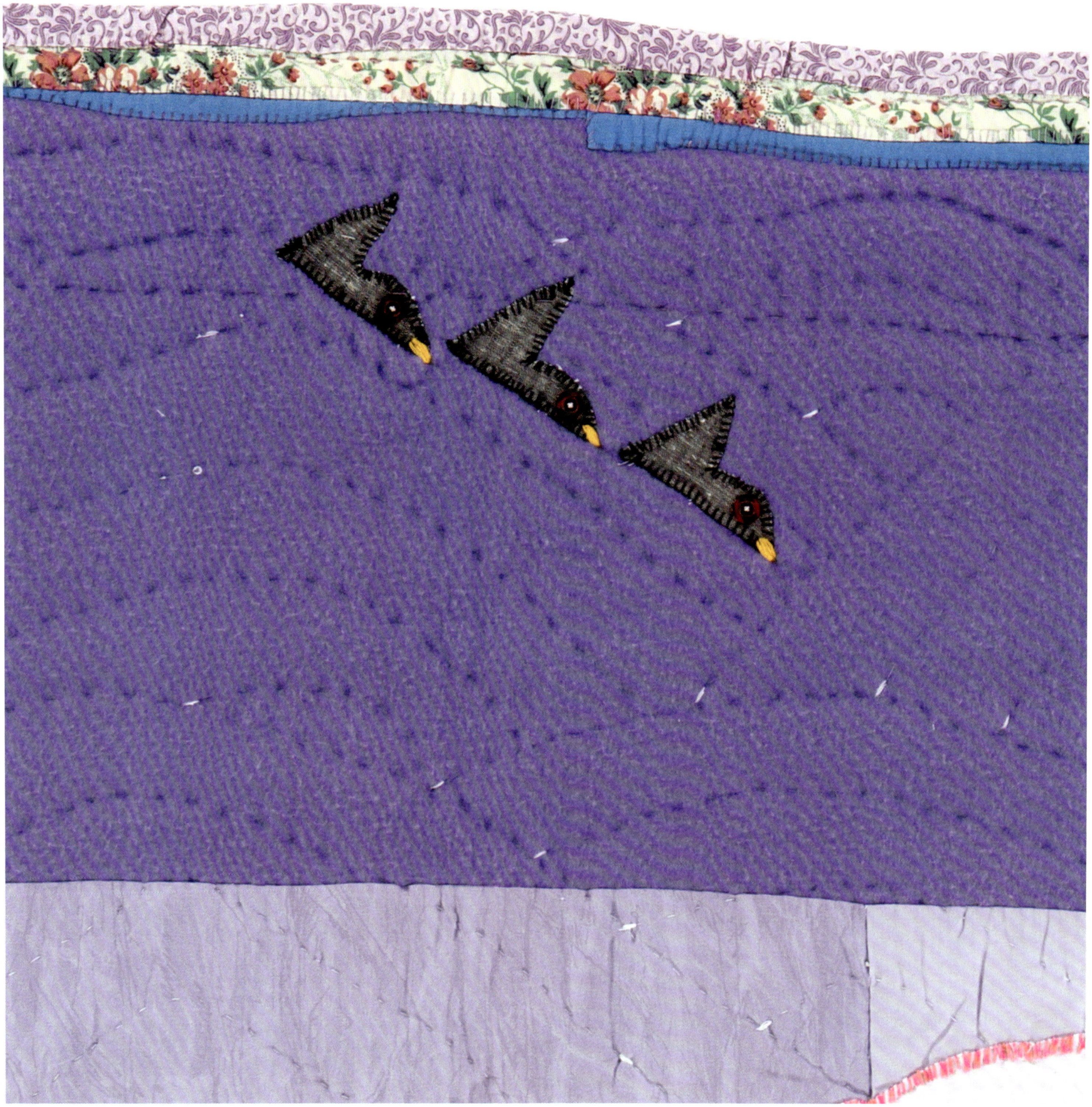

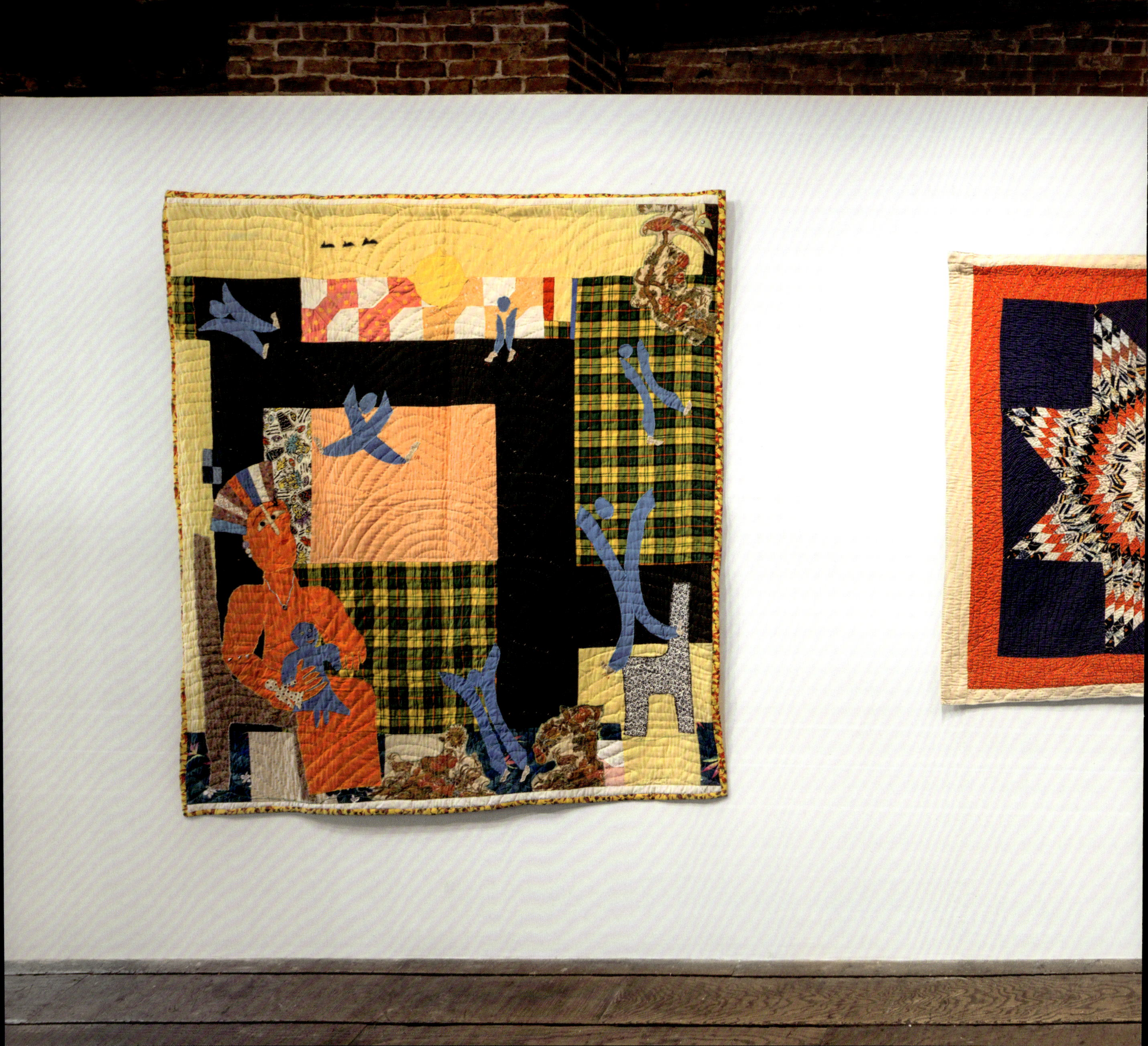

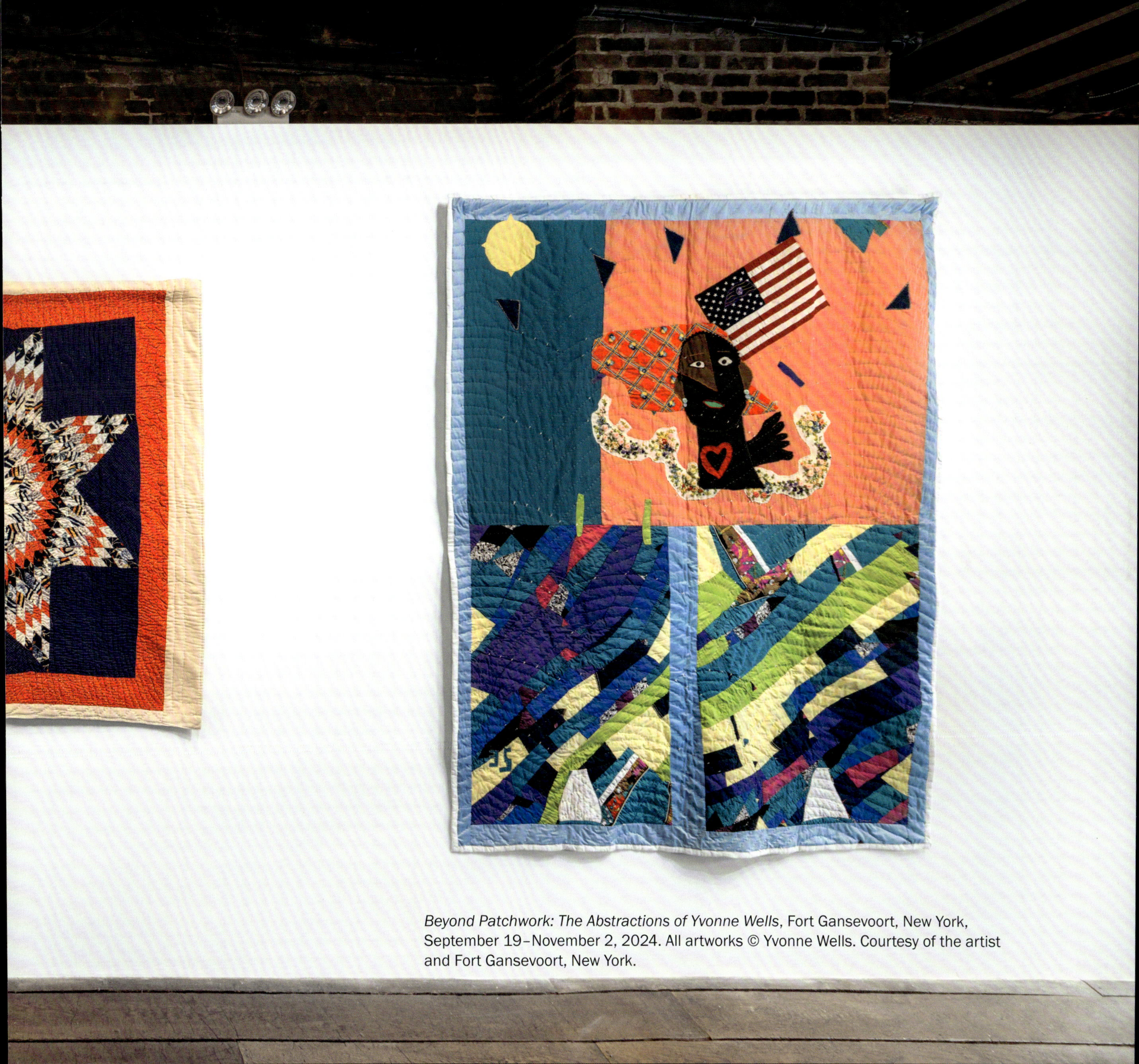

Beyond Patchwork: The Abstractions of Yvonne Wells, Fort Gansevoort, New York, September 19–November 2, 2024. All artworks © Yvonne Wells. Courtesy of the artist and Fort Gansevoort, New York.

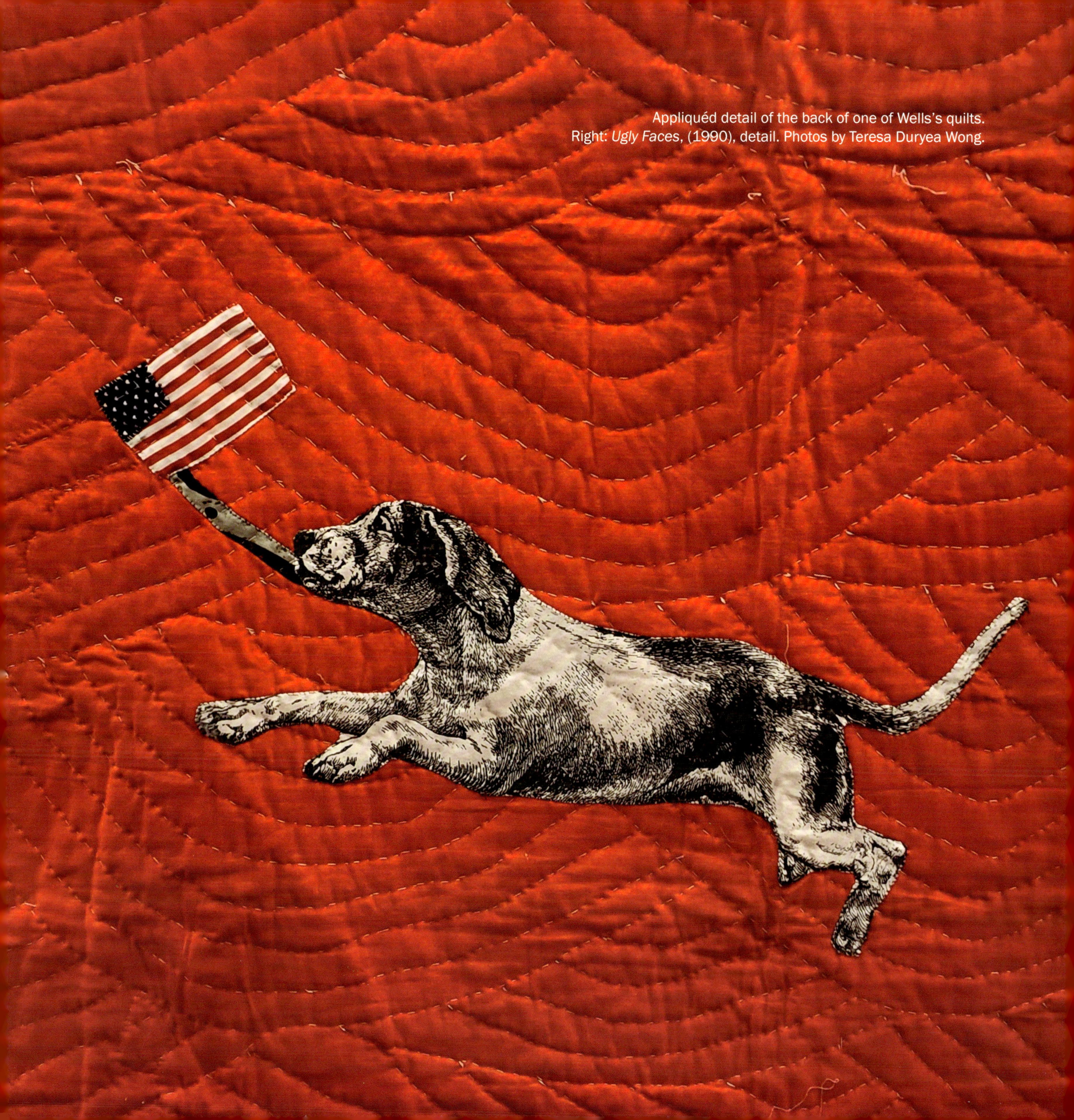

Appliquéd detail of the back of one of Wells's quilts.
Right: *Ugly Faces*, (1990), detail. Photos by Teresa Duryea Wong.

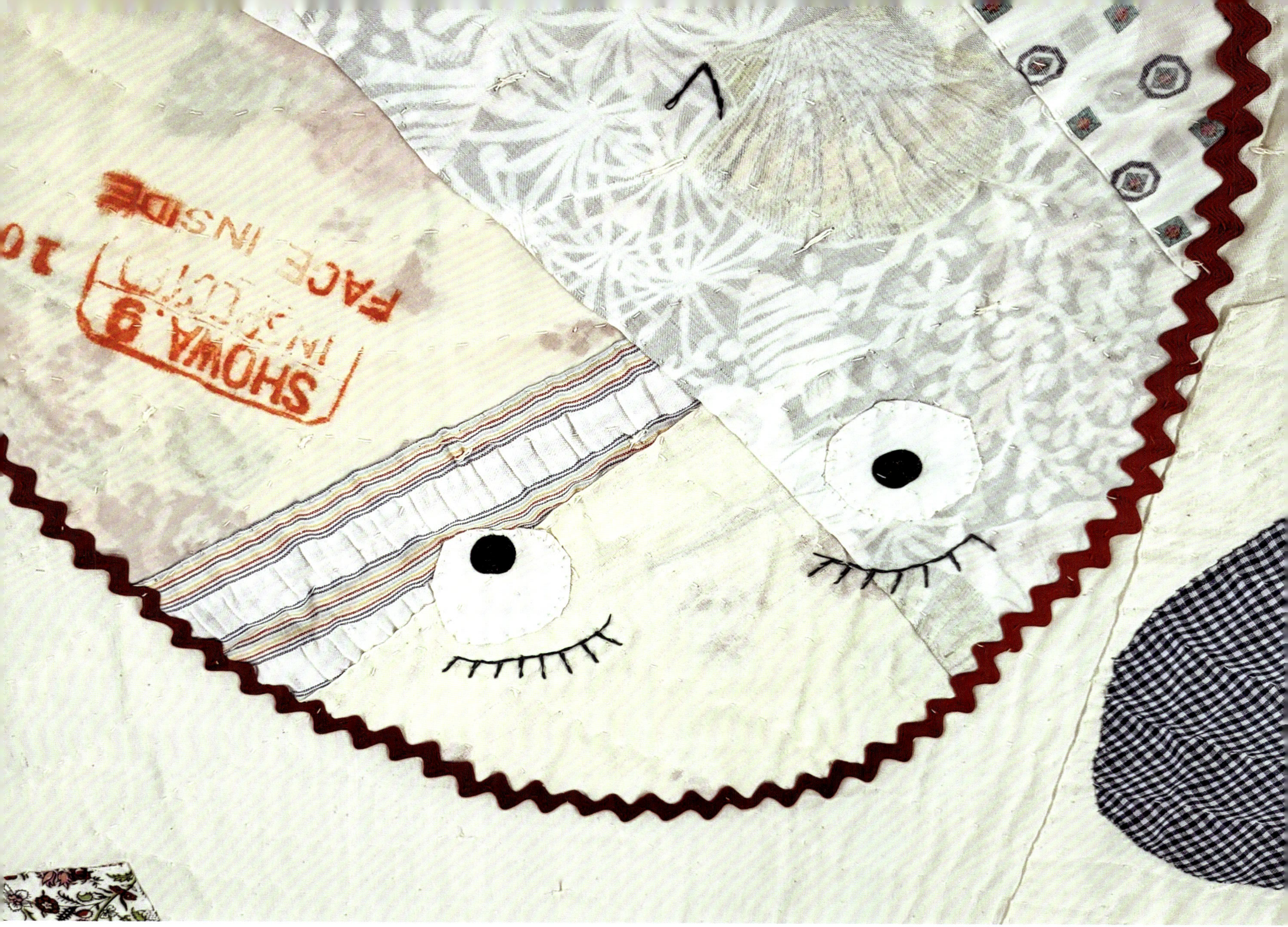

QUILT GALLERY

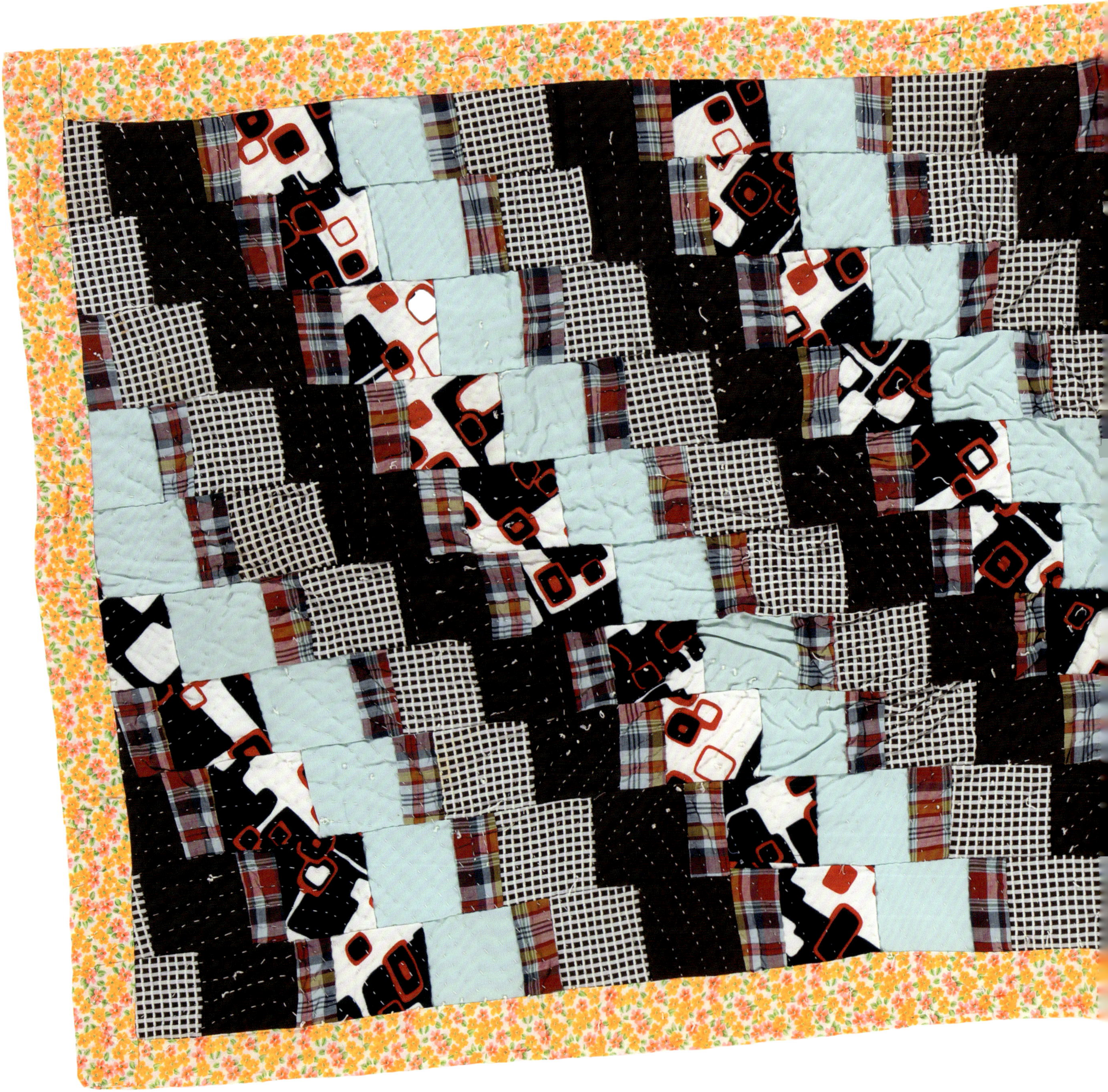

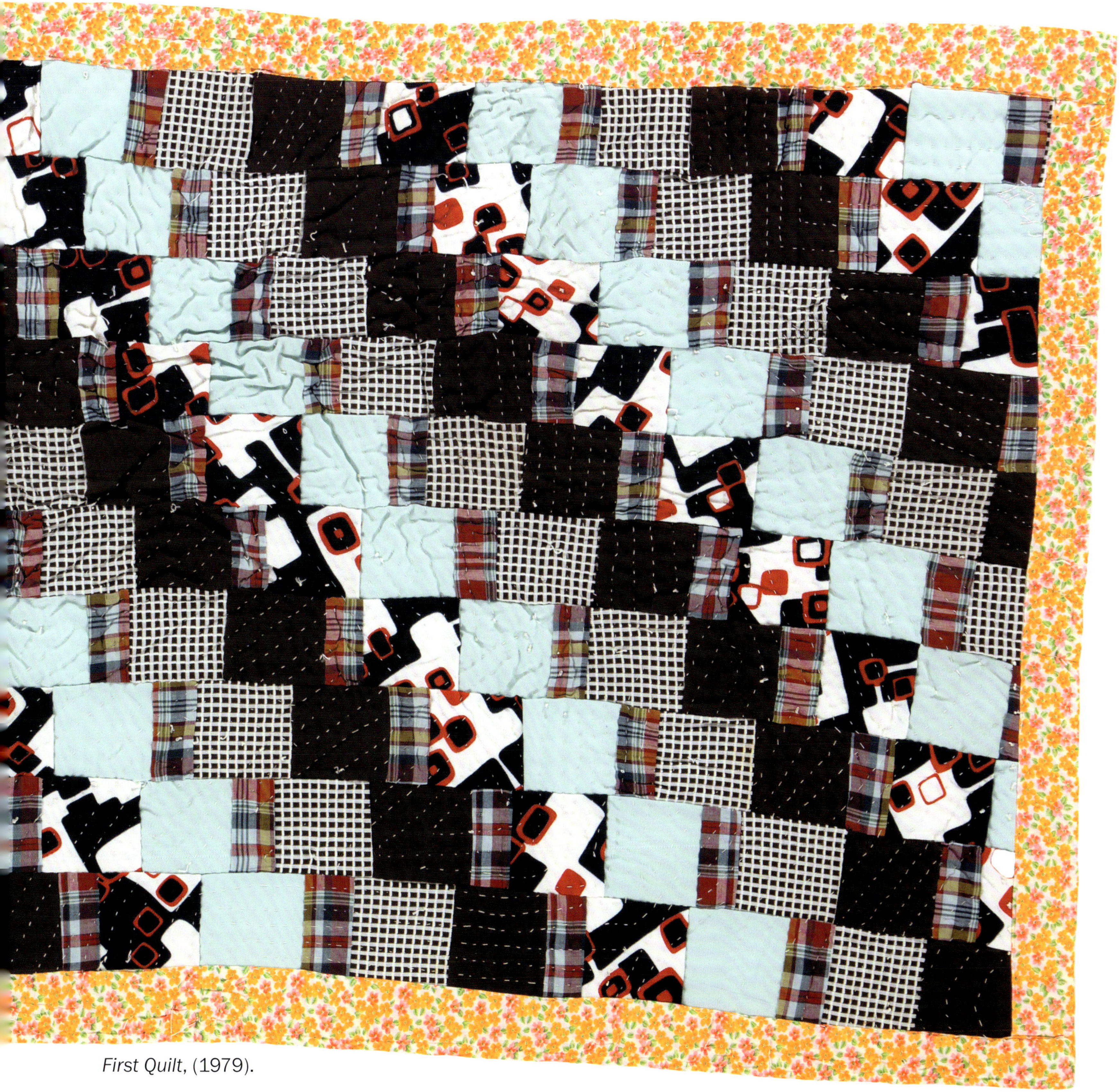

First Quilt, (1979).

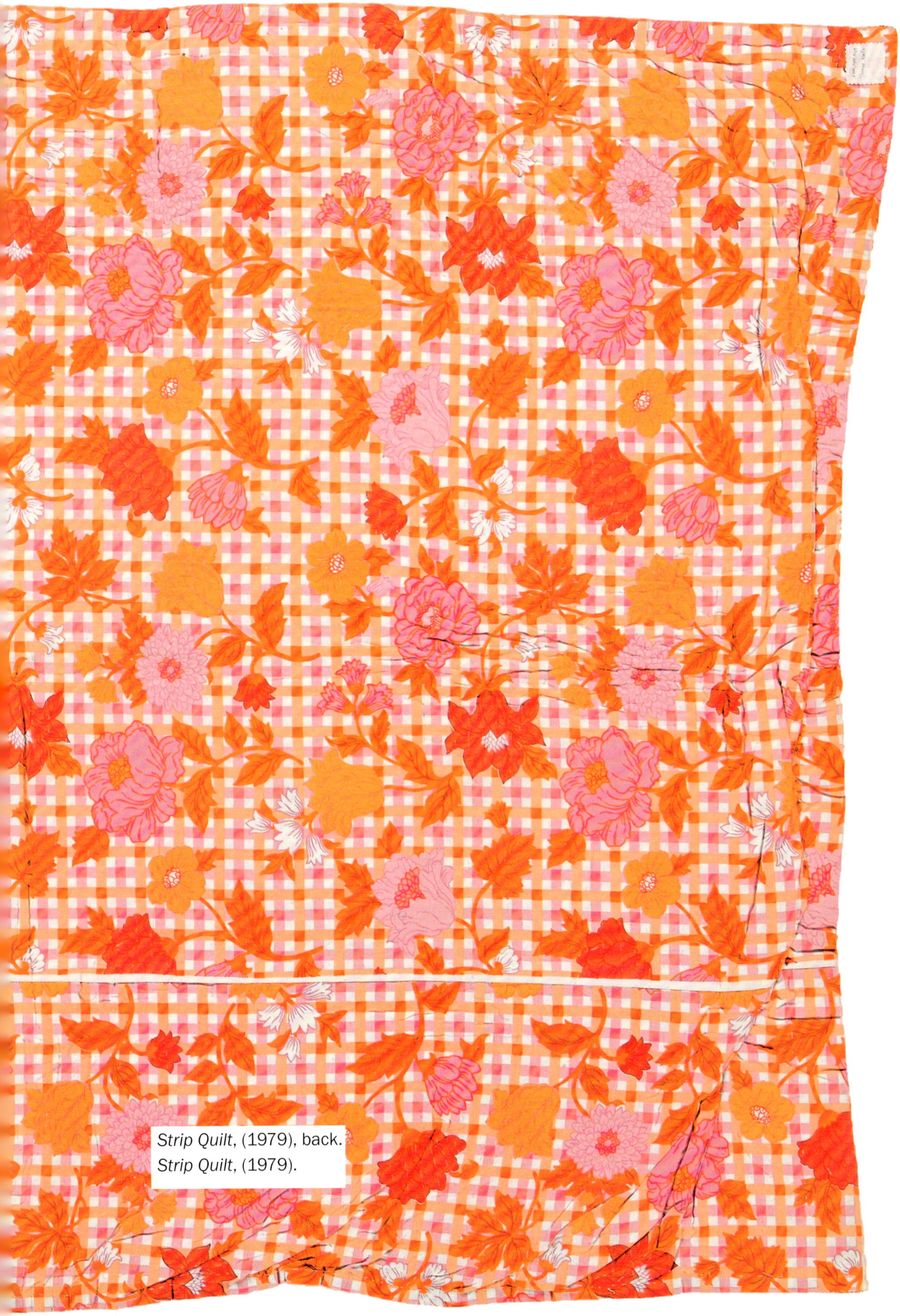

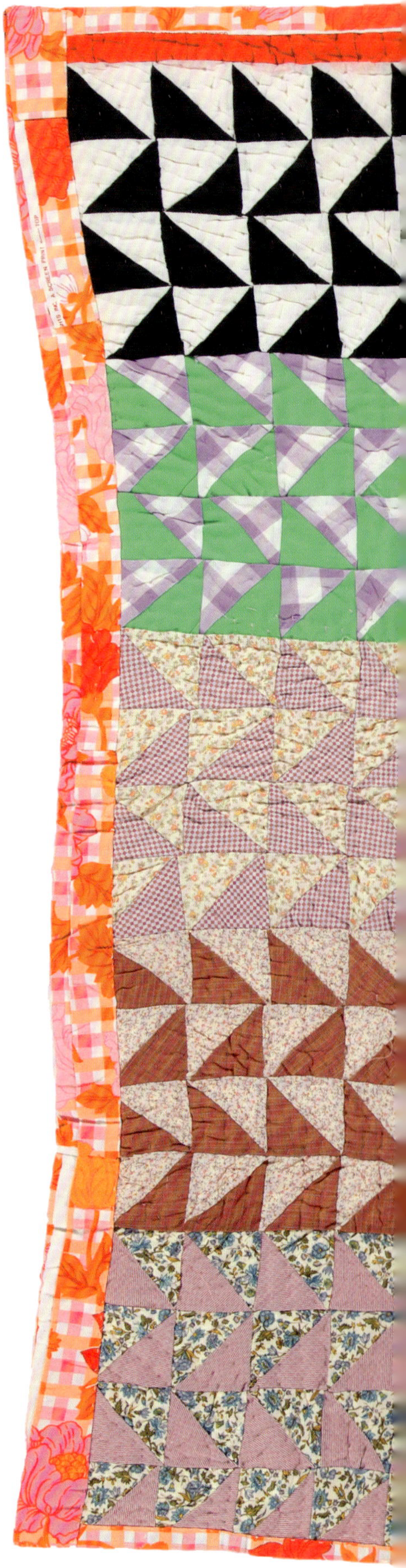

Strip Quilt, (1979), back.
Strip Quilt, (1979).

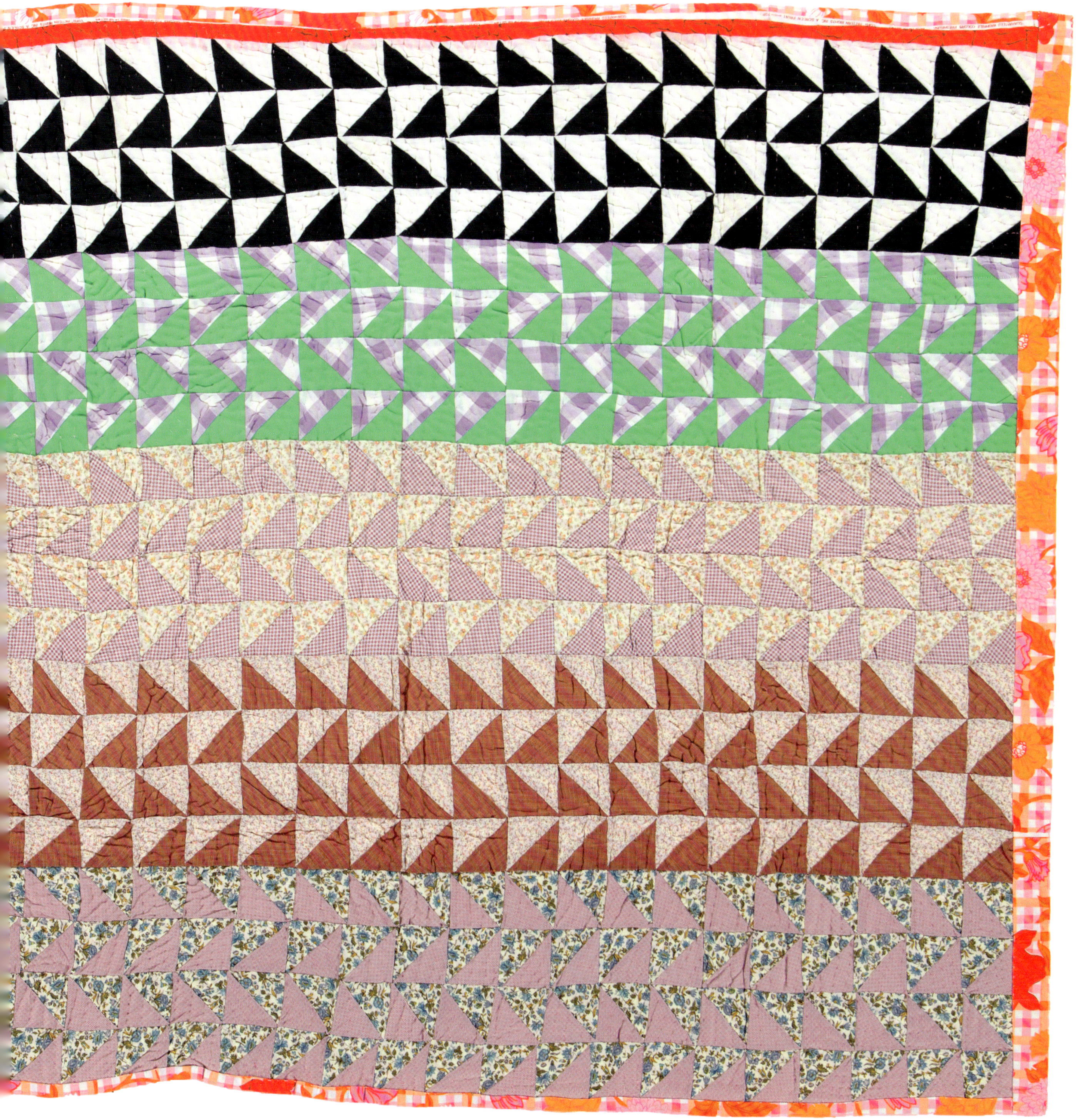

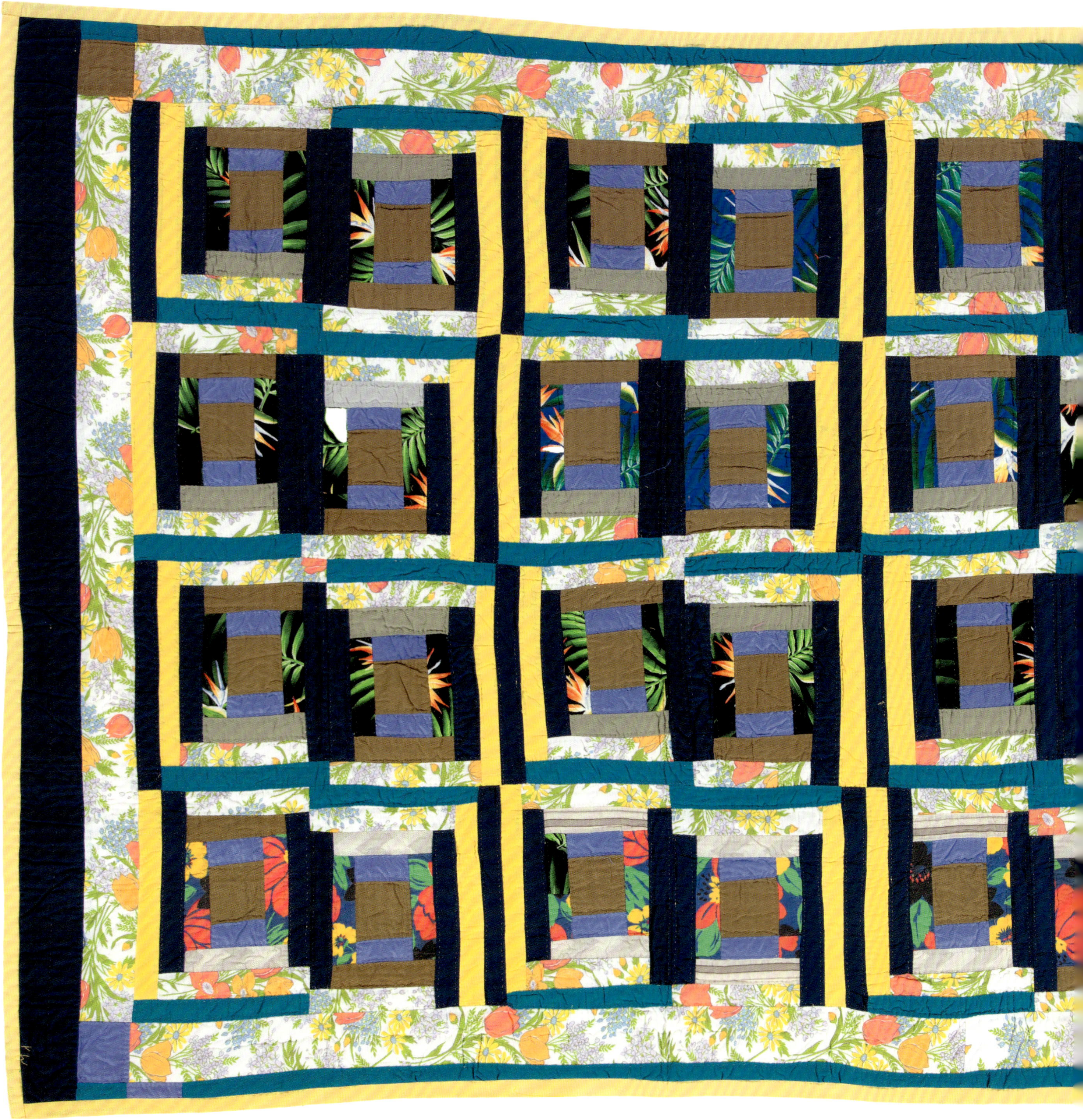

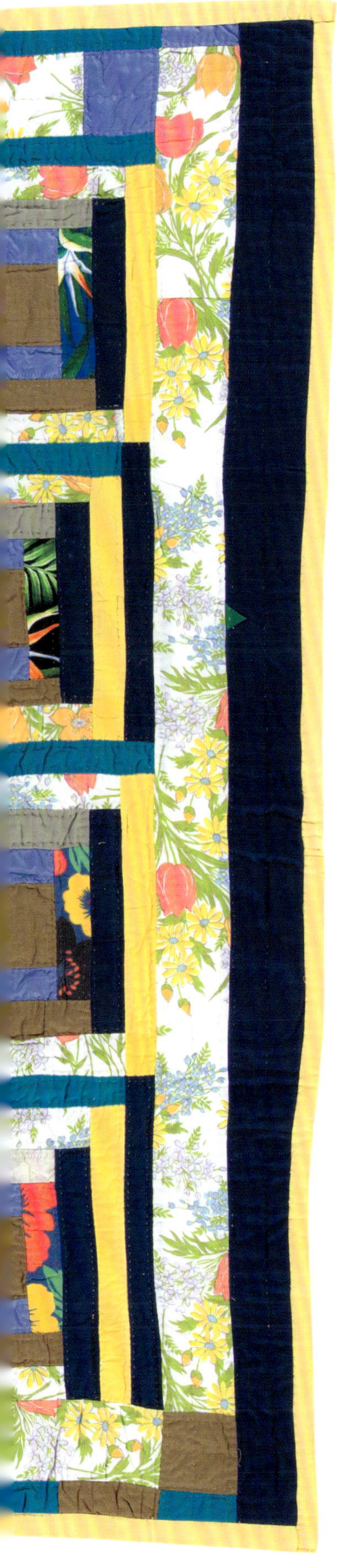

Log Cabin, (c. 1980s), back.
Log Cabin, (c. 1980s).

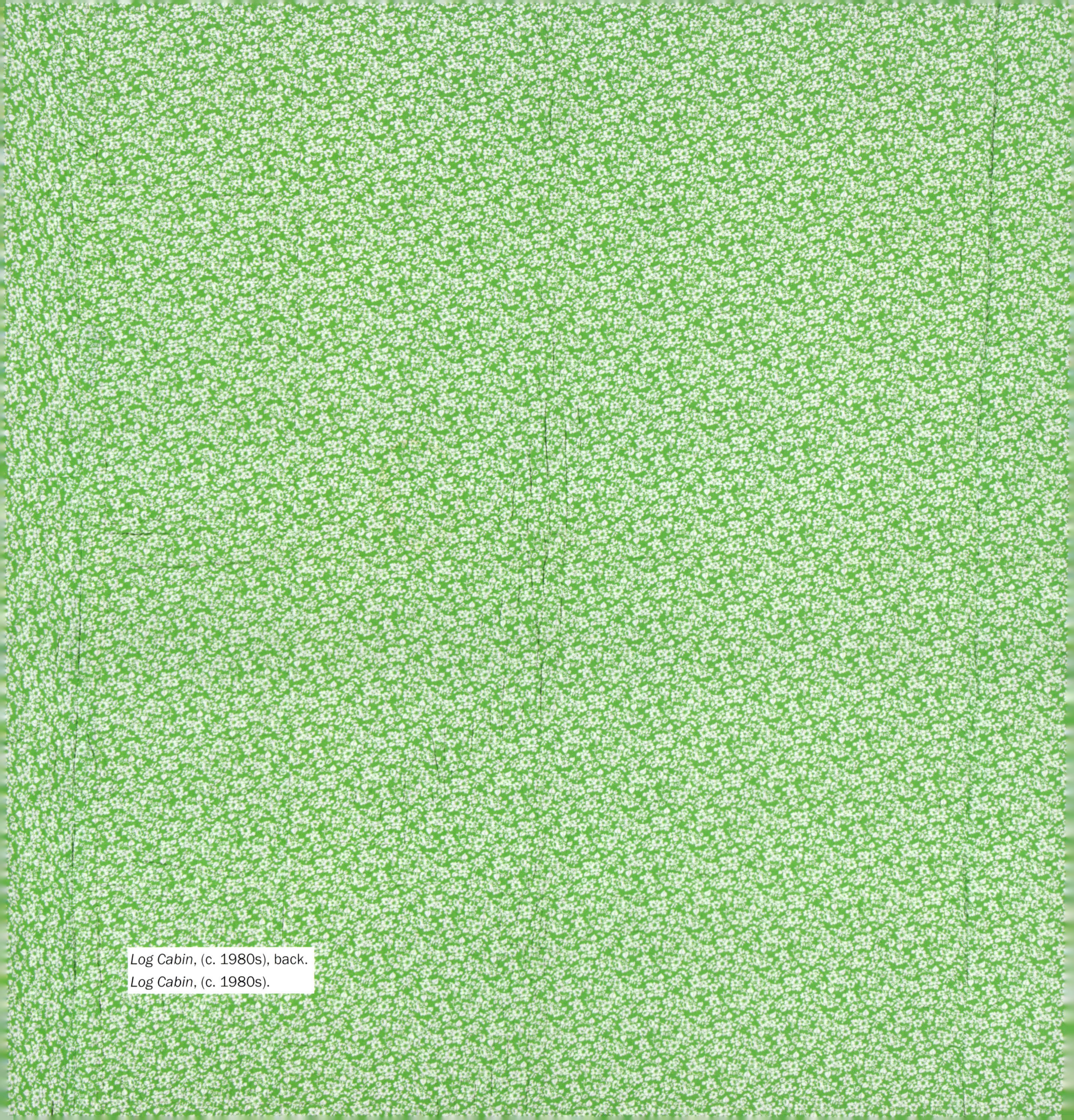

Log Cabin, (c. 1980s), back.

Log Cabin, (c. 1980s).

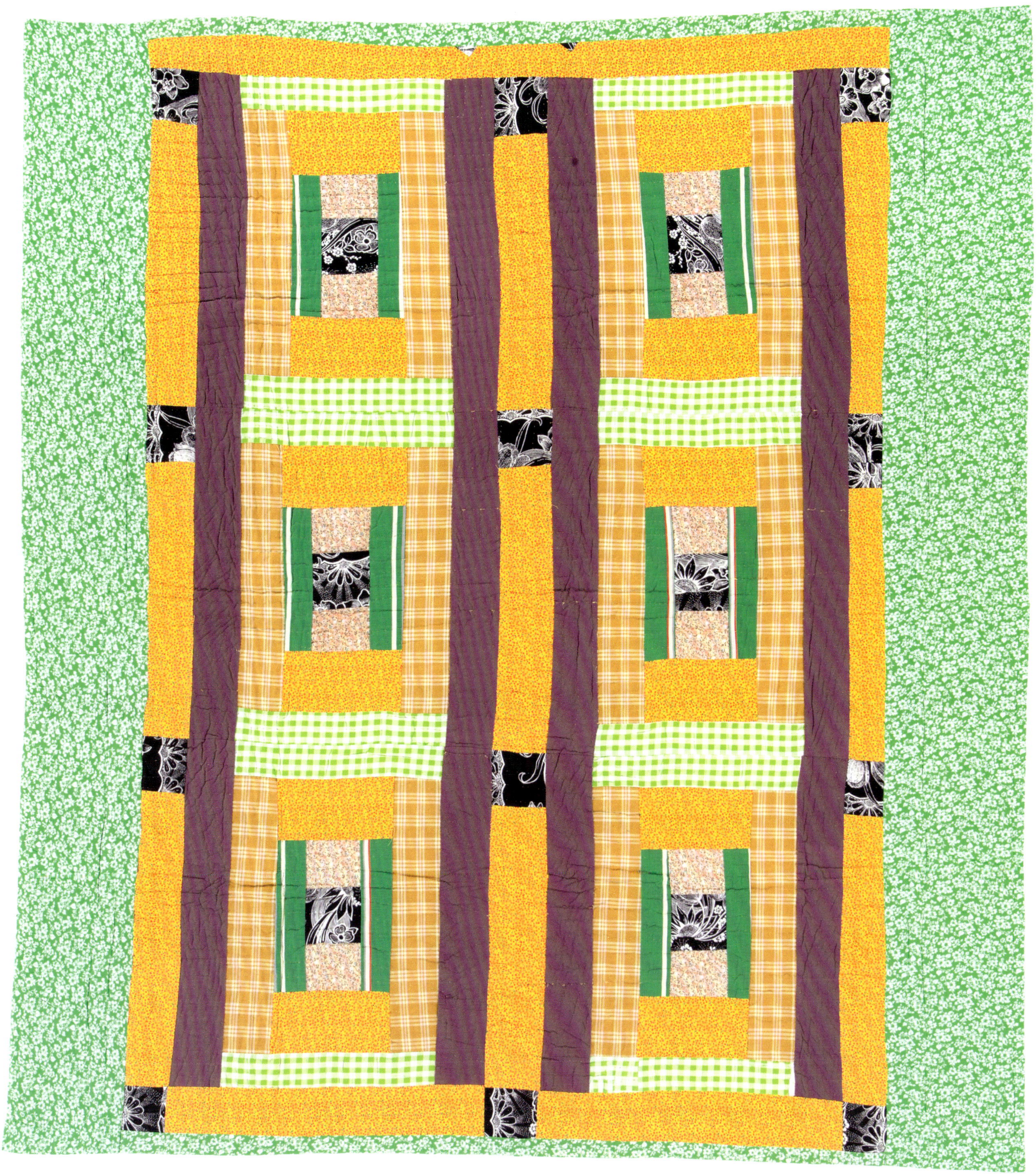

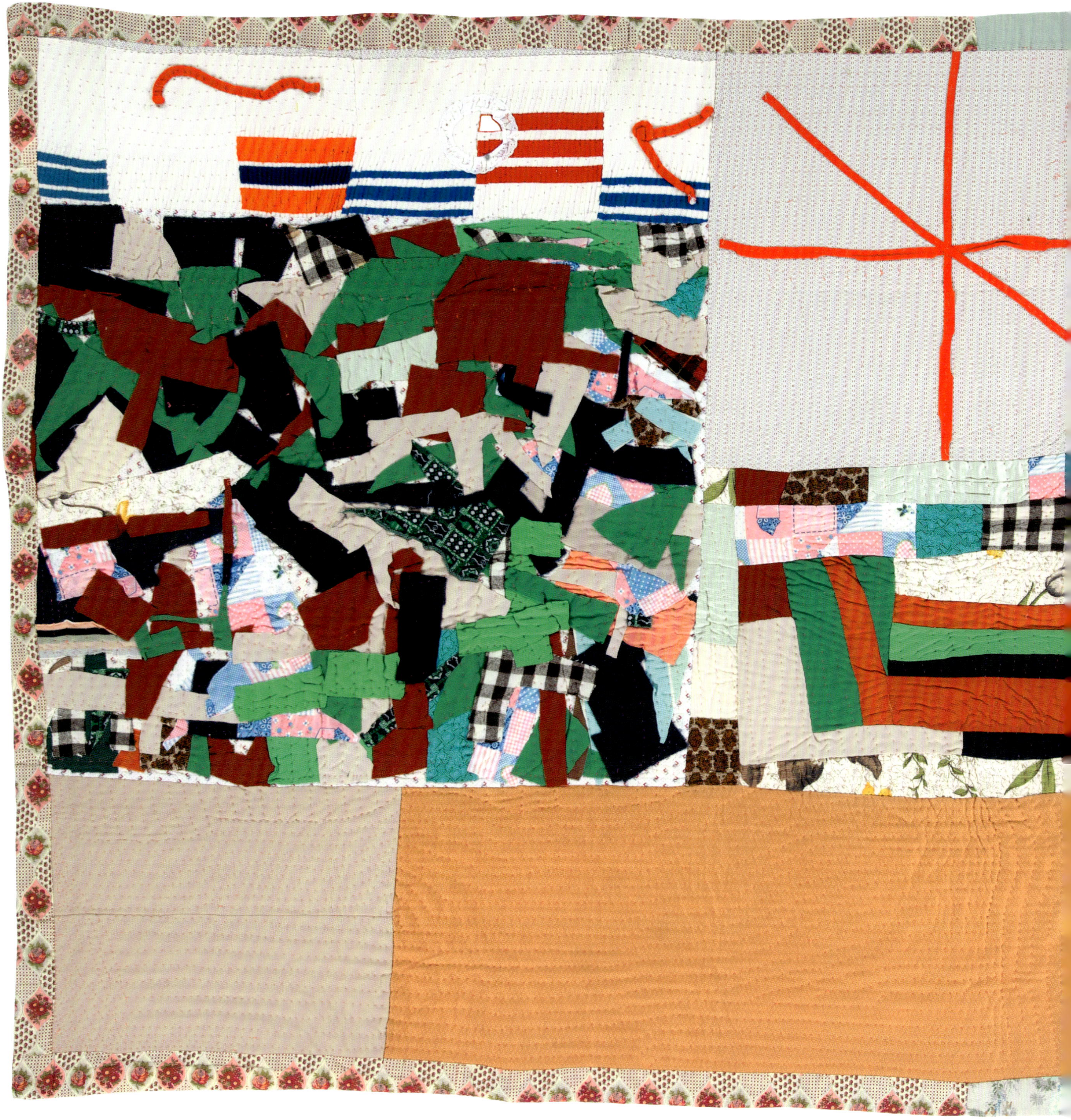

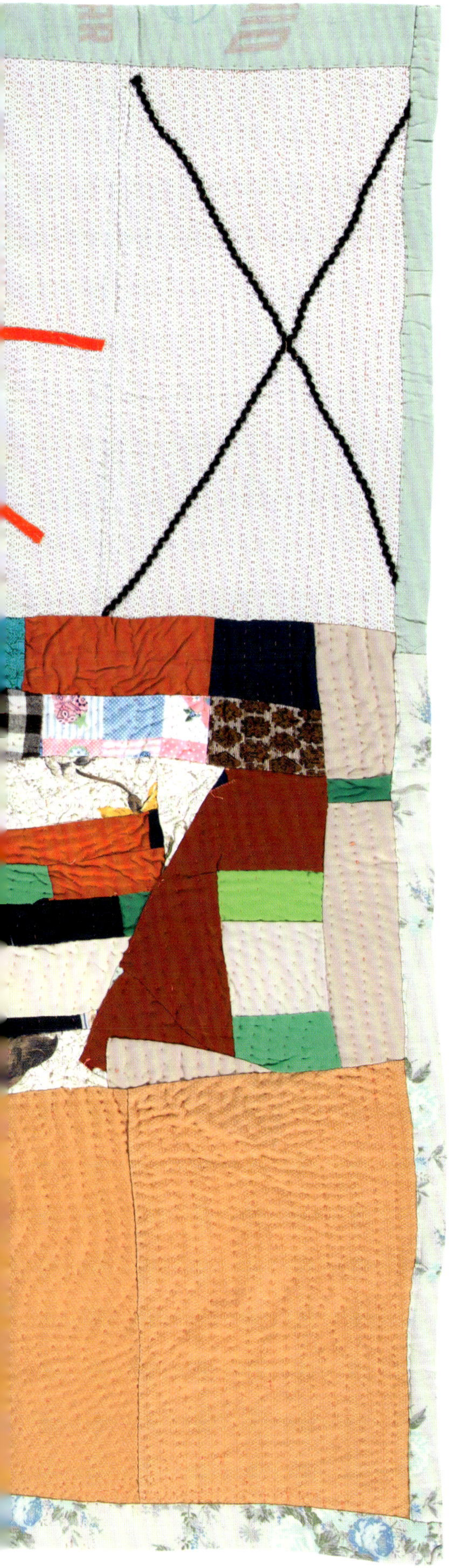

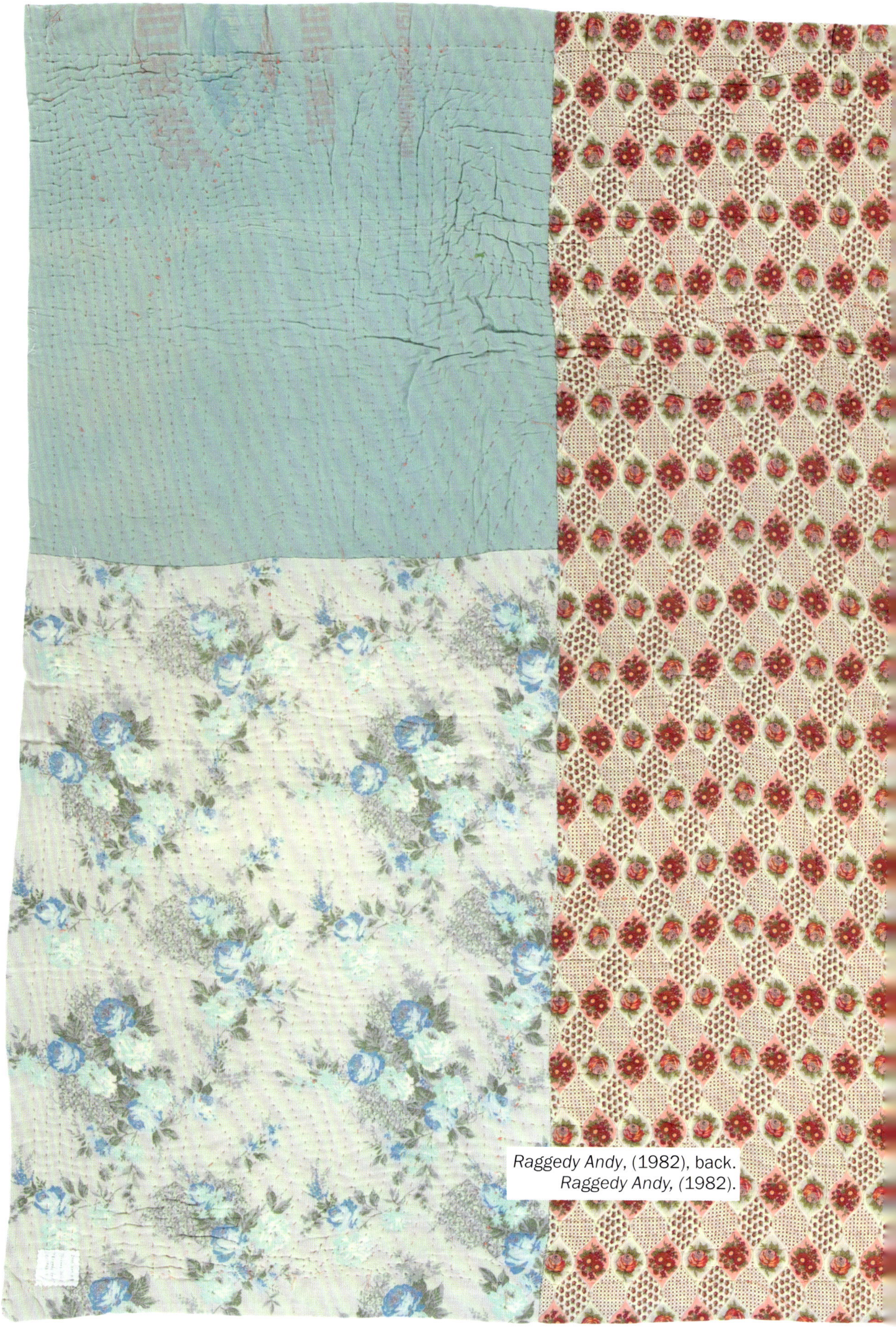

Raggedy Andy, (1982), back.
Raggedy Andy, (1982).

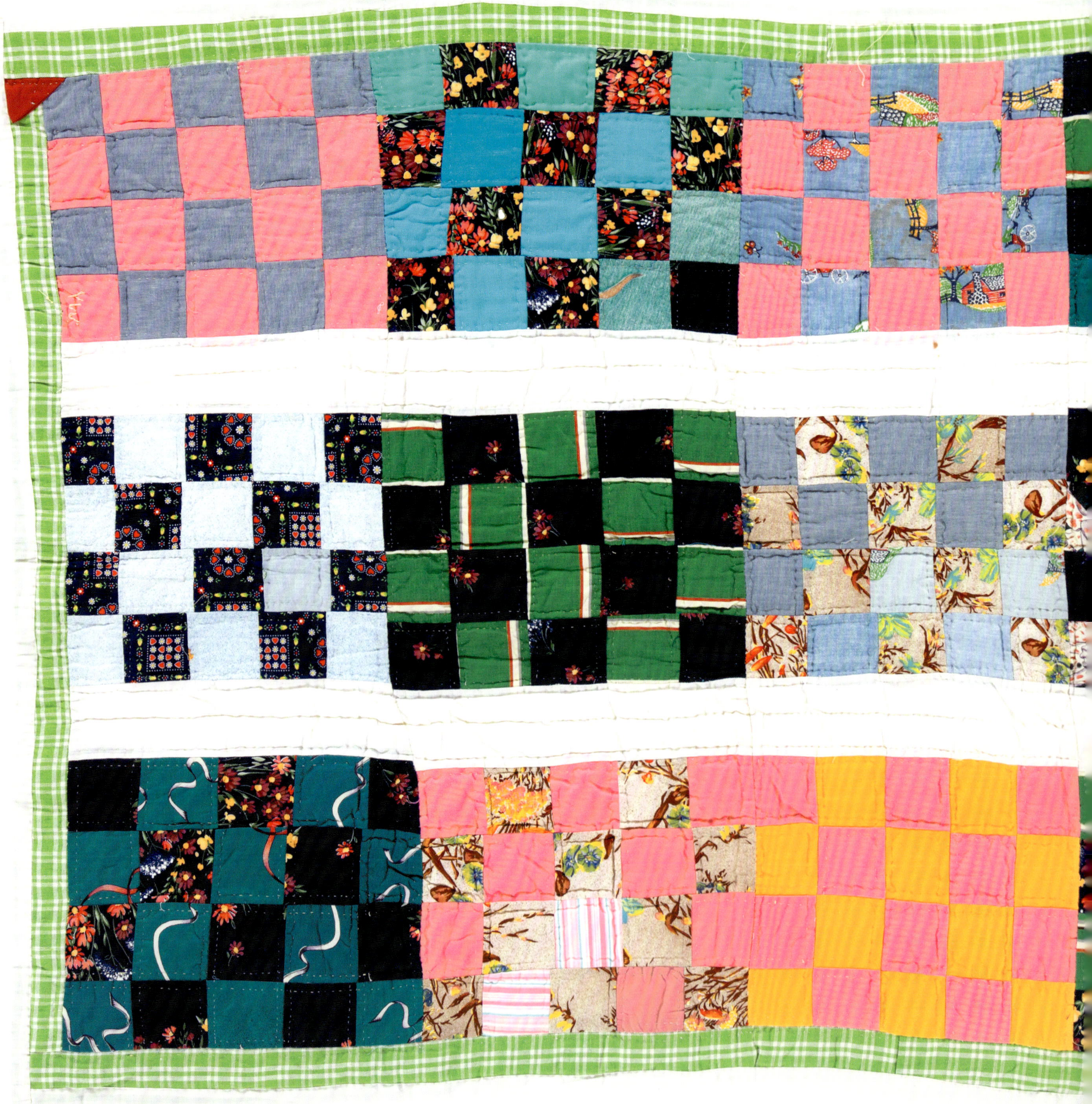

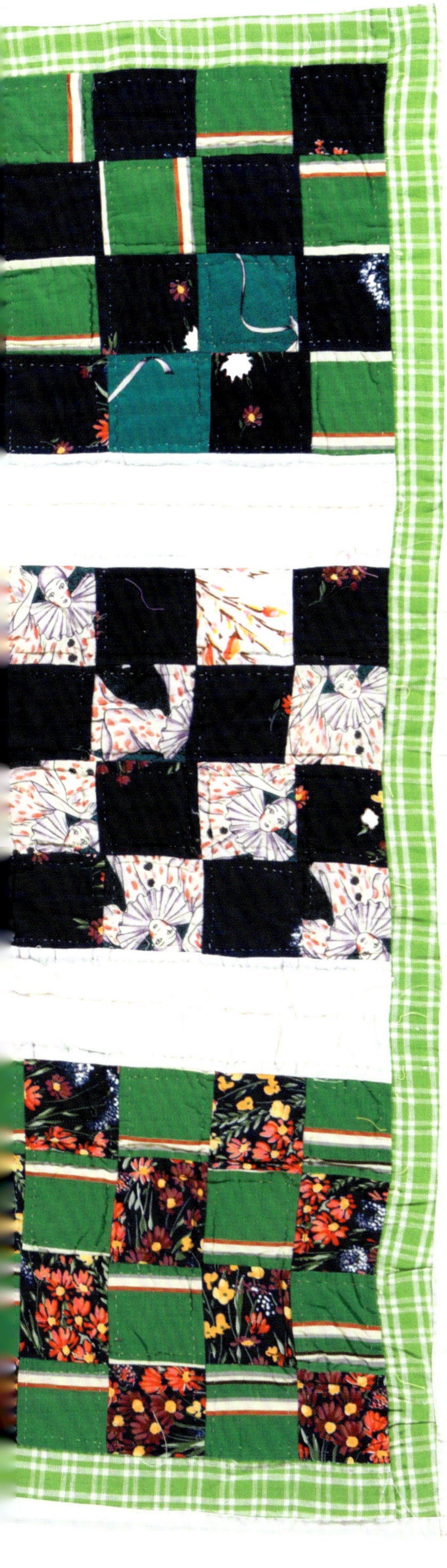

Twenty Patch, (*c.* 1980s), back.
Twenty Patch, (*c.* 1980s).

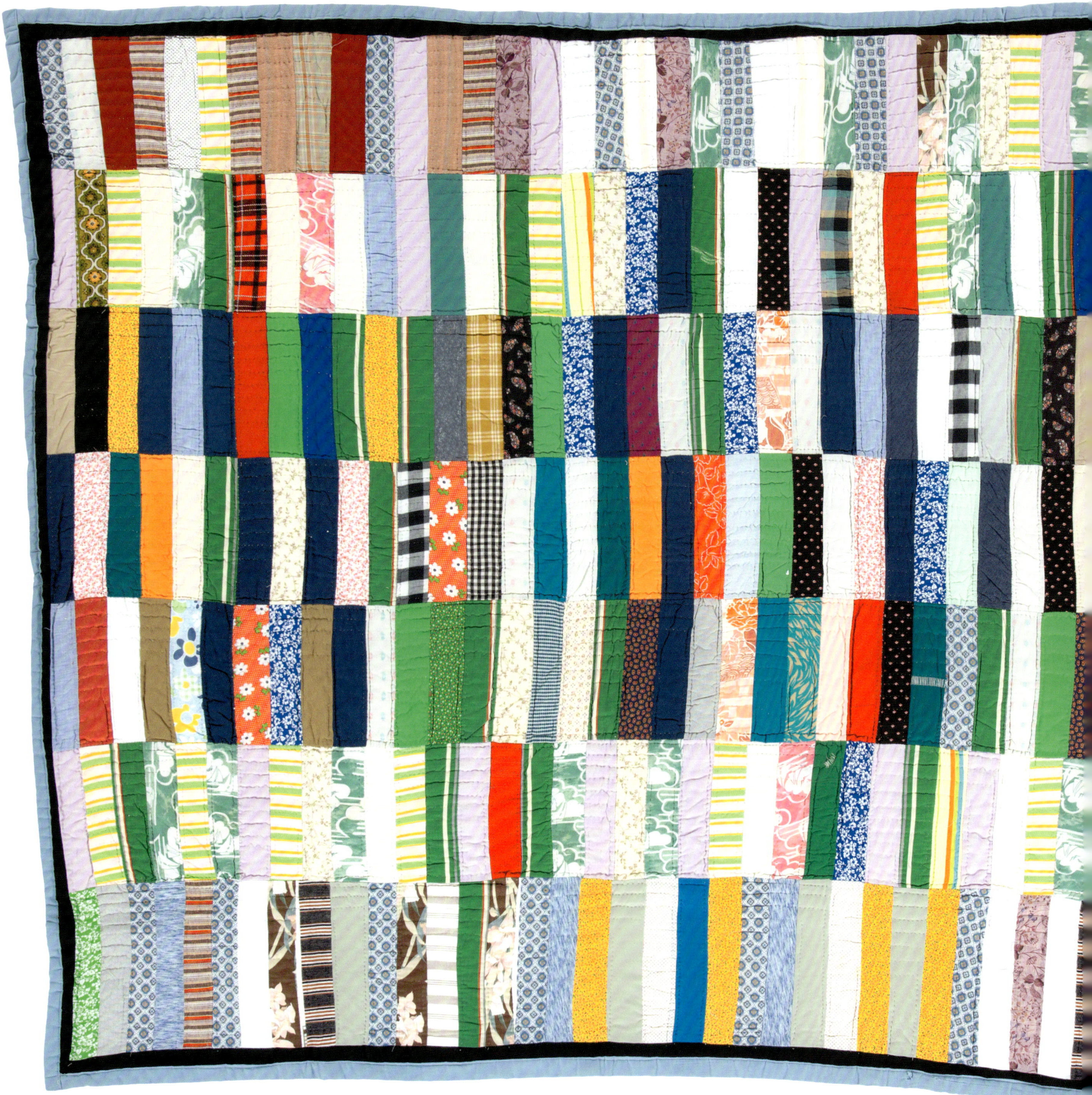

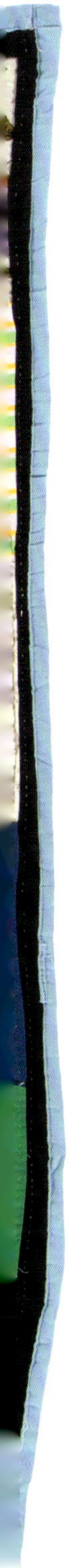

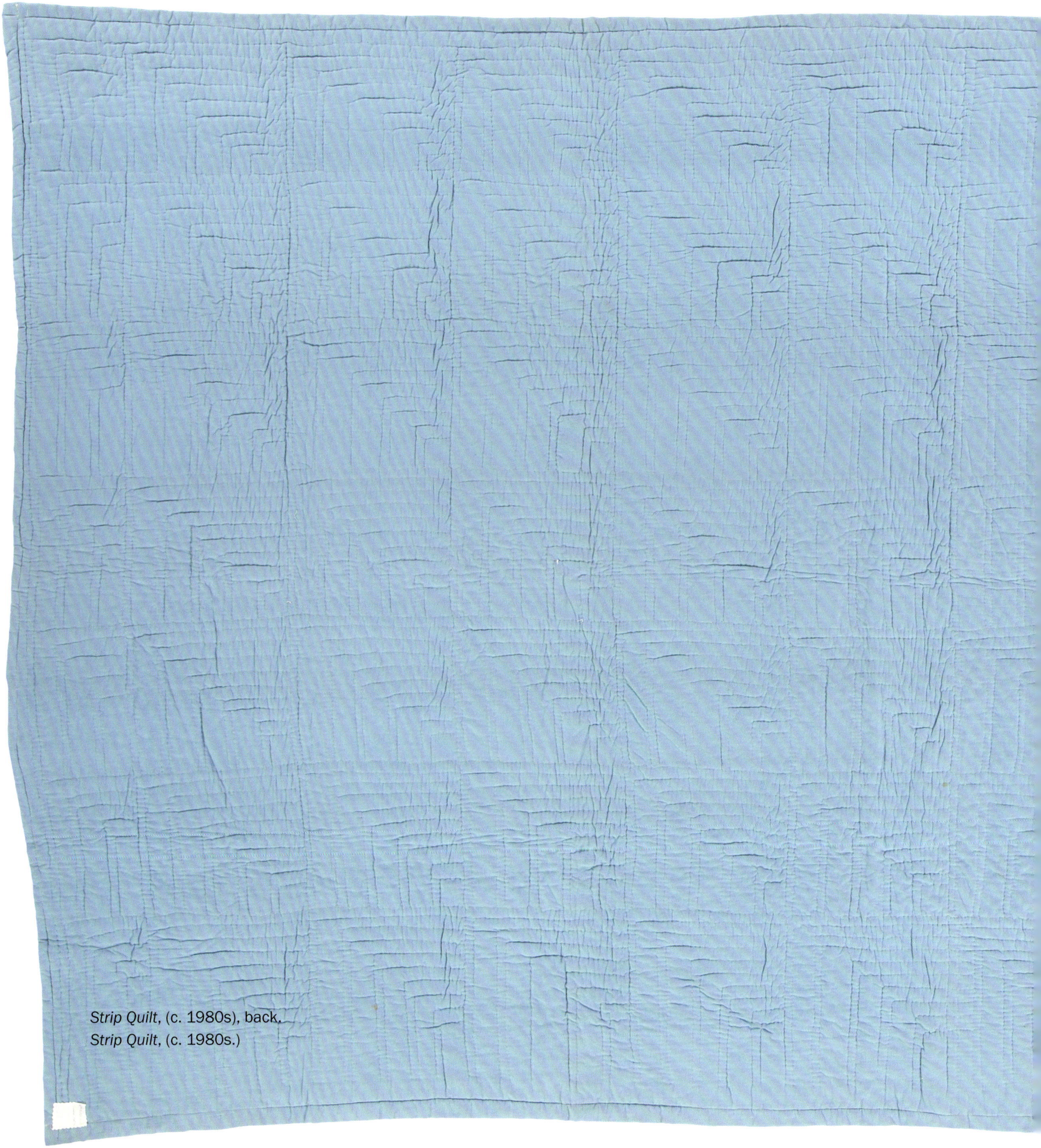

Strip Quilt, (c. 1980s), back.

Strip Quilt, (c. 1980s.)

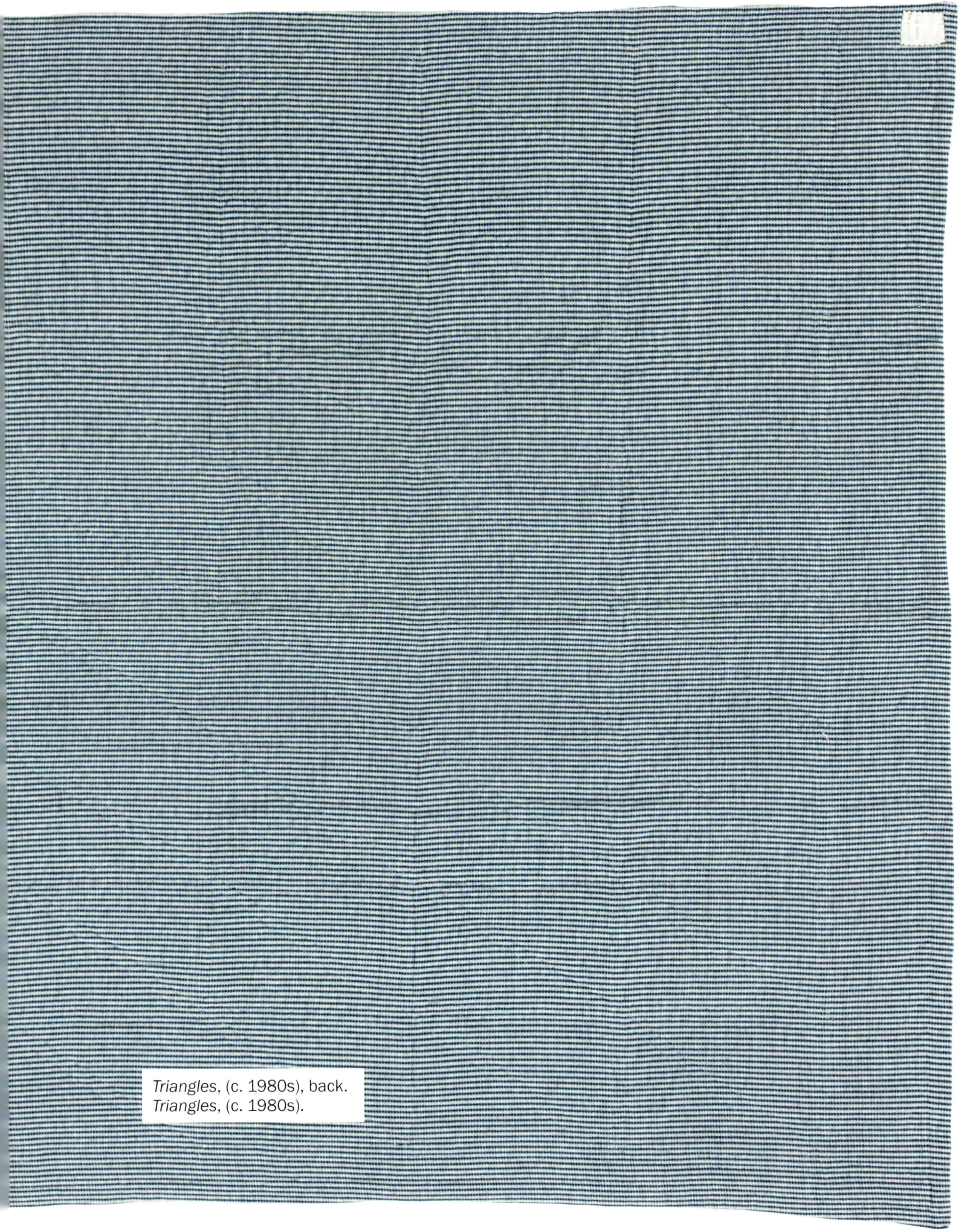

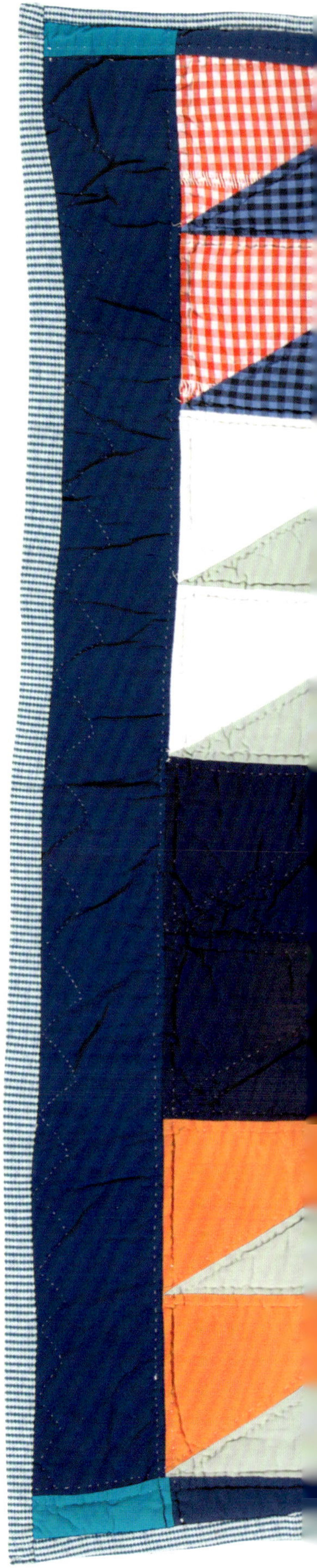

Triangles, (c. 1980s), back.
Triangles, (c. 1980s).

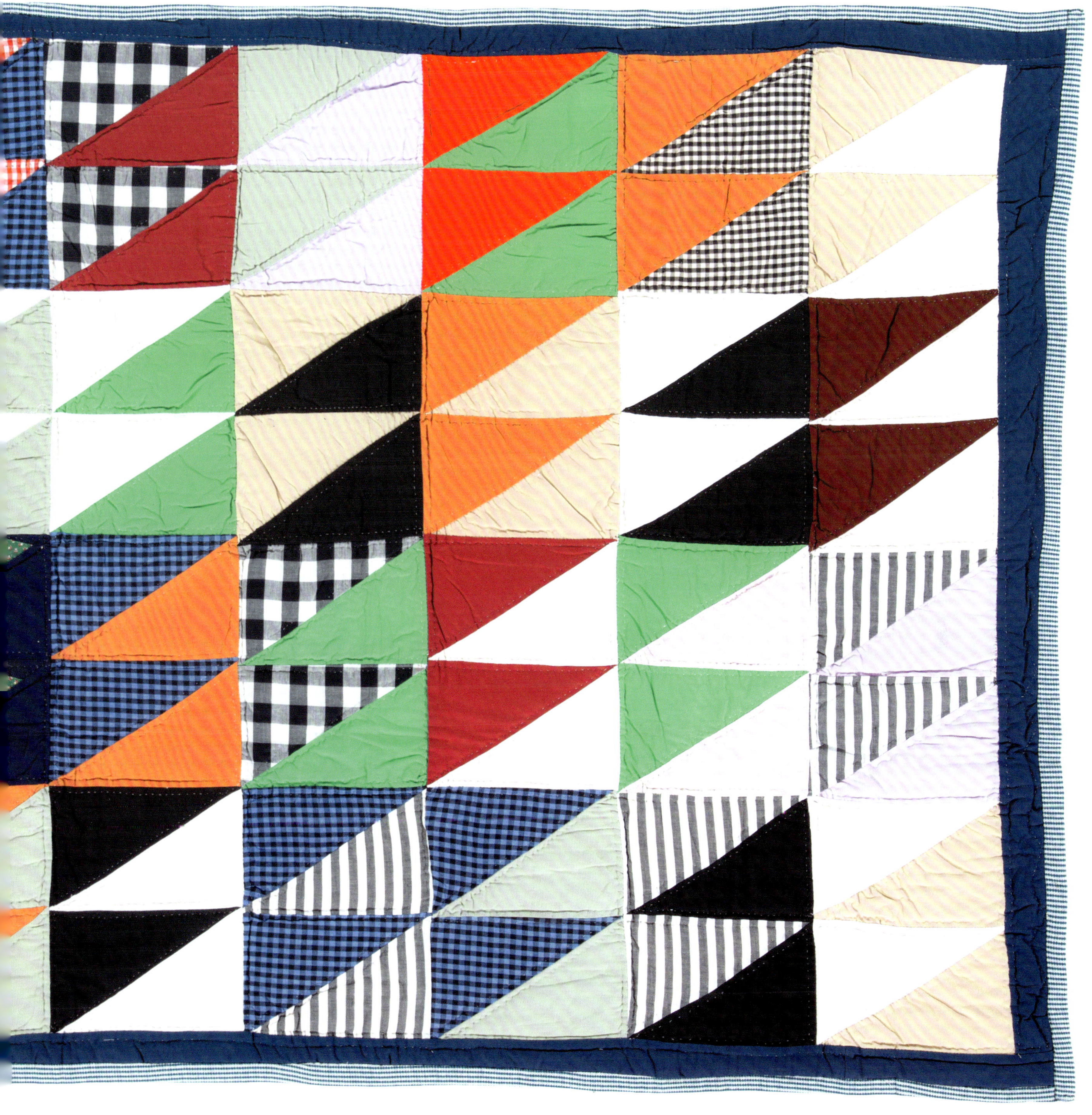

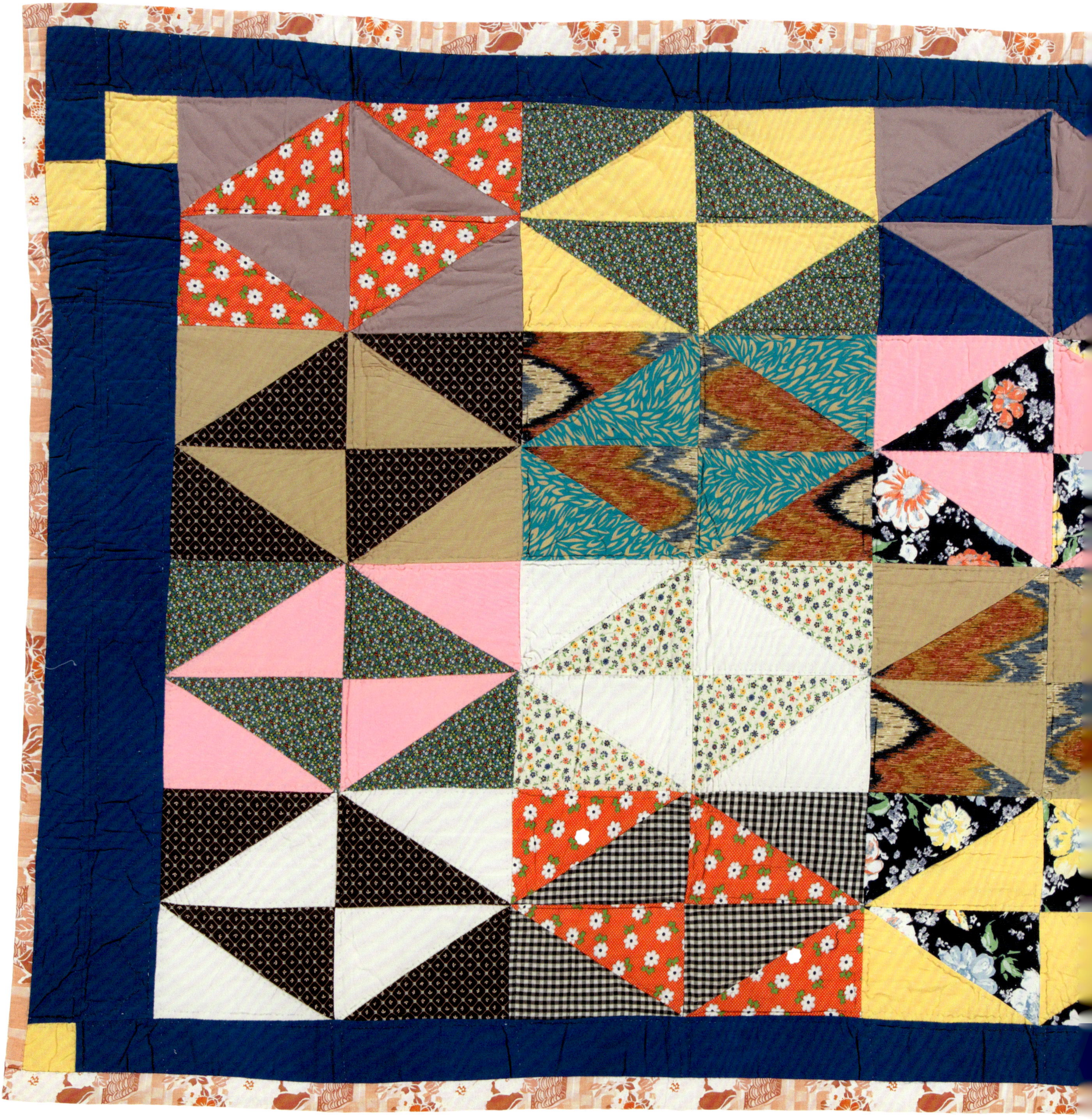

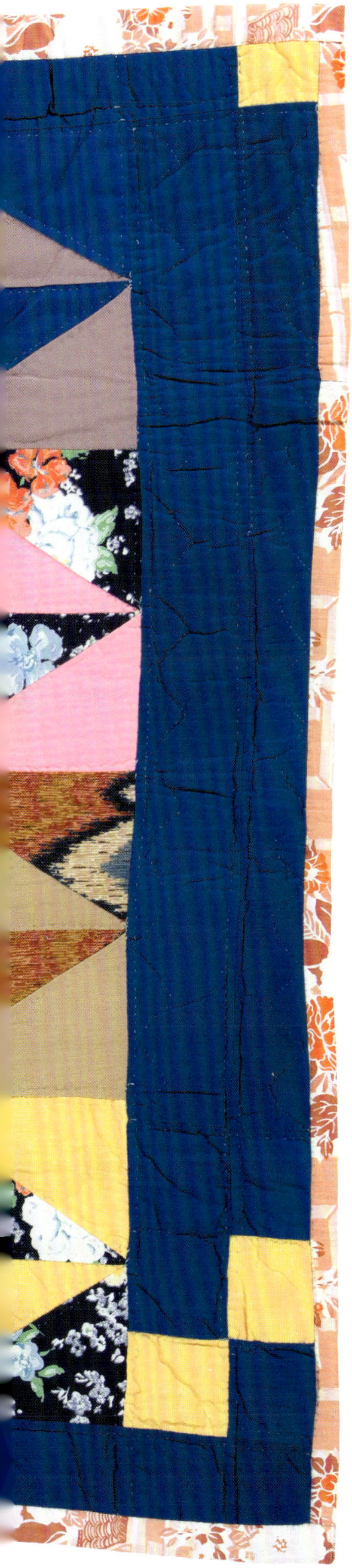

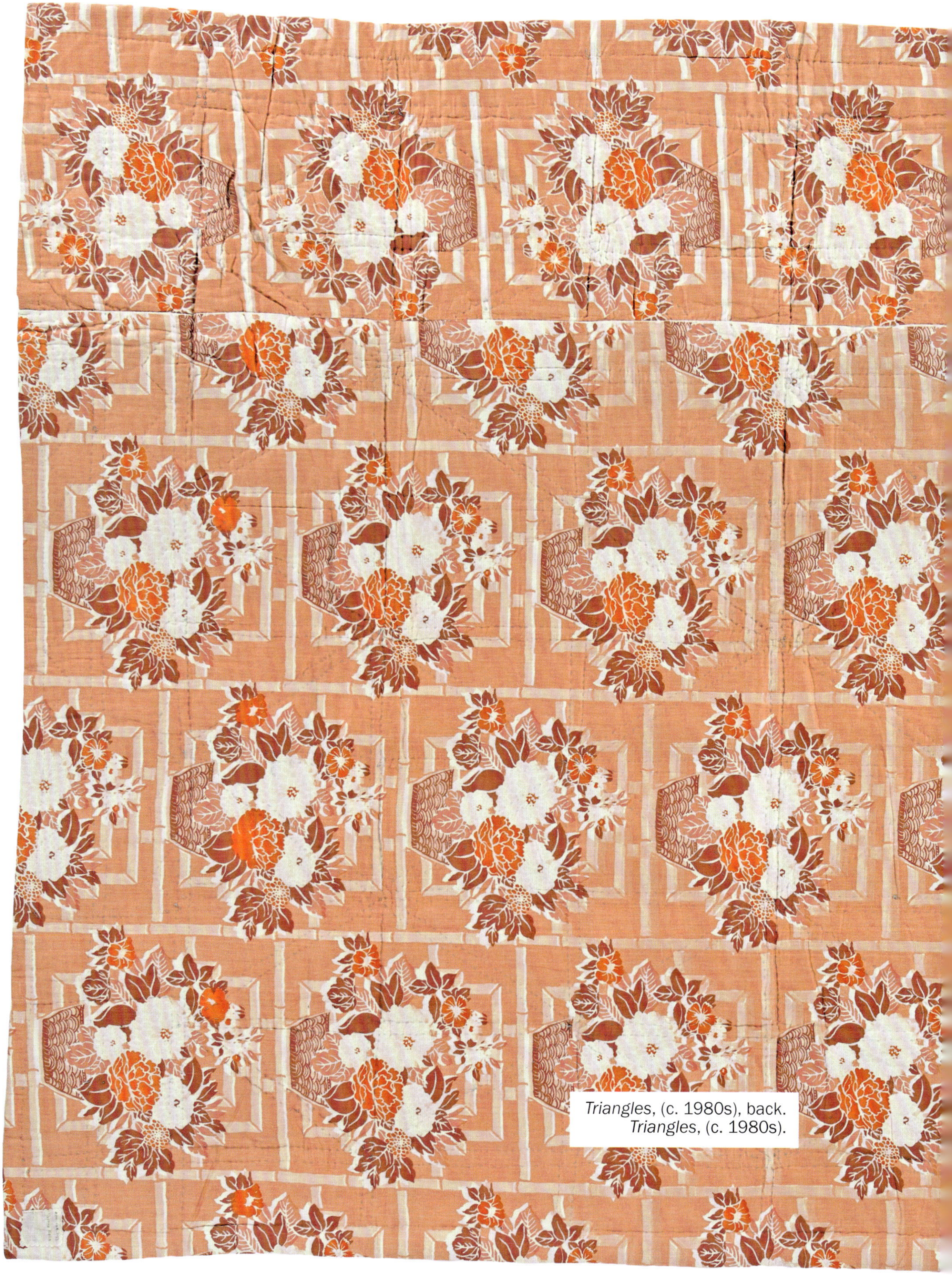

Triangles, (c. 1980s), back.
Triangles, (c. 1980s).

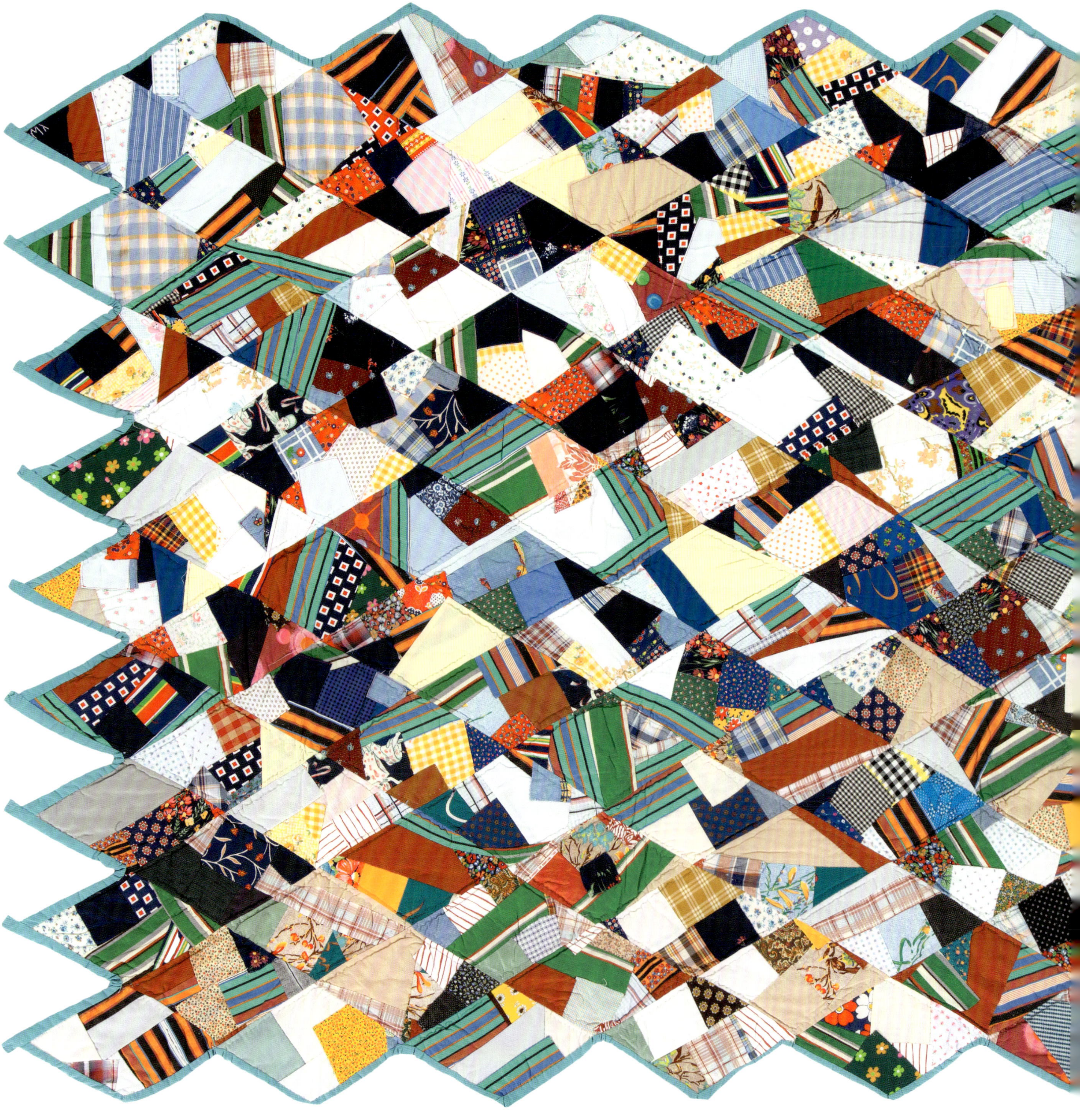

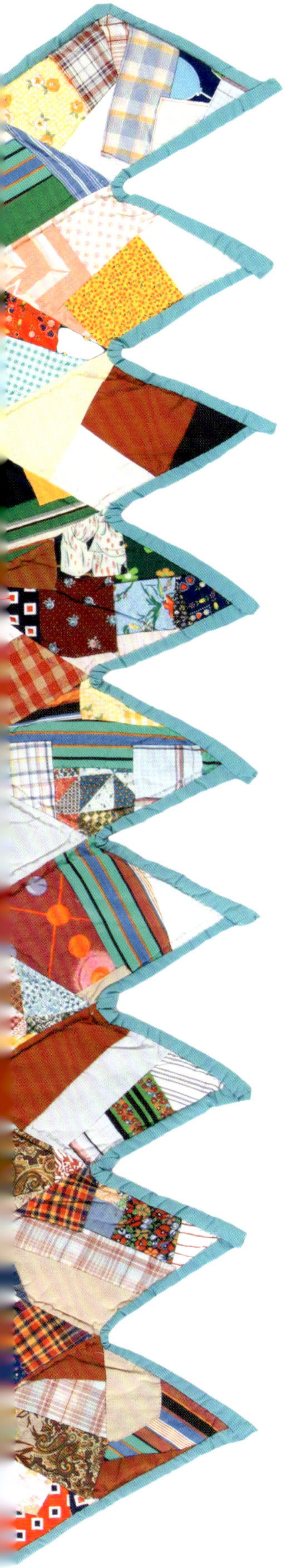

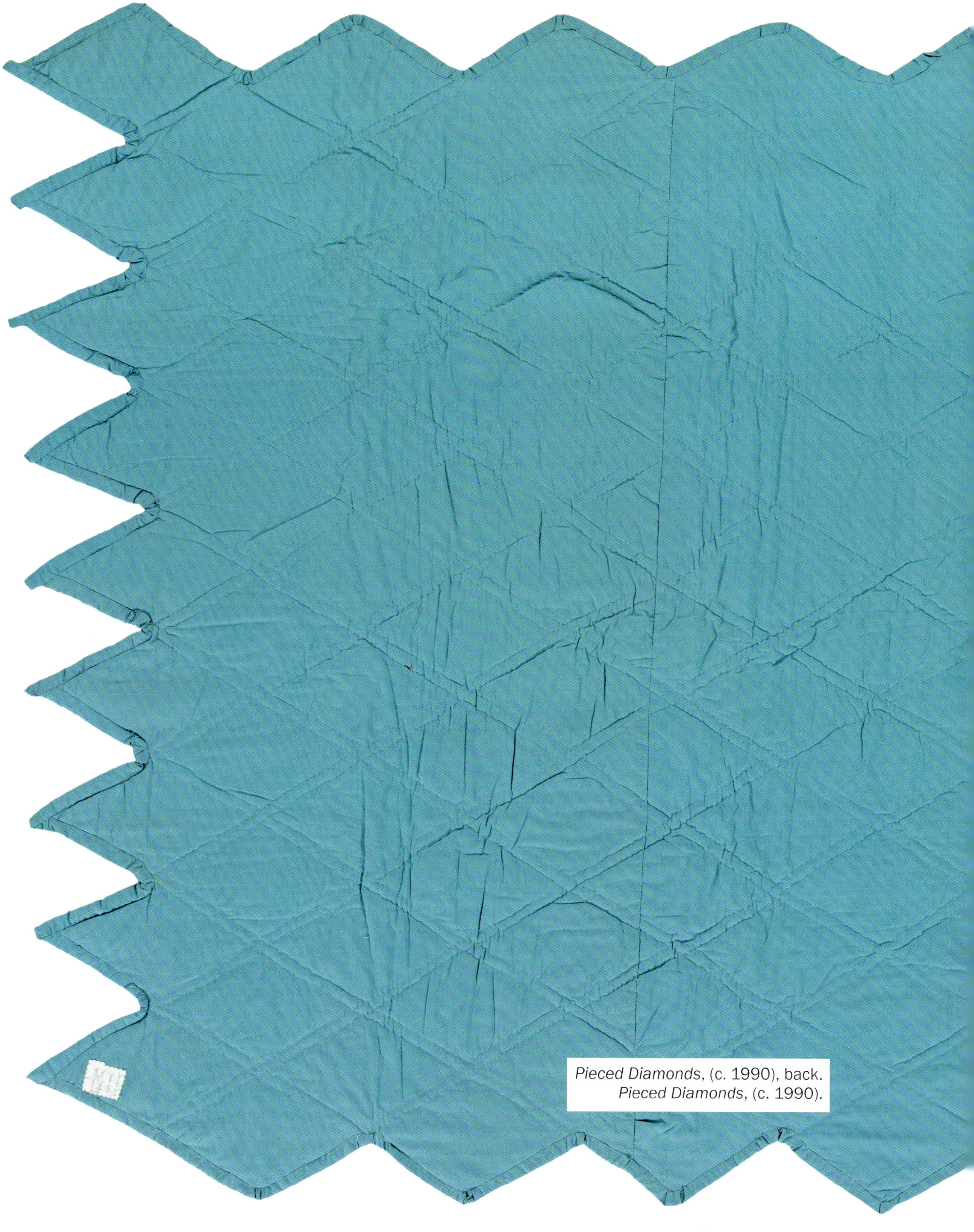

Pieced Diamonds, (c. 1990), back.
Pieced Diamonds, (c. 1990).

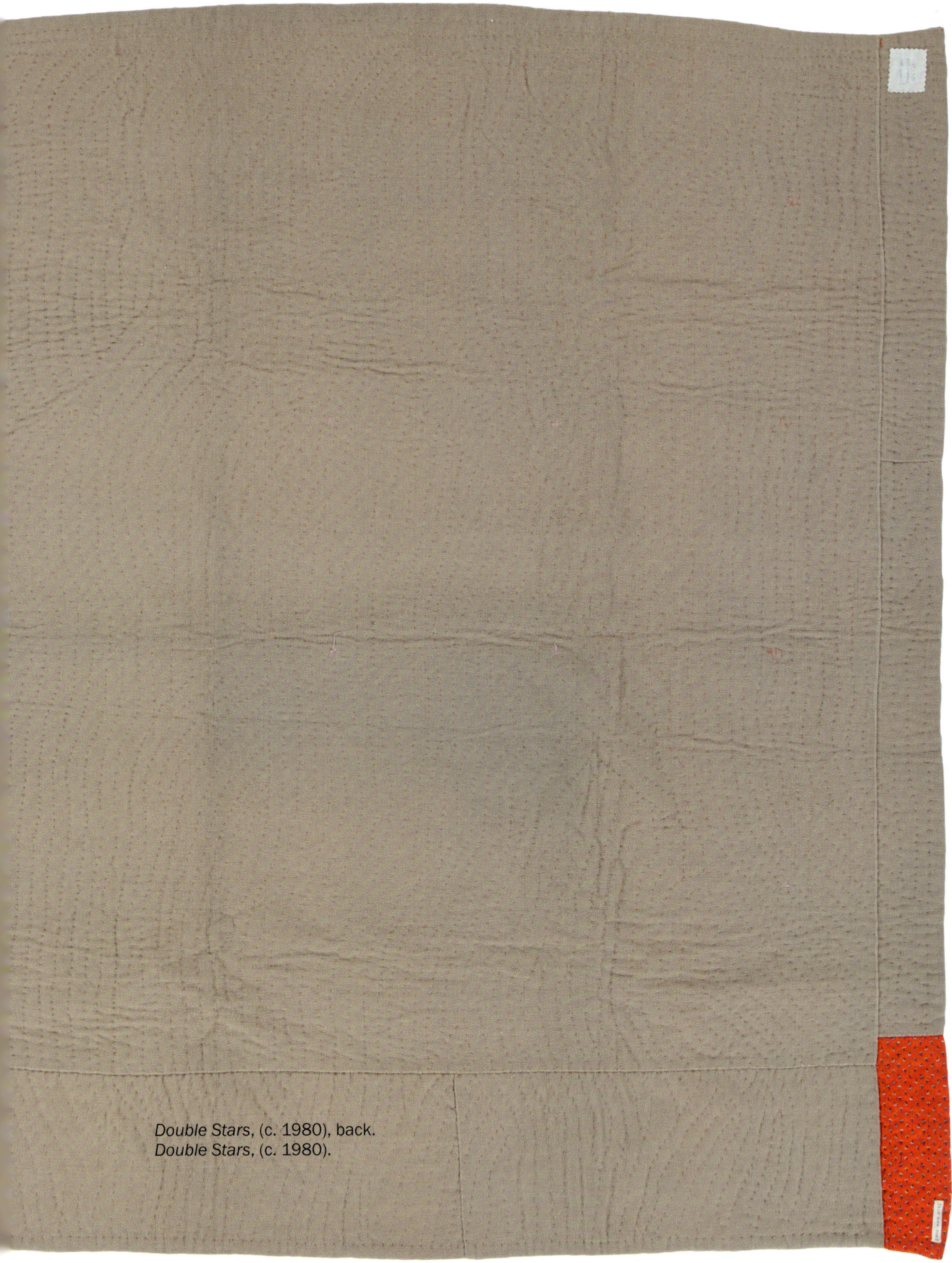

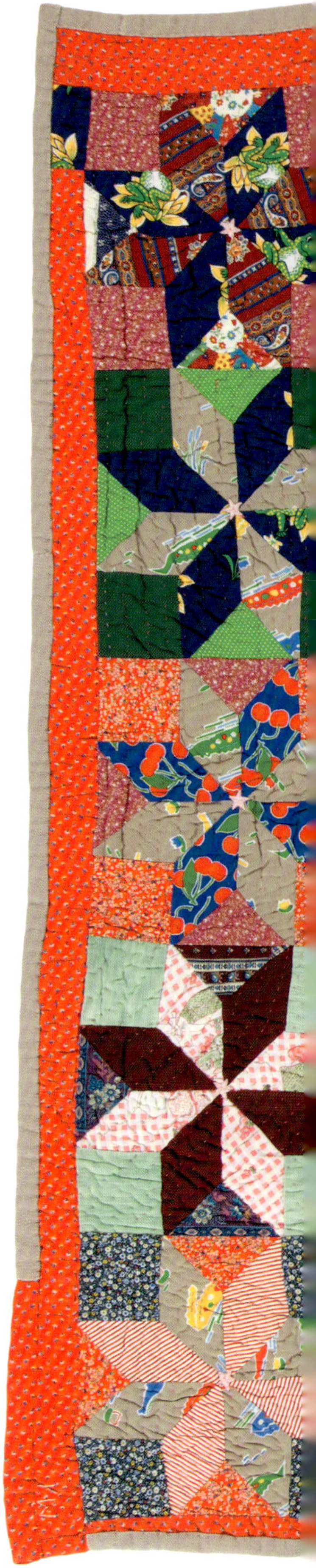

Double Stars, (c. 1980), back.
Double Stars, (c. 1980).

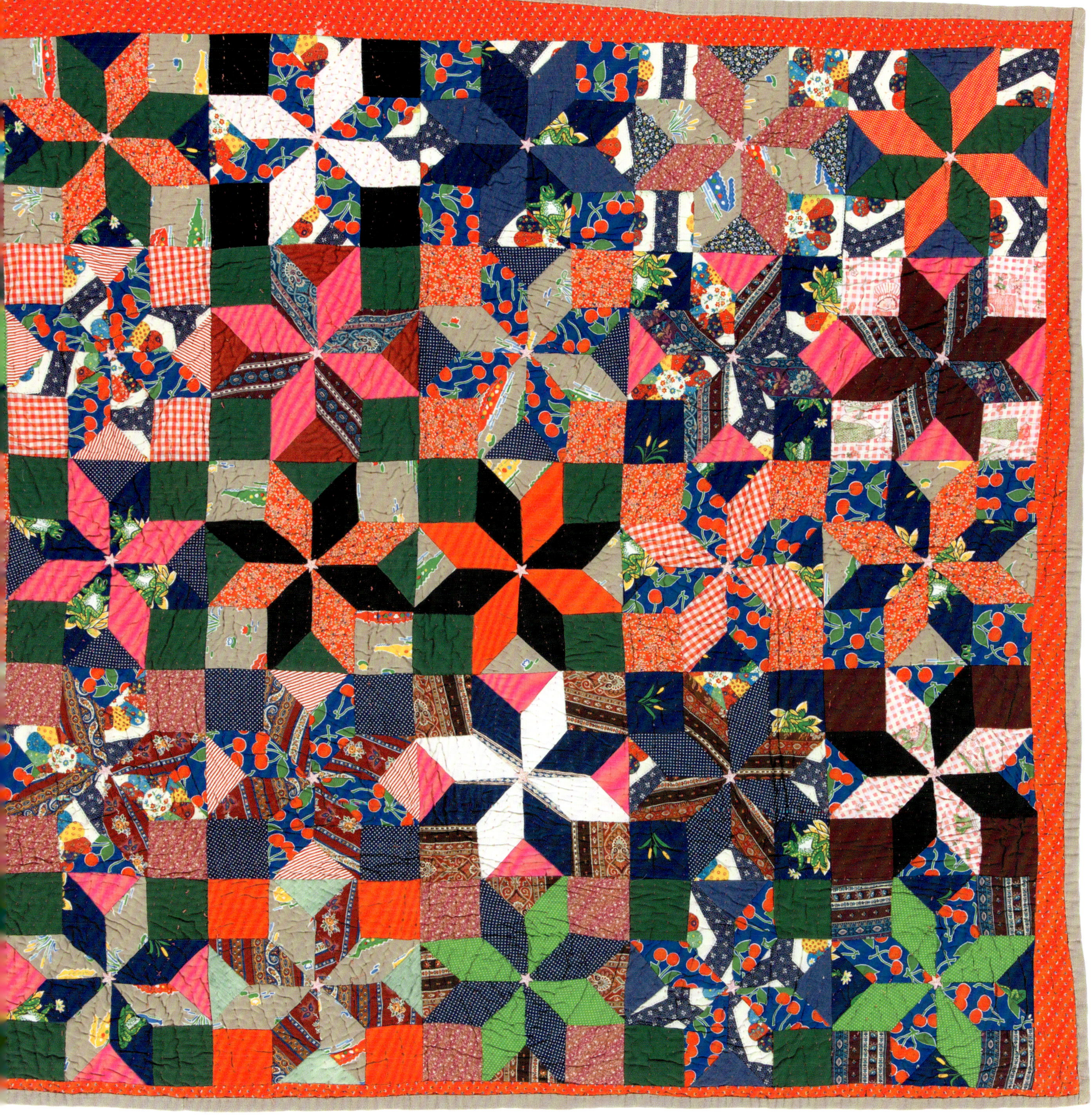

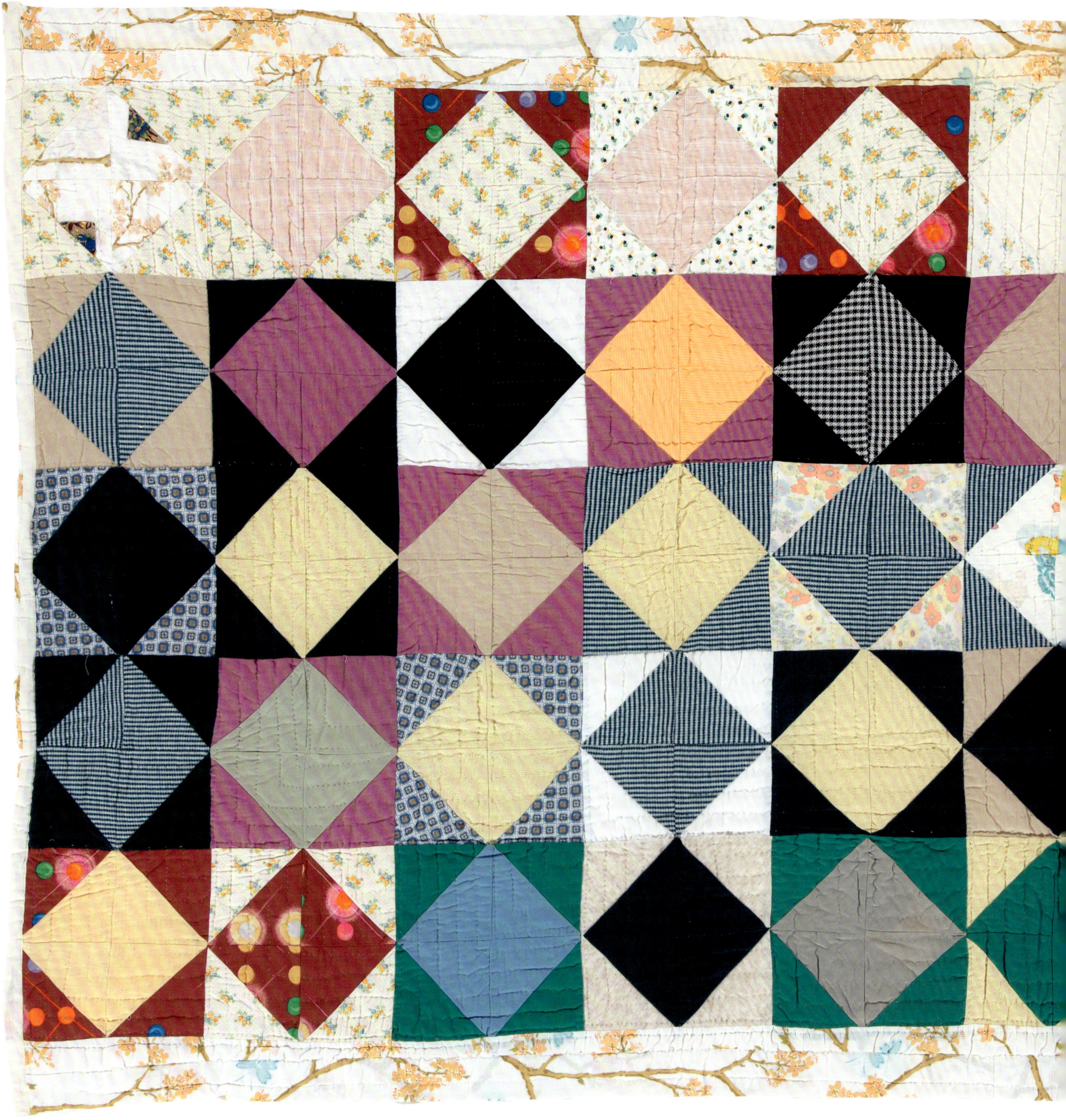

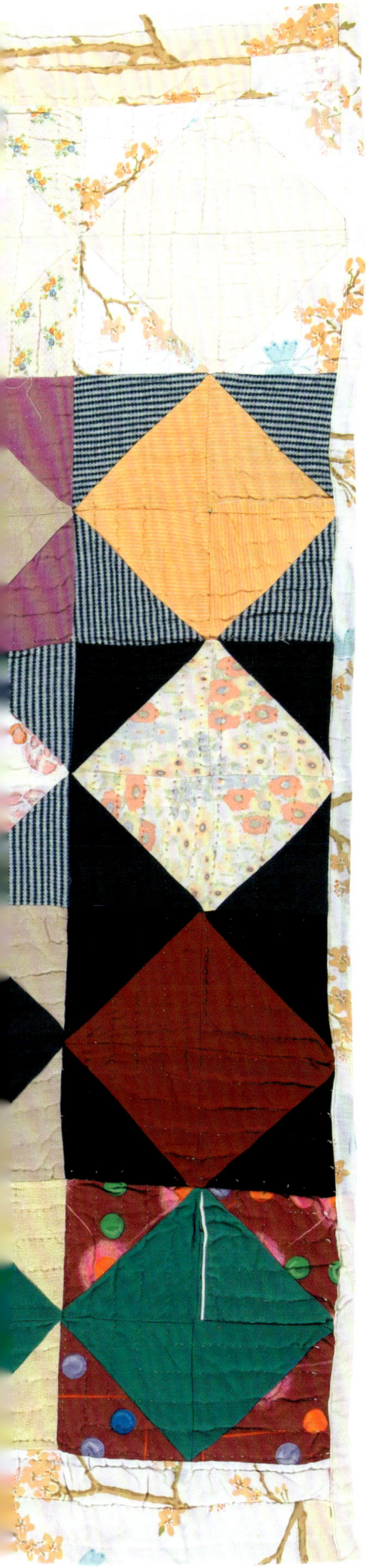

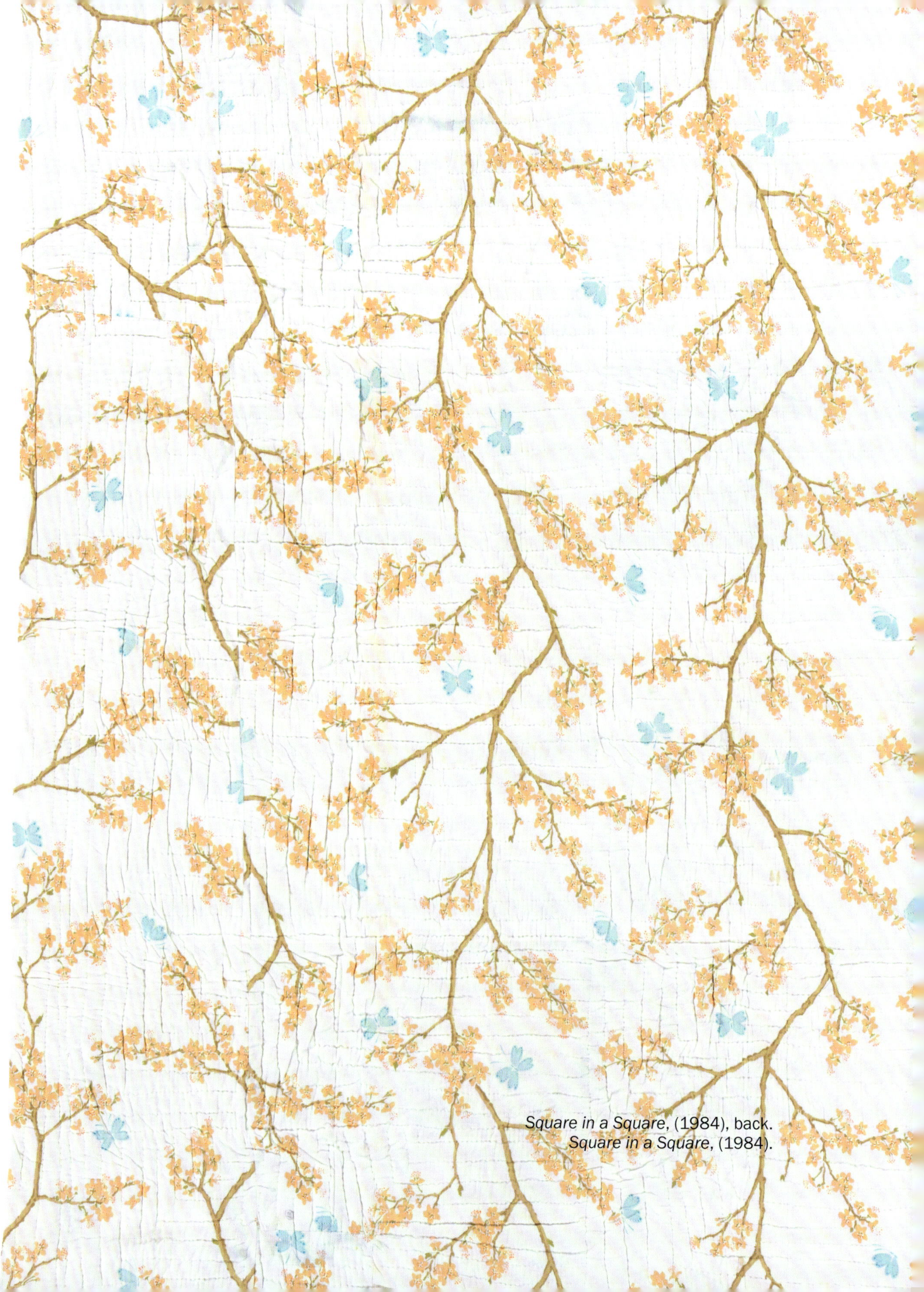

Square in a Square, (1984), back.
Square in a Square, (1984).

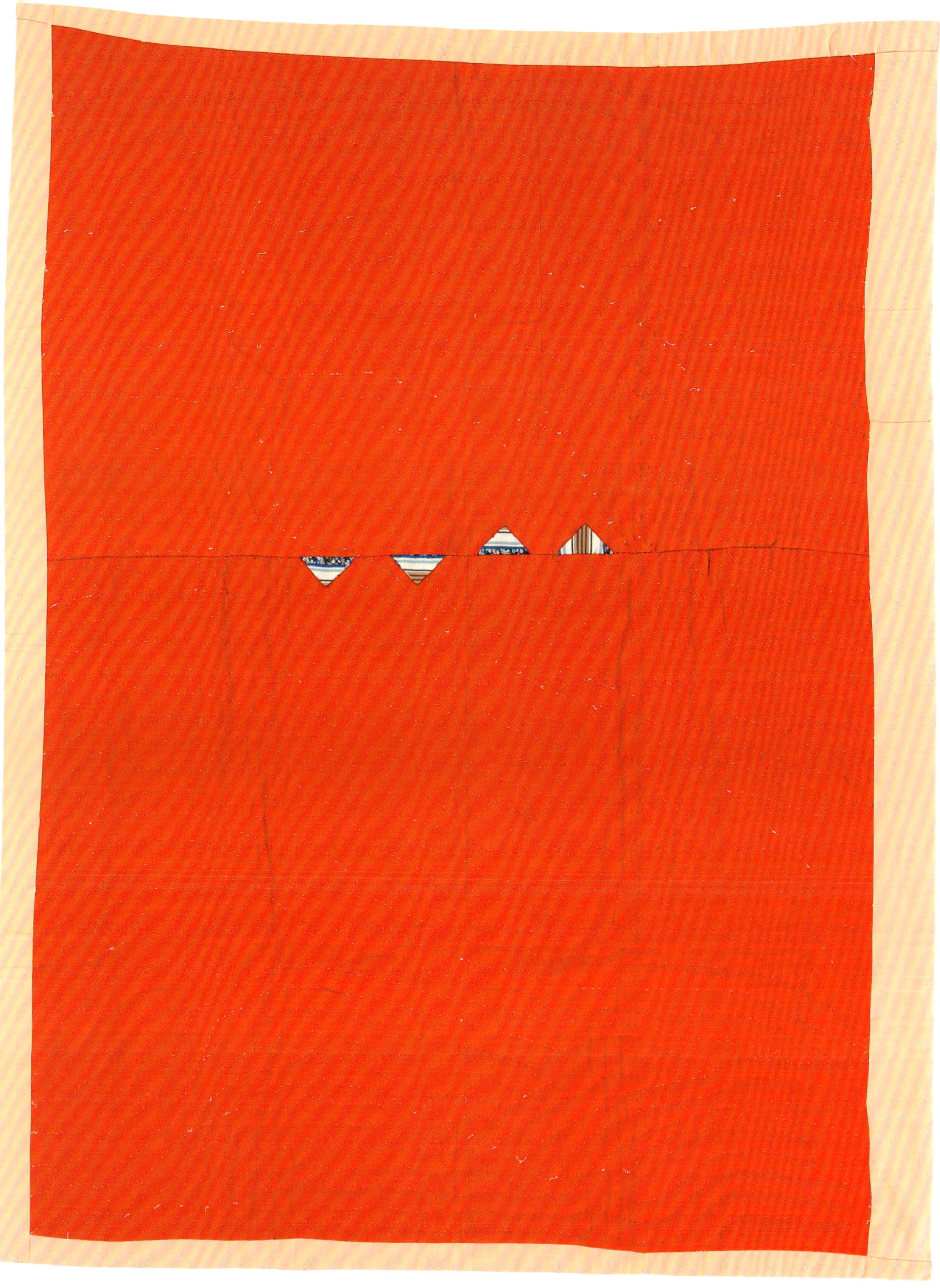

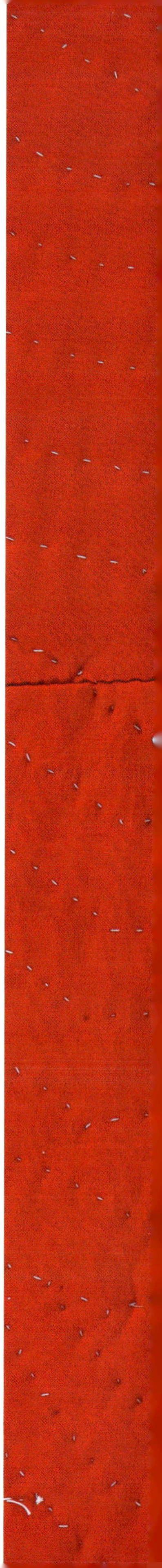

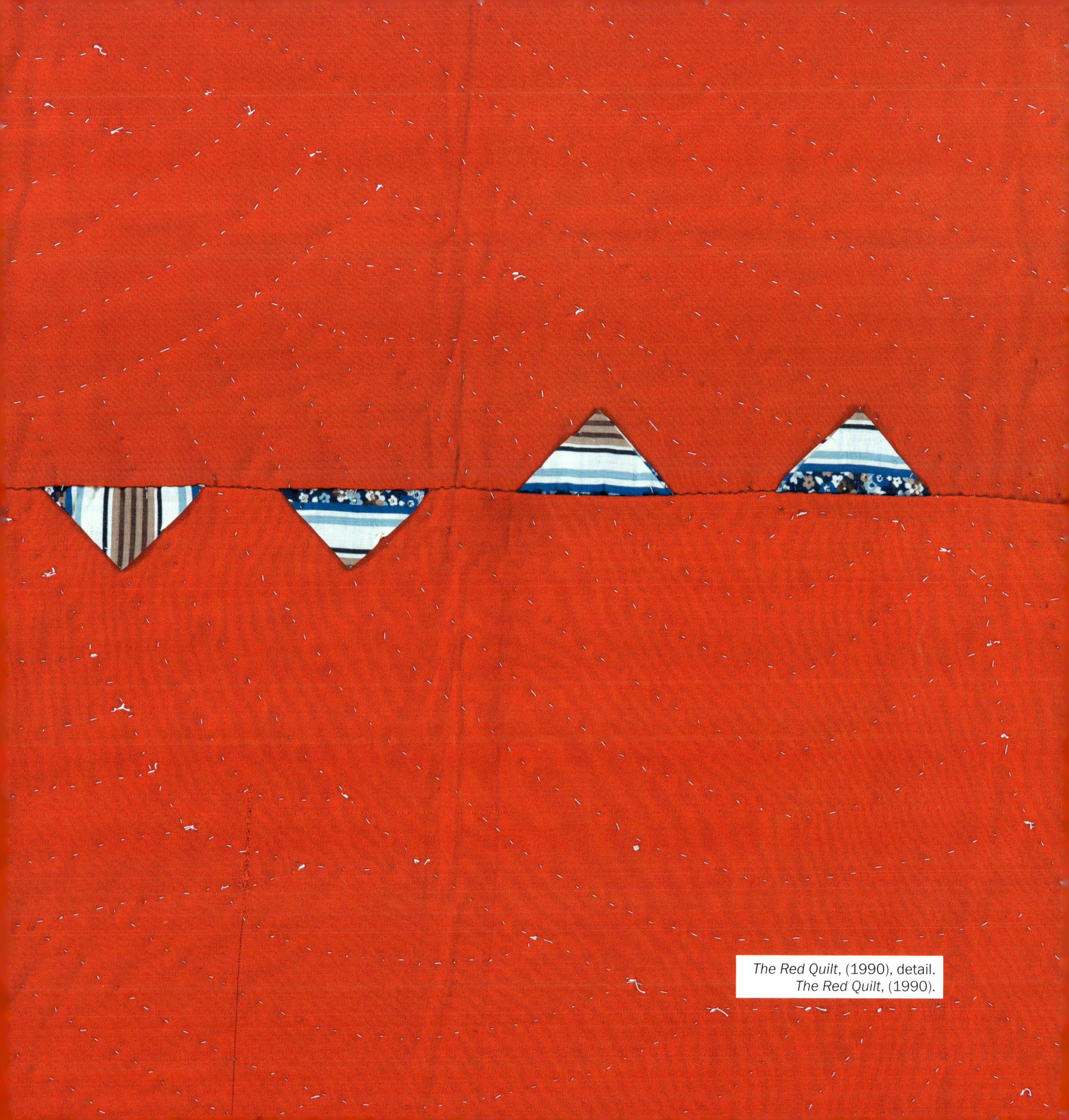

The Red Quilt, (1990), detail.
The Red Quilt, (1990).

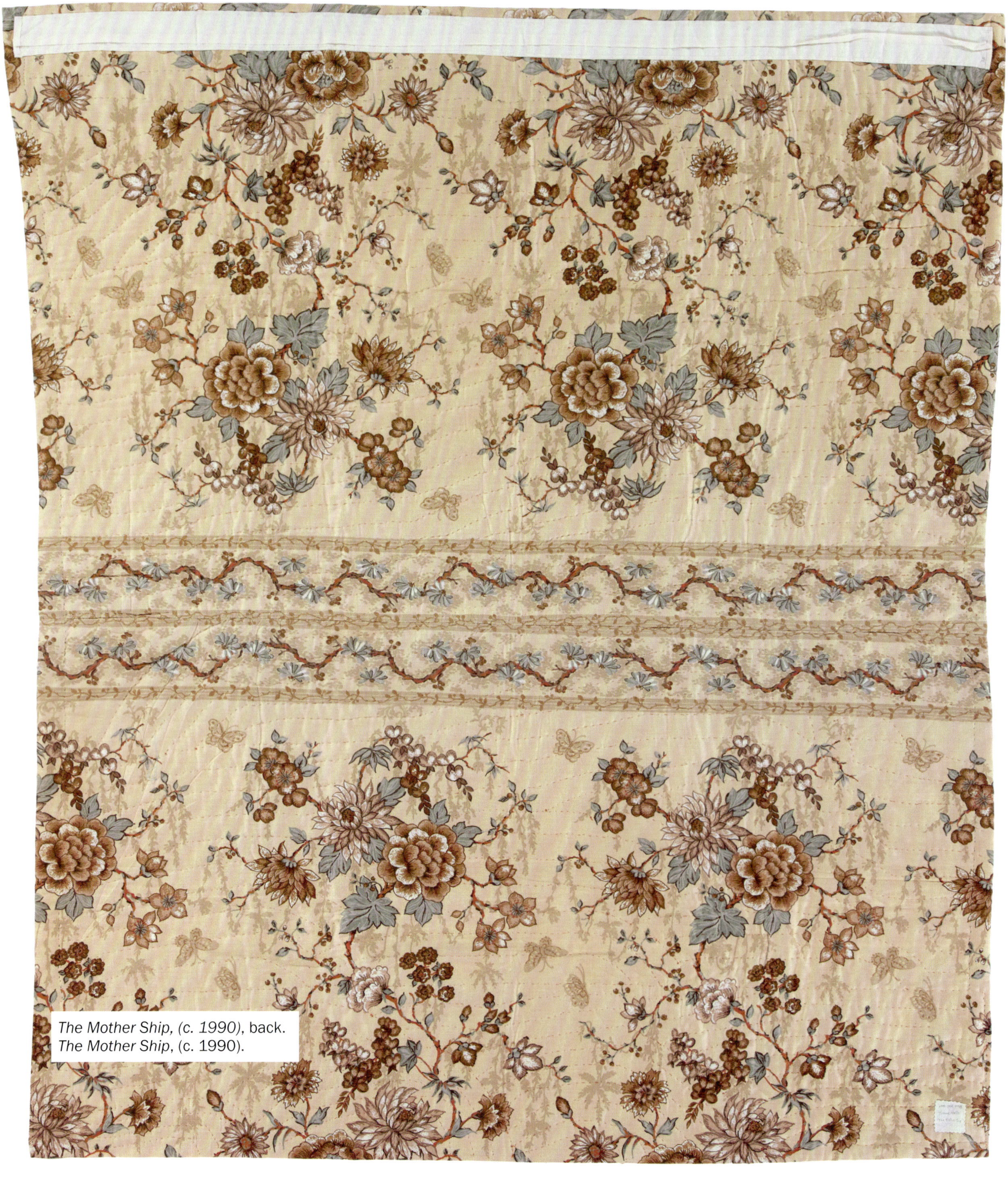

The Mother Ship, (c. 1990), back.
The Mother Ship, (c. 1990).

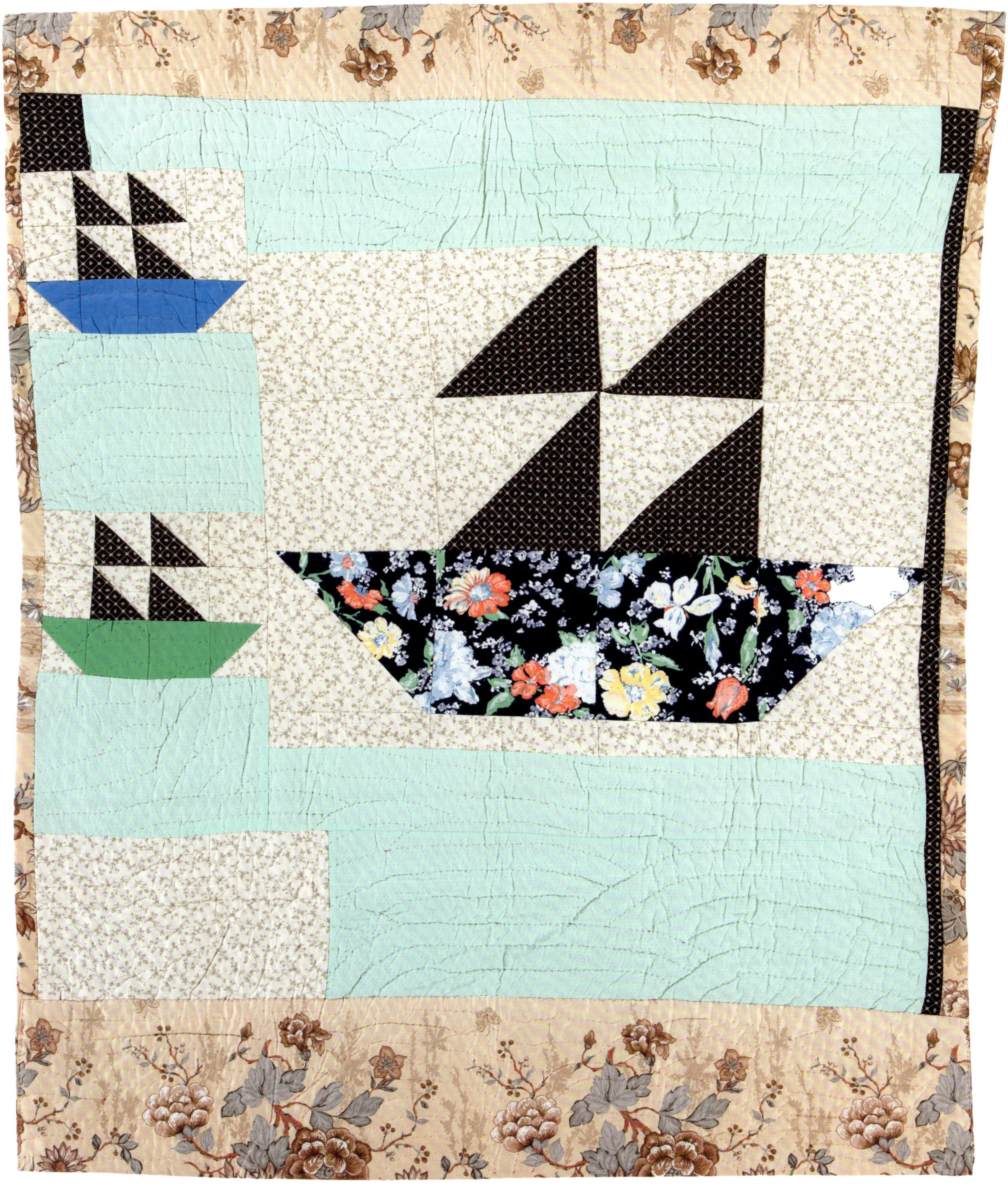

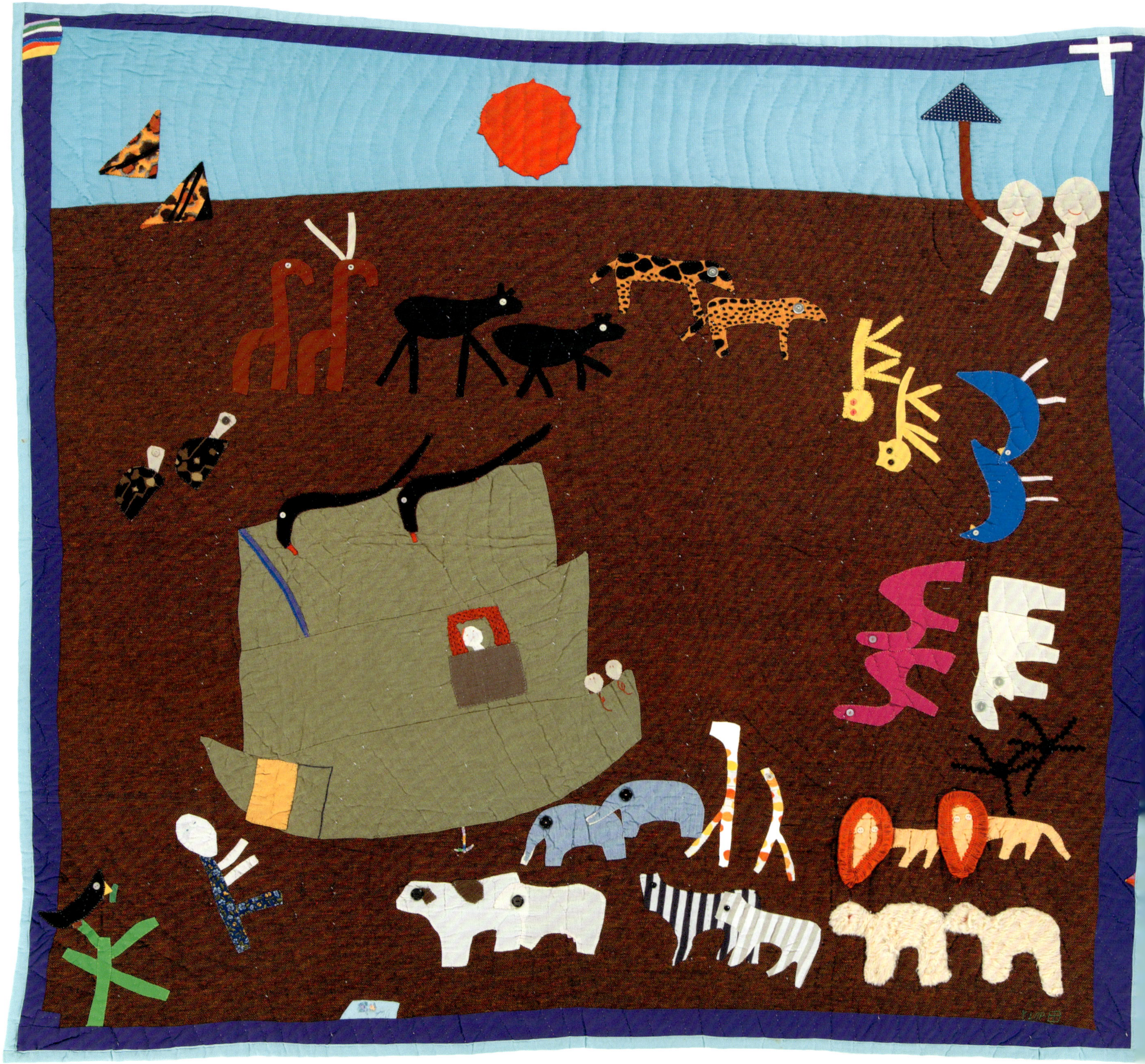

Noah's Ark, (1988).
Noah's Ark, (1988), detail.

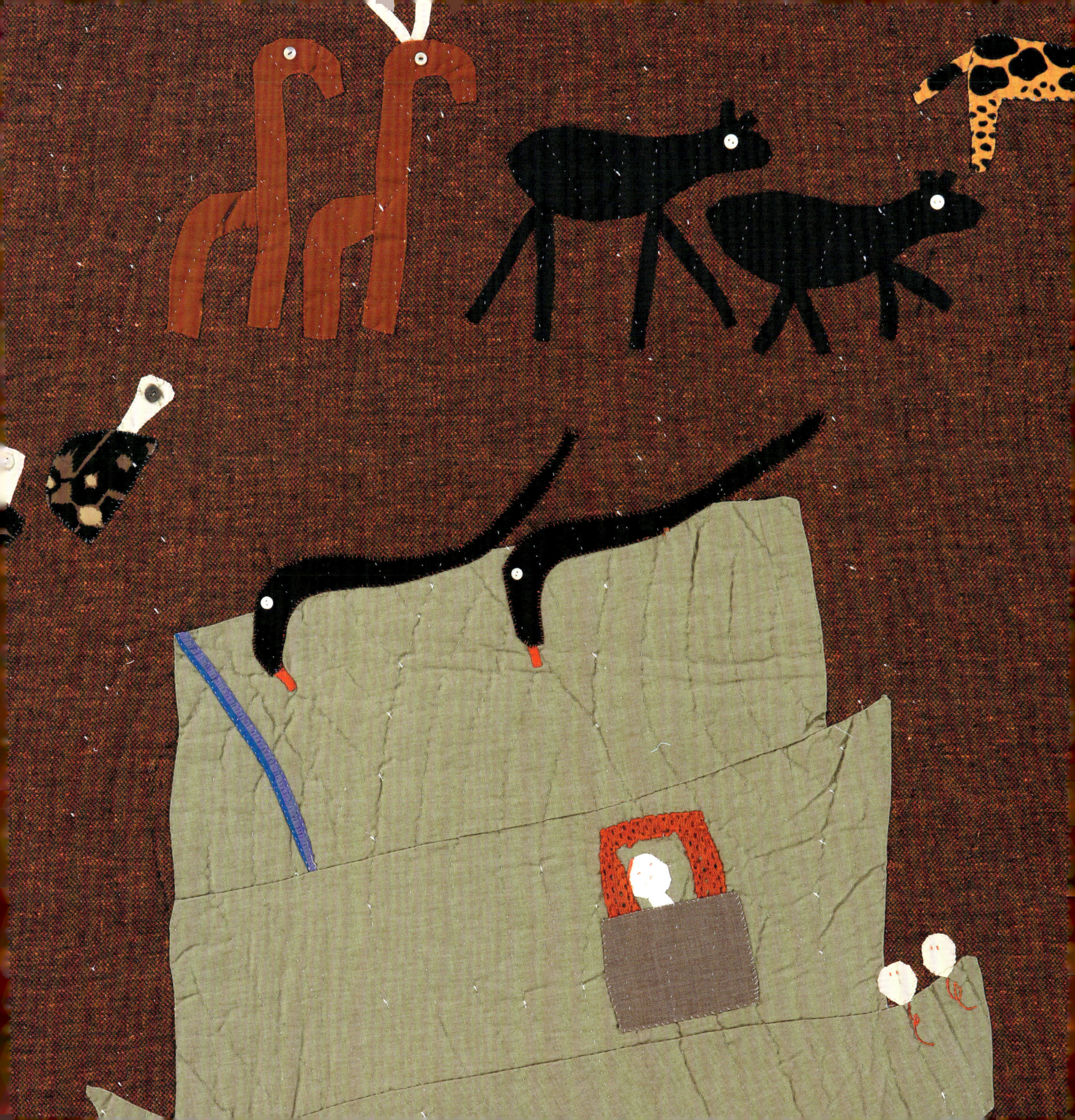

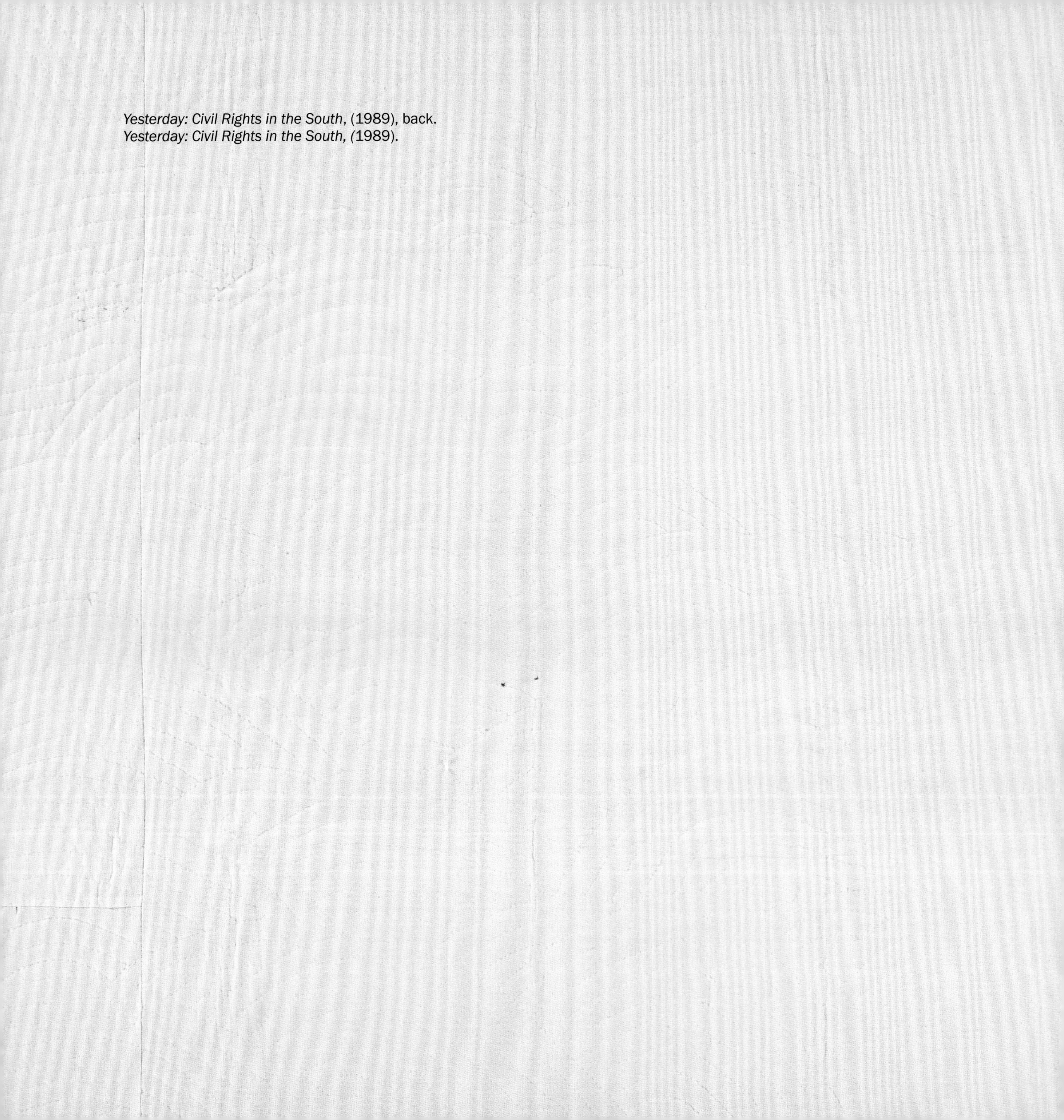

Yesterday: Civil Rights in the South, (1989), back.
Yesterday: Civil Rights in the South, (1989).

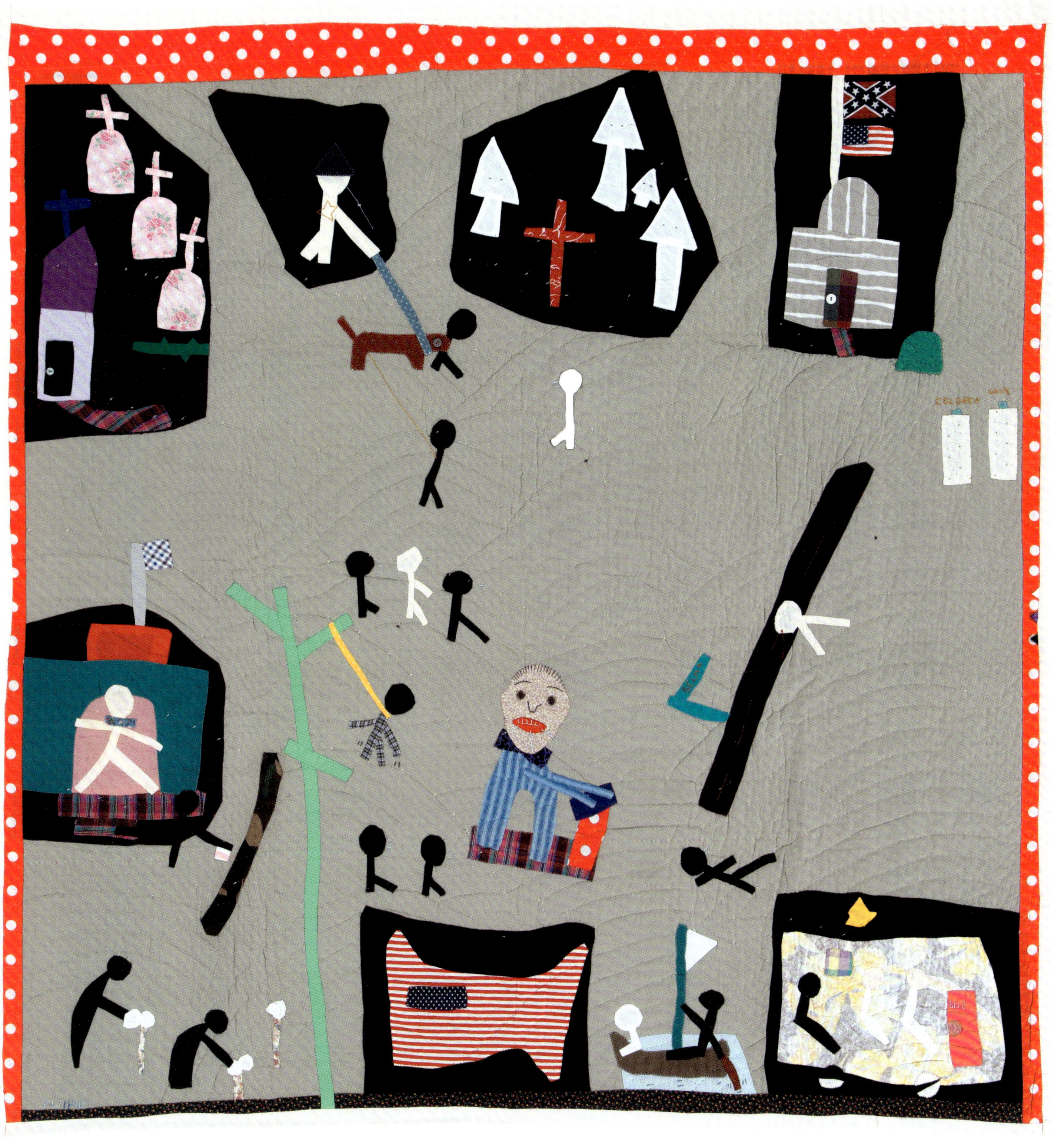

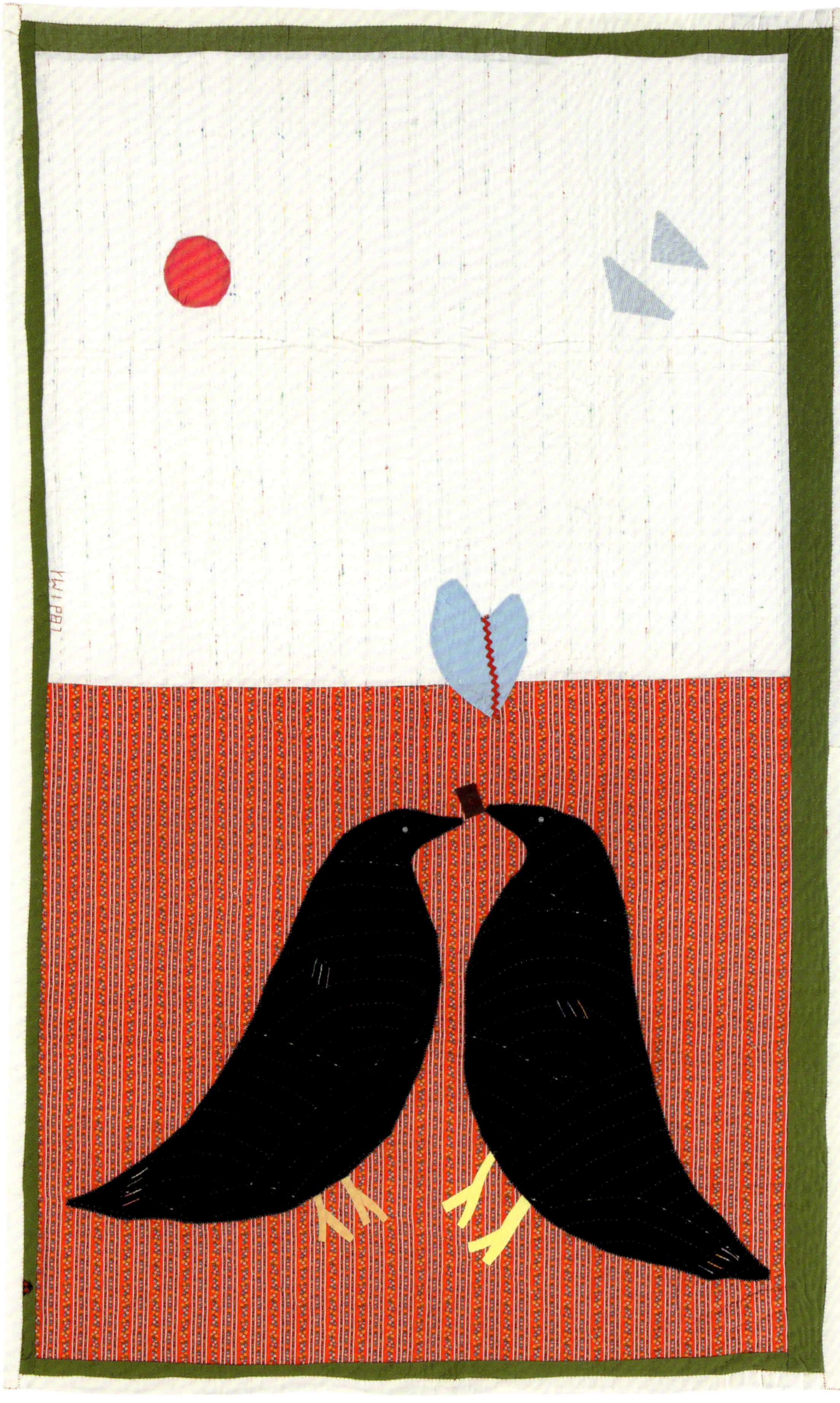

Lovers with a Broken Heart, (1987), detail. Photo by Teresa Duryea Wong.
Lovers with a Broken Heart, (1987).

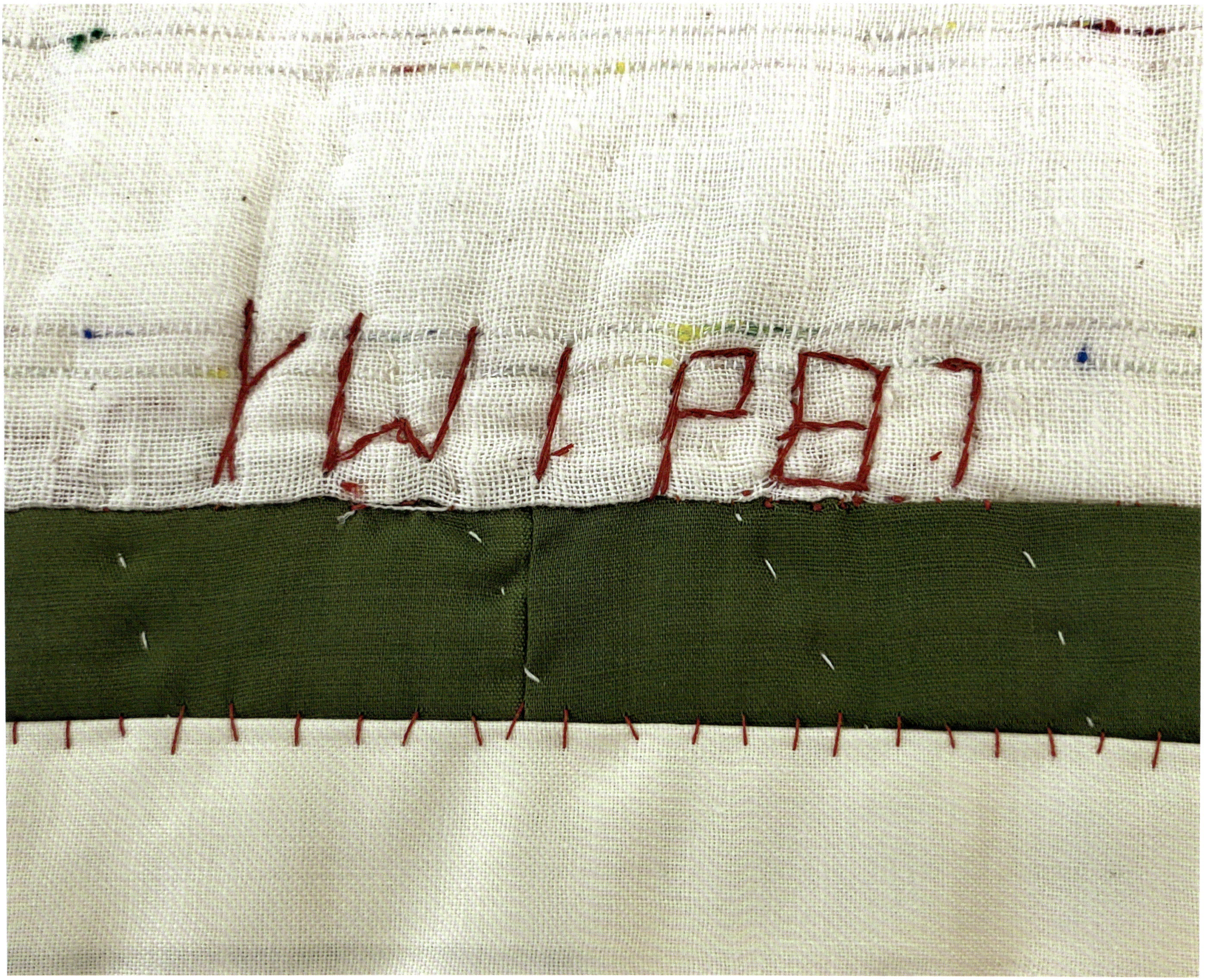

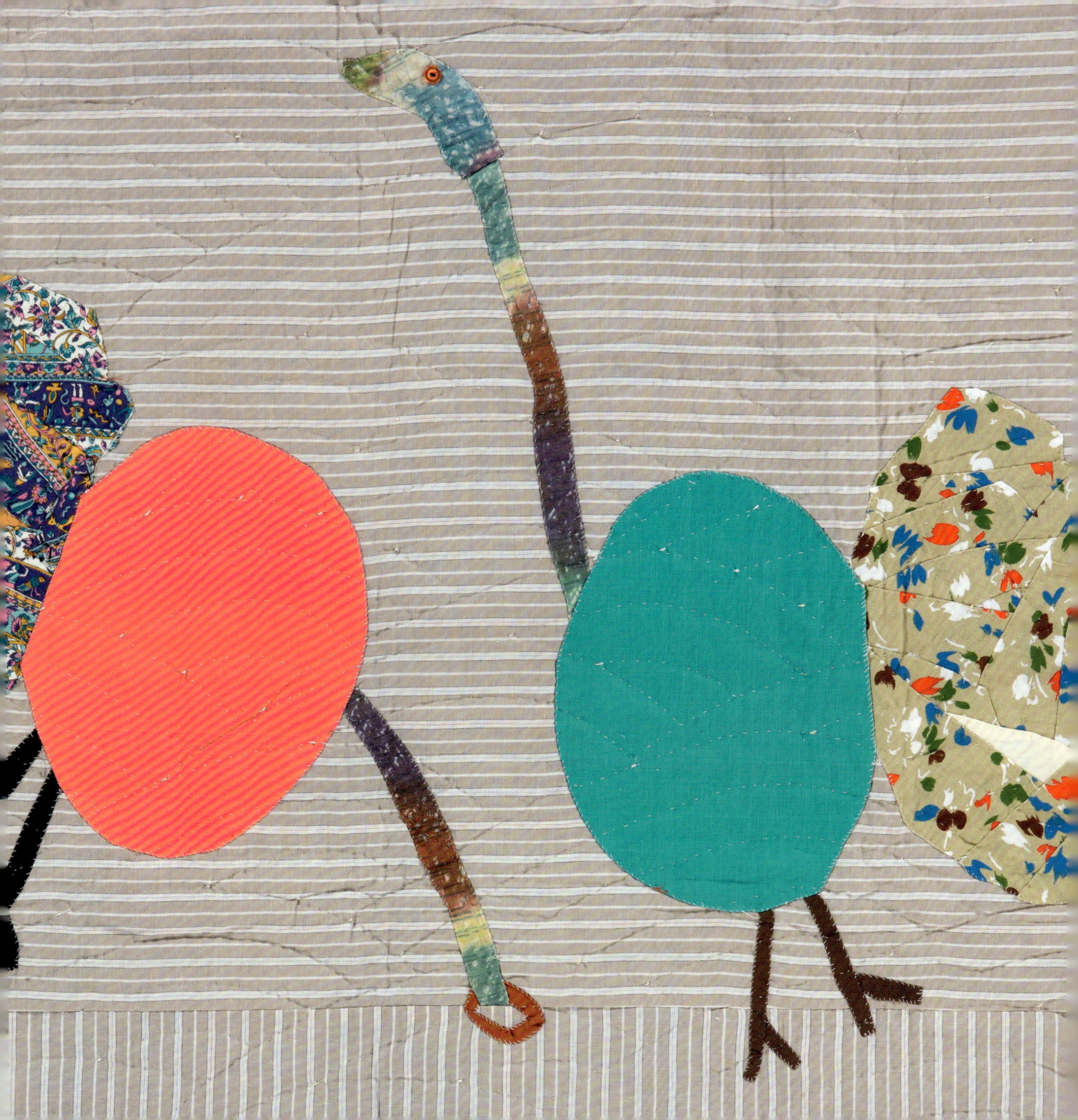

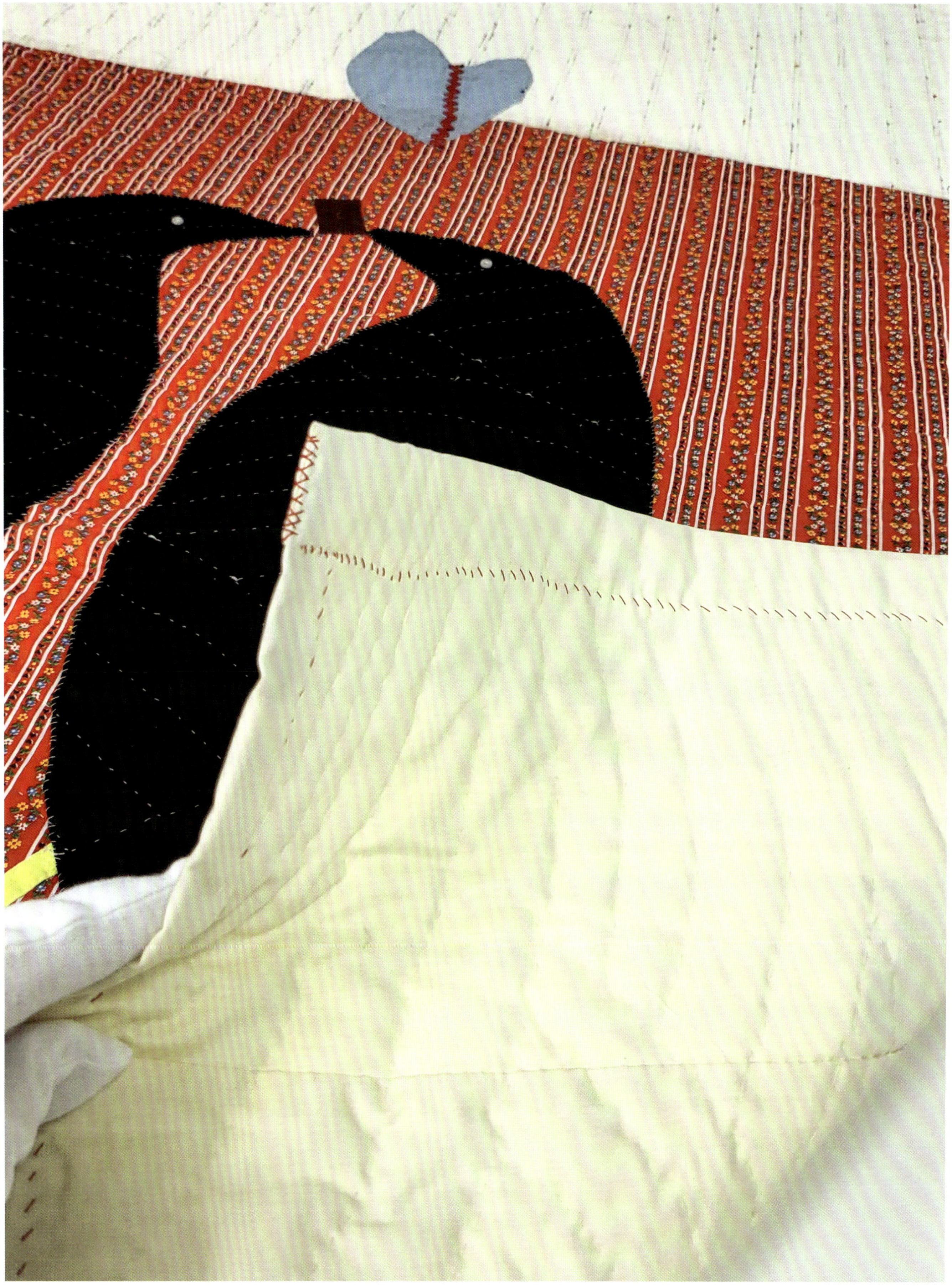

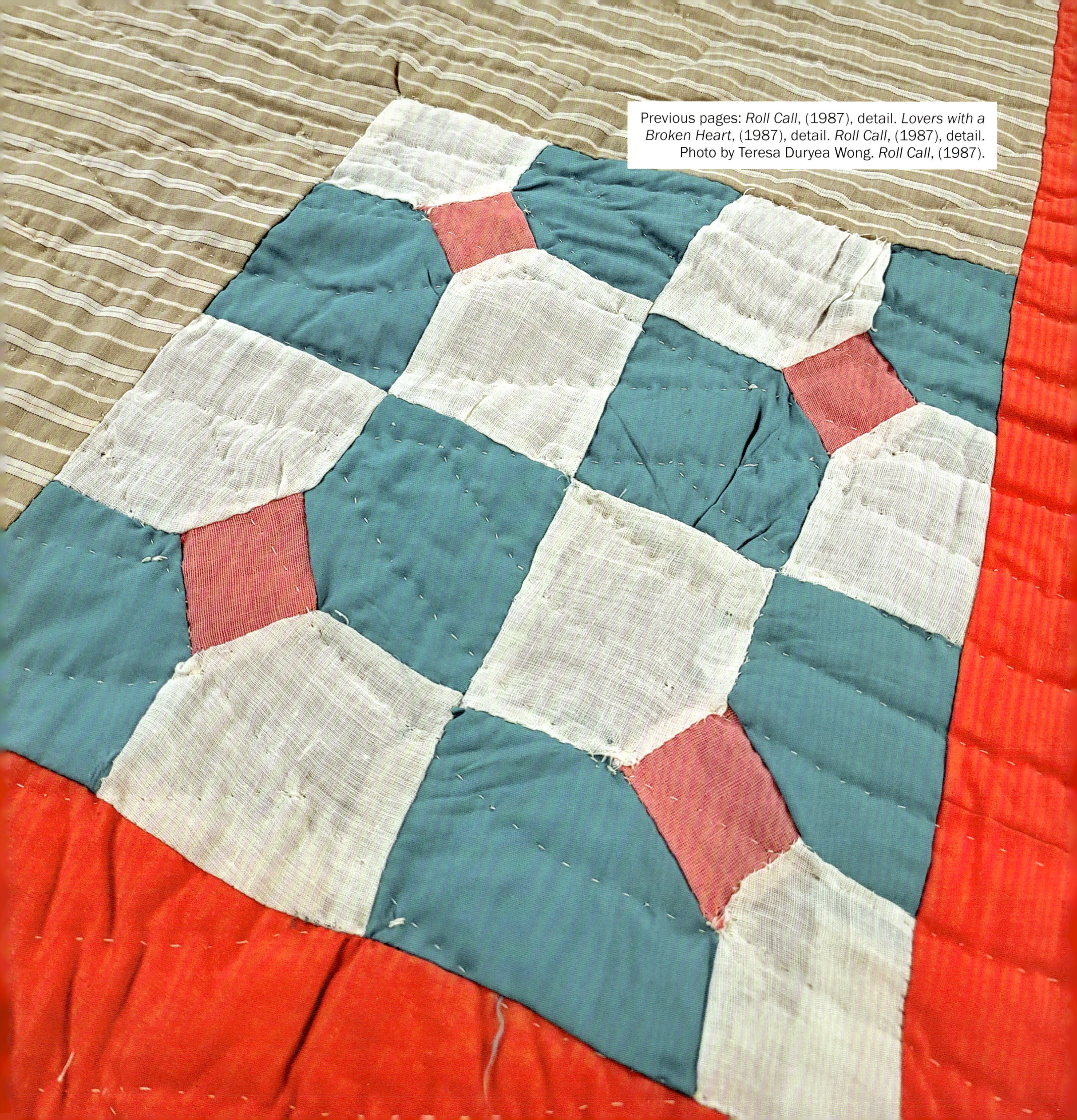

Previous pages: *Roll Call*, (1987), detail. *Lovers with a Broken Heart*, (1987), detail. *Roll Call*, (1987), detail. Photo by Teresa Duryea Wong. *Roll Call*, (1987).

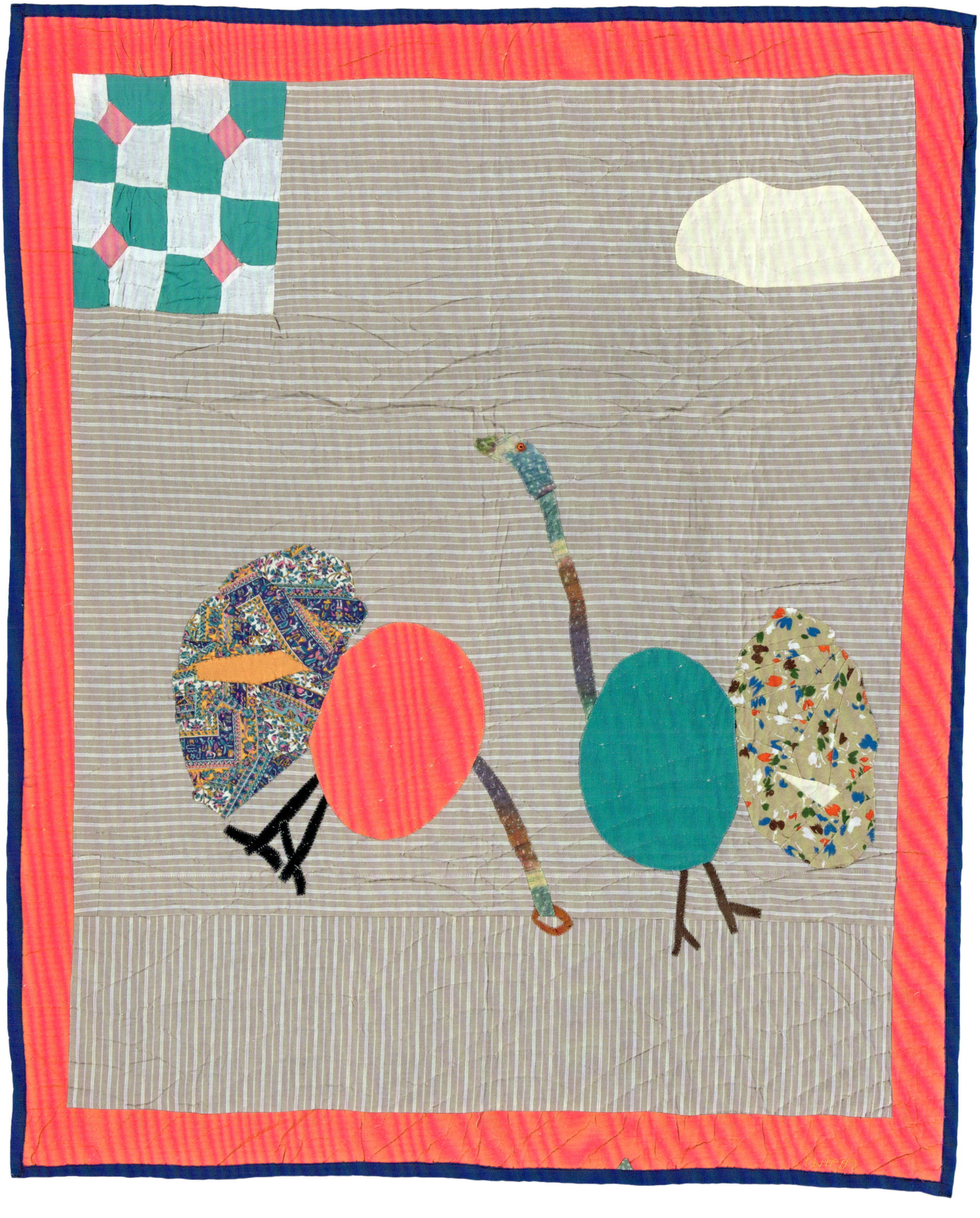

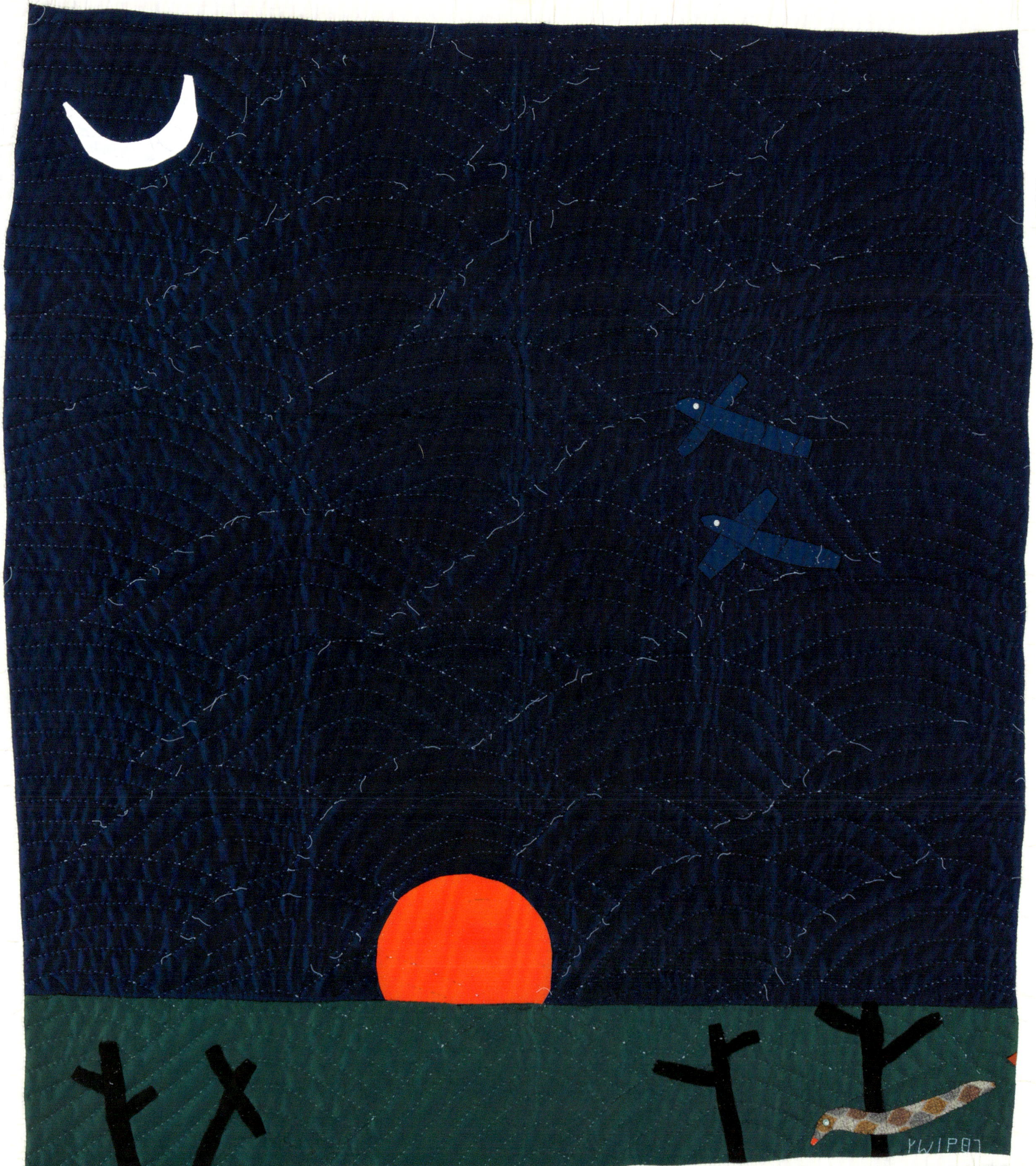
YWIP07

First Dark, (1987), detail. Photo by Teresa Duryea Wong.
First Dark, (1987).

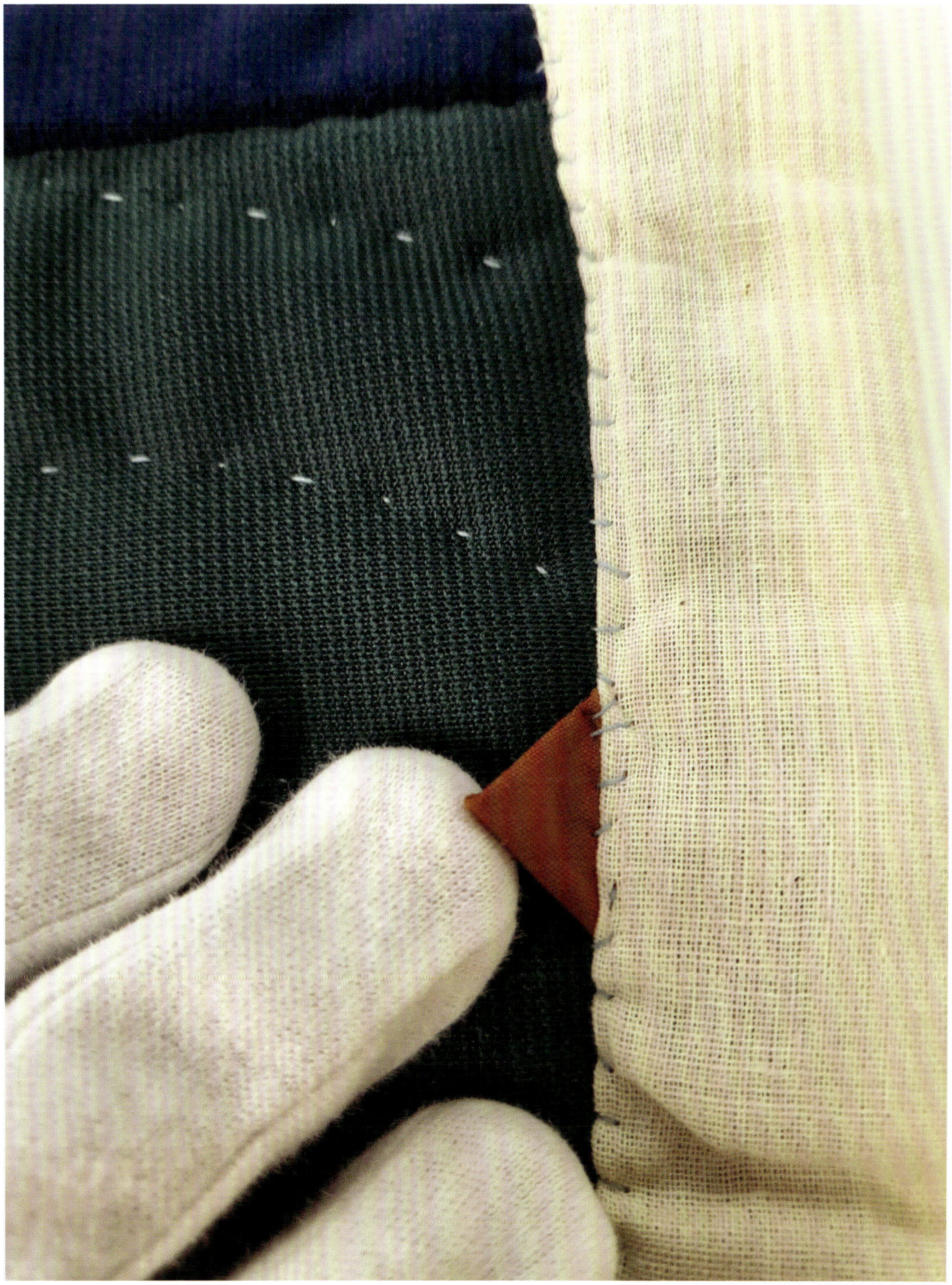

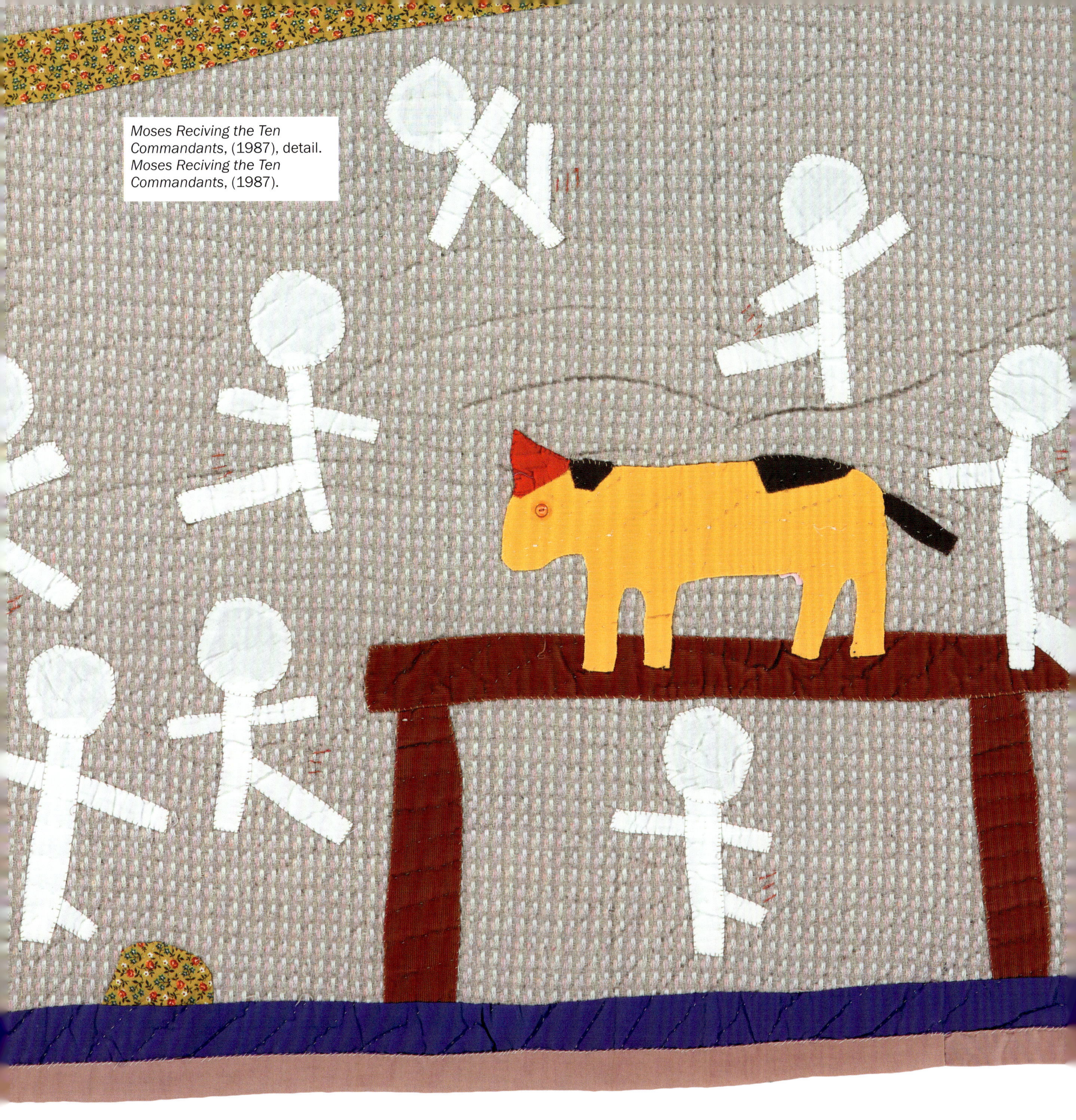

Moses Reciving the Ten Commandants, (1987), detail.
Moses Reciving the Ten Commandants, (1987).

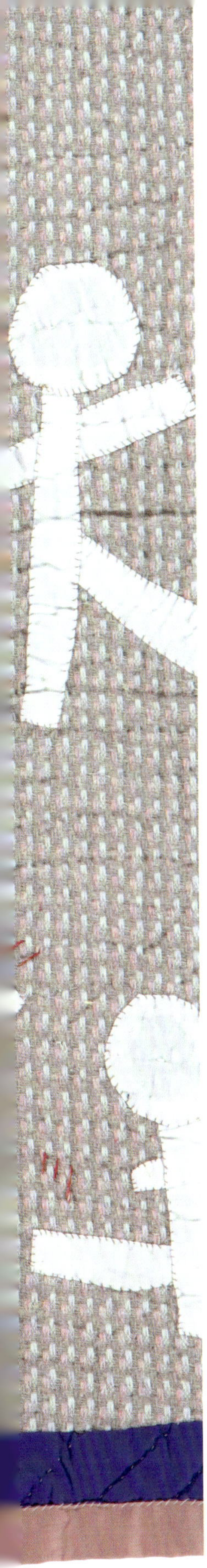

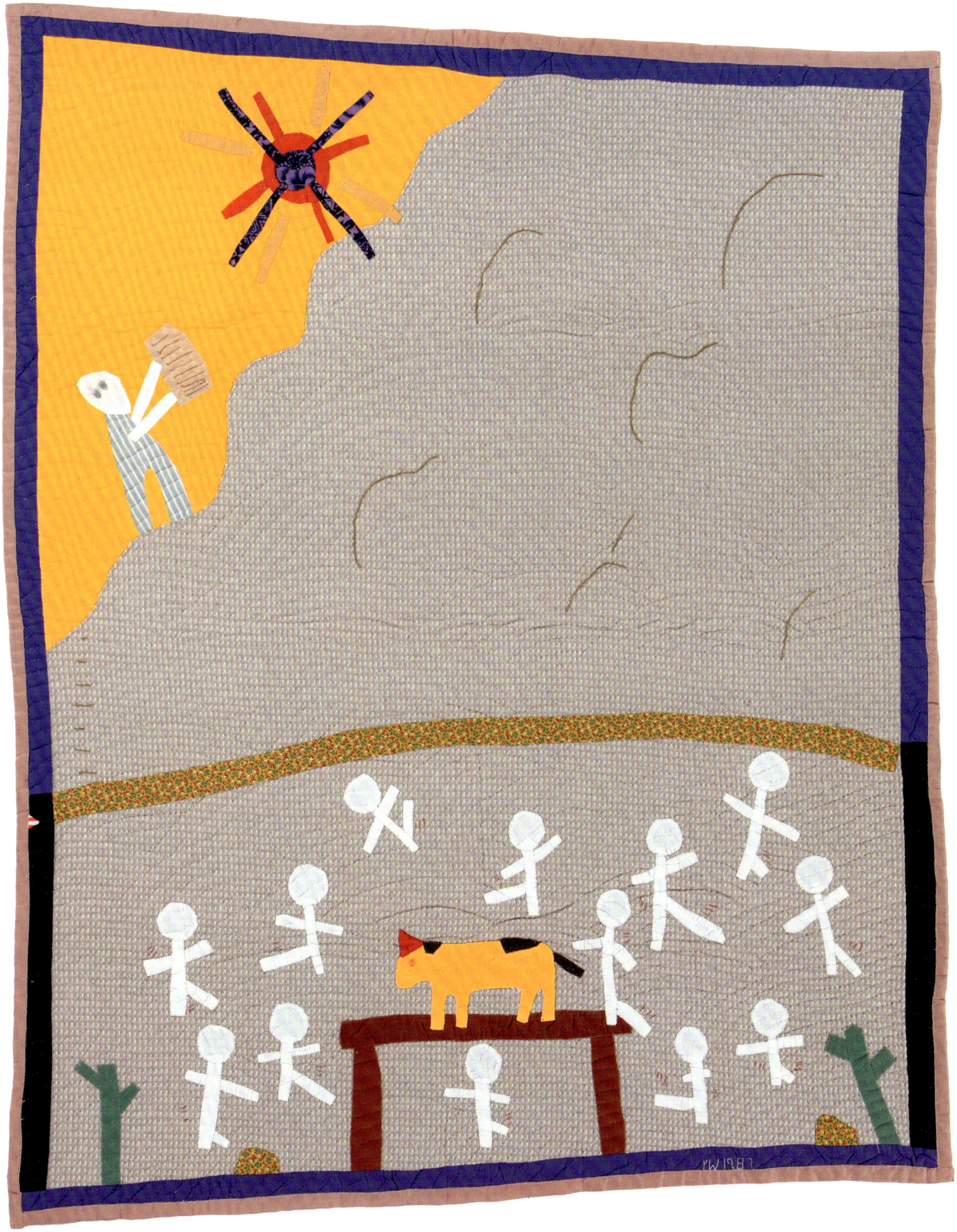
KW1987

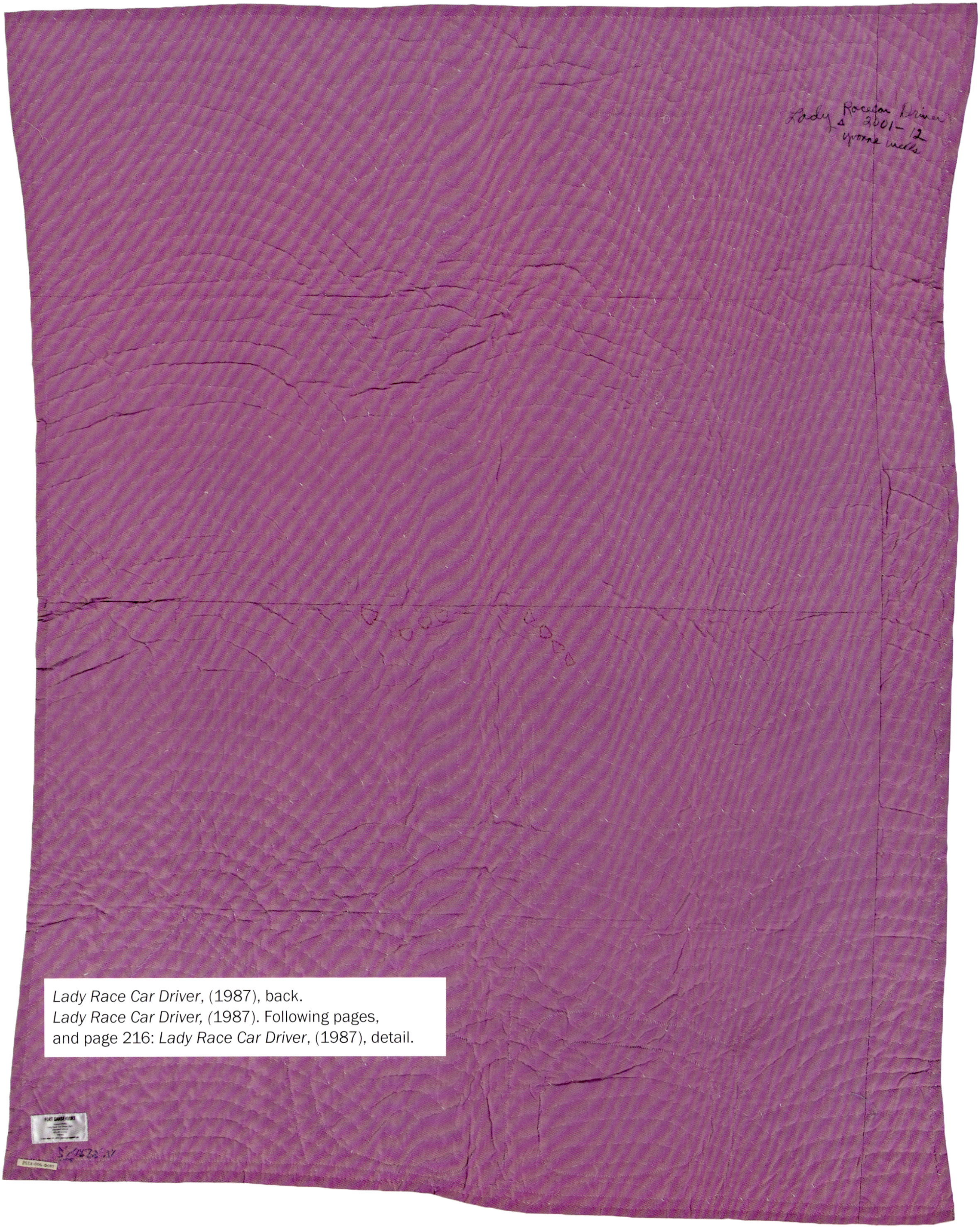

Lady Race Car Driver, (1987), back.
*Lady Race Car Driver, (*1987). Following pages,
and page 216: *Lady Race Car Driver*, (1987), detail.

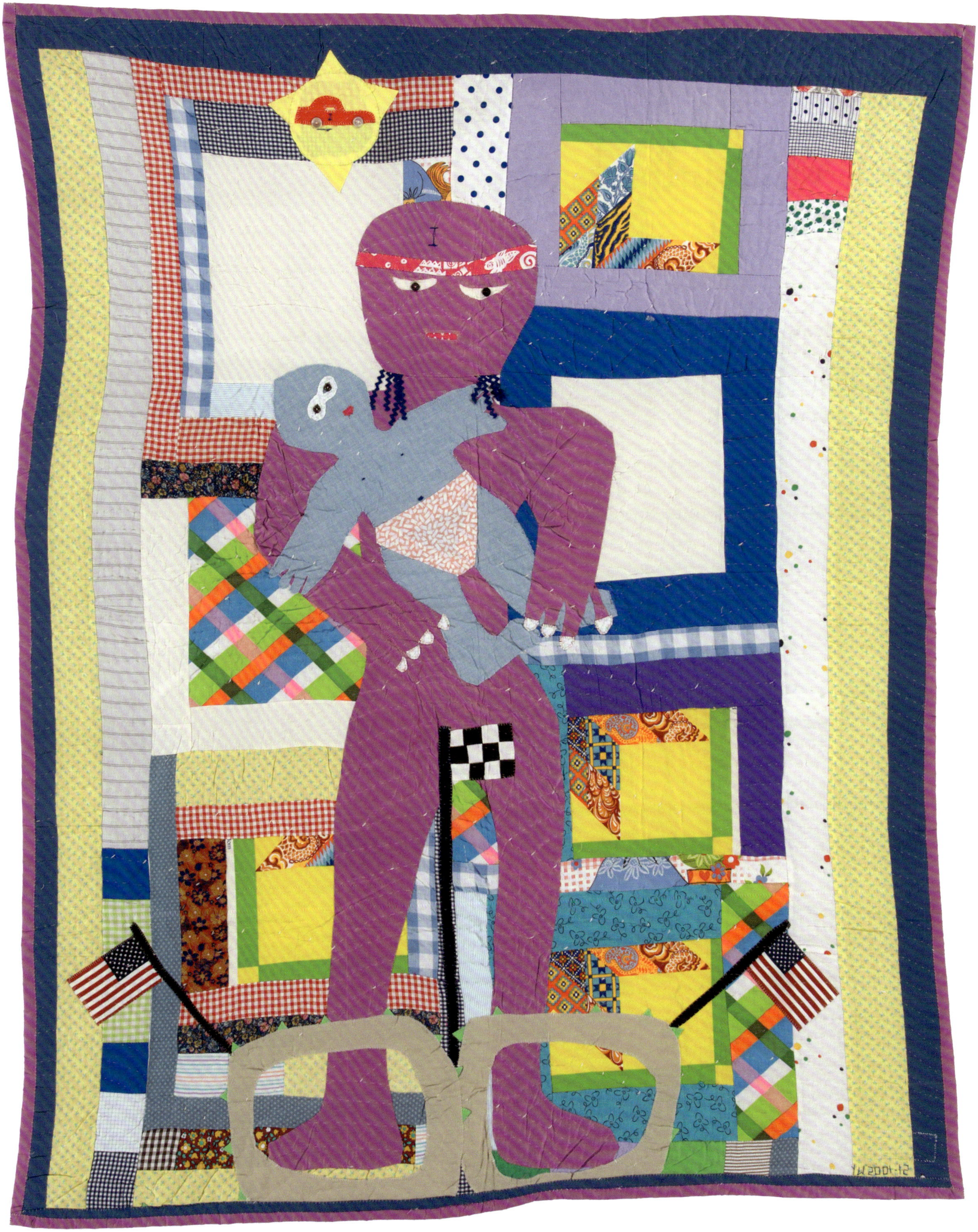

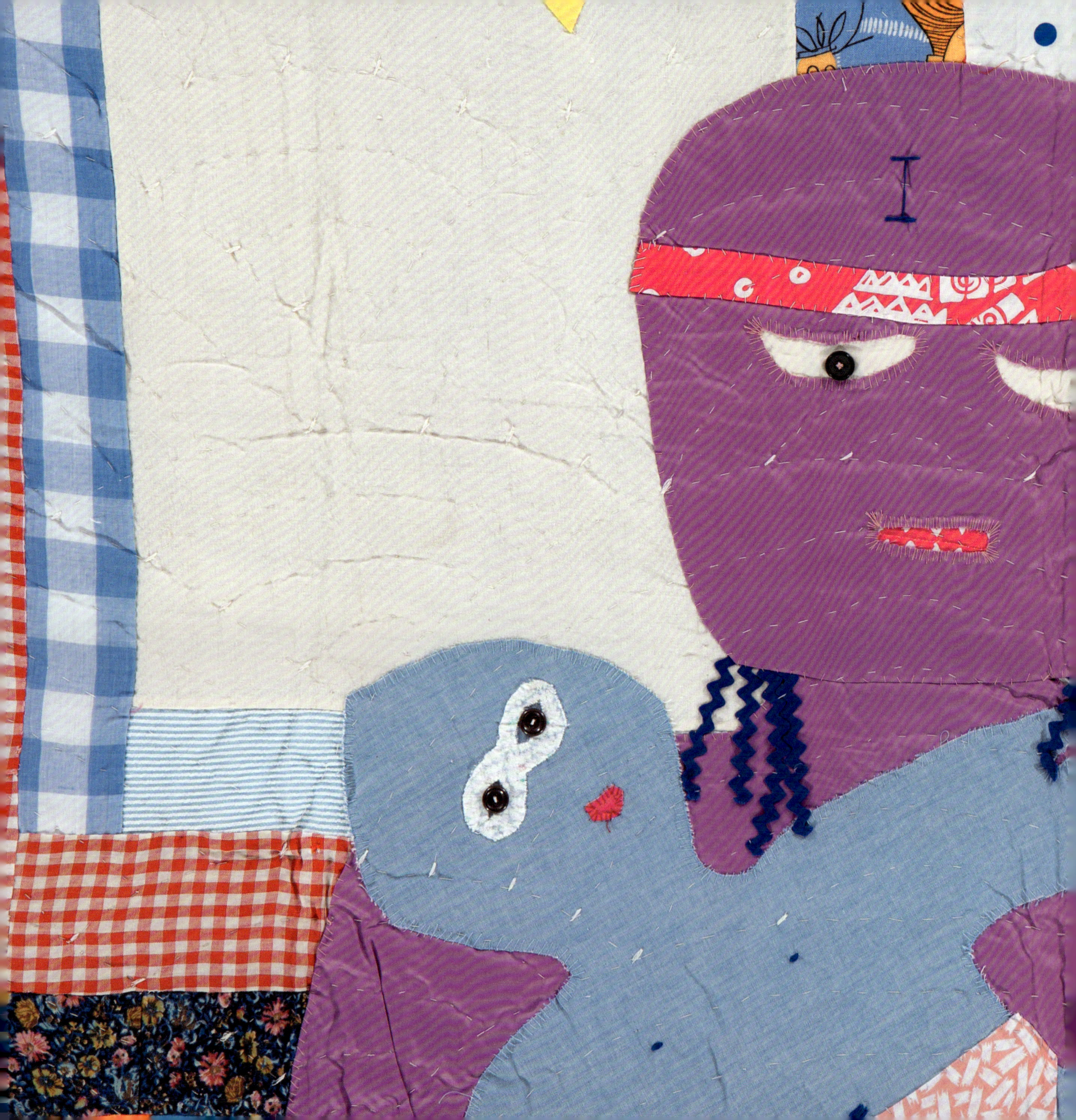

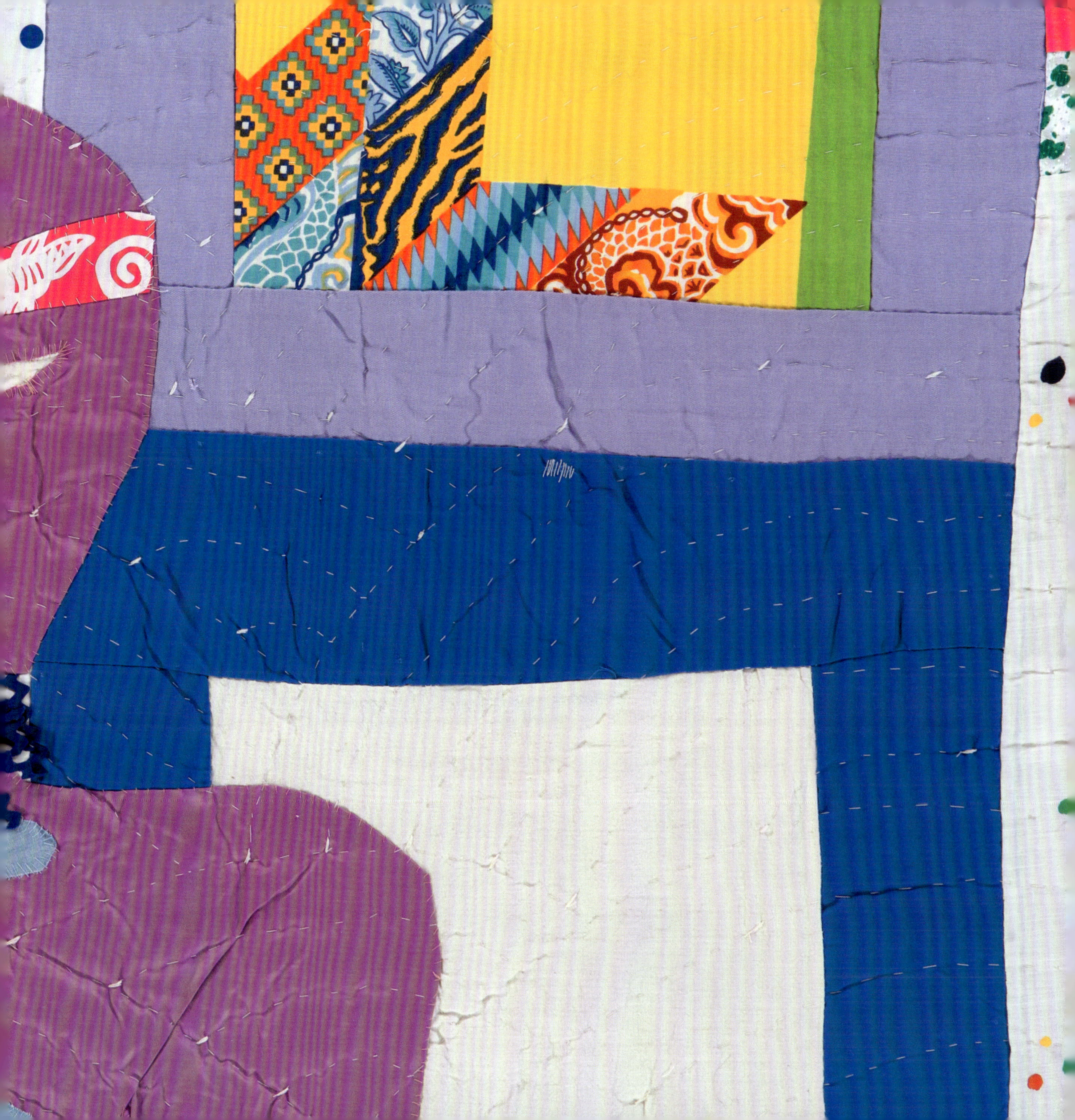

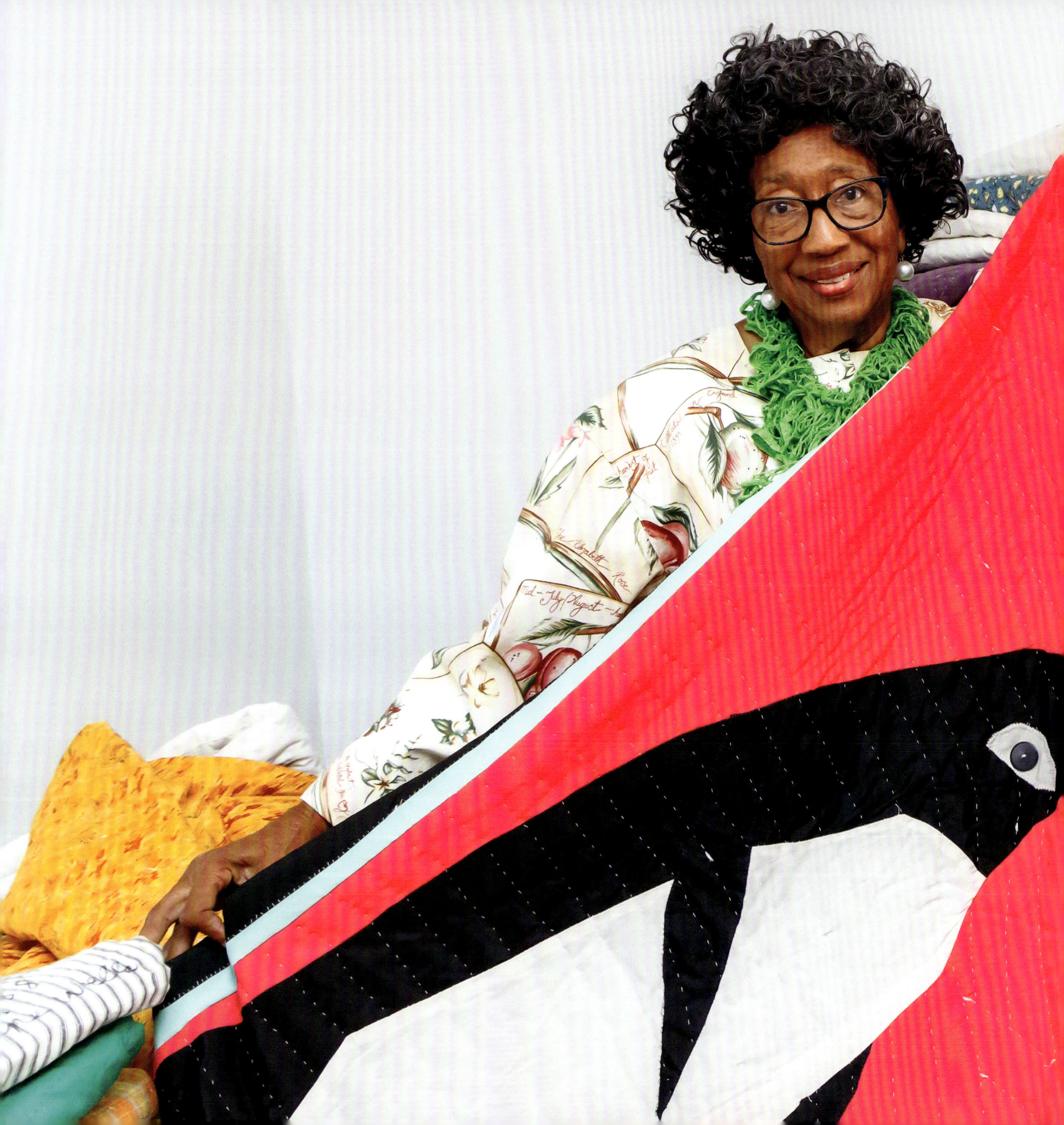

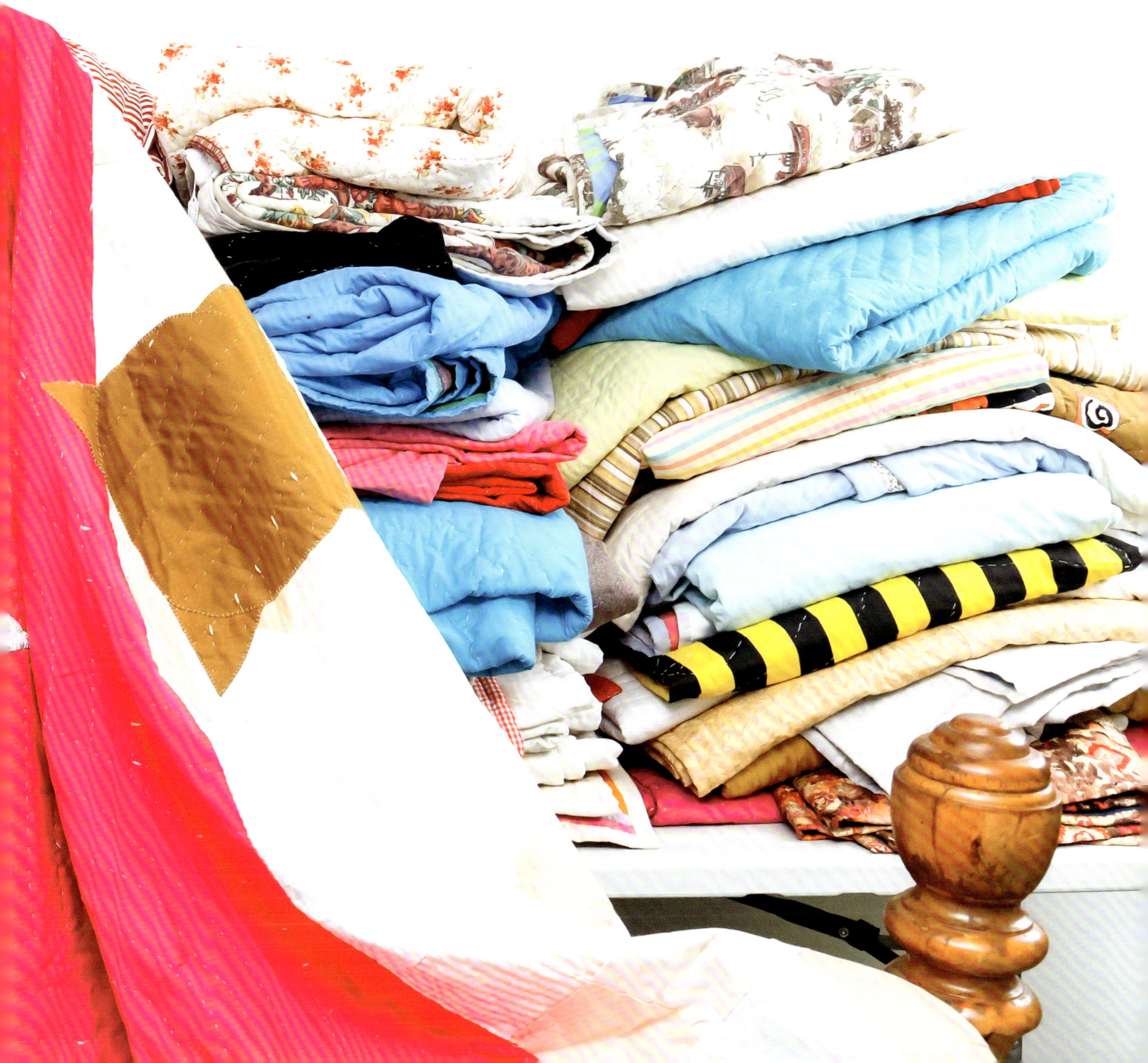

APPENDIX

Data for the Yvonne Wells Collection at the International Quilt Museum, University of Nebraska–Lincoln

The thirty-four works in the Yvonne Wells Collection at the International Quilt Museum are listed in chronological order. Every quilt was made in Yvonne Wells's home in Tuscaloosa, Alabama.

First Quilt
1979
Hand pieced. One Patch variation. Brackman #2289
84 × 38 in. (213 × 97 cm.)
Robert and Helen Cargo Collection
IQM 2000.004.0125
p. 160,161

Strip Quilt
1979
Hand pieced.
80.5 × 60 in. (204 × 152 cm.)
Robert and Helen Cargo Collection
IQM 2000.004.0129
p. 162, 163

Log Cabin/Courthouse Steps Variation
1980–1987
Hand pieced. Brackman #3240
65 × 82 in. (166 × 210 cm.)
Robert and Helen Cargo Collection
IQM 2000.004.0126
p. 8, 164, 165

Log Cabin/Courthouse Steps Variation
1980–1985
Hand pieced. Brackman #3240
77 × 72 in. (196 × 183 cm.)
Robert and Helen Cargo Collection
IQM 2000.004.0127
p. 166, 167

Raggedy Andy
1982–1983
Hand pieced.
90.5 × 69 in. (230 × 175 cm.)
Robert and Helen Cargo Collection
IQM 2000.004.0128
p. 67, 168, 169

Twenty Patch
1980–1985
Machine pieced.
62 × 44.5 in. (157 × 113 cm.)
Robert and Helen Cargo Collection
IQM 2000.004.0130
p. 170, 171

Strip Quilt
1980–1985
Hand pieced.
78 × 75.5 in. (198 × 192 cm.)
Robert and Helen Cargo Collection
IQM 2000.004.0131
p. 172, 173

Triangles
1980–1985
Hand pieced. Brackman #212.5
76 × 60.5 in. (193 × 154 cm.)
Robert and Helen Cargo Collection
IQM 2000.004.0132
p. 24, 25, 174, 175

Triangles
1980–1985
Hand pieced. Brackman #212.5
86 × 68.5 in. (218 × 174 cm.)
Robert and Helen Cargo Collection
IQM 2000.004.0133
p. 45, 176, 177

Pieced Diamonds
1980–1987
Hand pieced.
85.5 × 66.5 in. (217 × 169 cm.)
Robert and Helen Cargo Collection
IQM 2000.004.0134
p. 33, 178, 179

Double Stars
1980–1985
Hand pieced. Brackman Eight-Pointed Star #3735d
84 × 67 in. (213 × 170 cm.)
Robert and Helen Cargo Collection
IQM 2000.004.0135
p. 75, 180, 181

Square in a Square
1984–1990
Machine pieced. Brackman #2375a
77 × 59.5 in. (196 × 151 cm.)
Robert and Helen Cargo Collection
IQM 2000.004.0136
p. 72, 73, 182, 183

Crucifixion II
1986–1990
Hand pieced, hand appliquéd, embroidery.
76 × 68 in. (193 × 173 cm.)
Robert and Helen Cargo Collection
IQM 2000.004.0139
p. 48, 50, 51, 58

Moses Receiving the Ten Commandments
1987–1990
81 × 64 in. (206 × 163 cm.)
Hand appliquéd, hand pieced.
Robert and Helen Cargo Collection
IQM 2000.004.0141
p. 37, 200, 201

Lovers with a Broken Heart
1987–1990
Hand appliquéd, hand pieced.
76.5 × 48.5 in. (194 × 123 cm.)
Robert and Helen Cargo Collection
IQM 2000.004.0144
p. 28, 29, 192, 193, 195

Roll Call
1987
Hand appliquéd, hand and machine pieced.
60 × 51.5 in. (152 × 131 cm.)
Robert and Helen Cargo Collection
IQM 2000.004.0145
p. 194, 196, 197

Going Home
1987
Hand appliquéd, hand embroidery.
59 × 73 in. (150 × 185 cm.)
Robert and Helen Cargo Collection
IQM 2000.004.0146
p. 1, 44

The Gossip Quilt I
1987–1990
Hand appliquéd
73 × 57.5 in. (185 × 146 cm.)
Robert and Helen Cargo Collection
IQM 2000.004.0147
p. 41

First Dark
1987–1990
Hand appliquéd, hand pieced.
62 × 55 in. (157 × 140 cm.)
Robert and Helen Cargo Collection
IQM 2000.004.0148
p. 46, 198, 199

Noah's Ark
1988
Hand appliquéd.
71 × 77 in. (180 × 196 cm.)
Robert and Helen Cargo Collection
IQM 2000.004.0140
p. 14, 188, 189

Yesterday: Civil Rights in the South
1989
Hand appliquéd.
66.5 × 64 in. (169 × 163 cm.)
Robert and Helen Cargo Collection
IQM 2000.004.0142
p. 68, 70, 71, 190, 191

The Red Quilt
1990
79 × 60 in. (201 × 152 cm.)
Robert and Helen Cargo Collection
IQM 2000.004.0137
p. 184, 185

The Mother Ship
c. 1984
Hand pieced.
83 × 67 in. (211 × 170 cm.)
Robert and Helen Cargo Collection
IQM 2000.004.0138
p. 12, 186, 187

Ugly Faces
1990
Hand appliquéd.
78.5 × 58.5 in. (199 × 149 cm.)
Robert and Helen Cargo Collection
IQM 2000.004.0143
p. 60, 76, 77

The Greeting
2000
Hand appliquéd, hand pieced.
67 × 78 in. (170 × 198 cm.)
IQM 2023.006.0008
p. 38, 62, 64, 65

Lady Race Car Driver
2001
Hand pieced, hand embroidered appliqué.
83 × 65 in. (211 × 165 cm.)
IQM 2023.006.0010
p. 202, 203, 204, 205, 216

Seven Deadly Sins: Wrath
2004
Hand appliquéd, hand pieced.
102 × 72 in. (259 × 183 cm.)
IQM 2023.006.0004
p. 47, 128, 129, 130, 131, 133, 134, 135, 136, 137

Seven Deadly Sins: Lust
2005
Hand appliquéd, hand pieced.
90 × 71.75 in. (229 × 189 cm.)
IQM 2023.006.0006
p. 90, 91, 92, 93, 95, 96, 97

Seven Deadly Sins: Sloth
2005
Hand appliquéd, hand pieced, hand embroidery.
88 × 69.5 in. (221 × 177 cm.)
IQM 2023.006.0002
p. 118, 119, 120, 121, 122, 124, 125, 126, 127

Seven Deadly Sins: Gluttony
2005
Hand appliquéd, hand pieced, hand embroidery.
92 × 68.5 in. (234 × 174 cm.)
IQM 2023.006.0007
p. 88, 98, 99, 100, 101, 102, 104, 105, 106, 107

Seven Deadly Sins: Greed
2006
Hand appliquéd, hand pieced, hand embroidery.
93.5 × 69 in. (237 × 173 cm.)
IQM 2023.006.0001
p. 108, 109, 110, 111, 112, 113, 115, 116, 117

Seven Deadly Sins: Envy
2006
Hand appliquéd, hand pieced.
94.5 × 66 in. (240 × 168 cm.)
IQM 2023.006.0005
p. 15, 138, 139, 140, 141, 142, 144, 145

Seven Deadly Sins: Pride
2006
Hand appliquéd, hand pieced, hand embroidery.
91 × 70 in. (231 × 178 cm.)
IQM 2023.006.0003
p. 146, 147, 148, 149, 151, 152, 153, 154, 155

Invest in America (BP Oil Spill)
2010
Hand appliquéd, hand pieced.
81 × 58 in. (206 × 147 cm.)
IQM 2023.006.0009
p. 79, 80, 81, 84, 85

NOTES

Vision Without Precedent

1. Catherine L. Holmes, “The Darling Offspring of Her Brain,” in *Georgia Quilts: Piecing Together a History*, ed. Anita Zaleski Weinraub (Athens: University of Georgia Press, 2006), 177, 270. Powers’s full name appeared in the Clark County State of Georgia Returns and Mixed Records Book AA 1868–1884, p. 33. Her first name, Harriett, also appeared on her original headstone at the Gospel Pilgrim Cemetery in Athens, Georgia. The headstone was found damaged and vanished from view around 2008; its public whereabouts is unknown. A commemorative memorial was installed in 2023.

2. Holmes, “The Darling Offspring of Her Brain,” 179.

3. Ina B. Hawkes, “Reminiscence of a Negro Preacher,” ed. Maggie B. Freeman, unpublished manuscript, November 7, 1939, Manuscript/Mixed Material, Library of Congress, p. 2, https://www.loc.gov/item/wpalh000510.

4. Kyra E. Hicks, *This I Accomplish: Harriet Powers’ Bible Quilt and Other Pieces* (Washington DC: Black Threads Press, 2009), 38–39.

5. “The Colored Fair,” *Weekly Banner-Watchman* (Athens GA), November 20, 1886, 1.

6. Jennie Smith (1862–1946), handwritten essay regarding the *Bible Quilt*, ca. 1891, Harriet Powers object folder, Division of Home and Community Life, Smithsonian National Museum of American History, Washington DC.

7. Jennie Smith Papers, MSS 13, various letters and diary, Hargrett Rare Book and Manuscript Library, University of Georgia Libraries. The papers were sealed for fifty years and became available in 2000.

8. “Forward March of the Negroes,” *Pittsburgh Post*, December 6, 1895, 3.

9. Hicks, *This I Accomplish*, 33–34. At least two images that Lorene Diver commissioned have survived. One is in Harriet Powers object folder at the Smithsonian National Museum of American History, Washington DC, and the other is owned by the Lee County Historical Society, Keokuk, Iowa.

10. Harriet A. Powers to Mrs. James B. Diver, January 28, 1896, Lorene C. Diver Files, Lee County Historical Society, Keokuk, Iowa.

11 Gladys-Marie Fry, “Harriet Powers: Portrait of a Black Quilter,” in *Missing Pieces: Georgia Folk Art 1770–1976* (Atlanta: Georgia Council for the Arts, 1976), 19.

12. Adolph Cavallo, telephone interview with the author, May 26, 2008.

13. Hicks, *This I Accomplish*, 96. The transaction was $500, according to correspondence between Karolik and Rev. Hall housed at the Massachusetts

Historical Society, Karolik-Codman Family Papers.

14. Stacy I. Morgan and Yvonne Thomas Wells, *The Story Quilts of Yvonne Wells* (Tuscaloosa: University of Alabama Press, 2024), 291–307.

15. Morgan and Wells, *The Story Quilts of Yvonne Wells*, 5–7.

16. Morgan and Wells, *The Story Quilts of Yvonne Wells*, 111–25. I worked at Hallmark Cards in the 1990s and recall the excitement the late design director Alston Green and graphic artist Jan Bryan-Hunt had working with Wells and publishing her quilt images as part of the Mahogany card collection. That Hallmark licensed quilt designs by Wells and quilter Michael Cummings was unprecedented—and thrilling to see and purchase.

Seven Deadly Sins Quilts

1. Stacy Morgan is a folk art expert and a professor at the University of Alabama. He gave this quote to Teresa Duryea Wong during an interview in Nov. 2024.

Place and Purpose:

1. Elizabeth Fox-Genovese, *Within the Plantation Household: Black and White Women of the Old South* (Chapel Hill: University of North Carolina Press, 1988), 120.

2. Gladys-Marie Fry, *Stitched from the Soul: Slave Quilts from the Antebellum South* (Chapel Hill: University of North Carolina Press, 2002), 69.

3. Cuesta Benberry, *Always There: The African-American Presence in American Quilts* (Philadelphia: University of Pennsylvania Press, 1992), 19.

4. "Yvonne Wells: Quilted Messages," International Quilt Museum, accessed October 9, 2025, https://www.internationalquiltmuseum.org/exhibition/yvonne-wells-quilted-messages.

5. "Yesterday: Civil Rights in the South," International Quilt Museum, accessed October 9, 2025, https://www.internationalquiltmuseum.org/about/quilt-month/yesterday-civil-rights-south.

6. Eli Leon, *Who'd a Thought It: Improvisation in African-American Quiltmaking* (San Francisco Craft & Folk Art Museum, 1987), 16.

7. Fort Gansevoort, "Yvonne Wells: Play the Hand That's Dealt You," press release, accessed October 9, 2025, https://www.fortgansevoort.com/exhibitions/yvonne-wells/press-release.

8. Fort Gansevoort, "Yvonne Wells."

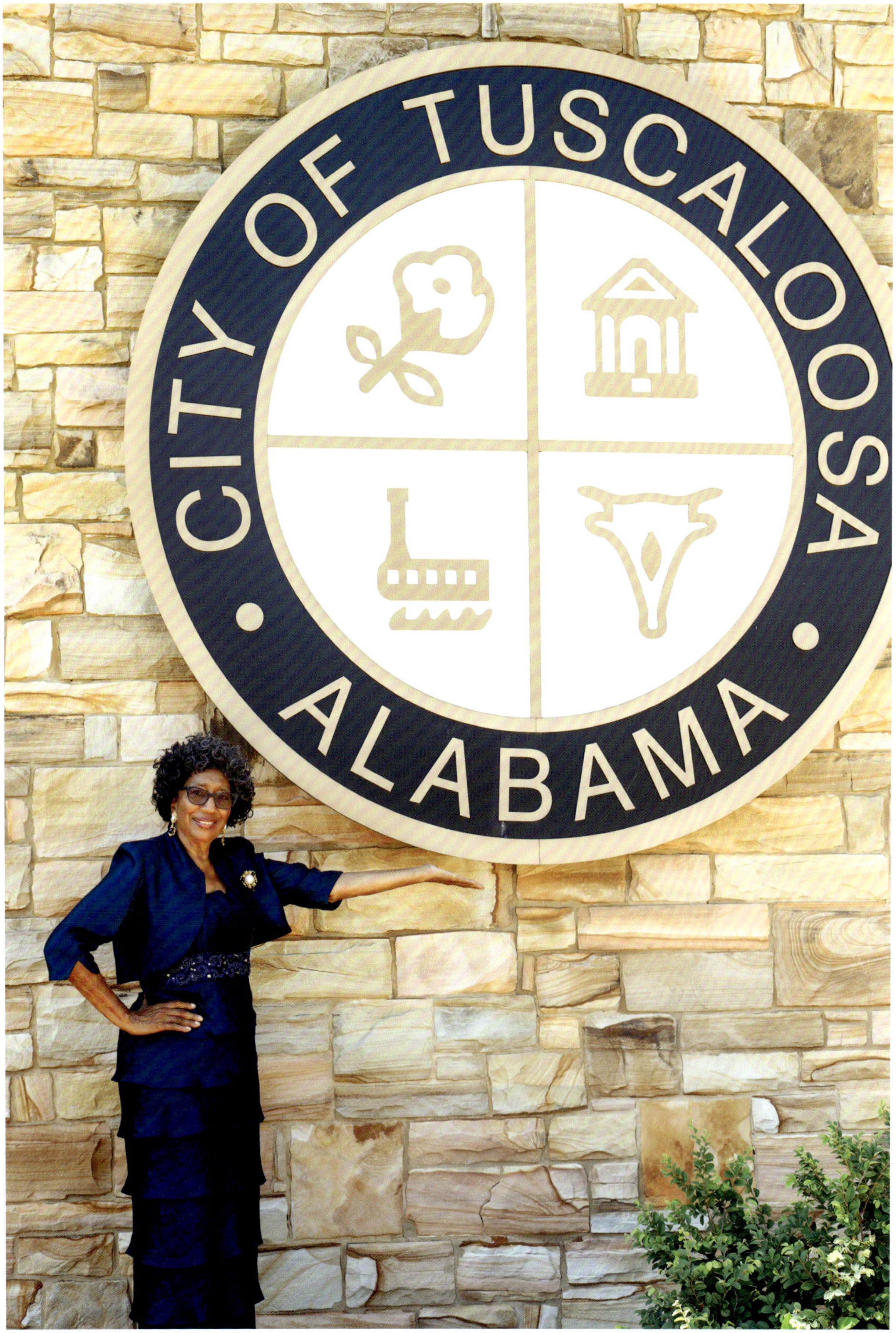
CITY OF TUSCALOOSA
ALABAMA

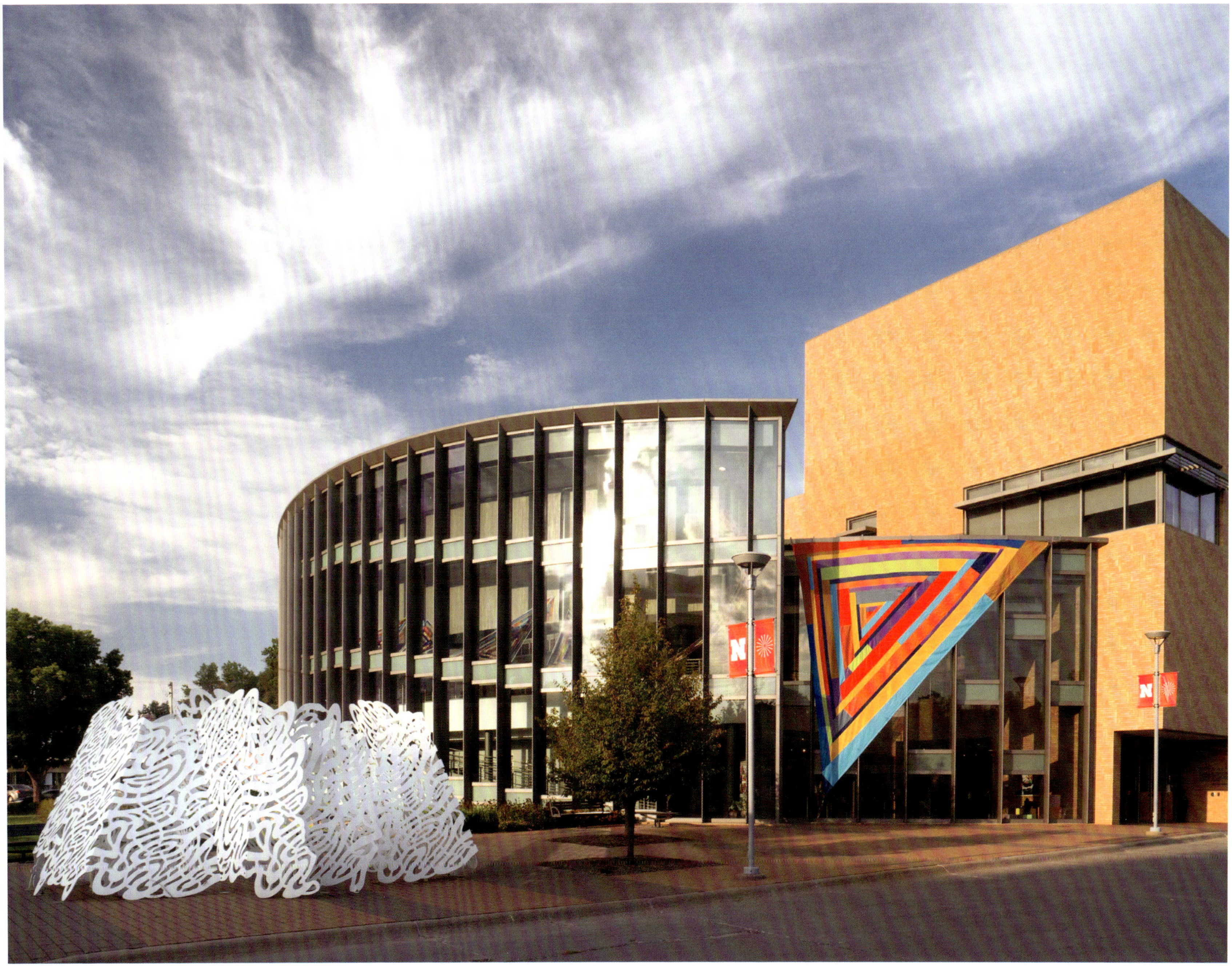

From Alabama to Nebraska and far beyond, Wells is a world-class artist, and the International Quilt Museum, located on the University of Nebraska–Lincoln's East Campus, is proud to be the caretakers of the Yvonne Wells Collection. The museum has the world's largest publicly held quilt collection, dating from the 1600s to present and representing sixty-nine countries. Museum photo by Larry Gawel. Wells's photo by Dave Walker.

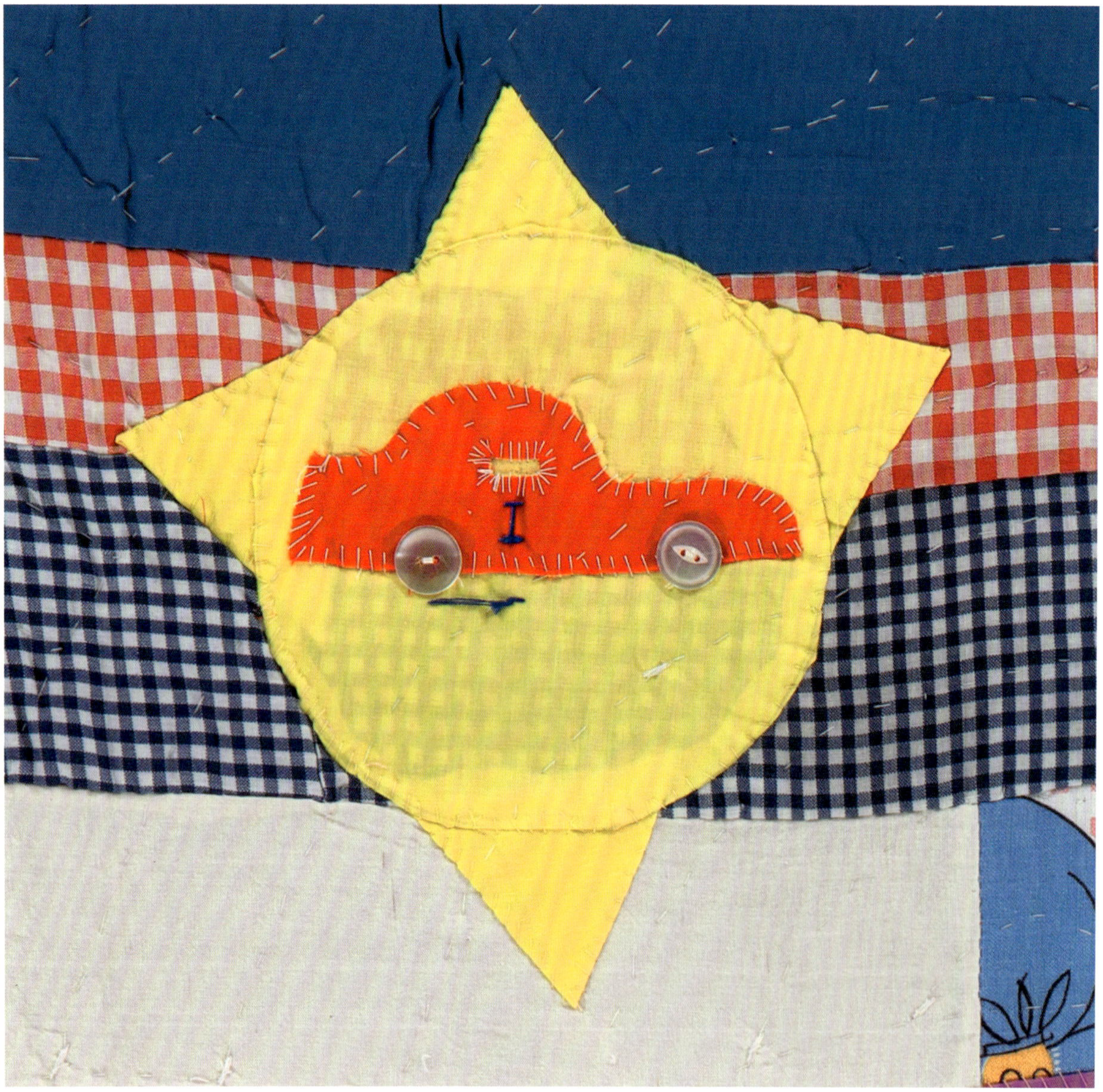

CONTRIBUTORS

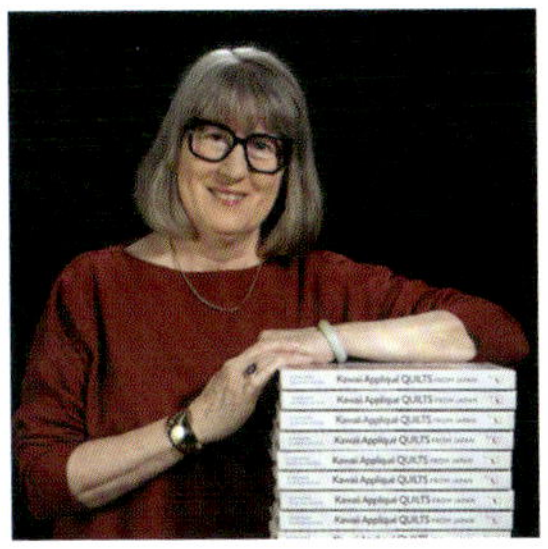

Teresa Duryea Wong is an author, lecturer, and quilt historian based in Houston. Her numerous books cover Japanese and American quilts and Native American quilt history. She is a member of the International Quilt Museum's International Advisory Board and a contributing writer for *Quiltfolk* magazine. Duryea Wong has presented hundreds of lectures to quilt guilds throughout the United States and even a few in Canada, the UK, and South Korea.

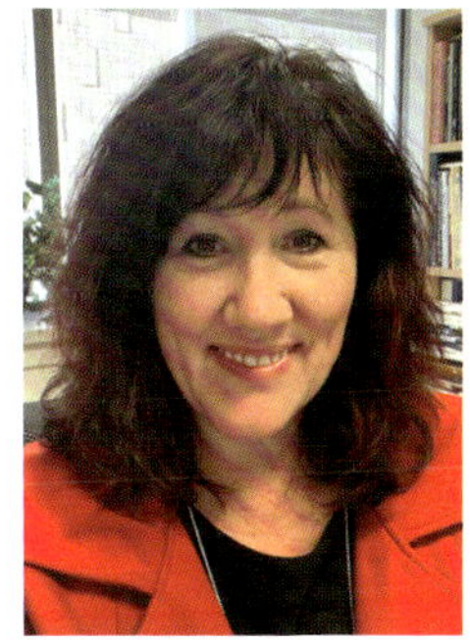

Carolyn Ducey recently retired as the Ardis B. James curator of collections at the International Quilt Museum at the University of Nebraska–Lincoln. She currently oversees special projects. Ducey curated numerous exhibitions and contributed to *An Evolving Vision: The James Collection, 1997–2022* (International Quilt Museum, 2022) and *American Quilts in the Industrial Age: 1760–1870* (Nebraska, 2018). She earned a master's degree from Indiana University and doctorate from the University of Nebraska–Lincoln.

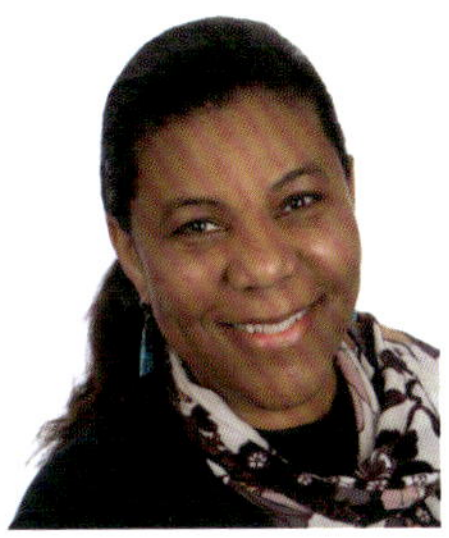

Kyra E. Hicks is a self-taught crafter of original story quilts. She loves historical, investigative research and rediscovering the lives of quilters' past. Hicks is the author of *Black Threads: An African American Quilting Sourcebook*, *This I Accomplish: Harriet Powers' Bible Quilt and Other Pieces*, and other books. She lives in Arlington, Virginia.

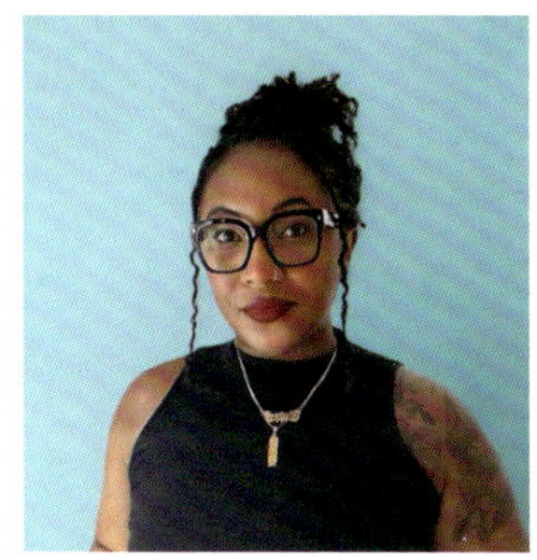

Dr. Sharbreon Plummer is an award-winning public scholar, artist, and curator from southeast Louisiana. She is the founder of AYA Thought Studio and has spent the past fifteen years shaping and facilitating transformative programs and initiatives that center liberation and justice through arts and culture. She specializes in Black art history and material culture, southern folkways, and craft studies with an emphasis on textiles.

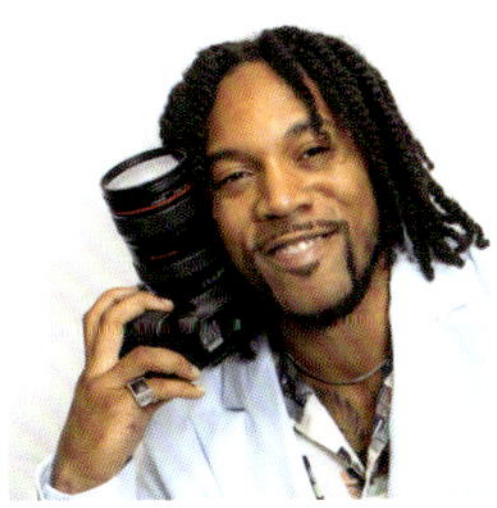

Dave Walker is a professional photographer and the owner of Simply Dave Photography. With over fifteen years of experience behind the camera, he's made photography his full-time career and lifelong passion. He loves connecting with people, telling their stories, and preserving life's most priceless experiences. Whether it's a wedding, portrait, or special event, his goal is always to create timeless, meaningful images.

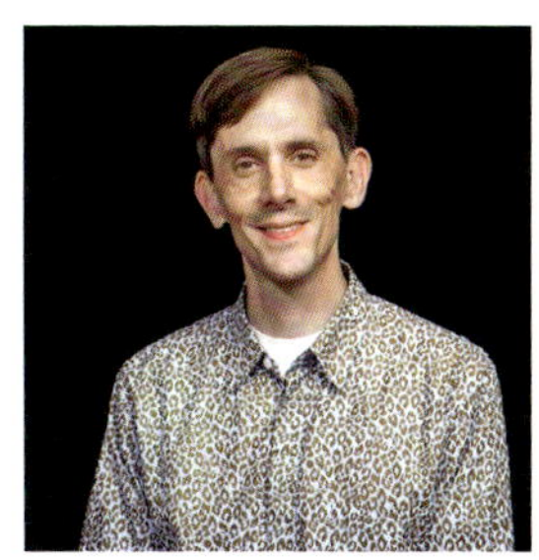

Jamie Swartz is the collections manager at the International Quilt Museum. He holds a bachelor of arts in art history from Minnesota State University–Moorhead and a master of arts in material culture and textile studies from the University of Nebraska–Lincoln. Swartz oversees all aspects of collections care, including preventive conservation, handling, storage, and environmental monitoring. He is also responsible for photography and lighting design.

"When someone says, I saw your work in the museum, I say, 'okay okay, it is out there.' To have my quilts in a museum, it means a whole lot to me. It means I have something to say that a big corporation is interested in purchasing and showcasing, and it makes me feel good because I will be leaving a legacy for my kids."

—Yvonne Wells